Crime, War, and C

Globalization creates lucrative opportunities for traffickers of drugs, dirty money, blood diamonds, weapons, and other contraband. Effective countermeasures require international collaboration, but what if some countries suffer while others profit from illicit trade? Only international institutions with strong compliance mechanisms can ensure that profiteers will not dodge their law enforcement responsibilities. However, the effectiveness of these institutions may also depend on their ability to flexibly adjust to fast-changing environments. Combining international legal theory and transaction cost economics, this book develops a novel, comprehensive framework which reveals the factors that determine the optimal balance between institutional credibility and flexibility. The author tests this rational design paradigm on four recent anti-trafficking efforts: narcotics, money laundering, conflict diamonds, and small arms. She sheds light on the reasons why policymakers sometimes adopt sub-optimal design solutions and unearths a nascent trend toward innovative forms of international cooperation which transcend the limitations of national sovereignty.

CHRISTINE JOJARTH is a Social Science Research Associate at the Center on Democracy, Development, and the Rule of Law at Stanford University.

Crime, War, and Global Trafficking

Designing International Cooperation

CHRISTINE JOJARTH

CAMBRIDGE
UNIVERSITY PRESS

CAMBRIDGE UNIVERSITY PRESS
Cambridge, New York, Melbourne, Madrid, Cape Town, Singapore, São Paulo, Delhi

Cambridge University Press
The Edinburgh Building, Cambridge CB2 8RU, UK

Published in the United States of America by Cambridge University Press, New York

www.cambridge.org
Information on this title: www.cambridge.org/9780521713764

© Christine Jojarth 2009

This publication is in copyright. Subject to statutory exception
and to the provisions of relevant collective licensing agreements,
no reproduction of any part may take place without
the written permission of Cambridge University Press.

First published 2009

Printed in the United Kingdom at the University Press, Cambridge

A catalogue record for this publication is available from the British Library

Library of Congress Cataloguing in Publication data
Jojarth, Christine, 1975–
Crime, war, and global trafficking : designing international cooperation / Christine Jojarth.
　　p.　cm.
Includes bibliographical references.
ISBN 978-0-521-88611-6
1. Crime.　2. Globalization.　3. Drug traffic.　I. Title.
HV6001.J65　2009
364.1′336–dc22
　　　　　　　　　　　　　　　　　2008049141

ISBN 978-0-521-88611-6 hardback
ISBN 978-0-521-71376-4 paperback

Cambridge University Press has no responsibility for
the persistence or accuracy of URLs for external or
third-party internet websites referred to in this book,
and does not guarantee that any content on such
websites is, or will remain, accurate or appropriate.

Contents

List of figures   *page* vii

List of tables   viii

List of abbreviations   x

Preface and acknowledgments   xiii

1 Introduction   1
   1.1 Crime, war, and global trafficking   2
   1.2 Explaining institutional design   9
   1.3 Methodology   15
   1.4 Outline   18

2 The concept of legalization   20
   2.1 Credibility versus flexibility   22
   2.2 The three dimensions of the concept of legalization   29
   2.3 Relationship between design variables   56

3 Problem constellation   59
   3.1 Competing theories of institutional design   60
   3.2 Toward a problem-tailored design model   67
   3.3 The three dimensions of problem constellations   72
   3.4 Interaction between problem constellation variables   89

4 Narcotic drugs: UN Convention against Illicit Traffic in
   Narcotic Drugs and Psychotropic Substances   92
   4.1 Narcotic drugs as an international policy problem   93
   4.2 Problem constellation   101
   4.3 Degree of legalization   119

5 Money laundering: the Financial Action Task Force and
   its Forty Recommendations   139
   5.1 Money laundering as an international policy problem   140
   5.2 Problem constellation   148
   5.3 Degree of legalization   165

6   Conflict diamonds: the Kimberley Process
    Certification Scheme   181
    6.1   Conflict diamonds as an international policy problem   182
    6.2   Problem constellation   191
    6.3   Degree of legalization   208

7   Small arms and light weapons: the United Nations
    Program of Action   221
    7.1   Small arms and light weapons as an international
          policy problem   222
    7.2   Problem constellation   233
    7.3   Degree of legalization   255

8   Conclusion   267
    8.1   Summary of results   268
    8.2   Rationality   271
    8.3   Instrumentality   278
    8.4   The step beyond: bounded rationality and
          multi-purpose instrumentality   285

References   287
Index   319

Figures

1.1 International agreements, institutions, and regimes   *page* 12
3.1 Potential loss as a function of futile sunk costs and
      forgone benefits   77
3.2 Propensity to shirk as a function of costs and benefits   79
3.3 Problem constellation with low and high asset specificity   81
4.1 Distribution of costs and benefits resulting from
      an international anti-drug institution   110
5.1 Distribution of costs and benefits resulting from
      an international anti-money laundering institution   156
6.1 Distribution of costs and benefits resulting from
      an international anti-conflict diamond institution   200
7.1 The world's legal small arms producers
      © Small Arms Survey. Reproduced with permission   236
7.2 Countries affected by armed conflicts, 1991–2000   241
7.3 Distribution of costs and benefits   243

Tables

2.1 Overview of key institutional design dimensions   *page* 54
3.1 Overview of key dimensions of policy problem
    constellations   87
3.2 Design hypotheses under different problem
    constellations   90
4.1 Output of leading opium and coca producers, 1988   105
4.2 Substance abuse-related death rates in most affected
    consumer states and in leading producer states
    in the early 1990s   108
4.3 Selected governance indicators for key drug producer
    states, 1996   112
4.4 Summary assessment of the problem constellation
    underlying the trafficking in narcotic drugs   118
4.5 Summary assessment of the level of legalization
    of the Vienna Convention   135
5.1 Selected anti-money laundering chronology   146
5.2 International and domestic importance of leading
    banking centers, 2003   151
5.3 Homicide rates in selected countries   153
5.4 Selected governance indicators for leading financial
    centers, 2003   158
5.5 Summary assessment of the problem constellation
    underlying money laundering   164
5.6 Summary assessment of the level of legalization
    of the Forty Recommendations of 2003   178
6.1 Diamond sanctions imposed by the United Nations
    Security Council   189
6.2 Economic importance of the diamond sector for leading
    producers in sub-Saharan Africa, 2000   193
6.3 Industry structure in leading diamond producers
    in sub-Saharan Africa, 2000   194

6.4 Occurrence of state failure in leading diamond-producing
countries in sub-Saharan Africa, 1990–2000   196
6.5 Output of major diamond producers, 2000   197
6.6 Selected governance indicators for leading diamond
mining, trading, and polishing states, 2002   202
6.7 Summary assessment of the problem constellation
underlying conflict diamonds   207
6.8 Summary assessment of the level of legalization
of the Kimberley Process Certification Scheme   218
7.1 Transfers of conventional arms to developing
countries, average 1997–2001   235
7.2 Selected countries with potential surplus stockpiles,
2003–2005   238
7.3 Average political terror score of countries with worst
human rights record, 1991–2000   240
7.4 Selected governance indicators for leading SALW
producers, 2000   246
7.5 Summary assessment of the problem constellation
underlying the trafficking in small arms and
light weapons   253
7.6 Summary assessment of the level of legalization of the
UN Program of Action on Small Arms and
Light Weapons   264
8.1 Summary of legalization of four international
institutions against global trafficking   270
8.2 Summary assessment of problem constellation
underlying four cases of global trafficking   271

Abbreviations

AML	Anti-money laundering
APG	Asia/Pacific Group against Money Laundering
ARS	Alternative remittance systems
AUC	*Autodefensas Unidas de Colombia*
BIS	Bank for International Settlements
CFATF	Caribbean Financial Action Task Force
CIA	Central Intelligence Agency
CITES	Convention on International Trade in Endangered Species
CND	Commission on Narcotic Drugs
CoE	Council of Europe
CTBTO	Commission for the Comprehensive Nuclear-Test-Ban Treaty Organization
CTF	Counter-terrorist finance
DDA	United Nations Department of Disarmament Affairs
DEA	Drug Enforcement Administration of the US Department of Justice
EAG	Eurasian Group on Combating Money Laundering and Financing of Terrorism
ECOSOC	UN Economic and Social Council
EITI	Extractive Industries Transparency Initiative
ELN	*Ejército de Liberacíon Nacional*
EMCDDA	European Monitoring Centre for Drugs and Drug Addiction
ESAAMLG	Eastern and Southern African Anti-Money Laundering Group
FARC	*Fuerzas Armadas Revolucionarias de Colombia*
FATF	Financial Action Task Force
FinCEN	Financial Crimes Enforcement Network
FSRB	FATF-Style Regional Bodies
GAFISUD	Financial Action Task Force on Money Laundering in South America
GDP	Gross Domestic Product
GIABA	Inter-Governmental Action Group against Money Laundering

IAEA	International Atomic Energy Agency
IFI	International Financial Institution
IMF	International Monetary Fund
INCB	International Narcotics Control Board
KP	Kimberley Process
KPCS	Kimberley Process Certification Scheme
LTTE	Liberation Tigers of Tamil Eelam
MENAFATF	Middle East and North Africa Financial Action Task Force (MENAFATF) against Money Laundering and Terrorist
MONEYVAL	Committee of Experts on the Evaluation of Anti-Money Laundering Measures and the Financing of Terrorism
NCCT	Non-complying countries and territories
NGO	Non-governmental organization
ONDCP	Office of National Drug Control Policy of the US White House
OPEC	Organization of Petroleum Exporting Countries
OSCE	Organization for Security and Cooperation in Europe
PoA	UN Program of Action to Prevent, Combat and Eradicate the Illicit Trade in Small Arms and light Weapons in All its Aspects
SADC	Southern African Development Community
SALW	Small arms and light weapons
UNGA	United Nations General Assembly
UNHCR	Office of the United Nations High Commissioner for Refugees
UNODC	United Nations Office on Drugs and Crime
UNSC	United Nations Security Council
VCLT	Vienna Convention on the Law of Treaties
WWF	World Wildlife Fund
WTO	World Trade Organization

Preface and acknowledgments

"But isn't this way too dangerous?" my mother-in-law asked whenever my research topic came up in our conversations. "I don't want you to get killed by these gangsters." Each time I tried to reassure her: "No, it is really not going to be that sort of crime-and-murder book you imagine." No blonde wigs, no sunglasses, no bulletproof vests. The way I set out to explore the shady world stretched between crime and war was not through undercover meetings with Viktor Bout, the legendary "Merchant of Death," or with his client, Manuel Marulanda, the world's oldest guerrilla leader and drug king. Instead, I spent the past five years interviewing policymakers and diplomats of all ranks and nationalities, industry representatives, and NGO leaders. I plowed through every imaginable written source on the subject. This was admittedly non-glamorous and required perseverance and analytic acuity rather than bravado and guile. The result of this endeavor may not be an adrenaline-packed thriller. But I hope to show that the big picture on how drugs, dirty money, diamonds, and arms circulate in the multi-billion dollar illicit global economy and how policymakers have tried to fight these different types of trafficking can be as fascinating as a series of anecdotes from the underworld.

On a more theoretical level, I want to explore how international cooperation on global trafficking can be facilitated through well-designed institutions. This focus on institutional design has led me to an unexpected puzzle which goes beyond the focus of this study but is too dear to me to go unmentioned.

Over the course of this research, I have become increasingly mystified as to why legally binding agreements are so popular despite the enormous investment in time and diplomatic capital required for their drafting and ratification process. The traditional international law argument suggests that states will comply with obligations created under a legally binding institution because their commitment is more formal and their credibility is to a much greater extent at stake when they officially endorse a legally binding rather than a non-binding institution. But this argument fails to take into account the fact that credibility is only at stake if non-compliance with that legally binding institution can indeed be detected and exposed. This is exactly where most legally binding agreements fall short. They often use formulations that are so vague that it is hard to differentiate between compliant and non-compliant behavior. Furthermore, they lack the mandate to monitor states' implementation record and to sanction non-compliance. So what is the point in crafting legally binding institutions that lack other – and probably more powerful – compliance mechanisms (e.g. precisely formulated obligations, monitoring, sanctioning)? Are there no more effective design options to facilitate international cooperation?

My interest in this question was triggered by a number of recently established international institutions that innovatively blend legal non-bindingness with tough compliance mechanisms. In this study, I will present the Financial Action Task Force, the central player in the global anti-money laundering movement, and the Kimberley Process on conflict diamonds as two prototypical examples of this move toward hybrid designs. I have explored these design innovations in more detail elsewhere (Jojarth 2007), but I want to alert the reader upfront to the embryonic new world order lurking in these case studies.

I guess that if this book is ever going to put me in danger, I have less to fear from criminal gangs than from devotees to classic international law and diplomacy who feel their traditional tools-of-trade threatened.

Over this half-decade long research journey, I have benefited from the advice and support of an incredible number of people who have continually stunned me with their intellectual rigor and generosity. These encounters in themselves have already made my efforts more than worthwhile.

From its genesis, this research has been nurtured by William Wallace and Martin Lodge, who proved superb mentors and intellectual sparring partners during my Ph.D. studies at the London School of Economics and well beyond. Stanford University and its Center on Democracy Development and the Rule of Law have offered me an unparalleled environment for taking my intellectual curiosity to the next level. Thomas Heller, Stephen Krasner, David Victor, Stephen Stedman, Kathryn Stoner-Weiss, Michael McFaul, and President Alejandro Toledo have all been instrumental in helping me synthesize my key findings and make them relevant to a wider audience.

Outside of my old and new academic home, I have also been privileged to receive encouraging feedback from a number of leading scholars in the field. I would like to mention in particular Robert Keohane, Barabara Koremenos, David Lake, Ronald Mitchell, Mats Berdal, and Phil Williams.

I am immensely grateful to my interviewees for sharing with me their insights into the practical world of international institutions and for luring me out of the ivory tower. The encouragement from two anonymous reviewers, John Haslam and Carrie Cheek of Cambridge University Press, was critical for making me go the painful last mile of endless revisions.

This book has been made possible thanks to the generous financial support I received from the Rotary Foundation, the British Chevening scholarship program, the Janggen Poehn Foundation, and from the Microsoft Corporation.

My family and friends have been indispensable for reminding me of the beauty life has to offer beyond my computer desk and for being the source of that beauty. My deepest gratitude goes to my husband Marton Jojarth to whom I dedicate this book and my life.

1 | Introduction

Why did states agree that the global fight against drug trafficking should be led by an international organization vested with an independent legal personality, a considerable budget, and powerful direct and indirect enforcement tools, but fail to adopt a similarly far-reaching form of institutionalized cooperation to combat illicit transfers in small arms and light weapons? This question is striking, because the trafficking of narcotic drugs and of small arms and light weapons seem – at first glance – to be very similar public policy problems: both kill and ruin the health of a comparable number of people; both provide a playground for profit-seeking criminals as well as ideologically motivated rebels and terrorists; and both require the coordinated response of a large number of producer, transhipment, and consumer countries. To rephrase the opening question in more general terms: Why do states adopt strikingly different designs for international institutions created to tackle seemingly similar problems? This puzzle is at the heart of this study's theoretical inquiry.

While the academic discussion of the reasons why independent states create institutions to facilitate international cooperation has started to reach its point of saturation, the more fine-grained inquiry into the factors explaining the pronounced variance in the design of these institutions is still in its infancy. So far, not even a common language has been developed to describe the most salient dimensions along which institutional designs vary.

This study seeks to contribute to this still largely unchartered territory of international relations by offering a detailed framework for analyzing and comparing institutional designs and by exploring one particular set of potential explanations. Specifically, I set out to examine the extent to which differences in the particular constellation of a given policy problem help explain the governance structure policymakers choose for the institution created to tackle the problem. This argument builds upon the functionalist school of international relations. However, in contrast

1

to many functionalist studies, I specifically set out to test whether form does indeed follow function rather than taking such a match between problem constellation and institutional design to be *a priori*. In fact, this inquiry assumes that sub-optimal designs may in fact be the norm rather than the exception in international institutions.

I am pursuing four main goals with this introductory chapter. First, I will introduce the empirical focus of this study – the policy area lying at the intersection between crime and war. I will shed light on the fascinating blurring we have witnessed over the past two decades of the differences between profit-oriented organized crime groups on the one hand and ideologically motivated rebel and terrorist groups on the other. Second, this introduction sets out to position the theoretical underpinnings of this study within the institutional design literature and clarifies central terms. Third, I will present the methodology used in this inquiry to make more transparent how and why this study reaches the assessments and conclusions it does. Fourth, the final part of this chapter charts the basic structure of this inquiry into the design of four real-world institutions created to tackle problems arising in the blurred borderland between transnational organized crime and international security.

1.1 Crime, war, and global trafficking

Traditionally, crime and war have been seen as two separate worlds. The former has been conceived of as harmful activities driven by greedy criminals' quest for profits and as a problem that is best countered by domestic law and order measures. This understanding of crime is, for instance, reflected in the definition the United States National Security Council formulated to describe organized crime: "continuing and self-perpetuating criminal conspiracy, having an organized structure, fed by fear and corruption, and motivated by greed" (e.g. National Security Council 2000).[1] War, in contrast, is typically assigned to the international sphere, where an anarchic world structure fuels the existential fear that one sovereign nation-state may seek to project its power on to

---

[1] This definition largely overlaps with the definition provided by Article 2(a) of the UN Transnational Organized Crime Convention of 2000, which defines organized criminal groups as a "structured group of three or more persons, existing for a period of time and acting in concert with the aim of committing one or more serious crimes or offences ... in order to obtain, directly or indirectly, a financial or other material benefit."

another state through large-scale organized violence (e.g. Luttwak and Koehl 1991) – a threat which can only be averted through military means. In the post-Cold War era, this neat distinction is becoming increasingly blurred. This fundamental shift in international security debates is reflected in the creation of the United Nations "High Panel on Threats, Challenges, and Change," which examines security issues like the proliferation of nuclear, radiological, chemical and biological weapons alongside transnational organized crime. As I will discuss in the following section, the breakdown of the separation of crime and war may be as much the result of changing perceptions as of fundamental real-world changes. The conceptual distinction between crime and war has thereby come under attack from two opposite angles. While one camp emphasizes the criminal elements in a number of contemporary wars, the other depicts crime, in particular, transnational[2] organized crime, as a security problem which needs to be fought with military power.

1.1.1 Criminal wars

The conceptual separation of crime and war has come under attack from scholars and policymakers who identify characteristics of contemporary armed conflicts that set these conflicts apart from the political-rationalist theory underlying the classical understanding of war (von Clausewitz 1992; Keegan 1993), and, in contrast, make them rather resemble organized crime operations. A first factor eroding away the delineation between crime and war in the post-Cold War era is the proliferation of intra-state as opposed to inter-state wars (Wallensteen and Sollenberg 1995) which has given prominence to new actors. While international wars pitch organized state armies against each other,

---

[2] I prefer the term "transnational organized crime" over "international organized crime," "multinational crime," and "global organized crime," which are often used synonymously. I prefer the former because it best captures the prominence of non-state actors in this type of activity. It resonates directly with Keohane and Nye's (1971) definition of transnational relations, which they describe as "the movement of tangible or intangible items across state boundaries when at least one actor is not an agent of a government or an intergovernmental organization" (1971: xii). Furthermore, in contrast to the term "global organized crime," "transnational organized crime" avoids creating the misleading impression that the fallout of criminal activities is felt equally around the world, while, in reality, different types of crime affect countries in different ways and to very varying extents.

intra-national wars are characterized by the fact that at least one warring party is an irregular, non-state led combat formation. In the fourteen intra-state conflicts that ravaged Africa in the 1990s, rebel groups as diverse as the Lord's Resistance Army in Uganda, the Groupe Islamique Armée in Algeria, or the Union for the Total Independence of Angola made headlines almost daily. Rebel groups are, however, not the only type of non-state actors that have been established as a major source of large-scale organized violence. Terrorist networks have also repeatedly and brutally manifested their determination and capacity to cause death and destruction in pursuit of their ideological goals.

Other factors leading to the increasing resemblance between armed conflicts and crime derive from the evolving nature of internal conflicts in the post-Cold War era. Most importantly, "new" civil wars differ from "old" civil wars (Kaldor 1999) with respect to the strategies employed by combatants and their driving motives. Although often violated in practice, the classical concept of war makes a clear distinction between combatants and civilians, and establishes the duty of the former to spare the latter. In recent civil wars this distinction has often been ignored on a massive scale or even turned on its head. Civilians are not only being unintentionally injured and killed in the course of military operations – as referred to by the problematic term "collateral damage" – but in many cases are specifically targeted by rebel groups and militias. The 1994 genocide in Rwanda and the massacres committed in the violent breakup of Yugoslavia in the early 1990s are just two of the most infamous examples of this trend. These new types of civil wars are also seen as differing from old civil wars in their driving motives: the latter are associated with the desire to bring about political change for the benefit of a larger collective, while the former are equated with a predatory enterprise involved in activities such as looting of natural resources and extortion undertaken for personal gain. Although armed conflicts may not initially have been triggered by economic greed, one can find many examples in Colombia, parts of Africa, and the Balkans where political motives became subordinate to the pursuit of financial and other material benefit during the course of conflict (Apter 1997). The continuation of widespread violence starts to serve a rational economic purpose as it confers pseudo-legitimacy on profit-driven actions that in peacetime would be punishable as crime (Keen 1998). Rebellion becomes a "quasi-criminal activity" (Collier 2000). In policy circles, this view has been adopted most prominently by the then-secretary general of the United

Nations (UN), Kofi Annan, who stated that "the pursuit of diamonds, drugs, timber, concessions, and other valuable commodities drives a number of today's internal conflicts. In some countries the capacity of the state to extract resources from society and to allocate patronage is the prize to be fought over" (Annan 1999). All these elements – the non-state nature of many fighting groups, the erosion of the distinction between combatants and civilians, and the prominence of economic motivations in many armed conflicts – all make many contemporary wars more resemble organized crime operations than classical wars.

1.1.2 The war against crime

Along with this move toward a stronger emphasis on the criminal aspects of contemporary wars, there has simultaneously been the inverse push toward the securitization of crime. Academics and policy-makers alike have tried to outdo each other in presenting transnational crime as an "existential threat" (Buzan, Wæver, and de Wilde 1998: 21). In 1994, an American think tank, the Center for Strategic and International Studies, published a report that declared organized crime the "new evil empire" (Raine and Cilluffo 1994) in a direct allusion to Ronald Reagan's vilification of the then-USSR. This view was echoed in a working paper of the Strategic and Defence Studies Centre of the Australian National University which argued that "[t]ransnational crime is now emerging as a serious threat in its own right to national and international security and stability" (McFarlane and McLennan 1996: 2). In politics, this view found supporters in the highest echelons of power. US Senator John Kerry warned of trans-national organized crime as "the new communism, the new monolithic threat" (quoted in Horvitz 1994), and James Woolsey, then director of the Central Intelligence Agency (CIA), maintained that "when inter-national organized crime can threaten the stability of regions and the very viability of nations, the issues are far from being exclusively in the realm of law enforcement; they also become a matter of national security" (quoted in Galeotti 2001: 215f.). This framing of crime as a national security issue was echoed in the Presidential Decision Directive 42 in which then-President Bill Clinton emphasized the "direct and immediate threat international crime present[ed] for national security" (White House 1997). This push toward a securitization of crime can only partially be attributed to real changes in the nature and dimension of transnational organized crime (Edwards and Gill 2003). At least equally important in this respect are the successful communications strategies deployed by Cold War security agencies, which sought to defend their organizational interests through the creation of a new mandate (Friman and Andreas 1999: 2; Lee 1999: 3; Naylor 1995a).

The war analogy is particularly pertinent in cases where criminal groups have virtually merged with the highest echelons of the political establishment. When the state itself becomes "criminalized" (Bayart, Ellis, and Hibou 1999) the goals and needs of criminal enterprises become indistinguishable from a country's national interest (Naím 2005: 27). Any attempt by a country suffering from transnational crime to address the foreign root causes of its problems results necessarily in a head-on inter-state confrontation – and not just one between a state and non-state actors. It is one thing to dispatch members of the National Guard to the national border with a mandate to help stem the inflow of illegal immigrants (e.g. Pessin 2006). It is a very different matter conceptually and practically to order almost 30,000 soldiers to invade a foreign country and capture that country's president on drug trafficking and money laundering charges, as occurred during the US invasion of Panama in 1989 (Bogges 1992). When a country is ruled by a president whose election campaign was sponsored by a drug cartel,[3] by a government that clears the country's external debts with drug money,[4] or that sells the nation's sovereignty to telephone sex operators and money launderers (Drezner 2001), international law enforcement matters unavoidably get twisted up in complicated security and foreign policy issues, even if outright military interventions remain rare.

1.1.3 Globalization and the transnationalization of crime

It has become commonplace to contend that in the twentieth century, transnational organized crime experienced a "phenomenal increase in

---

[3] The alleged US$3.75 million contribution of the Cali cartel to the presidential campaign of the later winner Ernesto Samper in 1994 probably provides the most notorious example (New York Times 1995).

[4] Bolivia's most senior drug lord, Roberto Suarez Gomez, reportedly offered the government to pay off two-thirds of the country's foreign debts of approximately US$3 billion at the time in exchange for legal impunity (Malamud-Goti 1992). Eventually, under heavy pressure from the United States, the Bolivian government rejected this generous offer.

scope, power and effectiveness" (Galeotti 2001: 203). This claim is rarely substantiated by empirical figures, which is understandable given the clandestine nature of the business, but more commonly deduced from a number of factors assumed to have fostered such a development (e.g. Naím 2005).

Most importantly, organized crime has been able to expand its operational activities and geographical scope by embracing economic globalization very much in the same way the licit business sector has. The increasing speed and significant drop in costs of communication and transportation, combined with a drastic reduction of barriers to trade and financial flows, allows legitimate businesses – but also organized crime groups – to shift to production networks that are organized globally rather than nationally (Evans 1997). This, in turn, allows both businesses and transnational criminal organizations to differentiate between their home base and countries of operation in a way that maximizes profits and minimizes operating costs. Criminal organizations thereby set up their "headquarters" in safe havens offering a low risk of detection and prosecution, while directing their operations toward countries "where the money is," to paraphrase Willie Sutton's famous explanation for why he robbed banks. For instance, criminal networks specializing in fraudulent advance fee schemes love the "ease of business" offered in Nigeria, while they find their "customer base" mainly in richer Western nations.

Economic globalization has not only contributed to the transnationalization of the production and distribution networks of illicit products and services, but also to the interlinking of formerly separate black markets for recreational drugs, counterfeit credit cards, fake designer watches, stolen diamonds, and terrorism – leading to the emergence of what Friman and Andreas called the "illicit global economy" (1999). According to Naylor, this illicit economy is supported by its own systems of information, sources of supply, distribution networks, and even its own modes of financing (1995b: 48). In the late 1990s, the "gross criminal product" generated from these activities (Friman and Andreas 1999) amounted to an estimated US$1 trillion annually[5] according to a former adviser to the British secret services (Green 1997).

The transnationalization of criminal activities is closely linked to the notion of trafficking, which refers to the international movement of goods and services that is deemed illicit for any of three different reasons.

---

[5] An equivalent of 3 percent of global legal gross domestic product.

First, most obviously, trafficking covers goods that are by themselves illicit, such as narcotics. Second, flows of licit goods may still be illicit if such goods have been obtained or processed in illicit ways (e.g. conflict diamonds, money laundering). Finally, illicit flows also include the movement of licit goods obtained in licit ways but intended for illicit purposes (e.g. terrorist financing, precursors for narcotics). Trafficking typically involves the states of origin for goods and services, one or more states serving as transhipment centers, and states where the illicit good or service is consumed. Illicit flows do not necessarily create public policy problems at all points along this chain. For example, in the case of conflict diamonds, the states that suffer most from diamond-related violence are primarily the states in which the diamonds are mined, rather than the ones in which these precious stones are processed or consumed. In contrast, small arms and light weapons (SALW) cause the greatest harm in countries amassing such weapons rather than the producing states. Consequently, countries that produce a certain illicit good or service cannot always be equated with "upstream states," to use a term that has gained popularity in international environmental politics to describe states that generate negative externalities.

The transnational dimension of these flows requires an internationally coordinated response. However, the necessity of international cooperation on trafficking-related issues does not mean that such cooperation is easy to achieve – far from it. Illicit flows affect countries in different ways and in varying degrees of intensity, so that international cooperation cannot rely on a natural harmony of interest. Cooperation in law enforcement and national security matters is further impeded by the fact that the control of the police and judiciary, as well as of intelligence services and military forces, are generally seen as defining features of national independence and sovereignty (Farer 2000; Smith 1992). However, history shows that these obstacles are not insurmountable. Pioneering international anti-trafficking agreements date back to the early twentieth century, but it was only after the end of the Cold War that international cooperation in this area gained real momentum.

The cases presented in this study are all situated in the blurred borderland between crime and war linked by trafficking. The first case study is dedicated to the trafficking in illicit drugs, a multi-billion dollar business often associated not with criminal organizations alone but also with insurgent groups and terrorist networks who seek to finance arms procurements through profits generated in drug-related activities.

Money laundering – the second of the case studies presented here – is directly linked to drug trafficking, as international control efforts to curb money laundering were first embraced as a tool to support the global war on drugs by opening a new – i.e. financial – front. Diamonds, even more so than illicit drugs, have attracted international concern because of their exploitation not just by criminals but also by rebel groups and terrorist networks. Small arms and light weapons, the subject of the fourth and final case study, are the obvious and indispensable tools of trade for every criminal as well as insurgent operation.

1.2 Explaining institutional design

Growing concerns about transnational security threats posed by global trafficking have led to the formation of a number of international counterinitiatives in the past decades. These initiatives resulted in the establishment of a great number of international institutions which differ considerably from one another in design. Whereas some of these international institutions are based on legally binding treaties and backed by international organizations vested with far-reaching competencies, other institutions amount to little more than lofty declarations of noble intent. The theoretical puzzle addressed by this study is to explain this variance – to explain why states endow international institutions dealing with policy problems in the same issue area with such different designs. Before embarking on this task, a few definitional clarifications are required.

This study adopts Koremenos, Lipson, and Snidal's definition of international institutions, which describes them as "explicit arrangements, negotiated among international actors,[6] that prescribe, proscribe, and/or

---

[6] By referring to "international actors" rather than "states," Koremenos, Lipson, and Snidal acknowledge in their definition the fact that international "nonstate actors participate with increasing frequency in international design" (2001: 763). I agree that it is important to acknowledge non-state actors' role in the creation, design, and ongoing development of international institutions (see also Koh 1996; Shelton 2000). However, I think it is also important to recognize that at least in today's world order, states retain a unique ability to adopt authoritative agreements, as recognized by Keohane (1988: 384) for whom international institutions are *per definitionem* agreed upon by states. This is not to say that agreements by non-state actors cannot have important effects around the globe (e.g. voluntary industry standards; codes of conduct adopted by a multinational corporation, etc.), but rather that arrangements in which states are not directly included differ in their design from arrangements adopted by states.

authorize behavior" (2001: 762).[7] As the following paragraphs will show, this definition is closely related to – but not congruent with – the concept of international governmental organizations, international agreements, and international regimes.

The definition of international institutions as used in this study is broader than that of international organizations.[8] International organizations share three defining features: they are characterized, first, by a membership base typically constituted of states, but in some cases also other intergovernmental organizations, second, by a separate international legal personality, and, third, by the existence of permanent organs with a will autonomous of that of its constituting members (Schermers and Blokker 1995: §§32ff.). All international organizations are part of an international institution according to the definition employed here, as they are established to shape states' behavior. However, not all international institutions rely on international organizations to facilitate cooperative objectives. For instance, the global anti-money laundering efforts spearheaded by the intergovernmental Financial Action Task Force (FATF) represent an international institution according to the definition employed here, despite the fact that the FATF lacks two central attributes of an international organization – namely, international legal personality and autonomous will. Rather than equating international institutions with international organizations, this study seeks to describe how and to explain why a particular international institution does or does not rely on a pre-existing or newly created international organization as part of its overall design.

International institutions as defined here are also broader than international agreements. Although international institutions are based upon international agreements – understood as written authoritative documents (Iklé 1964), they also encompass the normative and implemental practices that evolve around such agreements. In this sense, this study's understanding of international institutions also covers

---

[7] In contrast to Mearsheimer (1994–1995), Koremenos, Lipson, and Snidal do not explicitly limit the function of international institutions to the shaping of states' behavior. I welcome this broader understanding. Even though most international institutions only target state behavior and dualism remains the dominant view, we can witness a growing direct effect – in practical, not necessarily legal terms of international law.

[8] See also Simmons and Martin (2002) on the difference between international organizations and international institutions.

"interstitial law," i.e. the non-codified rules operating in and around explicit normative frameworks. International institutions thereby become comparable to a judicial interpretation which covers both *de lege lata* (codification of existing law) and *de lege ferenda* (progressive development of law) (Malanczuk 1997: 35). Such a broadening is justified by the fact that, in many cases, important regulatory practices are not directly established by a core agreement but evolve at a later stage, often without any authoritative codification. For instance, the international initiative to curb the illicit trade in conflict diamonds, the so-called Kimberley Process (KP), now encompasses elaborate monitoring and sanctioning mechanisms not provided for in the KP's founding document, the Kimberley Process Certification Scheme (KPCS) of November 2002, nor in any other formal declaration (see Chapter 6).

Today's international relations literature largely favors the term "institution" over "regime" in an attempt to make the boundaries of international institutions more distinct and to separate institutions from behavioral outcomes (Simmons and Martin 2002: 194). Over two decades ago, Stephen Krasner formulated the most widely agreed-upon definition of international regimes, which he described as "implicit or explicit principles, norms, rules and decision-making procedures around which actors' expectations converge in a given area of international relations" (Krasner 1983: 2). This and related definitions attracted increasing criticism for being too vague and "woolly" (Strange 1983: 337; Young 1983: 9). The most contentious element in this definition is the inclusion of implicit principles and norms[9] which are impossible to measure directly. Instead, observable changes in behavior were used to trace the existence of implicit principles and norms and thus of international regimes, which renders the examination of regimes' effects on behavior tautological (Simmons and Martin 2002). Like most modern definitions of international institutions, the one offered by Koremenos, Lipson, and Snidal (2001) seeks to avoid this problem by focusing on explicit arrangements and on the normative quality of institutions, independent of their actual effect on behavior.

Figure 1.1 summarizes the two fundamental dimensions along which international agreements, international regimes, and international

---

[9] Slaughter (2004a: 41) presents an additional argument against the lumping together of implicit norms and formal rules by pointing out that the two differ significantly in the way and intensity with which they affect state behavior.

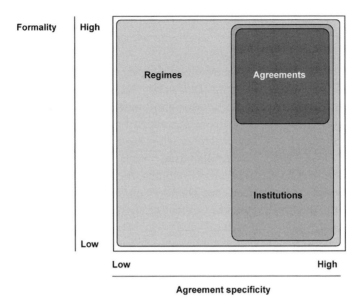

Figure 1.1 International agreements, institutions, and regimes

institutions can be differentiated from each other. For one, these terms and their various definitions differ from each other with regard to their degree of formality, i.e. the extent to which they are codified in a written, authoritative document (Carey 2000; Helmke and Levitsky 2004). For the other, these terms include normative elements that are more or less closely tied to a written core agreement. The combination of these two dimensions provides us with a 2x2 matrix which illustrates the definitional difference between international agreements, international institutions, and international regimes. International agreements are situated in the right upper corner because they are "parchment institutions" (Carey 2000) which are to be studied solely based on the written provisions they contain. This study's understanding of international institutions is broader because it emphasizes the importance of including elements that are meant to affect the behavior targeted by a written core agreement but are not necessarily codified in the institution's "founding" document. These elements are included as long as they are directly and explicitly tied to the central agreement(s), as are the above-mentioned compliance mechanisms developed by the Kimberley Process over the course of its existence. In contrast, the countless (and uncountable) norms and principles that also shape states' behavior in general (and also, therefore, indirectly with regard to the specific issue area targeted by an individual institution) fall outside the definitional scope of international institutions and into that of international regimes.

Despite all of these attempts to carefully delineate the boundaries of an individual international institution, drawing a watertight, undisputable demarcation line remains impossible. The most important complication arises from the fact that all international institutions are embedded in a network of overlapping, nested institutions (Alter and Meunier 2007) or regime complexes (Raustiala and Victor 2004). It often remains a matter of subjective judgment to decide where one institution ends and another one begins. For instance, while this study focuses on the United Nations Convention against Illicit Traffic in Narcotic Drugs and Psychotropic Substances of 1988, it is not very meaningful to examine this convention without taking into account the two earlier UN anti-drug conventions upon which the 1988 Convention is directly built. The 1988 Convention not only states explicitly that it seeks to complement the two earlier conventions, but also entrusts the various UN organs already created by the earlier treaties with important normative and executive functions.

Whereas the question regarding the reasons for the creation of international institutions (or regimes) has attracted a great deal of scholarly interest from the 1980s onwards (e.g. Keohane 1982, 1984; Krasner 1983; Young 1983), the question of why institutions were endowed with different institutional design arrangements has been addressed only recently (e.g. Goldstein *et al.* 2000; Koremenos, Lipson, and Snidal 2001). Design refers here to "the creation of an actionable form to promote valued outcomes in a particular context" (Bobrow and Dryzek 1987: 201). Although not necessary implied by this definition, this study focuses on design seen as the result of intentional activities, without denying that an institution's governance structure may also be the result of accidents and (undirected) evolutions (Goodin 1996), as suggested by historical and sociological institutionalists (e.g. Pierson 2004; Thelen 2004).

Recent interest in the design of international institutions has led to a proliferation of design classifications. One classification that has probably attracted the greatest scholarly interest is the so-called concept of legalization (Abbott *et al.* 2000). The name chosen for this concept is slightly misleading – in particular in the context of trafficking studied here. In everyday parlance, most people would associate the legalization

of narcotic drugs with de-criminalization of these mind-altering substances, and certainly not with a particular way of categorizing the
design characteristics of international institutions established to tackle
this problem. Among international relations scholars as well, "legalization" can refer to different, although strongly interrelated, meanings.
For some, the term refers to a process, namely to a particular form of
institutionalization, which March and Olsen define as "the emergence
of institutions and individual behaviors within them" (1998: 948).
What differentiates legalization from institutionalization is that these
emerging institutions take on the form of laws or law-like arrangements
(Brütsch and Lehmkuhl 2007). For others, including the author of this
study, legalization mainly connotes an analytic concept for describing
and comparing the design of international institutions based on features
that are considered to be particularly salient to the functioning of these
institutions. The authors of the original concept of legalization
(e.g. Abbott *et al.* 2000) identify three such variables, namely obligation,
precision, and delegation. Based on these three criteria, international
institutions can be arrayed on a spectrum ranging from soft law (low
levels of legalization) to hard law (high levels of legalization). Moving
along this continuum from soft to hard law involves a trade-off between
flexibility, found at the lower end of the spectrum, and credibility, which,
in contrast, is facilitated by high degrees of legalization.

This study's inquiry rests upon the central tenet that the optimal
design of an international institution is largely determined by the particular constellation underlying the problem on which international
actors seek to cooperate. Using transaction cost economics theory,
this study derives three problem attributes that are considered to be
most relevant – namely asset specificity, behavioral uncertainty, and
environmental uncertainty. The model developed and tested here conjectures that "harder" governance structures present an optimal design
when the intensity of asset specificity (actions which are required from
states by an international institution, but which states would not take
otherwise) and behavioral uncertainty (the difficulty involved with
detecting non-compliance of other states) are high. In contrast, "softer"
institutions are considered best suited for dealing with problems that are
fraught with a great risk of unforeseen changes in the understanding of
the causes, consequences, or remedies of a problem (environmental
uncertainty). In contrast to transaction cost economics theory and
functionalism in general, this study does not presuppose that

policymakers necessarily design an international institution in a way that is ideal for addressing a given policy problem. Instead, it conceptually allows for what we could call intentionally sub-optimal design outcomes and specifically sets out to test if (and under what conditions) an institution is indeed designed in a way that optimally caters for the challenges arising from a given problem constellation.

1.3 Methodology

There are countless reasons why policymakers design an international institution in varying ways. In order to distinguish the systematic from the more idiosyncratic factors that affect the design of an international institution, this study adopts a case-oriented approach that subjects qualitative data to a structured, focused comparison (George and McKeown 1985). This methodological approach presents itself as the most pertinent for two principal reasons.

First, the structure of the problems that policymakers decide to deal with through the creation of international institutions is impossible to control. I cannot study how designs change by purposefully adding a little bit more of this or that problem characteristic. For this reason, I am precluded from using the same experimental approach that has proven so successful in the "hard" sciences (Yin 1994).

Second, the utilization of quantitative methods is also hampered by the fact that institutional design theories are still underdeveloped, thus requiring the thick conceptualization of the context and central characteristics as offered by the case study method (Ragin, Berg Schlosser, and de Meur 1998). This richer description of both the dependent and the independent variables is considerably more research-intensive than an approach that relies exclusively on variables for which data are relatively easy to obtain, but which only captures superficial elements of an institution's governance architecture[10] or of a policy problem's underlying constellation. In this unavoidable trade-off between depth and breadth, this study favors the former, confronting a "many variables, few cases" dilemma (Lijphart 1971). To avoid the resulting problem of over-determination, the case study approach presents the best methodological strategy.

---

[10] See Finnemore and Toope's (2001) critique of an understanding of legalization that is too narrow.

In contrast to "large-n" observational tests, the case study method does not build upon random samples, but rather on cases that are intentionally selected based on theoretical considerations. One inherent danger of this approach is a potential omitted variable bias. I seek to mitigate this risk by selecting the cases based on two theoretical considerations. First, I selected cases in a way that maximizes the uniformity in background conditions. All cases examined here present cases of multilateral (not bilateral) institutions dealing with problems located in the same issue area (transnational crime and security threats) and established within the relatively narrow timeframe of fifteen years (namely between 1988 and 2003). Second, the cases selected here represent the complete design spectrum, ranging from international institutions with high levels of legalization (UN Drug Convention) to institutions which rely on soft law alone (UN Program of Action on Small Arms and Light Weapons). The Kimberley Process and the Forty Recommendations represent two intermediary design examples. Thus the case selection strategy used here follows Przeworski and Teune's "most different systems" design (1970: 34ff.). This selection method is not without its specific caveats (see King, Keohane, and Verba 1994: 141). However, it is justified here, given the early exploratory stage of institutional design theories where the most urgent challenge is still to eliminate irrelevant systemic factors – a task Przeworski and Teune's most different systems design is best capable of handling.

The empirical inquiry in each of the four case studies follows the same three-stage process. First, I analyze the problem constellation based on the three variables derived from transaction cost economics theory – namely asset specificity, behavioral uncertainty, and environmental uncertainty. In conjunction with the hypotheses presented in the previous section, this analysis allows me to formulate specific expectations regarding the optimal design of international institutions created to deal with the problem in question. In a second stage, I scrutinize the institutions' actual design along the three dimensions developed in Abbott *et al.*'s (2000) concept of legalization – namely obligation, precision, and delegation. Finally, I compare the design expectations raised in the first analytic stage with the actual institutional design as assessed in stage two. Throughout this investigative process, I use explicit and codified assessment methods in order to maximize transparency and replicability (King, Keohane, and Verba 1994: 8). A detailed assessment template developed here disaggregates the three design and problem constellation variables into narrower, and thus better measureable, sub-components. Each variable is measured on an ordinal scale that distinguishes between the three levels "low," "moderate," and "high." I opted for a tri-level assessment out of a conviction that any more fine-grained assessment scale would create a misleading impression of precision that is not attainable given the conceptual ambiguity that remains despite the best operationalization efforts.

While this study focuses on cases dealing with policy problems located in the intersection between crime and war, nothing of the theoretical framework developed here necessarily prevents its transfer to the analysis of international institutions dealing with problems related to other issue areas. In fact, a similar logic has already been successfully applied to international cooperative arrangements in other policy fields such as trade (e.g. Yarbrough and Yarbrough 1992), military security (e.g. Lake 1999), human rights (Lutz and Sikkink 2000), and monetary affairs (Simmons 2000). If done with the necessary concept adaptations (Munck 2004), such an inter-model transfer will strengthen our understanding of how institutions can be best designed to cater to the specific contractual challenges arising from certain problem constellations, and of the conditions under which policymakers are open to such optimality considerations in their final design choices.

I draw the empirical evidence underlying this study from a wide range of sources in order to prevent reproducing any potential bias from an individual source. I analyze the problem constellation and the design of international institutions based on evidence gathered from academic and semi-academic writings, newspaper reports, and public records of individual governments and of intergovernmental organizations. Semi-structured interviews with government officials and members of staff of international organizations, non-governmental organizations (NGOs), and affected businesses complemented these written sources and allowed for up-to-date evidence to be used in all four cases. Furthermore, these non-attributed interviews provided a valuable "reality check" of the assessments attained from prior desk research. Interviewees were identified and selected based on their publication record, participation lists of relevant conferences and hearings, as well as on cross-referrals by other interview partners. The number of interviews conducted for each of the four case studies varied inversely with the availability of reliable written sources – with the illicit trafficking in conflict diamonds requiring the greatest number of interviews, and narcotic drugs the least.

1.4 Outline

This book seeks to make both a theoretical and an empirical contribution. Chapters 2 and 3 lay out the theoretical foundation of this study and provide a detailed motivation and operationalization of the dependent (i.e. institutional design) and independent variables (problem constellation).

Chapter 2 addresses the question of how best to conceptualize the observed variance in the design of international institutions. It provides an overview and critical discussion of the relevant theoretical literature. In this chapter, I will also introduce the distinction between hard law and soft law as descriptive categories and show how the design of international institutions arrayed along this continuum offers unique combinations of advantages and disadvantages in the form of greater or lesser degrees of flexibility and credibility, respectively. Chapter 2 concludes with the presentation of the three design dimensions suggested by the concept of legalization – obligation, precision, and delegation – followed by the development of a list of operationalized criteria which will guide the assessment of the international institutions examined in the case studies that will follow in the second part of this study. Chapter 3 follows a similar argumentative structure in its introduction of the characteristics that form the basis upon which different problem constellations can be analytically described and causally linked to design outcomes. I will provide a brief overview of three leading institutional design theories and show how they inform the integrative design model underlying this study. The chapter then moves on to derive three explanatory variables from transaction cost economics theory – namely, asset specificity, behavioral uncertainty, and environmental uncertainty – and applies them to the context of international relations. These variables are then operationalized in a way that maximizes transparency in the assessment of the problem constellation underlying each of the four case studies.

These two theoretical chapters provide the foundation for the formulation of this study's central hypothesis, which conjectures that international institutions with high degrees of legalization present the optimal design for dealing with problems characterized by high levels of asset specificity and behavioral uncertainty combined with low levels of environmental uncertainty. Inversely, a governance structure with low degrees of legalization is assumed to be ideal for addressing policy problems with little asset specificity and behavioral uncertainty and considerable environmental uncertainty.

Chapters 4–6 subject these conjectures to rigorous empirical testing in four case studies. I will present these four case studies in the order of their decreasing degrees of legalization. Chapter 4 is dedicated to the 1988 United Nations Convention against Illicit Traffic in Narcotic Drugs and Psychotropic Substances, which I selected as an example of an international institution of comparably hard law. Chapter 5 scrutinizes the Forty Recommendations of the Financial Action Task Force of 2003, which establishes a moderately hard international institution to deal with money laundering. Chapter 6 discusses the Kimberley Process Certification Scheme of 2002, an international initiative to curb the illicit trade in conflict diamonds that is also situated halfway between hard and soft law. Chapter 7 concludes the empirical part with the analysis of the United Nations Program of Action on Small Arms and Light Weapons of 2001, which represents an international institution with a low degree of legalization.

Each of these empirical studies begins with an overview of the context of the policy problem, establishes how the issue emerged on the international agenda, and describes how it has been addressed through different international institutions. The main part of each case study is dedicated to the categorization of the characteristics of the underlying problem constellation and of the governance structure adopted by policymakers to institutionalize cooperation on this issue. This focus allows for a systematic comparison of the predicted and the actual design outcome and thus leads to the subsequent conclusion examining whether policymakers designed the institution in an effective way.

In the concluding Chapter 8, I synthesize this study's key findings and show how elements from other institutional design theories can enrich the understanding of cases wherein the actual design of an international institution matched the predicted design, as well as cases wherein the design prediction failed.

2 | *The concept of legalization*

What some scholars deplore[1] as a loss in coherence and theoretical purity, others[2] applaud as an innovative and necessary response to the regulatory challenges posed by globalization. Both camps agree, however, that we are currently witnessing a creative explosion in the diversity of regulatory frameworks policymakers design to govern issues on the domestic and international level. Within these scholarly discourses on trends in regulatory design, the term "legalization" has taken on two different, but closely related, connotations. To some, legalization refers primarily to the tendency of social conflicts to be transformed into legal or quasi-legal conflicts that are settled through institutionalized procedures. Brütsch and Lehmkuhl (2007: 9), for instance, define legalization as a move to law – a "complex set of transformations creating a multitude of overlapping, at times complementary, at times contradictory legal realms, or 'legalities'." This understanding deviates from the connotation this study focuses on, which sees in the concept of legalization a heuristic tool for describing and comparing the design of international institutions based on features considered particularly salient to the functioning of these institutions. This latter notion of legalization builds directly upon the theoretical framework developed by Abbott *et al.* (2000). This group of scholars identified three design features – that is, obligation, precision, and delegation – as central to the different ways international institutions function. Depending on the extent to which an international institution imposes substantive requirements on states (obligation), spells out determinate and coherent objectives and action plans (precision), and relies on third parties to perform certain tasks on its behalf (delegation), that institution is considered to represent a case of high or low legalization.

The concept of legalization was neither the first nor the last attempt to bring analytic order to the growing diversity in the landscape of

[1] E.g. Weil (1983).   [2] E.g. Reinicke (1998).

institutionalized international cooperation. Some rationalist scholars adopt dichotomous design concepts (e.g. formal versus informal agreements) (Lipson 1991; Morrow 2000), or the inclusion or absence of escape clauses (Rosendorff and Milner 2001), while others include a larger set of aspects in their analysis (e.g. scope, membership, centralization,[3] control, and flexibility) (Koremenos, Lipson, and Snidal 2001). Constructivist scholars, in contrast, place more emphasis on the legitimacy an international institution may or may not possess depending on the process through which it was created (Koh 1996) and on the extent to which its substantive and procedural provisions correspond with "deeply embedded practices, beliefs and traditions of societies" (Finnemore and Toope 2001: 743).

All these attempts to categorize international institutions have one characteristic in common: they more or less explicitly seek to identify the institutional features most relevant for facilitating the necessary changes in state (and increasingly also non-state)[4] behavior that allow institutions to mitigate transnational problems (e.g. Abbott *et al.* 2000: 402). In particular, the rationalist design argument builds directly on the insights gained from theoretical and empirical studies of the design of domestic institutions. This rich body of literature highlights the fundamental trade-off policymakers face whenever they design an international institution. They basically have to choose between a hard law governance structure that offers the advantage of lending strong credibility to their commitments at the expense of flexibility and soft law, which offers the inverse combination of merits and drawbacks. They can also opt for a middle-ground position between high and low levels of legalization.

I will explore this institutional design dilemma in the next section. From this foundation, the discussion moves on to develop the three dimensions of legalization – obligation, precision, and delegation – in more detail and to suggest ways to operationalize these explanatory variables. This chapter concludes with a tentative discussion of the relationship among these three design dimensions.

---

[3] Koremenos, Lipson, and Snidal's (2001) centralization and control variables are subsumed under the "delegation" dimension of the concept of legalization (see below).

[4] An increasing number of international institutions address the private sector directly, in contrast to the classical international law system in which states were the exclusive addressees.

2.1 Credibility versus flexibility

There is no such thing as perfect institutional design. All that policy-makers can aspire to is an institutional design that strikes the balance between credibility and flexibility in a way that is optimal (or at least, apt) for dealing with the particular governance challenges arising from a given policy problem (Goldstein and Martin 2000, 605; Koremenos 2001; Rosendorff and Milner 2001). As the following discussion will show, both credibility and flexibility are highly desirable features of a domestic, as well as international, institution, but an increase in one attribute necessarily comes at the expense of the other. As Levy and Spiller put it, "The same mechanisms that make it difficult to impose arbitrary changes in the rules may make it difficult to enact sensible rules in the first place or to adapt the rules as circumstances change" (1996: 5).

2.1.1 *Credibility: a central problem of the state*

Trade, the division of labor, and all the associated welfare benefits depend crucially on trust. Each transacting party must trust that all other partners will deliver what they offered in exchange for whatever good or service he or she produces. This trust has both social[5] and legal underpinnings. Trust in contractual promises made by private parties gains considerable credibility through the existence of a juridical system that is independent of the parties involved and vested with the authority and capacity to effectively enforce property rights and contractual obligations. Ensuring the rule of law is one of the most important functions states can assume to promote efficiency-enhancing coopera-tion among private parties. When, however, the state itself becomes party to a contract, the enforcement of contractual obligations for the transaction can no longer rely on the same mechanism, since the jur-idical system is part of the state itself. This results in a fundamental lack of credibility for all promises made by states, thereby undermining states' ability to conclude agreements with private parties as much as with other states.

A longstanding scholarly interest in this credibility dilemma has been growing. Political scientists study this dilemma in the domestic context and focus on the problems governments face in making credible

---

[5] E.g. Lane and Bachmann (1996).

commitments vis-à-vis private parties such as interest groups (e.g. Horn 1995; Moe 1990a), capital owners (Root 1994), or business communities (Levy and Spiller 1996). International relations scholars, in contrast, explore this question in the international arena and examine the credibility of promises exchanged between states. Both bodies of literature emphasize the importance of a state's ability to lend credibility to its commitments by binding itself through "some voluntary but irreversible sacrifice of freedom of choice" (Schelling 1960: 22).

Domestic credibility

The political science literature provides a rich discussion of the weak credibility a government faces at home and of several formal mechanisms through which it can seek to overcome this problem. Promises a government makes to domestic audiences are necessarily plagued with fundamental uncertainty because "whatever policies and structures ... [an incumbent government] put[s] in place today may be subject to the authoritative discretion of other actors tomorrow, actors with very different interests who could undermine or destroy ... [the incumbent government's] hard-won achievements" (Moe 1990b: 124). This uncertainty hampers a government's ability to engage in Pareto efficient transactions with private parties. In his historic study of royal fiscal policy during absolutism in France, Root (1994) noted that the monarch had to pay higher interest rates than private individuals to compensate for the fact that he could not be held accountable in case he defaulted and that he had a reputation for doing exactly that. Root calls this phenomenon the "irony of absolutism" and observes that, "because the king claimed full discretion, he had less power. Claiming to be above the law in fiscal matters made it more difficult for him to find business partners. The use of discretion reduced his payoffs in equilibrium because invoking absolute power destroyed royal credibility" (1994: 177). In a contemporary context, Moe (1990b), Horn and Shepsle (1989), and Horn (1995) demonstrate that a political regime which lends little or no credibility to the government's promises undermines interest groups' willingness to offer full support to the incumbent government, since they are fully aware that any benefits awarded today may be easily withdrawn by the next government. Levy and Spiller (1996) find in their comparative study of telecommunications regulation a strong causal link between the ability of governments to lend credibility to regulatory policies and their success in attracting domestic and foreign investments. Gilardi (2002) expands this point to other business sectors. Henisz (2000) presents a related argument in his article on multinational investments in which he describes investors' reluctance to invest in countries where government policies can easily be reversed. North and Weingast (1989) broaden the argument and demonstrate how a government's capacity to make credible commitments forms the indispensable underpinning of sustainable economic growth in general. It is paramount for governments of any type of political regime to develop mechanisms that allow them to signal their trustworthy intentions and to tie their own hands by insulating an enacted policy from the discretion of tomorrow's political decision-makers (Moe 1990b: 125; North and Weingast 1989).

This body of literature discusses several formal mechanisms a state can employ to enhance its credibility. The separation of legislative, executive, and judicial powers is the most prominent "credibility booster" (Gely and Spiller 1990; Landes and Posner 1975; McCubbins, Noll, and Weingast 1987, 1989), but other, more fine-grained remedies such as decentralization or the establishment of two legislative houses elected on different terms have also been studied in detail. Recent literature has been particularly interested in the relationship between the legislature and the bureaucracy (Epstein and O'Halloran 1999; Horn 1995; Huber and Shipan 2002; Miller 2000a). This literature demonstrates how the legislature can increase the value of a certain legislation in the eyes of beneficiaries by passing detailed statutes imposing rigid constraints (Moe 1990b: 136) and by entrusting the implementation of the policy to a permanent body removed from political oversight (Moe 1990b: 137). Central banks are the classic case in point, but other autonomous, technocratic regulatory agencies overseeing areas ranging from electricity to pharmaceuticals are also enjoying increasing popularity (Gilardi, Jordana, and Levi-Faur 2006). All these mechanisms generate a "lock-in" effect, as they insulate current policy beneficiaries from future change by increasing "the costs that future legislators must face if they attempt to undermine the original deal at the administrative level" (Horn 1995: 18).

International credibility

Many states have been quite successful in bolstering domestic credibility through the establishment of appropriate checks and balances while the equivalent development with regard to international credibility is lagging far behind. First steps have been undertaken in the direction of a credibility-enhancing separation of powers with the creation of international courts such as the weak International Court of Justice and the stronger International Criminal Court. However, these attempts are still confined to an embryonic stage.[6] States typically retain the discretion to decide on a case-by-case basis whether or not they want to acknowledge the competence of an international court. Furthermore, it is up to states to follow or disregard the court's ruling, as international courts cannot call upon a law enforcement body comparable to the police in the domestic context. In brief, international law rests largely on the consent of states (Brierly 1963: 7–16; Permanent Court of International Justice 1927). Many international relations scholars, in particular those associated with the realist camp, have questioned whether international law is law at all, emphasizing the anarchic nature of world affairs. The absence of any central authority above states vested with the authority and capability to effectively enforce the promises states give each other fundamentally undermines the credibility of these pledges (Mearsheimer 1994–1995; Morgenthau 1953: 296–7). The severity of this problem depends mainly on how strong the incentives are for states to renege on their promises. The problem is non-existent if states promise to take an action that offers them direct benefits that exceed the costs. In the cases presented in this study, no such quasi-automatic harmony of interest exists because each of the four cases depends on the cooperation of states which do not directly benefit from, or which may even be harmed by, effective international cooperation against the trafficking in certain goods or services. These cases resemble more a "deadlock" than the coordination scenario described by game theorists (e.g. Snidal 1985: 936–939; Stein 1983: 127–132). Therefore, for international efforts to curb illicit flows to be successful, it is critical for the enacting coalition to create institutions vested with sufficient credibility to induce all relevant states to join these efforts and to discourage cheating.

The central mechanism through which international institutions gain credibility is to raise the relative costs states incur in case they later revoke or defy previously made commitments. Fearon (1997) distinguishes two instruments that states can use to make the official endorsement of an international institution "costly" and therefore credible:

---

[6] The European Court of Justice presents the most important exception.

sunk-costs and tying hands. The former refers to financially costly actions undertaken by a party *ex ante*, such as the mobilization of troops. The latter mechanism – tying hands – is closely associated with audience or reputational costs a state incurs *ex post*. When a state fails to honor its formal promises, it spoils its international reputation, which has negative repercussions on both the international and domestic level. On the international level, the defecting state may find it more difficult to enter international agreements in the future (Keohane 1984: 105f.; Morgenthau 1953: 313). On the domestic level, the non-complying government may be sanctioned by the mass electorate in the case of democracies or by a clique of oligarchs in autocracies, since these groups value their state's good international standing (Bueno de Mesquita *et al.* 1999; Morrow 2000; Smith 1998). The actual size of international and domestic audience costs depends on the extent to which an international agreement puts a state's reputation at stake. Audience costs are higher, first, when a state makes an official declaration considering itself legally bound by an international agreement (Lipson 1991), secondly, when the provisions of this agreement are specific enough to allow for a clear distinction between compliance and breach and, finally, when an independent agency is commissioned to monitor and to expose (non-)compliance – in brief, when the agreement incorporates a high level of legalization.

2.1.2 *The downside of high levels of legalization*

Since obligation, precision, and delegation seem to boost the credibility of an international institution, one might expect states to favor higher levels of legalization, i.e. hard law, over lower levels of legalization, i.e. soft law. This assumption, however, is not supported by evidence, as demonstrated by the great number of international institutions with only soft legalization (Shelton 2000). Scholars of international relations and international law discuss various reasons as to why states might favor soft law over hard law (Abbott and Snidal 2000; Guzman 2004; Lipson 1991; Reinicke and Witte 2000; Rosendorff and Milner 2001; Shelton 2000).

The most fundamental obstacle for high levels of legalization (and thus credibility) is the sovereignty costs this move to hard law involves. "[T]he right of independent action is the natural result of sovereignty" (Lawrence 1910: 111) – a prerogative that states are as keen to defend today as when Lawrence wrote his seminal book *The Principles of International Law*.

Governments are deeply reluctant to renounce parts of their country's sovereignty, and the constitutions of most countries reinforce this tendency through rigid procedures that have to be followed whenever a government wants to make far-reaching international commitments.

Furthermore, hard law is associated with four major types of rigidities that all decrease the flexibility of international institutions, both with respect to their creation and their operation. First, the establishment of hard law usually entails a slow and costly process. It requires lengthy negotiations between top-level representatives of national executives. After closure, newly drafted international agreements of legally binding force typically require a ratification process that depends on the approval of parliament, or for a few countries, even the citizenry. Second, given the reputational stakes associated with hard law, states are very reluctant to enter an agreement with an ambitious agenda. For this reason, many hard laws represent little more than the lowest common denominator (Downs, Rocke, and Barsoom 1996). If an issue is contentious, "anything other than non-binding agreements would deter states and non-state actors from participating, precluding the possibility of informal and formal cooperation" (Reinicke and Witte 2000: 94). Third, the high levels of credibility of hard law come at the expense of a flexible adaptation of the provisions to changing circumstances. The complex interaction of many policy issues with a rapidly changing and technology-driven environment necessitates adaptive and responsive policy instruments (Reinicke and Witte 2000: 95). But as adaptations of existing hard law agreements require the consent of all parties, this process can be almost as cumbersome as the drafting of the agreement in the first place. Fourth and finally, hard law is very rigid toward the inclusion of non-state actors, as the Vienna Convention on the Law of Treaties (VCLT) of 1969 only recognizes sovereign states as negotiators and signatories of treaties. It has become commonplace to note the important roles various types of non-state actors assume throughout all stages of the international policymaking process, but only soft law allows for an official participation of non-state actors in the development and implementation of international rules (Shelton 2000: 13). For these reasons, Johnston concludes that soft law arrangements may enjoy increasing popularity, perhaps "motivated by the need to circumvent the political constraints, economic costs, and legal rigidities that often are associated with formal and legally binding treaties" (1997: xxiv).

2.1.3 Hard or soft legalization: a difficult trade-off

As the above discussion highlighted, international institutions endowed with either low or high legalization present certain advantages and drawbacks. International actors therefore face a difficult trade-off between flexibility and credibility when designing an international institution (Goldstein and Martin 2000: 605; Koremenos 2001; Rosendorff and Milner 2001).

Traditionally, scholars of international law made a clear-cut distinction between legally binding treaties and softer forms of international arrangements, dismissing the latter as non-law (Weil 1983), or as a mere second-best solution (cf. Schachter 1977: 304). But over the past decade, scholars in both international relations and international law increasingly recognize the growing importance of soft law. Koh argues that we are witnessing the emergence of a "brave new world of international law ... [where] transnational actors, sources of law, allocation of decision function and modes of regulation have all mutated into fascinating hybrid forms. International law now comprises a complex blend of customary, positive, declarative, and soft law" (1995: ix). Adopting Koh's perspective on the nature of contemporary international law, this study perceives hard and soft legalization not as mutually exclusive institutional designs, but as arrayed along a continuum ranging from arrangements that impose strong constraints on behavior to arrangements that allow for almost complete freedom of unilateral action (Abbott *et al.* 2000; Reinicke and Witte 2000; Shelton 2000: 4).

The distinction between hard and soft law is far from clear-cut. Many legally binding treaties "soften" their degree of obligation through vague formulations or weak enforcement mechanisms. In contrast, many non-binding arrangements may provide for supervisory mechanisms traditionally associated with hard law (Shelton 2000: 10), as I will show in the case studies on money laundering (Chapter 5) and conflict diamonds (Chapter 6). Furthermore, hard law and soft law often assume complementary roles. Shelton (2000: 10) notes that soft law can rarely be found in isolation, but is usually part of a complex regime consisting of hard law and soft law arrangements both seeking to regulate the same issue area. Soft law agreements often assume the function of authoritatively resolving a treaty's ambiguities or of filling in gaps and omissions. Furthermore, the separation between hard and soft law is not static. Soft law is often the first step on the path toward legally binding agreements (Abbott and Snidal 2004). Especially when an issue is highly contentious, soft law presents the only arrangement that diverging parties can agree upon. Reinicke and Witte (2000) point out how informal and formal cooperation based on soft law can lead to a convergence of perceived interests of states, and thus promote closer cooperation. However, as Raustiala (2005) points out, there is no automatism leading to the hardening of soft law over time. Although many examples exist in support of this assumption, there are also cases which remain permanently on the soft end of the spectrum or experience a "softening" over time.

The fact that the boundary between soft law and hard law is blurred does not imply that the two are indistinguishable. As I will show in the next section, it is both possible and heuristically useful to categorize international institutions according to level of legalization. I distinguish three ordinal levels of legalization – low, moderate, and high – and assign international institutions to one of these three broad categories based on the three design dimensions: obligation, precision, and delegation. The next section presents in more detail the theoretical motivation underlying these three dimensions and develops a framework for measuring them empirically .

2.2 The three dimensions of the concept of legalization

Abbott *et al.*'s (2000) three dimensions of legalization – obligation, precision, and delegation – allow for the localization of international institutions on the soft law–hard law spectrum. An international institution is more credible and thus "harder" when states unambiguously commit themselves to comply with an agreement (obligation), when the provisions of the agreement are precise enough to allow for a clear distinction between compliance and non-compliance (precision), and when substantive power is transferred to a third party vested with some degree of independence (delegation). In the following discussion, I will present these three aspects of legalization and their importance for the credibility–flexibility trade-off discussed above. Assessing the levels of obligation, precision, and delegation incorporated in an international institution is necessarily an approximation. I adopt two measures in order to allow for the greatest possible degree of intersubjectivity. First, the discussion below details which observable elements of an international institution are considered indicators for soft and hard legalization, respectively. These indicators will be compiled into a "checklist," which will systematically guide the assessment of international institutions in the second part of this study. Second, given the impossibility of generating any meaningful and precise quantitative measurements for the three explanatory variables, this study contents itself with discerning three ordinal levels (low, moderate, high) of legalization. The localization of an international institution on this three-step scale will be based on the relative prominence of the three major components of legalization: obligation, precision, and delegation. I will first assess each of these three dimensions separately before aggregating the overall degree of legalization as the unweighted average of obligation, precision, and delegation.

2.2.1 Obligation

This study refers to obligation as the intention of states to be bound by a commitment they have made. This intention is reflected in the extent to which an international institution is designed to make non-compliance costly. There are two basic ways states can tie their hands through costly commitments. First, institutions can be crafted in legally binding terms, which implies that commitments become a source of law in the sense of Article 38 Para 1 of the Statute of the International Court of Justice of 1945 and are governed by customary law and the Vienna Convention on the Law of Treaties. Most importantly, the legal principle of *pacta sunt servanda* enshrined in Article 26 VCLT applies, which obliges states to honor legally binding commitments. If they fail to do so, they become legally responsible, and parties injured by breach may claim reparations – either in the form of material compensation or an official apology (Abbott *et al.* 2000: 409). The authors of the initial concept of legalization (Abbott *et al.* 2000) focused their definition of obligation exclusively on this legal mechanism for tying hands. I expand this definition to include a second instrument states have at their disposal to signal the sincerity of their commitment. In addition to – or instead of – the procedures and remedies that international law provides in relation to legally binding obligations, states may also increase the cost of defection by devising institution-specific compliance mechanisms. Stringent monitoring and sanctioning mechanisms thereby serve as screening devices, since states that do not intend to comply with provisions enshrined in a highly obliging institution would oppose the creation of such governance structures in the first place and refuse to endorse an existing international institution with such compliance measures. Monitoring thereby serves a double purpose. For one, it provides the indispensable factual basis for making decisions on the imposition of sanctions. As for the other, stringent compliance monitoring constitutes in itself a sanctioning mechanism as it can entail significant reputational costs. The magnitude of incurred reputational costs depends on the extent to which the results of the monitoring exercise are published, whereby international praxis varies from confidentiality to full publicity.

In the following two sections, I will describe in detail how I operationalize these two sub-components of obligation to allow for a systematic assessment across cases.

Legal bindingness

The first sub-component of obligation – legal bindingness – contains both dichotomous and discrete elements. I share Shelton's (2000) proposition that policymakers make a conscious decision on whether to craft an international agreement in legally binding terms with the "intention ... to create legal rights and obligations or to establish relations governed by international law" (Schachter 1977: 296). Legality, to use Raustiala's (2005) terminology, is thus a binary variable – an agreement is either legally binding or not. However, I also think it is indispensable to take into account the various mechanisms legally binding instruments provide to attenuate the degree of bindingness, namely through reservations, escape clauses, and withdrawal.

To establish whether an international agreement is legally or only politically binding is not always straightforward, as states are often reluctant to explicitly declare that an agreement lacks legal power.[7] Therefore, the true intention often has to be inferred from the "language of the instrument and the attendant circumstances of its conclusion and adoption" (Schachter 1977: 297).

It has become common practice to use certain terms and formulations in agreements that are meant to be legally binding and to avoid these terms in

---

[7] An exception is, for instance, the "Non-legally Binding Instrument on All Types of Forests" adopted by the United Nations General Assembly (UNGA) in December 2007 which already clarifies its legal status in the title. The OSCE Document on Small Arms and Light Weapons of 2000 includes a final provision to the same effect, stating that "[t]he norms, principles and measures in this document are politically binding" (Section VI Para 6).

non-binding agreements. The most obvious starting point in a language-based assessment of an international agreement's legal status is to refer to its official name. The terms "convention,"[8] "treaty," and "protocol"[9] are typically used for legally binding agreements. In contrast, expressions like "program,"[10] "recommendations,"[11] "code of conduct,"[12] "memorandum of understanding,"[13] "arrangement,"[14] or "declaration" are more popular among legally non-binding agreements. Other words that indicate an agreement's legally binding character include "parties," "state parties," or "contracting state" (as opposed to "participants," "participating states," or "countries"); in addition to "obligations" (as opposed to "recommendations" or "standards") and "shall" (as opposed to "should").

In addition to an agreement's language, we can also consider its procedural provisions to determine whether or not it is meant to be legally binding. Legally binding agreements typically contain provisions on signature, ratification, acceptance, approval, accession, entry into force, amendments, denunciations, and depository. Many of these procedural issues are not explicitly addressed in legally non-binding agreements.

Among the "attendant circumstances" (Schachter 1977) of an international agreement's adoption are the domestic procedures through which a government must obtain authorization for endorsing an international agreement and the official registration of the agreement under the UN Charter.

Domestic laws typically require stronger forms of legislative or even public scrutiny for legally binding international agreements than non-binding instruments. The US Constitution, for example, requires the "advice and consent" of two-thirds of the Senate for the ratification of

---

[8] E.g. the UN Convention against Illicit Traffic in Narcotic Drugs and Psychotropic Substances.

[9] E.g. the UN Protocol against the Illicit Manufacturing of and Trafficking in Firearms, Their Parts and Components and Ammunition.

[10] E.g. the UN Program of Action to Prevent, Combat and Eradicate the Illicit Trade in Small Arms and Light Weapons in All Its Aspects.

[11] E.g. the Financial Action Task Force's Forty Recommendations on money laundering.

[12] E.g. the EU Code of Conduct for Arms Exports (8675/2/98 Rev. 2, of June 8, 1998).

[13] E.g. the Memorandum of Understanding between the Task Force for Cooperative Enforcement Operations Directed at Illegal Trade in Wild Fauna and Flora and the Secretariat of the Convention on International Trade in Endangered Species of Wild Fauna and Flora.

[14] E.g. the Wassenaar Arrangement.

an international treaty (Article II, Section 2, Clause 2). In Switzerland, some legally binding international agreements are subject to a mandatory or optional referendum (Constitution of the Swiss Federation, Article 140 Para 1 Lit. b and Article 141 Para 1 Lit. d, respectively).

A second but less conclusive element of Schachter's attendant circumstances is the registration of an international agreement under Article 102 of the UN Charter. This article stipulates that "every treaty or international agreement, whatever its form and descriptive name, entered into by one or more members of the United Nations has to be registered with the UN secretariat and be published in the United Nations Treaty Series." However, as both legally binding and non-binding agreements are required to be filed with the UN, the registration of an agreement is a very weak indicator of an agreement's legal bindingness. Some exceptions – most prominently, the Helsinki Final Act of 1975 – exist wherein the parties of the agreement explicitly decided against registration with the UN secretariat. Such a non-registration bears the important consequence that parties forfeit the right to invoke the agreement before any organ of the United Nations (UN Charter Article 102 Para 2). Therefore, a non-registration can be seen as an indicator of the parties' intentions to underline the non-binding status of the agreement, whereas registration does not in itself indicate bindingness. In praxis, using the non-listing of an agreement in the United Nations Treaty Series as an indicator of the soft law character of an agreement is complicated by the fact that the Treaty Series currently runs a backlog of around ten years.

Examining the language and formal provisions contained in an international instrument along with the procedures through which it was adopted usually allows for an unambiguous assessment of whether an agreement is legally binding or only politically binding.

The legally binding agreements typically provide for three mechanisms through which parties can unilaterally attenuate the bindingness of the agreement. These mechanisms are usually absent in non-binding agreements.

First, most legally binding international agreements allow for reservations,[15] which the Vienna Convention on the Law of Treaties defines

---

[15] An example to the contrary is the Ottawa Landmine Treaty which expressly states in Article 19 that "[t]he Articles of this Convention shall not be subject to reservations."

as "unilateral statement[s], however phrased or named, made by a
State, when signing, ratifying, accepting, approving or acceding to a
treaty, where … [they] purport to exclude or to modify the legal effect of
certain provisions of the treaty in their application to the State" (Article
2 Lit. d). The VCLT contains the extent to which parties can unilaterally
reduce the substantive and procedural strength of an agreement through
two main mechanisms. For one, as the article just cited clearly shows, a
party can only take recourse to this instrument prior to the ratification
of the agreement, but not thereafter. For the other, the VCLT tries to
safeguard the integrity of the treaty by limiting the application of
reservations. Article 19 Lit. c specifies that a state may not submit a
reservation which is "incompatible with the object and purpose of the
treaty." This provision is vague and leaves plenty of room for interpretation. Some international agreements therefore explicate which of
their provisions are open for reservations and which cannot be modified
unilaterally. For instance, Article 42 of the Council of Europe
Convention on Cybercrime[16] explicitly lists the provisions a party is
allowed to modify and interdicts reservations relating to all other provisions. The United Nations Single Convention on Narcotic Drugs of
1961 specifies both transitional (Article 49) and lasting (Article 50)
reservations, while the 1988 UN Convention against Illicit Traffic in
Narcotic Drugs and Psychotropic Substances does not contain any
provisions on reservations thus falling back on Article 19 VCLT (see
Chapter 4). The tenacity of the obligations enshrined in a legally binding agreement is therefore considered to be higher the more rigid the
limits it imposes on the use of reservations.

Second, many international agreements – and virtually all agreements
on trade[17] (Milner, Rosendorff, and Mansfield 2004) – soften their legal
bindingness by including safeguards, often also referred to as escape
clauses. Such provisions act as "safety valves" that allow states to
respond to unforeseen developments that "cause or threaten to cause
serious injury"[18] to a country's vital interests. The misuse potential of
escape clauses is even larger than with reservations, as the former allow

---

[16] Council of Europe Treaty Series (CETS) 185 of November 23, 2001.
[17] E.g. Article XIX, titled "Emergency Actions on Imports of Particular Products" of
the General Agreement on Tariffs and Trade (GATT) 1947, was evoked 151
times until the revision of GATT in the Uruguay round (Rogowsky 2001).
[18] Article 2 Para 1 Safeguard Agreement of the World Trade Organization (WTO).

for a unilateral deviation from previously made commitments whenever a party faces growing domestic pressure (Rosendorff and Milner 2001), not just in the period between its adoption and accession. International agreements are therefore careful to explicate the conditions under which a state may evoke these safeguards and temporarily suspend the fulfillment of its treaty obligations, and include provisions that impose some costs upon parties who invoke escape clauses (Hoekman and Kostecki 2001: 303). Under GATT, this is achieved through a stipulation that requires countries that temporarily erect trade barriers with reference to an escape clause to negotiate compensations with the affected exporters or to lower barriers in another area (Milner, Rosendorff, and Mansfield 2004). The number and the scope of escape clauses incorporated in an international agreement can therefore serve as a second criterion to assess the degree to which legally binding obligations are weakened.

Mindful that at some point the temporary suspension of some specific obligations may not suffice, states endow most legally binding agreements with provisions on withdrawal. These allow states to renounce their previously made commitments altogether. Theoretically, the credibility-weakening potential of the withdrawal option is even more severe than the escape option, as the latter usually applies only to one or two provisions of an agreement. In order to balance states' reluctance to sign on to obligations that cannot be renounced at a later stage on the one hand, and the need for credibility on the other, almost all legally binding international agreements allow for withdrawal,[19] but specify procedures that constrain the exercise of this option. International agreements vary, however, with respect to the constraints they impose on withdrawal. The aforementioned Council of Europe Convention on Cybercrime of 2001, for example, specifies that a denunciation of the Convention by any party becomes effective three months after the secretary general of the Council of Europe has been notified (Article 47).[20] The Nuclear Nonproliferation Treaty (NPT) of 1968 provides for the same lapse period between a party's announcement of withdrawal and its effect. Many other arms treaties stipulate a six-month withdrawal

---

[19] A notable exception is again the European Union, the founding treaties of which do not contain any clauses on withdrawal.
[20] The same period of notice applies to the Council of Europe Convention on Laundering, Search, Seizure and Confiscation of the Proceeds from Crime of 1990 (Article 43).

period.[21] The United Nations Convention against Illicit Traffic in Narcotic Drugs and Psychotropic Substances of 1988 (see Chapter 4) and the 2006 Convention on Small Arms and Light Weapons, Their Ammunition and Other Related Materials of the Economic Community of West African States (ECOWAS) (see Chapter 8), in contrast, require the lapse of one year after notification until withdrawal takes effect. Apart from such a treaty-imposed time lag between announcement and effect of withdrawal, many legally binding instruments also require a withdrawing party to justify its decision with reference to "extraordinary events it regards as having jeopardized its supreme interests,"[22] thus rendering it impossible for the party to continue treaty membership. The "height" of the hurdles an international agreement erects to prevent easy withdrawal affects the degree of obligation imposed by an international institution and can therefore serve as a third criterion for the extent to which obligation is attenuated through procedural provisions.[23]

In sum, the language of an international agreement and its procedural provisions and attendant circumstances determine whether the agreement is legally binding or only politically binding, thereby relegating the latter to the lower spectrum of legal bindingness. In the case of a legally binding agreement, I will, in a second step, assess the restrictions it imposes on reservations, safeguards, and withdrawal. These provisions can significantly weaken the credibility of an international agreement. Under these circumstances the overall degree of legal bindingness can be reduced to moderate, even if the agreement is formally of legally binding nature. In contrast, legally non-binding agreements necessarily receive low scores on this sub-component of obligation.

---

[21] E.g. the Treaty between the United States and the Union of the Soviet Socialist Republics on the Limitation of Anti-Ballistic Missile Systems (ABM) Treaty of 1972; the Comprehensive Test Ban Treaty (CTBT) of 1996; the Ottawa Landmine Treaty of 1997.

[22] E.g. Article X of the NPT.

[23] In praxis, withdrawal from international conventions remains a relatively rare phenomenon. The United States' withdrawal from the ABM Treaty in 2002 and North Korea's withdrawal from the NPT in 2003 are among the highest profile exceptions. To my knowledge, no systematic analysis has been carried out so far to assess whether withdrawal is more common from international agreements with low denunciation hurdles than from agreements that impose tighter restrictions on withdrawal.

Compliance mechanisms

Legal bindingness is only one way states can signal the sincerity of their commitment to an international institution. In addition to, or instead of legal bindingness, they can also increase the costs of non-compliance through rigorous procedures to monitor actual implementation and to sanction breaches of commitments. While many legally binding agreements have incorporated provisions on monitoring and sanctioning of varying strength for some time, it is a more recent development that some non-binding instruments also provide for far-reaching compliance-enhancing instruments (Shelton 2000). The original concept of legalization does not explicitly include monitoring and enforcement under the "obligation" variable. In fact, these two elements only receive a scant review, mainly in the discussion of delegation. I agree that monitoring and enforcement gain significant credibility if carried out through an independent body – be it an international governmental organization[24] or private groups.[25] However, I take the position that the question as to who assumes these functions is analytically distinct from other important modalities that lend teeth to an international institution. I therefore include the latter element in the "obligation" variable and discuss the former under delegation.

The popularity of monitoring or implementation reviews varies considerably over time and across policy fields,[26] and a great number of international institutions do not have any explicit monitoring provisions. Institutionalized monitoring is most common in environmental or human rights institutions, and recent institutions are more likely to provide for monitoring than older institutions (Haas 2003).[27] Those international institutions that do provide for monitoring come up with a great range of different mechanisms which vary in terms of their

[24] E.g. the International Atomic Energy Agency (IAEA).

[25] An interesting example is TRAFFIC, a joint program between the non-governmental organization World Wildlife Fund (WWF) and the World Conservation Union (IUCN), a network that brings together 83 states, 110 government agencies, more than 800 NGOs, and some 10,000 scientists and experts from 181 countries in a unique worldwide partnership.

[26] For instance, neither the Council of Europe Convention on Laundering, Search, Seizure and Confiscation of the Proceeds from Crime of 1990 nor the UN Firearms Protocol of 2001 contains any provisions to that end. For an excellent discussion of monitoring mechanisms – or systems for implementation review in their parlance – see Victor, Raustiala, and Skolnikoff (1998).

[27] Haas (2003) estimated that the median year for environmental treaties requiring monitoring was 1982.

credibility-boosting effect: the format, scope, frequency, and publicity with which monitoring occurs can all vary considerably.

The most common form of monitoring mechanism is self-reporting, whereby states periodically outline the steps they have undertaken to fulfill the general goal of an international institution or of specified substantive provisions. Already in this rather weak form of self-monitoring, we find some arrangements that signal greater sincerity to ensure compliance, while others leave more scope for policymakers to hide non-compliance behind vague rhetoric. Most prone to such rhetorical detractions are implementation reviews that rely exclusively on members discussing behind closed doors the efforts they made pursuant to the substantive provisions of an international institution, as, for instance, envisaged by the Organization for Security and Cooperation in Europe (OSCE) in its Document on Small Arms and Light Weapons (Section VI Para 2; see Chapter 7). A stronger variant is found in reviews based on written reports, in particular if these reports are compiled in accordance to a common format and address the implementation of specific provisions. Depending on the issue area, the reporting format may be designed to increase transparency by making it easier for other parties to cross-check the validity of submitted data. For instance, international institutions governing trade matters may ask both importing and exporting states to report independently the number or value of a specific category of goods. The Kimberley Process Certification Scheme (Chapter 6) provides one such example. Another approach to data validation was pioneered by the Extractive Industries Transparency Initiative (EITI), which asks extractive industry companies and host governments to independently submit information on the amounts of money they spent and received, respectively, in connection with extraction licenses.

Credibility is further enhanced when frequent reporting is required. Haas (2003) finds that the majority of environmental treaties (62 percent) do not specify the frequency of reporting, while annual and biannual reporting are roughly equally prevalent (17 and 19 percent, respectively). Also, monitoring mechanisms gain considerable strength if they are mandatory – as is the case in 81 percent of all multilateral environmental treaties (Haas 2003). If implementation reviews are published in full length,[28] they enable civil society groups to

---

[28] E.g. the member states of the Financial Action Task Force agreed in 2004 to make the summaries of the mutual evaluation reports available to the public through the FATF's website.

comment on the validity of the submitted information[29] and to point out areas they find wanting.

Finally, monitoring systems may also include provisions on how to deal with countries that fail to submit implementation reports. So far, very few international institutions include a mechanism for addressing non-submission of reports, with the consequence that compliance with this type of monitoring is very uneven.[30] Civil society groups engaged in the Kimberley Process lobbied very hard for the inclusion of some sort of mechanism for ensuring that all participating states live up to their reporting requirements. To date, the only form of sanction against non-submitters that participants have been able to agree upon consists of a "naming and shaming" strategy, whereby the name of the non-submitting state is published with some visual prominence on the KP's website.

One way around the problem of non-submission of reports is the establishment of direct verification mechanisms that provide information about other states' actions. A classic verification example is the International Monitoring System established by the Preparatory Commission for the Comprehensive Nuclear-Test-Ban Treaty Organization (CTBTO) which seeks to detect possible nuclear explosions through a network of 321 monitoring stations and 16 radionuclide laboratories (CTBTO 2001). However, external verification is feasible in only a limited number of issue areas. For instance, controls of arms transfers (in particular, of major weapons systems), of the emission of environmentally damaging substances, and of large cultivations of narcotic drugs are more amenable to remote sensing than the observance of human rights and banking standards.

Sanctions are subject to a similar variety of mechanisms, and differ from each other both in the type and severity of costs imposed on non-complying states. The spectrum ranges from weak symbolic sanctions, e.g. when Malta recalled its ambassador from the United States in protest of a US policy, to severe material sanctions, e.g. the imposition of an international trade embargo against Iraq in the 1990s. In reality, the distinction between symbolic and material sanctions is often blurred.

---

[29] E.g. the two NGOs Global Witness and Partnership Africa Canada cast a vigilant eye on the trade statistics submitted by states participating in the Kimberley Process (Chapter 6).

[30] The US General Accounting Office found in 1991 that only 30 percent of the parties to the 1973 International Convention for the Prevention of Pollution from Ships (MARPOL) complied with reporting obligations (US General Accounting Office 1992).

Given the importance of a good international reputation for companies as well as states, the practical effect of purely symbolic sanctions can well be material. For instance, "black listing" by the Financial Action Task Force is primarily a symbolic action of "naming and shaming," but it can result in material damage in the form of a drop in foreign direct investments and higher commissions for international money transfers (Chapter 5). Similarly, the exclusion from the EITI's list of candidate countries does not result in any direct, EITI-imposed material consequences, but it may jeopardize the affected country's efforts to receive international debt relief or aid packages. In contrast, the imposition of membership sanctions related to the Convention on International Trade in Endangered Species (CITES) or the Kimberley Process on diamonds results in direct, institution-specific, material consequences. Under both agreements, the non-complying state is excluded from the international trade in endangered species and rough diamonds, respectively.

International agreements often refrain from directly spelling out monitoring and sanctioning provisions. Particularly in the case of legally non-binding agreements, monitoring and enforcement mechanisms are often developed in practice without being enshrined in any official document or perhaps only in the minutes of meetings. In the case of both legally binding and non-binding agreements, monitoring and sanctioning are often guaranteed by provisions and through bodies – private or public – that are external to an international institution. For instance, international rating agencies take into account a country's compliance record with the legally non-binding Forty Recommendations on money laundering (Macao Trade and Investment Promotion Institute 2006) or with the equally non-binding EITI provisions, thereby affecting the influx of foreign direct investments and the capital costs on sovereign debt. The United States has a long history of unilaterally monitoring and sanctioning other states' compliance with international agreements of both legally binding[31] and

---

[31] E.g. the US State Department publishes its annual assessment of states' compliance with the UN Convention against Illicit Traffic in Narcotic Drugs and Psychotropic Substances of 1988 in the International Narcotic Control Strategy Report. States that are found to be non-complying and non-cooperative can be subjected to aid cut-offs (see Chapter 4). On unilateral sanctions imposed by the US in response to non-compliance with international environmental policies, see DeSombre (1995).

non-binding[32] nature. Because of the importance of monitoring and sanctioning practices that are not explicitly enshrined in the core agreement underlying an international institution, I extend the analysis of an institution's compliance mechanisms to include the larger institutional context, even though this leads to a blurring of the demarcation line between institutions and regimes (see Chapter 1).

In sum, this study assesses the degree of obligation created by an international institution based on the institution's formal legal status and on the monitoring and enforcement mechanisms it envisages. A legally binding international institution that limits the possibilities for a unilateral modification of obligations and provides for strong monitoring and sanctioning mechanisms thereby presents the prototypical case of a high degree of obligation.

2.2.2 Precision

The assessment of the degree of obligation enshrined in an international institution is an important, yet insufficient, first step to locate the institution on the soft law–hard law continuum. As Chinkin notes,[33] "the conclusion of an agreement in treaty form does not ensure that a hard obligation has been incurred. Treaties with imprecise, subjective, or indeterminate language ... fuse legal form with soft obligation" (2003: 25f.). The authors of the concept of legalization therefore identify precision as a second important design dimension of an international institution (Abbott *et al.* 2000).

Whereas some scholars name the lack of precision as a major reason for non-compliance (Chayes and Chayes 1993, 1995; Hirsch 2004; Shannon 2000), this study takes a contrasting perspective. It argues that the primary problem with vague rules is not that they increase non-compliance, but rather that they make non-compliance logically impossible (see with respect to human rights, Handl *et al.* 1988). The most fundamental consequence of having vague rules is that multiple

---

[32] Countries' compliance with anti-money laundering provisions detailed in the legally non-binding Forty Recommendations of the Financial Action Task Force is also analyzed in the State Department's International Narcotic Control Strategy Report.

[33] N.B.: her understanding of the term "obligation" deviates slightly from that enshrined in the concept of legalization and corresponds more with the idea of hard law or a high level of legalization.

interpretations are allowed, thus rendering it impossible to distinguish clearly between acceptable and unacceptable behavior. For instance, Morgenthau sees in the widespread imprecision of international law a "ready-made tool [used by governments] for furthering their ends. They have done so by advancing unsupported claims to legal rights and by distorting the meaning of generally recognized rules of international law" (1953: 299). Abbott and Snidal refer to this phenomenon as "self-serving auto-interpretation" (2000: 427). Such a deliberate manipulation is not surprising as imprecision of international rules and standards often results from profound disagreement among parties in the negotiating stage.[34] To avoid endless and costly negotiations over a highly contentious issue, parties may choose to phrase their commitment in ambiguous terms which are later mirrored in uneven implementation efforts (Iklé 1964: 12; Shelton 2000: 14). Low levels of precision can therefore seriously undermine the credibility of an international institution.

A high level of precision helps to strengthen compliance with an international institution – and thus its credibility – in two major ways. First, precise formulations help narrow the scope of permissible interpretation (Franck 1990), thus facilitating convergence of state behavior. Second, by formulating rules that are precise enough to allow for a clear-cut distinction between acceptable and unacceptable behavior, states increase the reputational stakes of non-compliance. Only if a certain type of behavior can clearly be discerned to be in breach of the agreement can it become the basis for a "naming and shaming" campaign or other sanctions. In this sense, precision can serve as a screening device to distinguish states that are more sincere about living up to their pledges from states that are less inclined to do so.

Although there is widespread agreement that precision matters, as of now, few scholars have tried to specify the term in ways that would allow for a systematic comparison and assessment of the degree of precision found in different international institutions. The "precision" variable still remains the least specified and operationalized of the three dimensions of the concept of legalization. Abbott *et al.* (2000) have undertaken a first step toward bringing more precision to their third

---

[34] Horn's (1995) analysis of legislative decision-making in the domestic context empirically confirms such a relationship between the level of conflict and the degree of vagueness of a law that is being passed (see also Huber and Shipan 2002).

design variable. They specify that "[p]recise sets of rules are often, though by no means always, highly elaborated or dense, detailing conditions of application, spelling out required or proscribed behavior in numerous situations" (2000: 413). These authors also suggest assessing the degree of precision enshrined in an international agreement based on the precision in which individual provisions are formulated (determinacy), as well as of the precision of the agreement in its entirety (coherence) (Abbott *et al.* 2000).

Determinacy

Franck (1990) uses the notion of "determinacy" to describe rules' ability to specify "clearly and unambiguously what is expected of a state or other actor ... in a particular set of circumstances" (quoted in Abbott *et al.* 2000: 412). Precision can be achieved either through relatively precise "rules" or through more general "standards." The former refer to provisions such as "no person may pilot a commercial airplane after his sixtieth birthday" (example taken from Diver 1983), which use words with "well-defined and universally accepted meanings" (Diver 1983: 67). Such rules are "transparent" in Diver's notion. They increase the "accuracy of prediction" (Franck 1990: 118–119) of how the provision will be applied, as the enactors of the provision determine *ex ante* which behavior is deemed acceptable (Abbott *et al.* 2000). The wording of standard-like provisions, on the other hand, is more general, opening room for an *ex post* interpretation in order to allow for greater "congruence," i.e. to foster "the law's substantive moral aims by promoting outcomes in individual cases consistent with those aims" (Diver 1983: 71). The standard-based equivalent to the example of a rule-based provision given above could be formulated in the following fashion: "No person may pilot a commercial airplane if he poses an unreasonable risk of accident" (example again taken from Diver 1983). The formulation "unreasonable risk of accident" is obviously susceptible to widely varying interpretations. Standard-like formulations commonly used in international agreements include "as appropriate," "to the greatest extent possible," and "as may be necessary."[35] The actual range of diverging

---

[35] These terms could also be interpreted as mechanisms for weakening the tenacity of an obligation similar to escape clauses, thus constituting an element of obligation (I owe this point to Robert Keohane). My preference for considering the use of these vague terms under the "precision" dimension is based on the fact that escape clauses, at least in the legal meaning of the word, only exist in legally

interpretations of such formulations depends on who is entrusted with the task of interpreting and applying a standard-like provision and on the "thickness" of the interpretative context surrounding such provisions. The authors of the concept of legalization point out that when the interpretation of standard-like prescriptions is entrusted to independent courts, standard-like provisions can also reach a high degree of determinacy (Abbott *et al.* 2000: 413). While this argument may be often correct,[36] it fuses the precision dimensions with delegation, which I prefer to keep distinct. I therefore focus more on the determinacy that vague terms can gain from a "thickening" body of literature that seeks to specify the meaning of an international institution and its provisions. Precedents are the most authoritative source of interpretation in which independent courts have clarified the meaning of indeterminate terms through specific cases. The second most authoritative sources come from official commentaries, interpretative notes, and glossaries, which the United Nations and other international bodies issue for their legally binding[37] and non-binding[38] agreements. A number of international institutions have also developed handbooks for assessing compliance, which also help to reduce uncertainty about the appropriate interpretation of indeterminate formulations.[39] Finally, publications by legal scholars who examine a particular international institution[40] can also help to compensate for a low level of determinacy.

---

   binding agreements, whereas vague terms are equally prevalent in legally binding and non-binding agreements. Furthermore, the conditions under which recourse to safeguards is permissible are specified in the agreement, whereas diverging interpretations of underspecified terms are not tied to any specific circumstances.

[36] The validity of the argument largely depends on the number of precedents that have helped to specify the meaning of an open term. The combination of ambiguously formulated provisions and an absence of precedents has in many cases led to courts' refusal to rule on the grounds that the laws they were meant to use were too imprecise, thus rendering a (binding) law practically ineffective (Diver 1983).

[37] E.g. the Commentary on the United Nations Convention on Contracts for the International Sale of Goods of 1980; official commentary on the United Nations Convention against Illicit Traffic in Narcotic Drugs and Psychotropic Substances of 1988.

[38] E.g. the Commentary on the United Nations Norms on the Responsibilities of Transnational Corporations and Other Business Enterprises with Regard to Human Rights.

[39] E.g. the Financial Action Task Force published in 2007 the AML/CFT Evaluation and Assessment Handbook for Countries and Assessors.

[40] E.g. Boister (2001).

In sum, this study assesses the overall level of an international institution's determinacy based on the relative reliance on rule-like versus standard-like provisions, the frequency of *ex ante* indeterminate formulations, and the density of authoritative interpretations.

Coherence

The second element of precision – coherence – refers to the relation among the provisions contained in an agreement (internal coherence) and to the relation between an individual institution and the international legal system in which it is embedded (external coherence). Referring to Dworkin (1986), Franck (1990) uses the term "coherence" to describe a situation in which the provisions of an agreement do not contradict each other and fit with other principles and rules of the international legal system in a non-contradictory way. The central idea behind the coherence requirement is that legal uncertainty arises when provisions within the legal system contradict each other and it is not clear which one prevails. This legal uncertainty, in turn, threatens to undermine the credibility of an international agreement and of the system as a whole.

The desirability of a coherent legal system is apparent, but, as Georgiev (1993) argues, it is very difficult to achieve in practice. This is mainly due to the fact that international law, as the product of human beings, necessarily reflects their conflicting interests, and that furthermore, many situations require a very delicate balancing of two or more incompatible but equally desirable values. The text on self-determination in the UN Declaration of Principles concerning Friendly Relations among States of 1970 (A/8028) provides a good illustration. The declaration upholds, on the one hand, the virtue of the principle of self-determination of all peoples and, on the other hand, and equally forcefully, the principle of territorial integrity and political unity of sovereign and independent states. Contradictory provisions are not unfamiliar to the domestic legal system, either.

Jurists of both domestic and international law have developed several principles on how to resolve legal contradictions, such as *lex posterior derogate legi priori*, *lex specialis derogat legi generali*, and *lex superior derogat legi inferiori*. In international law, an example of the latter principle is the superior status assigned to *ius cogens* from which it follows that *ius cogens* cannot be abrogated by contractual stipulations between states. These juridical rules of interpretation enhance the predictability of an unavoidably contradictory legal system. However, this enhanced predictability can only be achieved when conflicting norms are indeed submitted to a body which seeks to resolve contradictions according to juridical professional standards. As in the first dimension of precision, i.e. determinacy, the predictability of an international agreement which is either self-contradictory or which is in conflict with provisions of the wider legal system can only be saved when the settling of interpretative disagreements is delegated to an independent judicial body (Abbott *et al.* 2000). In the absence of such delegation, the resolution of norm conflicts is left to the unpredictable haggling between the politically motivated actors who created the agreement, and who may subsequently engage in forum-shopping to justify their incongruent behavior (Alter and Meunier 2006; Drezner 2006; Raustiala and Victor 2004). Incoherence therefore undermines the predictability of an international agreement and the credibility of the enacting coalitions' commitment.

To some extent, determinacy and coherence are interdependent, as coherence can only be assessed when an international agreement possesses at least a minimum level of determinacy. When an international agreement is formulated in highly ambiguous terms, no contradiction between individual provisions or between the agreement and other rules of international law can be clearly established, as these vague formulations allow for multiple interpretations, some of which may or may not be contradictory.

In sum, an international institution is considered highly precise when the share of ambiguously formulated terms relative to the total number of provisions is low, and when the institution makes a conscious effort to ensure coherence of its provisions with other international institutions and general principles of international law.

2.2.3 Delegation

The authors of the concept of legalization define their third dimension – delegation – as the "extent to which states and other actors delegate authority to designated third parties – including courts, arbitrators, and administrative organizations – to implement agreements" (Abbott *et al.* 2000: 415). While this definition refers to implementation in general, the bulk of the authors' elaboration of the specific meaning of delegation focuses on the delegation of legislative (e.g. norm elaboration) and *a fortiori* of judicial (e.g. norm interpretation, dispute settlement, monitoring, and enforcement) tasks, while the delegation of executive functions (e.g. capacity-building programs, research, and analysis) receives only scant attention. This focus on legislative and judicial delegation is justified when a stricter understanding of legalization is adopted – that is to say, when the structuring of international affairs is held in place primarily through laws and quasi-laws. If the emphasis is on international institutions more broadly, however, it becomes necessary to place equal emphasis on all three functions, since executive tasks also have a direct and indirect bearing on states' behavior. Training programs directly help to reduce the number of unintended non-compliance cases (Chayes and Chayes 1993, 1995) whereby willing states fail to live up to obligations because of weak governance capacity. Compliance is also strengthened more indirectly when states mandate a centralized body to compile annual reports on parties' implementation records. This form of delegation provides the indispensable analytical basis for naming and shaming non-compliant states and identifying necessary policy adjustments. This study therefore posits that an international institution can possess at least a moderate degree of delegation even if it does not entrust dispute settlement to an independent third party,[41] provided that it delegates important legislative and executive functions.

The question as to why the legislator on the domestic level and the state on the international level delegate certain functions poses an intriguing theoretical puzzle, since delegation always involves a certain loss of authority. Recent literature points to three motivating factors: efficiency gains through specialization, blame-shirking in the face of potentially unpopular policy decisions (Alesina and Tabellini 2005; Fiorina 1982), and credibility enhancement. This study focuses on the last aspect, which has attracted the greatest interest among scholars studying the phenomenon in both the domestic (e.g. Bawn 1995; Diver 1983; Epstein and O'Halloran 1999; Horn 1995; McCubbins and Page 1993; Miller 2000a; Moe 1990b) and in the international context (e.g. Hawkins *et al.* 2006; Lake and McCubbins 2006; Martin 1993; Stone 2002). Majone, for example, posits explicitly that "political sovereigns are willing to delegate important powers to independent … [bodies] in

---

[41] In fact, only a few international institutions provide for an effective delegation of dispute resolution.

order to increase the credibility of their policy commitments" (1997: 139–140). Delegation to an independent agent increases credibility because it implies that governments renounce their discretion and bind themselves to more or less rigid rules, the implementation of which is beyond their immediate control. This is an effective tool for "tying a government's hands," as the entrusted agencies ideally operate according to incentive structures that do not encourage the short time horizon and volatility associated with elected and democratically accountable bodies (Dixit 1996; Shepsle 1991). Delegation is thus an important mechanism for "locking-in" current policies to insulate them from future change (McCubbins, Noll, and Weingast 1987).

In the domestic context, we find such delegation in its most fundamental form in the separation of powers, and in particular, with the independence of the judiciary. Other examples include the delegation of monetary policy to independent central banks (Barro and Gordon 1983; Keefer and Stasavage 1998) and the delegation of regulatory policies, e.g. related to telecoms, electricity, and railways, to arm's-length agencies (Gilardi 2002; Thatcher 2002). In the international context, delegation is often seen as the aspect of legalization that states are most reluctant to establish and commit to. This hesitance results from the fact that delegation impinges directly on national sovereignty. As Andrew Moravcsik notes, "Governments often refuse to assume the political risk of delegation, preferring instead imperfect enforcement and inefficient decision-making to the surrender of sovereignty" (1993: 509). Given the centrality of national sovereignty to the concept of statehood, it may be surprising that a considerable number of instances of international delegation do exist on a wide range of issues. States delegate aid-giving to multilateral organizations like the World Bank (Milner 2006), their monetary policy to the European Central Bank, and even, in at least one case, national security to another state,[42] to mention just a few examples. Understanding these and other examples of international delegation requires a step beyond the binary view on delegation (i.e. the question of whether to delegate authority or not in a certain issue area). As Abbot and Snidal (1998) convincingly demonstrate, states can choose to delegate a narrower or broader scope of tasks ("centralization") and vest the agent with more or less autonomy ("independence").

---

[42] E.g. the Principality of Liechtenstein delegated the responsibility for its territory's defense to its western neighbor, Switzerland.

Independence

The first aspect of delegation, independence, refers to a body's "authority to act with a degree of autonomy, and often with neutrality, in defined spheres" (Abbott and Snidal 1998: 9). An agency's independence is assessed, thereby, based on the extent to which it can take decisions that are not predetermined in advance by the principal (Bawn 1995: 62). Three aspects seem to be particularly important constituents of an agency's autonomy: personnel, financial resources, and decision-making procedures.[43]

The first aspect refers to the issue of to whom the authority is delegated. Independence is nil when a certain function is assumed by the assembly constituent of all parties. Inversely, independence is maximized when this function is delegated to an agency that is not constituent of or directly managed by state representatives. This agency may be a public (e.g. an intergovernmental organization), a private body (e.g. an industry umbrella organization), or a private–public hybrid organization.[44] As mentioned above (see 2.2.1), a number of international conventions explicitly delegate certain monitoring functions to groups of independent experts.[45] In other instances, the incorporation of non-state actors developed without a formal authoritative decision. For instance, the World Trade Organization's Appellate Body barely granted non-state actors standing in the dispute settlement process any formal codification (Cortell and Peterson 2006).

Independence is further enhanced when the head of the agency and the board of managers enjoy a long and renewable term of office and the procedures governing their appointment or dismissal restrict the influence of political considerations (Elgie and McMenamin 2005; Nielson and Tierney 2003). An annually rotating secretariat chosen on the basis of considerations for equitable geographic representation[46] presents a much lower degree of independence than an executive office whose one secretary is hired on the basis of technical competency and retains the position for over a decade.[47] The temporal status of the agency itself is also closely related to its independence. In some cases, policymakers expressly limit the duration of an international institution

---

[43] My understanding of independence is largely congruent with Koremenos, Lipson, and Snidal's (2001) notion of "control."
[44] E.g. the World Conservation Union.
[45] E.g. ECOWAS SALW Convention: Article 28 Para 1; Article 28 of the International Covenant on Civil and Political Rights of 1966.
[46] E.g. the Kimberley Process.   [47] E.g. the Financial Action Task Force.

with the consequence that its mandate automatically expires unless policymakers decide to renew it. Embargoes imposed by the United Nations Security Council typically include an expiry date, but this sunset mechanism is equally popular in a wide range of other areas such as climate change,[48] peace keeping, and money laundering.[49]

Second, an agency can be assumed to be more autonomous when it possesses a source of income that is independent of the principal. For instance, in order to strengthen the independence of the European Community vis-à-vis its member states, the funding system was changed in the first half of the 1970s from one based on national contributions to one based on "own resources," such as common customs tariff duties, agricultural levies, and a proportion of the value added tax. The Office of the United Nations High Commissioner for Refugees (UNHCR), in contrast, relies almost exclusively on voluntary contributions. Consequently, its independence is considerably constrained as it has to raise new funds for every new initiative it seeks to launch. Intermediary forms of financial independence are found in international organizations which rely on mandatory contributions, the level of which is predetermined either as a fixed sum that is equal for all member states – as in the case of the Organization of Petroleum Exporting Countries (OPEC) – or, more commonly, based on certain criteria, such as member states' gross domestic product (e.g. the Organization for Economic Cooperation and Development (OECD)) (Klein 1997).

Ceteris paribus, "bigger" might be better for the independence of an agency both with regard to personnel and financial resources. A large body of permanent staff and significant resources allow an agency to build up strong in-house expertise which strengthens the agency's position vis-à-vis the delegating states.

Finally, the level of delegation also depends on decision-making procedures. If binding decisions require unanimity, as is the case, for example, under the Kimberley Process Certification Scheme and in the Financial Action Task Force, parties retain full sovereignty, since no act can be imposed on them against their will. The degree of delegation is consequently low. Other bodies take decisions based on simple (usually only to block proposals (Ballmann, Epstein, and O'Halloran 2002)) or

---

[48] The first commitment period of the Kyoto Protocol expires in 2012.
[49] The Financial Action Task Force's mandate was first limited to five years and has now been extended to an eight-year period.

qualified majority votes. For example, the International Narcotics Control Board and the Council of the International Organization for Migration adopt certain decisions based on a two-thirds majority. When the required quorum is smaller, the degree of delegation is higher.

In a number of instances, third parties have started to assume certain functions related to international institutions (typically of an executive nature), but without such roles being codified in a written document. The independence of these bodies is usually very high, but it becomes difficult to decide whether or not they truly represent a case of delegation. For example, the NGO World Wildlife Fund provides technical assistance to countries related to the implementation of conventions like CITES,[50] while Greenpeace actively monitors states' compliance with the Convention on the Conservation of Antarctic Marine Living Resources and many other multilateral environmental agreements without being entrusted with this mandate by the agreements themselves. The United States unilaterally decided to assess states' efforts to implement the Vienna Convention and to sanction those found to be non-complying or non-cooperative. This study adopts the position that whenever a credible governmental or non-governmental body defines one of its activities explicitly with reference to an international institution, it needs to be included in the assessment of the degree of independence associated with that international institution.

Centralization

The second element of delegation – centralization – refers to the range of activities a principal delegates to an agent (Koremenos, Lipson, and Snidal 2001: 771). In international affairs, either of three distinct collective activities or a combination thereof can be delegated (McCall Smith 2000): rule-making (including facilitating negotiations of agreements), implementation (including operational activities like providing technical assistance, monitoring, information collection, and analysis), and dispute resolution and enforcement. The degree of centralization can vary considerably in any of these three functions.

---

[50] E.g. the WWF developed a wood-tracking software program that assists forest and industry managers, as well as state control agencies, to efficiently monitor wood flow from the stump to the market and thus to protect CITES protected mahogany trees (WWF 2006).

With respect to rule-making, the agency to which certain functions are delegated may, for example, be limited to a supporting role for negotiations. For instance, the sole role assumed by the secretariat for the Convention on Long-Range Transboundary Air Pollution of 1979 was to ensure that meetings ran smoothly (Levy 1993: 84). Agencies that assume such a limited range of functions have been referred to as "housekeepers" (Manger 1968) and "post offices," because their main function consists in receiving and circulating documents from member states. In other cases, the agent is granted the right to come up with its own initiatives that could potentially develop into legally binding decisions. The European Commission provides the paramount example of this far-reaching type of delegation, as it is vested with the authority not only to draft extensive policies but also to claim direct effect of these policies. Intermediary forms include the drafting of model regulation which transforms a convention's substantive provisions into a legal text that is compatible with most states' legal framework. Examples include the United Nations Model Regulations on the Transport of Dangerous Goods or the Model Regulation for the Control of the International Movement of Firearms, their Parts and Components and Ammunition drafted by the Inter-American Drug Abuse Control Commission of the Organization of American States.

An agency can assume a wide range of implemental functions ranging from technical assistance to monitoring to support the achievement of an international institution's goal. For instance, the United Nations Office on Drugs and Crime (UNODC) helps countries detect drug trafficking by training their border control officers in cargo screening. Similarly, the Division for Sustainable Development of the UN Department for Economic and Social Affairs assists countries in their efforts to combat desertification through alternative livelihood programs which the division develops and implements. As mentioned in the discussion of "obligation" (2.2.1), states can strengthen the credibility of their monitoring provisions when they entrust an independent third party to carry out the implementation reviews. Most international institutions do not delegate monitoring and rely solely on self-reporting. Even under these circumstances, *de facto* monitoring can be strong if third parties – typically civil society organizations – assume the role of unofficial "fire alarms." As fire alarms, they collect independent data on states' compliance records and publicly denounce irregularities they identify in the information submitted by member states (McCubbins and Schwartz 1984; Raustiala 2004).

The delegation of dispute resolution and enforcement are the functions that have attracted the greatest interest in international relations literature. A considerable degree of variation exists in terms of how far delegation goes with respect to these two functions. The role of third parties in dispute settlement may be limited to offering "good office," i.e. acting as channels of communication between protagonists and encouraging them to seek peaceful means of settling their differences. An example of this weak form of delegation is the Conciliation and Good Offices Commission, which was created to settle any future disputes between parties to the Convention against Discrimination in Education (429 UNTS 93) of 1960. Third parties may, in contrast, be vested with the authority to pass decisions which the protagonists accept *ex ante* as legally binding, as in the case of the World Trade Organization's (WTO) Dispute Settlement Body. The commitment of states can be seen as particularly credible when the circle of legitimate plaintiffs is extended to include non-state actors and individuals, as is the case for the European Court of Human Rights (Helfer and Slaughter 1997; Keohane, Moravcsik, and Slaughter 2000; McCall Smith 2000; Rittberger and Zangl 2004). Intermediary forms of delegated dispute resolution are found in binding and non-binding arbitration arrangements or mediation.

The two components of delegation – independence and centralization – are interdependent in as much as centralization only matters when a certain minimum threshold of independence is passed. If, in contrast, an agreement assigns an extensive range of functions to a plenary, the overall level of delegation remains low, because the plenary is fully congruent with the principal.

Table 2.1 lists the three dimensions identified in the concept of legalization as the most salient design features of international institutions. It shows how each of these dimensions can be operationalized in a way that allows for a consistent assessment across cases and lists empirically observable characteristics for the low and the high ends of the spectrum of each sub-component.

Table 2.1 *Overview of key institutional design dimensions*

Design element	Low level of legalization	High level of legalization
1. Obligation		
A. Legal bindingness		
a. Language	• Intention of signatories was merely to recommend or to state a fact.	• Intention of signatories was to create legal rights and obligations.
	• Agreement is called "recommendation," "program," "declaration," etc.	• Agreement is called "convention" or "treaty."
	• Participating states are referred to as "participants," "countries," etc.	• Participating states are referred to as "member states," "parties," or "signatories."
	• The word "obligations" is avoided and agreement lists what states "should" do.	• Obligations are called "obligations" and are formulated using "shall."
b. Procedural provisions	• Agreement contains no procedural provisions on entry into force, accession, or amendments, etc.	• Agreement contains procedural provisions on entry into force, accession, and amendments, etc.
	• Agreement effective with adoption, no formal signing or ratification process is required.	• Agreement effective after domestic ratification process typically involving the approval of the legislative.
c. Tenacity of obligation	• Use of reservations significantly attenuated.	• Agreement strictly limits the scope of reservations.
	• Lax escape mechanisms allow evasion of obligations.	• Agreement does not provide for temporary suspension of obligations or makes "escape" costly.
	• Parties can withdraw from agreement at short notice.	• Signatories cannot withdraw from the agreement.
B. Compliance mechanisms		
a. Monitoring	• No provisions on monitoring or only occasional self-reporting.	• Independent monitoring on regular basis.
b. Enforcement	• Consequences for non-compliance neither spelled out in the agreement nor developed in practice.	• Procedures established for breaches of commitments, (e.g membership sanctions reciprocal measures, "naming and shaming".

Table 2.1 (*cont.*)

Design element	Low level of legalization	High level of legalization
2. Precision		
A. Determinacy	• Definitions of the rights and obligations allow for multiple interpretations.	• Provisions do not leave room for self-serving interpretation by states.
	• Impossible to distinguish between acceptable and unacceptable behavior.	• Acceptable behavior can be clearly distinguished from non-acceptable behavior.
	• Many statements of general aims, declarations of principles.	• Agreement contains mainly rule-like provisions.
	• No independent body named to settle ambiguities.	• Independent body is authorized to settle ambiguities.
B. Coherence	• Provisions within an agreement contradictory.	• Provisions within the agreement fully coherent.
	• Agreement contradicts other principles and rules of the international legal system.	• Agreement fits with other principles and rules of the international legal system.
3. Delegation		
A. Independence		
a. Human resources	• No permanent staff.	• Permanent staff.
	• Delegating parties appoint agency's personnel.	• Delegating parties cannot appoint & dismiss personnel.
	• Short term for agency head.	• Agency head has long term.
b. Financial resources	• Agency financed by principal.	• Agency possesses its own sources of financing.
c. Decision-making	• Unanimous decisions.	• Majority rule.
	• All delegating parties have seat in decision making body.	• Less members in decision making body than delegating parties.
B. Centralization		
a. Rule making	• Agency's functions are limited to support roles, no right to own initiatives.	• Agency sets its own agenda.
		• Agency takes binding decisions for delegating parties.
b. Implementation	• Agency disseminates information provided by parties.	• Agency active in data collection and service provision.
c. Dispute resolution	• Agency's function limited to offering "good offices".	• Agency decisions as legally binding for delegating parties.
		• Non-state actors and individuals can be plaintiffs.

2.3 Relationship between design variables

The authors of the original concept of legalization assume their three design dimensions are independent of one another (Abbott *et al.* 2000: 404). While policymakers are conceptually free to mix and match different levels of obligation, precision, and delegation, they may, in practice, favor certain combinations over others. Regrettably, no systematic analysis has yet been undertaken to analyze the relative prevalence of different combinations. Given its small sample size, this study will not be able to fill this empirical gap either. All I aim to do at this point is to provide some initial food for thought on how the three design dimensions may complement or substitute each other.

2.3.1 *Obligation and precision*

Precision is largely a prerequisite for a high degree of obligation. The second element of obligation – compliance mechanisms – is thereby most dependent on a high degree of precision. It is conceptually possible that an indeterminate and incoherent institution could be legally binding, but monitoring and enforcement are significantly jeopardized when the substantive obligations of states are not spelled out in unambiguous terms and when they are in conflict with the wider international legal system. Indeterminate provisions make it hard for a monitoring mission to decide which type of state behavior deserves a checkmark in the "fully compliant" box rather than the "largely non-compliant" box. Consistency in the assessment of different cases becomes impossible, which in turn undermines the legitimacy of any sanctions imposed on states that are found to be non-compliant on the basis of such a problematic assessment.

2.3.2 *Obligation and delegation*

There does not appear to be a strong relationship between obligation and delegation on this level of aggregation. However, a richer story emerges upon breaking down obligation into its two sub-components, legal bindingness and compliance mechanisms. Legal bindingness is often a prerequisite for high levels of delegation. The legal framework of many states provides for very stringent procedures that need to be observed whenever a government seeks to delegate formal power to an international body. As part of these procedural demands, the initial act of delegation is crafted as a legally binding international agreement which is then ratified through the appropriate domestic procedures. Delegating power to an international body based on a legally non-binding agreement would, in many countries, be subject to serious constitutional challenges. The association of delegation with compliance mechanisms is weaker. As I will show in the case study portion of this book, a number of international institutions exist in which strong compliance mechanisms are combined with low levels of delegation (Chapters 5 and 6), while stronger forms of delegation can coexist with weaker compliance mechanisms (Chapter 4).

2.3.3 Precision and delegation

One of the most intriguing interactions involves the interplay between precision and delegation. The imprecision of provisions for defining an agent's mandate presents the most relevant case in this context, but vagueness in the formulation of substantive provisions can also have a significant impact on an international institution's degree of delegation.

On the one hand, a high level of precision may strengthen the authority of an agent as it provides the agent with a clear mandate it can invoke whenever its actions are contested. A highly precise provision may even specify that the agent possesses exclusive authority over a certain function (Bradley and Kelley 2006). On the other hand, and along the line of reasoning emphasized by most political scientists, a high degree of delegation may, on the contrary, be achieved through particularly low levels of legalization. Precisely because its mandate is not clearly circumscribed, an entrepreneurial agent may seek to expand its sphere of authority by adopting a very liberal interpretation of its mandate. On the domestic level, the perceived encroachment of the judiciary into legislative realms has sustained a longstanding debate (Lambert 1921). A similar dynamic for the instrumental use of discretion is also found in international legislative, executive, and judicial bodies. For instance, Malone (2004) describes how the United Nations Security Council expanded its mandate over time by advocating a very loose interpretation of "threats to international peace" (Article 39 UN Charter) to include a coup against a democratically elected regime, humanitarian catastrophes, and terrorism. Einhorn (2001) provides a similar account of the World Bank's mission creep. Keohane,

Moravcsik, and Slaughter (2000: 461) argue that "the greater the uncertainty concerning the proper interpretation or norm in a given case, the more potential legal independence it possesses."

Whether or not an agency tries and succeeds in using imprecision in its mandate to expand its mission depends on at least three major factors. First, an agency will only be successful in mission creep if it is led by an ambitious and skillful policy entrepreneur. Second, an agency can only expand its mission as long as it succeeds in mirroring this expansion in its budget and personnel. Third and finally, successful expansion of the agency's portfolio depends on the image of the particular agency as much as of international organizations in general. Klabbers (2002) provides a convincing account of the changing image of international organizations from one of a benevolent body that helped to overcome states' tendency toward war and other forms of destructive behavior to one of a monster bureaucracy lacking efficiency as well as accountability. Consequently, international organizations have found it much harder and become more modest in their attempts to get involved in an ever-increasing array of issues. The evocation of "implied powers" has lost much of its appeal.

The purpose of this chapter was to introduce a heuristic tool for categorizing international institutions based on their most salient design features. Building upon the concept of legalization as developed by Abbott *et al.* (2000), I argued that policymakers are confronted with a fundamental dilemma when designing international institutions because strong credibility associated with high levels of obligation, precision, and delegation comes ineluctably at the expense of flexibility offered by institutions relying on a softer legal architecture.

After this introduction of these descriptive design categories and their operationalization, the next chapter examines the factors that help explain why policymakers sometimes opt for the higher end of the legalization spectrum and why they favor soft law in other cases.

3 | *Problem constellation*

The concept of legalization introduced in the previous chapter provides a valuable tool for capturing essential differences in institutional designs. It does not in itself, however, provide a framework for *explaining* the so-categorized variance in the design of international institutions nor does it attempt to do so. In fact, it is one of the major strengths of the concept that it is equally compatible with different rationalist[1] theories including power-based, domestic politics, and functionalist approaches, as illustrated by the diverse contributions to the special volume of *International Organization* on the concept of legalization. This study remains rooted in the concept's rationalist orientation as it assumes that policymakers consciously choose among different design options when they establish a new international institution.[2] Already the term "design" itself alludes to "intention-based theories of social change" (Goodin 1996: 28) and precludes the possibility of "spontaneous order" (Young 1983).

Within the school of rationalist theories, this study builds on the functionalist tradition – namely on transaction cost economics theory. However, the problem-tailored design model developed here deviates from two central tenets of the functionalist paradigm. First, this study does not share the functionalist assumption that international institutions necessarily generate Pareto efficiency gains. All cases studied here result in both winners and losers, and it remains questionable whether the institution created in each of these cases even results in Kaldor–Hicks efficiency improvements. Second, this study focuses on

---

[1] Finnemore and Toope (2001) point out that the concept of legalization is less suitable for the analysis of the less tangible variables like "deeply embedded practices, beliefs and traditions" that constructivists focus their attention on. I will refer to this point in the conclusion.

[2] The focus is thus on design at the genesis of an international institution. For the equally interesting question of how the governance structure of an institution evolves over the course of its existence, see the works of scholars rooted in historic institutionalism (e.g. Pierson 2004; Thelen 2004).

identifying the optimal institutional design for tackling a given policy problem; I do not assume that policymakers necessarily adopt the most suitable design solution. In fact, the central puzzle which I attempt to make sense of in this study is why policymakers, in some cases, agree on an institutional architecture that seems appropriate for catering to the governance challenges arising for international cooperation in a certain issue area, while in other cases they opt for a sub-optimal design.

The argument in this chapter proceeds in three stages. The first section briefly outlines the three main rationalist approaches to institutional design. The second stage discusses the central tenets of the design model underlying this study and highlights the areas where it is compatible with the analytic insights gained from realist and domestic politics approaches. The remainder of the chapter explores at length the three problem constellation variables, their sub-components, and the way in which they can be operationalized. It also touches upon the issue of the interaction among these three variables, and how this interaction influences the expectations we derive with regard to the optimal design of an international institution.

3.1 Competing theories of institutional design

From the 1970s onwards, international relations scholars have addressed the question of why states create international institutions or regimes to facilitate cooperation. This inquiry has led to an abundant body of literature.[3] In contrast, scientific inquiry into the question of why states design international institutions in very different ways is a rather recent phenomenon and remains a largely underdeveloped field in international relations. As Abbott and Snidal critically observe, "regime theory deals with institutions at such a general level that it has little to say about the particular institutional arrangements that organize international politics" (1998: 6). It was not until the turn of this century that a group of scholars first made a systematic attempt to fill this void and to disaggregate and systematize differences in the design of international institutions. As discussed in the previous chapter, the concept of legalization that emerged from this common endeavor introduced a helpful heuristic tool for comparing different institutions with respect to their structural arrangements. However, the developers and early followers of this

---

[3] For a comprehensive overview, see Hasenclever, Mayer, and Rittberger (1997).

concept did not attempt to establish a single, coherent theory to explain these differences. Rather, each scholar has so far approached the design question from his or her own theoretical perspective, variously applying power-based or realist, domestic politics-based, and functionalist theories. Each of these approaches captures a different aspect of reality, and none of these three approaches is theoretically "pure." To a lesser or greater extent, they all blend in elements of the other two theoretical approaches in order to at least partially offset the deficiencies specific to each individual approach. The functionalism-inspired design model developed here is no exception in this regard. In the following cursory overview of the three design approaches, I will show how the differences in these schools' design explanations result directly from diverging views on the emergence and role of international institutions.

3.1.1 Power-based theories of institutional design

Classical realists are highly skeptical about the relevance of international law and – by extension – international institutions. Stanley Hoffmann, for example, concludes that "in the clash between inadequate law and supreme political interests, law bows – and lawyers are reduced to serve either as a chorus of lamenters with their fists raised at the sky and state or as a clique of national justifiers in the most sophisticatedly subservient or sinuous fashion" (1968: 31). In a very similar vein, Hans Morgenthau argues that "[g]overnments ... are always anxious to shake off restraining influence which international law might have upon their international politics" (1953: 214). Other realists do not necessarily deny the relevance of international institutions, but see them primarily as a tool which powerful states may avail themselves of to further state power and egoistic self-interest (e.g. Carr 1946). Neo-realist scholars adopt a similar perspective on the emergence of international institutions or regimes. Stephen Krasner (1985), for instance, explains the United States' decision to create multilateral institutions such as the United Nations or the World Bank – rather than relying entirely on unilateralism – as a strategy to confer legitimacy on, and thus strengthen, the United States' post-war supremacy. The self-interest of a powerful state may or may not be in harmony with the interests of other states, but given its power, it can make other states endorse an international institution even when the institution does not generate joint cooperative gains and may lead to a Pareto sub-optimal solution (Krasner 1991: 364).

National interests and the distribution of power not only influence the creation of international institutions, but their designs as well. As of now, a handful of scholars have set out along this line of inquiry – namely Miles Kahler (2000), James McCall Smith (2000), and Beth Simmons (2002). Their realist design theories all assume that states' design preferences vary with their relative power. These theories all agree that great asymmetries in power lead to lower levels of legalization, but they differ considerably in the causal mechanisms provided for explaining varying design preferences. These differences result in part from the different metrics employed in these studies for measuring a state's relative power. The majority of realist design theories conceptualize power as capabilities measured in terms of gross domestic product (GDP), military capacities, or population. These studies maintain that weaker states favor higher degrees of legalization as a means to constrain the behavior of more powerful parties (Alter 1998; McCall Smith 2000). However, if one follows Miles Kahler's (2000) example and chooses to conceptualize power in terms of legal resources, a very different picture emerges. In his study of the Asia-Pacific Economic Cooperation (APEC) forum, Kahler shows how developing states with poorly developed legal systems and resources are often skeptical or even hostile to high degrees of legalization, as they fear being outmaneuvered by states with more abundant and sophisticated legal resources. Strong states may favor higher degrees of legalization if they assume that the international institution designed in this way will primarily serve their interests – an assumption which, at times, has proved unwarranted. For instance, the United States advocated binding WTO dispute settlement procedures assuming that the dispute settlement body would be unlikely to rule against US trade policies. It can further be assumed that powerful states support hard law arrangements when they expect future declines in relative power, as they hope to lock-in current advantageous policies to preserve them for the period beyond that power-shift.

Realist theories on institutional design are still very far from presenting a coherent picture of the relevant explanatory variables and the causal mechanisms linking them with different levels of legalization. Furthermore, these theories are ill-suited to explain the design of international institutions when the creation of these institutions does not primarily result from the self-interested assertion of a powerful state, but may be better attributed to the emergence of a "principled and shared understanding of desirable forms of social behavior" (Kratochwil and Ruggie 1986: 764). This book's case study on conflict diamonds (see Chapter 6) presents the most compelling example wherein none of the powerful states had an immediate self-interest in the creation of an international institution designed to tackle this problem, but still promoted the creation of the Kimberley Process to tackle the uncontrolled trade in this conflict commodity.

3.1.2 Domestic politics-based theories of institutional design

In contrast to realist and functionalist approaches, domestic politics-based theories do not conceive of the state as a unitary actor. Rather, they disaggregate the state into competing interest groups and vote-maximizing politicians. From this perspective, international institutions are created when they serve the interest of influential domestic groups in several countries, as does, for instance, the World Trade Organization, which promotes the interests of competitive export industries. Domestic politics approaches stipulate that the interest groups which stand to benefit from a certain international institution will lobby for higher degrees of legalization, as only highly legalized institutions could protect against trade barriers a new government with protectionist tendencies might erect in the most important trading states. Only when international institutions are designed in ways that insulate them from tomorrow's exercise of authority can they continue to generate benefits for the domestic interest groups that pressed for their creation (Moe 1990b: 124). This lock-in effect of hard law arrangements is very similar to the argument presented above with reference to powerful states' support for high degrees of legalization in the light of a likely power shift.

While it is clear that interest groups benefit from "harder" institutions, it is less clear – and highly controversial among domestic politics scholars – whether a vote-maximizing government fares best by succumbing to these interest groups' lobbying efforts for higher levels of legalization. At the bottom of this controversy are different conceptualizations of the key explanatory variable that scholars in this camp refer to – i.e. "political uncertainty" – which leads to opposite design predictions. This intra-camp theoretical disagreement mirrors the above discussion on how realist design scholars predict opposite design outcomes depending on how they define "power."

Arguments by scholars primarily interested in the design of domestic institutions like Moe (1990b, 1991), Horn (1995), and Levy and Spiller (1996) are based on the assumption that vote-maximizing governments fare best when they continue throughout their tenure to serve the interest of the same constituency that brought them to power. Consequently, governments are assumed to embrace hard law as a means of tying their hands and signaling their sincere and irreversible commitment to safeguard the interests of that constituency. By doing so, governments reduce political uncertainty, which these scholars understand as the risk interest groups face of potential policy changes later.

A number of international relations scholars have adopted a similar line of reasoning. Judith Goldstein (1996) describes in her study of the Canada–US Free Trade Agreement how the US executive sought to insulate this pro-free trade agreement from protectionist forces within the US Congress by endowing the agreement with binding arbitration arrangements. Frederick Abbott (2000) makes a similar case with respect to the North American Free Trade Agreement (NAFTA). Lutz and Sikkink (2000) also find that in the protection of human rights, many governments preferred high levels of legalization in order to enhance the credibility of their commitment vis-à-vis their domestic constituencies. A complicating factor to this argument is the fact that preferences of interest groups may change under certain circumstances. For instance, farmers of country A may have initially lobbied their government to press trading partners to formally commit to an abolition of tariffs on agricultural goods. However, when a new member with a more competitive agricultural sector joins the free trade agreement, the farmers of country A will likely turn protectionist.

In contrast, other international relations scholars adopt a different understanding of political uncertainty and, consequently, reach opposite conclusions regarding its influence on design preferences. The assumption underlying this argument is that a vote-maximizing government seeks to serve whichever domestic interest group holds the upper hand, and not necessarily the one which was instrumental in the election of the incumbent government. A government is therefore primarily concerned about a potential tip in the balance of power among domestic interest groups or a change in their priorities to which it cannot easily adapt if its sovereignty is curtailed by highly legalized international institutions. Rosendorff and Milner (2001) show how states seek to reduce the level of political uncertainty (as defined above) by reducing the degree of legalization through the inclusion of escape clauses in trade agreements. These escape clauses allow governments to adjust their policies to potential changes in the domestic support for an international institution. For instance, a government may have come to power on a pro-farmer ticket, but if the electoral power of the agricultural lobby wanes, the government may shift its allegiance to a stronger interest group with different preferences. A high degree of political uncertainty understood in this way is thus associated with a preference for soft law arrangements.

The domestic politics approach encounters some particular – though not insurmountable – challenges when trying to explain the design of international institutions created to address global criminal markets. This approach assumes the existence of organized interest groups that lobby for competing interests through established political channels – an assumption which is only partly valid in the gray area of illicit flows. It is important to note that the weak degree of organization of many victims of illicit flows prevents them from lobbying forcefully for their interests. In the case of human trafficking, for instance, victims find it difficult to lobby for their interests due to language barriers, severely constrained financial resources, and uncertain legal status in the country to which they have been trafficked. The lobbying power of criminal or rebel groups may not suffer from a lack of organization or financial resources, but mainly from their limited access to legitimate channels of political influence. However, the potential explanatory power of domestic politics-based design theories varies, depending on the type of crime and the type of solution policy-makers use to combat it. Cyber crime, for instance, is an area highly amenable to the line of reasoning presented above, since the main victims of this type of crime are companies with substantial financial and legal resources which thus yield considerable lobbying power. Furthermore, the relative weakness of the domestic politics approach is also partly mitigated by the fact that many policies primarily seek to curb illicit flows not by targeting illicit organizations, but – more indirectly – by imposing tighter regulations on the licit industry with commercial connections to the criminal underworld, e.g. as with suppliers of chemical precursors of narcotic drugs. These legal industries, in turn, dispose of the full range of lobbying instruments assumed by the domestic politics approach.

3.1.3 Functionalist theories of institutional design

Functionalist scholars see international institutions as a means of realizing efficiency gains from which all participating states benefit.[4] In

---

[4] Or – at a minimum – that leave no states worse off; see Helen Milner's definition of international cooperation (1997: 8).

contrast to realist scholars, they assume that states are primarily concerned about absolute – rather than relative – gains, which opens a greater scope for international cooperation. However, as rational[5] egoists, states will only create international institutions if two basic conditions are met. First, all participating states need to share a common interest – be it of identical or complementary nature. Second, this common interest can only be attained through international cooperation and not through unilateral action (Keohane 1984: 6, 1989: 2). Whether or not a common interest exists around a policy issue and whether its solution requires cooperation depends on the specific constellation of the underlying problem.

Functionalist scholars primarily interested in the design – rather than the emergence – of international institutions adopt a similar logic. For instance, Koremenos, Lipson, and Snidal (2001: 781) argue that "states and other international actors, acting for self-interested reasons, design institutions purposefully to advance their joint interests." The design option best suited to further joint interest is thereby assumed to depend primarily on the specificities of the policy problem that states seek to solve through an international institution. Form follows function is the overriding idea shared by functionalist design theorists.

A first step along this argumentative route was undertaken by Charles Lipson (1991), Kenneth Abbott and Duncan Snidal (1998), and later, James Morrow (2000), who all explore the conditions under which states favor formal versus informal arrangements to govern their cooperation. Abbot and Snidal's article of 2000 directly relates to this concept of legalization. The authors demonstrate that an international institution's location on the soft law–hard law spectrum is determined by a number of characteristics of the issue area addressed by the institution. Soft law arrangements are, for instance, favored when a problem is fraught with a high degree of controversy and environmental uncertainty because less legalized forms of cooperation can adapt quickly to changed political or environmental circumstances (Abbott and Snidal 2000).

The rational design theory developed by Koremenos, Lipson, and Snidal (2001) is closely related. Although they do not directly adopt the

---

[5] Functionalist theories, and the variant presented here, are compatible with the assumption of bounded rationality (Barnard 1938; Keohane 1984: 110–116; Lake 1999: 41; Simon 1976).

three dependent variables used by legalization scholars – obligation, precision, and delegation – Koremenos, Lipson, and Snidal's (2001) own five variables – membership, scope, centralization, control, and flexibility – overlap considerably with the former, as discussed in the previous chapter. Furthermore, their independent variables – distribution problems, enforcement problems, number of actors, and uncertainty – fall squarely within the functionalist tradition. The research area within international relations that has made the greatest progress in studying the impact of problem structures on design outcomes so far is undoubtedly that of international environmental politics (see for instance Mitchell 2006).

3.2 Toward a problem-tailored design model

The design model underlying the empirical inquiry of this study builds largely on the functionalist tradition by sharing the assumption that the specificities of a problem influence the optimal design for an international institution established to cater to that problem. At the same time, it deviates from two central tenets of functionalism to integrate elements that are more akin to the realist argument about the relevance of power.

3.2.1 Back to the roots of functionalist design theory

Functionalist theories in international relations build heavily – although not always explicitly – on the conceptual foundations laid out by Oliver E. Williamson and his transaction cost economics[6] theory. This study returns to these roots of functionalism out of a conviction that the rich empirical body of literature that transaction cost economics theory has given rise to in its original context, i.e. the institutional design of business transactions, presents a still largely uncharted fishing ground for international relations design scholars. This may sound surprising given the great popularity the term "transaction costs" enjoys among functionalist international relations scholars. However, as I will argue, international relations can still benefit greatly from embracing not only the general notion of transaction cost but also from engaging more deeply the operationalization and empirical testing that this theory has generated in microeconomics over the past thirty years.

---

[6] Also referred to as relational contracting.

In his seminal book *Markets and Hierarchies* (1975), Williamson addresses the question originally brought up by Coase (1937) as to why certain transactions are not carried out in markets – as neo-classical economics would suggest – but rather under the hierarchical structure of firms. Transaction cost economics scholars[7] explain the existence of hierarchical firms and intermediary forms[8] of governance with reference to economic actors' desire to minimize transaction costs arising from contractual problems that are specific to individual trans-actions. Such costs can arise *ex ante* through the costly process of partner selection, negotiations, and contracting. Transaction costs can also result *ex post*, first, through the execution and policing of con-tracts, secondly, through renegotiations of contracts that become neces-sary as a result of omissions, errors, and unanticipated events, and, finally, through the settling of contractual disputes. Furthermore, trans-action costs may result from opportunity costs, as sub-optimal govern-ance structures may make transacting partners reluctant to undertake efficiency-increasing investments and deepen cooperation (Dyer 1996; Klein, Crawford, and Alchian 1978). The central tenet of transaction cost economics theory posits that transactions involving high transac-tion costs are better carried out in hierarchies, or formal organizations, in which the risk of cheating is mitigated through a pooling of interests. Inversely, markets are best suited when transactions involve low trans-action costs, thanks to the fact that cheating can relatively easily be mitigated through contracts that are complete and allow all parties to reliably appropriate the (positive or negative) net receipts resulting from their efforts. The magnitude of transaction costs is thereby assumed to be determined by the particularities of a transaction.

Robert Keohane pioneered the transfer of transaction cost economics theory from the world of inter-firm to that of inter-state cooperation. In his book *After Hegemony*, Keohane (1984) refers to transaction costs as one of the main reasons that states create international institutions that endure. This theoretical approach has gained a growing number of followers in international relations circles – most notably Beth and Robert Yarbrough (1990, 1992), Charles Lipson (1991), David Lake

---

[7] For an overview of the abundant body of transaction cost economics studies see Boerner and Macher (2001).

[8] E.g. franchising, joint-ventures, reciprocal trading, and other forms of relational and long-term contracts.

(1996, 1999, 2000), and James Morrow (2000). Abbott and Snidal (2000) link transaction cost economics theory with the above-discussed concept of legalization. They show how international institutions with high degrees of legalization, on the one hand, require more time and resources in the negotiation phase (thus increasing *ex ante* transaction costs) but, on the other hand, strengthen the credibility of a government's commitment in the eyes of other parties, thereby reducing implementation costs (*ex post* transaction costs) (in a similar vein to Keohane, Moravcsik, and Slaughter 2000). The optimal level of legalization thus depends on the relative importance of *ex ante* and *ex post* transaction costs, respectively, which in turn results from the characteristics of the underlying policy problem.

Three problem variables have attracted the greatest scholarly interest and gained the strongest support in empirical microeconomic studies carried out over the past thirty years: asset specificity, behavioral uncertainty, and environmental uncertainty. I will explore these three variables in greater detail in the remainder of this chapter, but before that, I want to clarify the way in which the problem-tailored design model presented here deviates from this functionalist tradition.

3.2.2 *Beyond the functionalist paradigm*

The problem-tailored design model developed in this study deviates from its functionalist origin in three important respects. First, it does not depend on the assumption of Pareto efficiency gains. Second, it acknowledges the existence of rationally sub-optimal designs that can result when powerful states are not directly affected by a problem and therefore are unwilling to contribute to an effective solution. Finally, the approach presented here also recognizes that the problem constellation itself is in part endogenous to the substantive solution envisaged by an international institution. I will expand on these three themes in the concluding chapter of this book, but I would like to foreshadow them at this point.

Transaction cost economics theory in both its original microeconomic setting and in functionalist theories in international relations assumes that cooperation results in Pareto efficiency gains that are not attainable through unilateral action. The backbone of this argument is the assumption that cooperation occurs on a voluntary basis. Consequently, no firm or sovereign state would be willing to sign up to an agreement that damages its interests. The obstacles to realizing these joint benefits may be lower or higher depending on whether a particular problem constellation resembles more a coordination game, battle of the sexes, or a prisoners' dilemma game,[9] but in all these games a cooperative outcome leaves every player better off than under a non-cooperative outcome. In contrast, the policy problems studied here more resemble deadlock games that produce both winners and losers. The illicit transnational flows of narcotic drugs, dirty money, conflict diamonds, and small arms and light weapons affect states at varying levels of intensity and in very different ways. As I will argue in the individual case studies, some states may even benefit from these flows in economic or political terms. Consequently, they have strong reasons to oppose the creation of international institutions that would curtail these flows, or at least, to refrain from cooperating in the case of the establishment of such institutions. However, many of these states with positive stakes in global trafficking can still be found among the members of anti-trafficking institutions. This raises the important question of why these states decided to join an institution that apparently hurts their interests.

It remains questionable whether the institution created in each of these cases even helps to generate Kaldor–Hicks efficiency improvements. This question is of little practical relevance in the cases studied here, because the losers are clearly not fully compensated for the damage they incur. These cases, therefore, highlight the coercive side of international institutions that realists have studied extensively. They discuss a number of more or less coercive tools such as side-payments, issue-linkages, or blunt blackmailing (e.g. aid cut-offs) which the winners of an international institution can use to incentivize potential losers to join (Keck 1993; Mitchell and Keilbach 2001). Lloyd Gruber (2000) presents an interesting twist to the issue-linkages argument. He argues that in many circumstances, states may feel compelled to sign up to an international initiative because the enacting coalition that created the international institution may possess what he calls "go-it-alone power," i.e. the power to alter – intentionally or not – the status quo of non-parties in ways that make them worse off than before the institution was created. For instance, it is very plausible that Luxembourg, with its

---

[9] See Oye (1986) for a characterization of these games in the context of international relations.

important financial center, would have preferred to maintain the pre-1988 status quo when money laundering was not tabled on the international political agenda. However, once it realized that international action was unavoidable, it made a strategic U-turn. It joined the newly created anti-money laundering institution in an attempt to minimize the risk that cooperating states would reach an agreement that would hurt its economic interests (see Chapter 5).

The design model developed here also deviates from its functionalist origin by acknowledging that the design of many international institutions is not optimal for dealing with the governance challenges arising from cooperation in the targeted issue area. This model thereby attributes the observed sub-optimality less to cognitive limitations of the drafters and more to deliberate choices. It concurs with Miller's observation that "[r]ational choice by actors with conflicting preferences for institutions may result in institutions that are suboptimal" (2000a: 535; similarly, see Pierson 2004: 106).

Whether an international institution will indeed be optimally designed to cater for the governance challenges arising from particular problem constellations depends on the bargaining power of the group that is most strongly affected by a problem. If the most powerful state or coalition of states is not directly affected and thus does not stand to benefit from an effective international institution, it is likely to oppose the creation of an international institution that results in net costs for it. Along with its efforts to prevent the adoption of substantive provisions that demand a costly behavioral change, it will focus its energy on the design of this institution to ensure that it remains so weakly legalized that it can easily disregard the substantive provisions.

Analyzing this question in detail is beyond the scope of this study, but its importance will become particularly apparent in the case study on small arms and light weapons (Chapter 7). The more modest ambition of this study is to specify what an optimal design solution would look like if policymakers sided with the party most severely affected by a transnational problem. This allows us to see in which cases the optimal design corresponds with an international institution's actual design and to provide the basis for future research seeking to explain mismatches between optimal and actual design. As the empirical part of this study will show, the problem-tailored approach developed here is compatible with cases of what we can call rationally sub-optimal design, which results when the enacting coalition is opposed to the creation of an effective international institution but, for domestic politics or other reasons, feels compelled to pretend to be actively concerned about an international problem (see also Chapter 8).

The third and final way in which this study's problem-tailored design approach deviates from its functionalist roots is by questioning the assumption that the particular constellation of a policy problem is fully independent of the international institution created to tackle the problem. Depending on how a problem is framed, it requires different types of actions and leads to different distributions of costs and benefits among states. A problem constellation is thus in part endogenous to the substantive measures enshrined in an international institution. The same logic of sub-optimality discussed above can thus also affect the substance of an international institution and thereby undermine its effectiveness, as will become apparent in the case study on narcotic drugs (Chapter 4).

3.3 The three dimensions of problem constellations

The growing popularity of transaction cost economics theory has led to a plethora of variables that supposedly explain the variance in governance structures in business settings and in institutional designs in international cooperation. Three explanatory variables have attracted the greatest scholarly interest and gained the strongest support in empirical studies carried out over the past thirty years: asset specificity, behavioral uncertainty, and environmental uncertainty. In order to avoid fueling the ongoing inflation of new explanatory variables and neologisms, I am adopting these three core transaction cost economics variables and seeking to stay as close as possible to their original definitions.

3.3.1 Asset specificity

The most prominent of all transaction cost economics variables is asset specificity, which virtually all empirical transaction cost economics studies include as a key independent variable. The following paragraphs first clarify this concept in its original microeconomic setting and trace its transfer into the context of inter-state cooperation by international relations scholars. The discussion then moves on to explain in more detail how this study operationalizes asset specificity to allow for a systematic assessment across cases.

Conceptualization

Asset specificity refers to relationship-specific investments that decline in value if a cooperative project is terminated prior to its completion (Williamson 1996: 377). Economists distinguish between two components of relation-specific costs: one-time sunk costs and opportunity costs resulting from the non-realization of expected benefits. The size and distribution of sunk costs and opportunity costs influence the bargaining position of the parties during contract negotiations and the contract's lifetime. The party that faces comparatively smaller sunk costs and derives smaller net benefits from a continuation of the relationship sees its relative power increase in the *ex post* bargaining process during which it may shirk its ongoing commitments or seek to extract additional benefits from its counterpart. The outcome of this *ex post* bargaining process is uncertain and plagued by opportunism (Eggertsson 1990: 172) and therefore reduces the *ex ante* incentives of the party with the higher asset-specific costs to engage in this type of transaction (Klein, Crawford, and Alchian 1978). This obstacle to cooperation can be overcome only if the two parties adopt a governance structure that contains sufficiently strong safeguards to reduce the unequal propensity to shirk associated with a high degree of asset specificity. This positive correlation between high degrees of asset specificity and deeper integration has been confirmed by a large body of empirical economic studies (e.g. Anderson and Schmittlein 1984; Masten, Meehan, and Snyder 1991; Monteverde and Teece 1982).

Only a handful of international relations scholars incorporate the concept of asset specificity explicitly in their studies. In security affairs, Lake (1996, 1999) and Weber (1997, 2000) refer to asset specificity as investments in specialized military equipment or know-how, or in strategically important locations undertaken in the framework of security cooperation. Beth and Robert Yarbrough adapt the concept of asset specificity to the context of international trade and find that investment in trade relations can alter "the pattern of production and investment in the participating economies" (1992: 25). They mention the Soviet–European gas pipeline built in the 1970s and 1980s as a prototypical example of such an asset-specific investment. Once completed, the European-financed pipeline became susceptible to Soviet opportunism as the Soviets possessed the power to reduce the value of the investment by reducing the volumes of gas exported through it.

Many other international relations scholars do not adopt the term "asset specificity" as such but nevertheless embrace the essence underlying this notion. International cooperation involves the "exchange of conditional promises by which each state declares that it will act in a certain way on condition that the other parties act in accordance with their promises" (Iklé 1964: 7). The promise of state A to undertake or refrain from a certain action in expectation of a particular behavioral response by other states is akin to an asset-specific investment because this action decreases substantially in value for A if other states do not honor their promises. In this sense, asset specificity corresponds largely with Downs, Rocke, and Barsoom's understanding of the cooperative depth of an agreement, defined as the "extent to which [an agreement] requires states to depart from what they would have done in its absence" (1996: 383) or Raustiala's notion of "substance," which he defines as "the degree of deviation from the status quo ante that an agreement generally demands" (2005: 581). By definition, all measures that states adopt solely in response to an international agreement decline substantially in value when non-compliance by other states spoils the benefits the agreement was meant to generate.

Asset-specific investments can come in the form of physical investments, like investments in certain types of interoperable weapon systems, or of normative investments, like the aligning of national legislation with an international agreement, along with the domestic enforcement of these provisions. These costs represent investments in so far as they are made in view of certain benefits the international agreement is expected to generate. These benefits can only be generated, and thus the investments be justified, when all other parties, or at least the major ones, honor the obligations they subscribed to. If, for example, the Netherlands reduces its carbon dioxide emissions as prescribed by the Kyoto Protocol in the hope of a reduced risk of flooding but other parties fail to do so, it cannot reap the expected benefits from its action, and its investments in the Protocol are futile.

The risk of states failing to agree on or to honor a cooperative solution of a shared problem is not only a function of the absolute size of the required asset-specific investments but also their relative distribution. Obstacles to successful cooperation are particularly high when costs and benefits are asymmetrically distributed among states. For example, adherence to international anti-drug policies imposes significant costs on Afghanistan in both economic and political terms, since opium is the country's most important foreign exchange earner and poppy eradication programs boost support for the Taliban. In contrast,

Russia reaps considerable benefits from such action in terms of a reduction in its high prevalence of heroin addiction and in drug-related crime and health problems. To use Mitchell and Keilbach's (2001) terminology, Afghanistan in this context presents an example of an "upstream" state as it incurs net costs from an international institution, whereas Russia corresponds to a "downstream state" that suffers under the negative externalities created by another state's behavior and would thus reap net benefits from an effective international drug control institution.

Upstream states have no genuine interest in the success of the cooperative project and will therefore seize every opportunity to shirk their obligations as long as non-compliance remains inconsequential (Mitchell and Keilbach 2001). Consequently, the net winners from a new institution will seek to counterbalance this tendency by incorporating legal arrangements. The stronger other states' incentives to shirk and the greater the potential damage non-compliance can cause, the more net winners will push for harder legal arrangements. We can therefore expect – *ceteris paribus* – the greater the absolute level of asset-specific investments required by an agreement and the greater the asymmetry in the distribution of these investments, the higher the level of legalization.

Operationalization

To assess the level of asset specificity associated with a certain policy issue, this study differentiates between two central elements. First, it examines the potential loss countries would incur from the breakdown of an international institution established to deal with a problem they face. Second, this study analyzes the likelihood that such a breakdown occurs due to widespread shirking. A high degree of asset specificity is found in problem constellations in which some states face great potential loss while others have strong incentives to dodge obligations. The assessment of asset specificity, as well as the other two problem attributes, examines the problem constellation as it presented itself at the time the related international institution was created. As in the assessment of an institution's degree of legalization, I distinguish again between the three ordinal levels "low," "moderate," and "high."

The asset specificity of a problem is positively correlated with the loss a state suffers if an agreed problem solution falls apart. This loss consists of two components. For one, a country sees all the direct and indirect implementation costs it incurred in association with a given international institution turned futile. Additionally, and in many cases more importantly, a state faces opportunity costs as a result of the forgone benefits the collaborative project was meant to generate. The extent to which a state values the benefits an international institution is expected to generate depends on the prominence a certain problem has on the domestic political agenda. Domestic politics scholars would be well equipped to explore this aspect with finer nuances than does this study,[10] but I hope to show that even a more aggregate look at state preferences can yield valuable insights.

Figure 3.1 illustrates this interplay between costs and benefits. It displays the relative distribution of costs and benefits among three states that cooperate to solve a common problem. Countries A and B both reap moderate benefits from an effective policy solution. Country B faces moderate costs, while country A only bears a low level of costs. Since country B invested more to solve the problem than country A, country B incurs greater overall costs if the intended solution for the problem fails despite investments. Consequently, the potential loss resulting from a collapse of their cooperation is higher for country B than for country A. The solution of the problem generates higher benefits for country C than for country A, even though their costs are the same. For this reason, the potential loss in terms of opportunity costs is higher for country C than it is for country A. Depending on how different countries value the non-realization of benefits relative to futile sunk costs, countries B and C might associate an identical level of loss with the breakdown of an established policy solution.[11] However, both states will certainly assess their loss as higher than A's.

The falling line L1 connecting countries C and B suggests that all countries located on this utility curve may attribute the same level of loss to a potential *ex post* collapse of the problem solution. The falling line

---

[10] The domestic politics approach could also provide a welcome refinement of the analysis of indirect implementation costs which in part depend on the lobbying power of domestic interest groups negatively affected by the creation of an international institution and on the permeability of the political system (Risse-Kappen 1991).

[11] Public choice literature suggests that it is most plausible to assume that states are risk averse, i.e. that they attach greater importance to the loss of value of an investment they have made than to the non-realization of an expected benefit, even if the two types of losses are the same in monetary terms (Olson 1971).

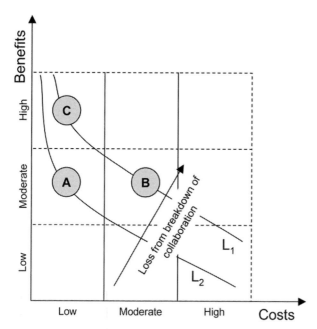

Figure 3.1 Potential loss as a function of futile sunk costs and forgone benefits

L2 going through country A also depicts the possible locations of countries that share the same level of loss, but their potential loss is lower than that of countries located on line L1.

Costs and benefits associated with the cooperative solution of an international policy problem do not necessarily have to be framed in monetary terms. International institutions on illicit flows typically impose significant normative costs on states as they require states to criminalize and prosecute a type of behavior which would otherwise have gone unpunished. There are various reasons – of cultural, political, and economic nature – why a state might oppose the criminalization of certain types of behavior which others have prohibited through criminal statutes.

First, an international institution may target a certain type of behavior that is deemed acceptable or at least tolerable in some countries but criminalized in others.[12] As Bogges pointedly notes with respect to drugs, "one nation's menace ... [can be] another nation's pastime"

---

[12] As has been pointed out elsewhere, the concept of "crime" lacks objective reality and must primarily be seen as a construct of criminal law (Sheptycki 2003).

(1992: 167). Second, even when states do share the understanding that a certain type of behavior is socially undesirable, it does not automatically follow that criminalization is deemed the most effective way of dealing with the issue at hand (Burchell, Gordon, and Miller 1991; Smandych 1999). Whereas the United States has a long history of fighting drug addiction largely through its criminal justice organs, many European countries view this problem primarily from a medical perspective and emphasize the importance of policies aimed at harm reduction (Nadelmann 1990; Walker 1992: 270). Third, even when states agree that a certain type of behavior is both socially undesirable and best tackled with criminal law enforcement instruments, the priority they may attach to prosecuting it may still differ. Scarce policing resources require a prioritization of the efforts targeted against different types of criminal activities. This prioritization should be based on the level of social harm created by a certain criminal activity, but the selection of these targets is inevitably of a political rather than technical nature (Sheptycki 2003: 53). Difficult trade-offs are also involved when the criminalization and prosecution of a certain type of behavior negatively affect the country's economic or political stability.

Any international cooperation will collapse when a sufficient number of countries fail to meet their commitments toward an agreed cooperative project. This study argues that, *ceteris paribus*, shirking is more attractive the greater a state's net costs. By focusing on net rather than absolute costs, this study deviates from other rationalist scholars who emphasize states' inclination for bandwagoning, i.e. their attempt to reap a share of collectively produced benefits while dodging their own contributions to the cooperative project. While not denying that such a tendency does exist, I argue here that egoist, utility-maximizing states will also – unless they suffer from severe myopia[13] – take into account the risk that their shirking may lead to the demise of an international institution and thus to a loss of the benefits they reaped from it. This line of reasoning leads to the same conclusion that constructivists reach based on their argument which highlights the extent to which states

---

[13] E.g. a state suffering from great political instability may pursue more shortsighted policies than one where the government has reason to believe that it can reap the praise for the benefits generated by an international institution it helped to create. In addition to a country's domestic political landscape, the risk of shirking may also depend on the sequencing of the cost and the benefits stream. The larger the temporal gap between costs and benefits, the greater the risk of shirking.

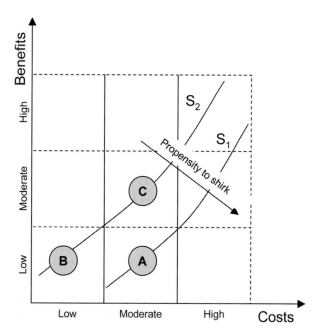

Figure 3.2 Propensity to shirk as a function of costs and benefits

(like individuals) are guided by a logic of appropriateness rather than mere cost–benefit calculations (logic of consequences) (March and Olsen 1989).[14]

Figure 3.2 illustrates this argument by depicting the relative distribution of costs and benefits a certain policy solution creates for the three countries A, B, and C. Country A faces a moderate level of costs while gaining few benefits from an international institution. Country B reaps the same low level of benefits as country A, but contributes less to the common solution. In this constellation, country A is more likely to shirk its obligations than country B, as the costs it incurs are more likely to outweigh its benefits. Its incentive to shirk is also larger than that of country C, which bears the same moderate level of costs, but gains more from successful cooperation. Depending on how B and C value potentially forgone benefits relative to potentially futile investments, their propensity to shirk their obligations may be identical.[15] In any event, the propensity of both B

---

[14] This argument is also supported by results from experimental economics.

[15] The risk aversion assumption mentioned in footnote 11 above is equally valid with respect to states' considerations on whether to shirk.

and C to shirk is lower than A's. This relationship is demonstrated by line S1 connecting countries B and C and line S2 going through A.

Each state assesses the creation of an international institution with respect, first, to the potential loss it incurs in case of an *ex post* breakdown of that institution and, second, to its perception of other participating states' inclination to shirk their obligations. Based on this problem assessment, a state will formulate its design preferences whereby it favors harder legalization the greater its potential loss and the risk of shirking. Transaction cost economics theory posits that effective cooperation requires that participants agree to endow an institution with the level of legalization that is sufficient to safeguard the interests of the state that faces the highest potential loss.

Figure 3.3 illustrates two extreme problem constellations. Figure 3.3(a) depicts a situation where no participating states face significant incentives to shirk. None of these states is strongly concerned about protecting the collaborative project from a breakdown, as this institution does not generate any substantial benefits. Given the low level of asset specificity, we can expect participating states to endow the international institution with only weak legalization. The other extreme is represented in Figure 3.3(b). In this constellation, state A would incur high losses from an *ex post* breakdown of an international institution it invested in, because of both the high sunk costs it incurred and the high value of forgone benefits. Given all other states' strong incentive to shirk their obligations, country A will insist on high levels of legalization in order to protect the institution from collapse.

3.3.2 Behavioral uncertainty

Behavioral uncertainty is the second explanatory variable many transaction cost economics studies have found to be significant in explaining institutional design outcomes. As above, I will introduce this variable first in conceptual terms before explaining how I plan to operationalize it to measure the extent it affects specific problem constellations in the shady area of illicit trade.

Conceptualization

Whereas asset specificity determines parties' propensity to shirk and the potential loss such shirking inflicts on other parties, behavioral uncertainty refers to the *opportunities* parties have to shirk their contractual

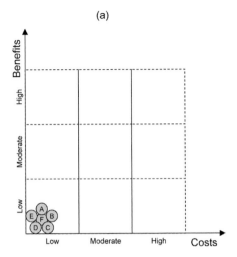

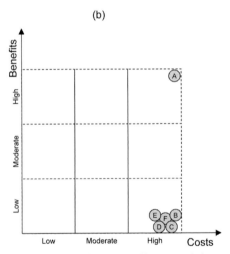

Figure 3.3 Problem constellation with low and high asset specificity

obligations without facing the risk of detection. Behavioral uncertainty thus depends on the relative ease with which parties can observe other parties' compliance with contractual obligations. Economists have extensively studied how this type of uncertainty impacts make-or-buy decisions relating to both goods and services, and have found a move toward more hierarchical governance structures with increasing complexity of performance evaluation.[16]

Behavioral uncertainty is no stranger to international relations either. Some scholars even use the very same term (e.g. Koremenos, Lipson, and Snidal 2001), while others refer to the concept under different terms, such as "actor uncertainty" (Abbot and Snidal 2004: 65f.) or simply "uncertainty" (Weber 1997: 331f.). The central issue addressed by all these scholars is the observability of behavior. Detecting non-compliance is considerably easier in some issues (e.g. nuclear tests) than in others (e.g. development of biological weapons) because of the availability of suitable verification technologies. In other problems like human rights violations or excessive trade tariffs, detection is facilitated by the fact that individuals or firms are directly affected by a state's non-compliance and can therefore serve as "fire alarms" (McCubbins and Schwartz 1984; Raustiala 2004) to sound the alarm when a state's behavior is in breach of officially endorsed international obligations.

This study adopts the hypothesis put forward by the microeconomic transaction costs economic theory and assumes that states favor higher levels of legalization the greater the extent of behavioral uncertainty associated with a given policy problem. This expectation largely corresponds with Koremenos, Lipson, and Snidal's (2001: 787) conjecture C1, which posits that centralization, i.e. the delegation of functions to an international institution, increases with behavioral uncertainty. My argument deviates from theirs in as much as I assume a positive correlation between behavioral uncertainty and the level of legalization at large, and not only with the delegation dimension of it.

Operationalization

International law enforcement agreements typically require the criminalization and prosecution of certain types of behavior. Compliance with the first element is relatively simple for other states to observe. Criminalization requires amendments of the domestic penal code, and since these laws are publicly available, it appears almost trivial for states to detect non-compliance. However, as Andrew Ashworth puts it, "it would be foolish to think that the criminal law as stated in the statutes and the textbooks

---

[16] E.g. the performance of a company's sales force is easier to measure than that of its research division, thereby making it easier to outsource the former task than the latter.

reflects the way in which it is enforced in actual social situations" (2003: 12). In order to capture the behavioral uncertainty associated with the practical reality of criminal provisions, we need to examine three elements that affect the level of difficulties states face in observing each others' compliance.

First, insufficient implementation may result from a country's poor policing and prosecuting capabilities. This study refers to this first element of behavioral uncertainty as "governance incapacity,"[17] whereby I assume that the more the solution of an international policy problem depends on the effective cooperation of states with weak domestic law enforcement institutions, the greater the behavioral uncertainty of a cooperative undertaking. I measure governance incapacity as understood in this way based on three of the World Bank's six governance indicators,[18] namely, "government effectiveness,"[19] "rule of law,"[20] and "control of corruption."[21] Any international institution whose effectiveness relies on compliance with a poor governance capacity is fraught with a high degree of behavioral uncertainty. It is difficult to monitor the actual behavior of such states because their performance is typically erratic in many areas and little reliable information is publicly available. Furthermore, even if other states do detect non-compliance, it remains close to impossible for them to

---

[17] For a detailed discussion of lack of capacity as a major source of non-compliance see Chayes and Chayes (1993). I prefer the somewhat cumbersome term "governance incapacity" over the more elegant "governance capacity" so as to ensure a positive correlation between a concept and its sub-components (e.g. greater governance incapacity leads to greater behavioral uncertainty). This same reasoning also explains the choice of the term "industry opacity" rather than "industry transparency."

[18] A World Bank research team led by Daniel Kaufmann started in 1996 to assess the governance performance of over 200 states along six dimensions, namely, voice and accountability, political stability, regulatory quality, government effectiveness, rule of law, and control of corruption.

[19] Which according to the World Bank reflects the "quality of public service provision, the quality of the bureaucracy, the competence of civil servants, the independence of the civil service from political pressures, and the credibility of the government's commitment to policies" (World Bank 2007).

[20] This indicator "measures the extent to which agents have confidence in and abide by the rules of society. These include perceptions of the incidence of crime, the effectiveness and predictability of the judiciary, and the enforceability of contracts" (World Bank 2007).

[21] This indicator measures "the extent of corruption, conventionally defined as the exercise of public power for private gain. It is based on scores of variables from polls of experts and surveys" (World Bank 2007).

determine whether the non-complying state willfully disregarded its obligations or simply lacked the capacity to honor them.

The level of behavioral uncertainty can be mitigated by societal groups with strong interests in the success of an international institution. Effective societal monitoring of state compliance largely depends on the degree to which affected groups are organized and command physical and normative lobbying power. For instance, international institutions that produce concrete benefits for multinational companies (e.g. international investment accords) suffer under a lower level of behavioral uncertainty than institutions that mainly affect weakly organized individuals, such as drug addicts or illegal immigrants. This second element of behavioral uncertainty is captured by the term "reliance on governmental monitoring." This study hypothesizes that behavioral uncertainty increases given greater relative reliance on governmental monitoring, or inversely, given weaker monitoring by non-state actors.

The overall transparency of the affected industry is a third indicator for the behavioral uncertainty associated with a policy area. Important differences exist between institutions that primarily target an illicit sector (e.g. trafficking in narcotic drugs) and institutions that pursue a strategy of responsibilization under which a licit sector (e.g. banking) is enlisted in the government's fight against certain illicit activities (e.g. money laundering). Illicit sectors, by their very nature, seek to maintain the highest possible degree of opacity. Consequently, it is very difficult for other states to observe whether state A is indeed as successful in fighting an illicit sector as it claims to be. Also within the licit segment of the economy, we can find some sectors that are decidedly more opaque than others. In industries where business is conducted on the basis of a handshake and little written documentation is stored (e.g. the diamond trade, alternative remittance systems), the actions of regulated subjects are much more difficult to track than in strongly regulated industries where a tradition of accurate written reporting exists (e.g. established financial services). I refer to this third element of behavioral uncertainty as "industry opacity." I hypothesize that behavioral uncertainty associated with a certain international institution increases with greater opacity of the targeted industry.

In each of the four case studies presented in the second part of this study, I measure the degree of behavioral uncertainty based on these three elements: governance incapacity, reliance on governmental monitoring, and industry opacity. All three elements are positively correlated with behavioral uncertainty and thus with the expected level of legalization.

3.3.3 Environmental uncertainty

Environmental uncertainty is the third and final variable this study uses for analyzing a policy problem's particular constellation and for formulating expectations about the optimal design of an international institution created to tackle this problem. This variable is commonly referred to by both transaction cost economics and international relations scholars. The next section clarifies the meaning of environmental uncertainty in these two disciplines and how it relates to the choice of governance structures. This conceptual discussion is again followed by an elaboration of how this study disaggregates and operationalizes this variable.

Conceptualization

Environmental uncertainty refers to situations where the range of possible outcomes or the probability distribution of the outcomes is unknown (cf. Knight 1921; Williamson 1975: 31). Transaction cost economics scholars argue that both human infallibility and *force majeure* are the reason transactions can be plagued with environmental uncertainty. Given bounded rationality and the costliness of drafting contracts that include provisions on every imaginable contingency, contracts governing complex and longer-term transactions are almost inevitably fraught with omissions. This in turn necessitates renegotiations of original terms in response to the realization of unforeseen events. In support of this line of reasoning, empirical studies have found a negative relationship between environmental uncertainty, such as technological change, and the level of integration among firms (Balakrishnan and Wernerfelt 1986; Walker and Weber 1984).

This third transaction cost economics variable has also attracted considerable attention from international relations scholars. Koremenos, Lipson, and Snidal (2001: 778) refer to this variable as "uncertainty about the state of the world." Abbott and Snidal's use of the term "technical uncertainty" also captures the same idea, since they define it as "doubts or partial ignorance of the existence and nature of a problem, as well as appropriate solutions" (2004: 63). Other scholars essentially discuss the same ideas under the term "scientific uncertainty" (Rosendorff and Milner 2001; Shelton 2000). They all agree that when dealing with complex problems such as global warming, cause-and-effect relationships may be poorly understood, making it difficult to forecast the effectiveness of certain policy measures. Under these circumstances, policymakers are assumed to prefer international institutions that are flexible enough to allow for renegotiation and adaptation when new evidence suggests more effective ways of dealing with the problem (Abbott and Snidal 2000: 442). Shelton maintains that "[l]egally binding norms may be inappropriate when the issue or the effective response is not yet clearly identified, due to scientific uncertainty or other causes, but there is an urgent requirement to take some action" (2000: 13). This same idea is echoed by Rosendorff and Milner (2001: 832). Two of Koremenos, Snidal, and Lipson's (2001) conjectures point in the same direction. They hypothesize that with increasing environmental uncertainty, states become keener on retaining autonomy and flexibility in decision-making, i.e. become more reluctant to be bound by highly legalized institutions.[22] Abbott and Snidal (2000), finally, argue with direct reference to the concept of legalization that weakly legalized international institutions present an optimal design solution for issues plagued by high levels of environmental uncertainty. This study adopts this same hypothesis.

Operationalization

International efforts to exert control over the fuzzy border between crime and war suffer under environmental uncertainty arising from two major sources. First, environmental uncertainty can result from a lack of international experience in tackling the targeted type of illicit flow. States may therefore feel unsure about the relative effectiveness of different policy options and prefer to first test out a certain approach prior to enshrining it in hard law. As Koremenos (2001) points out, soft law arrangements can offer states an important learning opportunity on how to deal with a poorly understood policy problem. I refer to this first element of environmental uncertainty as the "novelty of policy issue."

Second, environmental uncertainty in the context of international law enforcement also depends on the level of innovation associated with the targeted type of crime. Innovation may either relate to the development of new types of criminal activities, such as hacking into bank accounts, or to process-related adaptations, such as the dissemination of child pornography over the Internet instead of, or in addition to, videotapes. Another type of process innovation relates to the displacement of criminal activities either to less tightly regulated sectors or to states with lax legislation or law enforcement capacities. As the case

---

[22] See their conjectures V3 and F1.

studies will show, criminal fields differ from each other significantly with respect to their amenability to product and process innovations.

Both the novelty of a policy issue and the innovativeness of the targeted problem area are positively correlated with environmental uncertainty and, consequently, hypothesized to require an international institution with softer legalization.

Table 3.1 summarizes the three independent variables and their subcomponents which will guide the empirical inquiry into the problem

Table 3.1 *Overview of key dimensions of policy problem constellations*

Problem attribute	Low	High
1. Asset specificity		
A. Potential loss	• The benefits resulting from effective cooperation are low.	• The benefits resulting from effective cooperation are high.
B. Propensity to shirk	• Solving the problem involves small implementation costs.	• Problem solution involves significant implementation costs.
	• Problem solution has negligible negative economic or political side effects.	• Problem solution has significant negative economic or political side effects.
2. Behavioral uncertainty		
A. Governance incapacity	• Countries whose compliance is key for an effective solution have a strong record in government effectiveness, rule of law, and control of corruption.	• Countries whose compliance is key for an effective solution have a weak record in government effectiveness, rule of law, and control of corruption.
B. Reliance on governmental monitoring	• Problem solution benefits specific non-state actors.	• Problem solution creates diffuse benefits for non-state actors.
	• Affected groups have strong monitoring capacity.	• Affected groups have poor monitoring capacity.
	• Affected groups are politically influential.	• Affected groups are politically influential.

Table 3.1 (*cont.*)

Problem attribute	Low	High
C. Industry opacity	• Targeted industry is well regulated. • Transactions are well documented. • Targeted industry is dominated by a small number of highly professional companies.	• Industry is largely unregulated. • Transactions are not documented. • Targeted industry is fragmented with many small-scale enterprises.
3. Environmental uncertainty		
A. Novelty of policy issue	• Cause–effect relationship of the problem and potential solutions are well understood. • Proven strategies exist for dealing with potential side effects. • Countries have long experience in dealing with the targeted problem.	• Cause–effect relationship of the problem and potential solutions are only poorly understood. • No strategies exist for dealing with potential side effects. • Countries have little experience in dealing with the targeted problem.
B. Innovativeness of field	• Development of substitutes to the targeted goods or services involves significant investments and delay. • Substitutes would pose less of a problem. • Production, transhipment, and consumption of targeted goods or services cannot easily be switched to less regulated channels or countries.	• Substitutes to the targeted goods or services can be developed with little investment and delay. • Substitutes would be of equal public concern. • Production, transhipment, and consumption of targeted goods or services can easily be switched to less regulated channels or countries.

constellation underlying the trafficking in narcotic drugs, money laundering, the illicit trade in conflict diamonds, and the diffusion of small arms and light weapons. Based on this analysis, I will derive specific design expectations and compare these expectations with the actual design of an international institution created to mitigate a certain policy problem. As argued above, this study hypothesizes that harder legalization is the best design solution for dealing with moral hazards arising from high levels of asset specificity and behavioral uncertainty. In contrast, soft law arrangements are better suited for problems plagued with a high degree of environmental uncertainty, in particular when asset specificity and behavioral uncertainty are not very pronounced.

3.4 Interaction between problem constellation variables

Recent empirical studies on transaction cost economics have turned their attention to potential interaction effects between problem constellation variables[23] and revealed a bias toward weak governance structures that result from the way asset specificity, behavioral uncertainty, and environmental uncertainty collectively impact the optimal design solution.

Masten, Meehan, and Snyder (1991) conclude that low levels of integration (i.e. spot markets) are the default governance structure for business transactions since vertical integration is associated with considerable *ex ante* transaction costs. Economic actors are only willing to shoulder these costs if tighter integration helps them reduce the risk of opportunism arising from high levels of asset specificity and if the expected value of losses resulting from opportunistic behavior by the other party outweighs the integration costs.

In international relations, the analogous assumption is also widespread, maintaining that *ad hoc* coalitions are the preferred mode of cooperation as they involve the least sovereignty costs (Abbott and Snidal 1998; see also 2.1.2). States only consider higher degrees of legalization when such international institutions reduce the risk that other states shirk their obligation and when such shirking inflicts considerable losses on the other participating states – in brief, when asset specificity is high.

---

[23] For instance, a large number of empirical studies show the correlation between behavioral uncertainty and the level of integration is particularly strong in the presence of a non-trivial degree of asset specificity (Anderson and Schmittlein 1984; Gulati and Singh 1998; Morrill and Morrill 2003; Widener and Selto 1999).

Table 3.2 *Design hypotheses under different problem constellations*

Problem constellation			Expected design outcome (level of legalization)	Number of different problem constellations leading to the same design outcome
Asset specificity	Behavioral uncertainty	Environmental uncertainty		
Low	Any value	Any value	Low	9
Moderate	Any value	Any value	Moderate	
High	Low	Low	Moderate	
High	Low	Moderate	Moderate	
High	Low	High	Moderate	
High	Moderate	Low	Moderate	17
High	Moderate	Moderate	Moderate	
High	Moderate	High	Moderate	
High	High	Moderate	Moderate	
High	High	High	Moderate	
High	High	Low	High	1

Assuming low levels of legalization as the "default" design option has two important consequences for our institutional design model. First, behavioral uncertainty alone cannot be expected to lead to a deviation from the default design, i.e. from soft legalization. Even if states find it easy to cheat surreptitiously from the obligations created by a certain institution, such a high level of behavioral uncertainty remains inconsequential if (a) states have little incentive to exploit this situation and if (b) such a breach does not result in any significant loss or harm for other states. Both the incentives to shirk and the level of harm inflicted on other participating states by such behavior influence the asset specificity of a certain cooperative project. Hence, only when asset specificity has passed a certain threshold can increasing behavioral uncertainty – *ceteris paribus* – be expected to motivate states to choose higher levels of legalization.

Similarly, the effect of environmental uncertainty on the optimal design of an international institution is also conditioned by the level of asset specificity. Only when a non-trivial level of asset specificity is involved can we assume that decreasing levels of environmental uncertainty are correlated with harder forms of legalization. But in contrast to behavioral uncertainty, environmental uncertainty never exerts a pull toward higher levels of legalization. Low environmental uncertainty simply means that flexibility is not a major concern and thus should not be an obstacle to the adoption of a hard law arrangement. It does not imply that a high level of legalization is necessary or desirable. To put it plainly, environmental uncertainty can only drag the optimal level of legalization down but never push it up.

In sum, I expect to find institutions with low levels of legalization whenever asset specificity is insignificant, independent of the values of behavioral and environmental uncertainty. Assuming that the three problem constellation variables are equally distributed, this conjecture suggests a strong bias in the distribution of design outcomes toward the middle and lower end of the legalization spectrum. Table 3.2 displays the various combinations of problem constellation variables that all lead to the same expected design outcome. It shows that a high level of legalization can only be expected to be the optimal design solution for cases that present a combination of high asset specificity and behavioral uncertainty and low environmental uncertainty. In contrast, there are nine different problem constellations under which a soft law arrangement is deemed ideal and almost twice as many problem constellations under which a design solution with a moderate degree of legalization is expected to be best suited for dealing with associated governance challenges.

The small number of cases studied here does not allow me to reach a conclusion on the extent to which this hypothesized distribution of design outcomes corresponds with the actual design distribution of international institutions. However, should such a skew toward soft legalization be confirmed by a large n-study, it would resonate well with the realist position which stresses the reluctance of states to commit to any form of international cooperation that would impinge on their sovereignty.

4 | *Narcotic drugs: UN Convention against Illicit Traffic in Narcotic Drugs and Psychotropic Substances*

Today's war on terror is stealing the headlines of another fuzzy war the world is fighting against a non-conventional enemy: the war on drugs. Illicit drugs[1] are a prototypical case of a problem stretching all across the blurred crime–war continuum. On the one hand, narcotics are associated with problems that fall clearly within the crime category, such as crimes committed under the influence of drugs. Not a day passes without the tabloids reporting new sensational stories about a crack addict battering an innocent victim. On the other hand, drugs have also triggered and sustained a number of prominent inter-state and intra-state wars. The tense stand-off between Colombia and its neighbors Venezuela and Ecuador is just the most recent manifestation of the bellicose dimension of the drugs industry. The extra-territorial killing of a senior leader of Colombia's most notorious narco-guerrilla group has led Latin America close to a cross-border war (The Economist 2008).

In this chapter, I will explore the violent side of this half-trillion-dollar business[2] and assess the extent to which the architecture of the international institution created in response – namely the United Nations Convention against Illicit Traffic in Narcotic Drugs and Psychotropic Substances of 1988 – provides the optimal governance structure for dealing with the problem. The starkly contrasting ways and degrees of intensity with which different states are affected by the problem and the scarcity of reliable information on industry trends and on

---

[1] I will use the terms "narcotic drugs," "narcotics," "drugs," and "illicit drugs" interchangeably as generic terms for substances of natural or synthetic origin which are classified by the United Nations as illicit based on their dependence-producing nature and negative health impact. However, Boaz (1991) is right in pointing out that this logic is not consistently applied, as alcohol and tobacco would have to be included in this definition of drugs.

[2] This is the upper limit of a widely cited estimate produced by the UN with the lower estimate being US$300 (see also Hopkinson 1991: 1; Reuter and Greenfield 2001).

governments' control efforts suggest hard law to be the best design option. Environmental uncertainty does not mitigate this push toward high levels of legalization, as this second type of uncertainty is low, thanks to the century-long experience in international drug control cooperation, thus reducing the need for flexibility offered by soft law. The following analysis will show a match between the actual architecture of the Vienna Convention and the design expectations I derive from the assessment of the problem constellation as it presented itself to the drafters of the Convention.

4.1 Narcotic drugs as an international policy problem

4.1.1 Drugs between crime and war

Drugs and crime are intimately intertwined. Virtually all jurisdictions around the globe criminalize the consumption,[3] production, and distribution of mind-altering substances like heroin, cocaine, marijuana, and methamphetamines. Despite – or because of – the ubiquity of the prohibitionist approach, this question is highly controversial as will become apparent throughout this chapter: drug-related offenses top many countries' crime statistics. At the turn of this century, almost a quarter of a million drug offenses were recorded by the Russian police (Barclay and Tavares 2003); and in the United States over 60 percent of inmates in the federal prison system were drug law violators (Perl 2006). However, these *drug-defined offenses*[4] account for only a part of all crimes associated with drugs. Equally important are *drug-related offenses*, i.e. crimes committed under the influence of drugs (or drug-induced crime) or to finance drug addiction as well as violence among rival drug dealers. According to US government figures, over one-fifth of all prison inmates – or almost 400,000 – were under the influence of drugs at the time they committed their offense (ONDCP 2000). In the UK, around 15 percent of all arrestees report that drugs had impaired their judgment and thus led them to their offense. In murder and robbery cases, this share climbs to almost 30 percent (Bennett 1998).

---

[3] The consumption of narcotic drugs has been decriminalized in some countries, as we will discuss below.

[4] See the definition by the US Office of National Drug Control Policy (ONDCP 2000).

More prevalent than crimes under drug influence are offenses that narcotics misusers commit to finance their addiction or drug retailers to defend their turf. In the United States, drugs are involved in about half of all cases of street crime (Lee and Perl 2002). Clutterbuck (1995) reports a similar figure for the United Kingdom. Finally, drug-related acts also account for a noticeable share in the most serious of all criminal offense categories. The US Office of National Drug Control Policy (ONDCP 2000) reports that around 5 percent of all homicides are connected to a narcotics felony, such as drug trafficking or manufacturing. All these cases have in common that they occur in drug consumer countries and clearly fall within the crime category, as they are largely about one individual or group inflicting harm for non-ideological reasons.

The distinction between crime and war becomes considerably more blurred in drug-producing and trafficking countries where non-political violent acts often occur on a much larger scale. In order to protect their lucrative business from governmental raids, the Colombian Medellín cartel adopted a strategy of targeted assassinations of public proponents of a strong anti-drugs policy. In 1984, for instance, the cartel accounted for the killing of Rodrigo Lara Bonilla, the Colombian justice minister, Attorney General Carlos Mauro Hoyos, High Court Judge Carlos Valencia (Hopkinson 1991) and many other public figures, including elected politicians, presidential candidates,[5] cabinet ministers, and journalists (Thoumi 1999, 2003). The Medellín cartel also offered a bounty for the head of each policeman (Thoumi 1999: 134), which contributed to over 3,000 military and police personnel being killed or wounded during the second half of the 1980s, and 420 in 1990 alone (Bagley 1988; Hopkinson 1991; Office of the President of the Republic 1989). Simultaneously, the drug industry – particularly in Colombia – has at times also pursued the strategy of creating general chaos through the detonation of bombs at police headquarters, but also in random public places. Although not ideologically motivated, these acts of violence certainly reached a level where they became a political force as they threatened the very existence of the state.

These acts of violence are indistinguishable – at least in their outward manifestation, though not in their purported motivation – from the

---

[5] The 1989 presidential campaign established a sad record with three candidates being assassinated (Thoumi 1999).

tactics employed by terrorist or guerilla groups that are becoming increasingly involved in the drug business to finance their ideologically motivated, armed struggle against incumbent governments. Colombia provides again the most illustrative example,[6] where drug-related income has strengthened the position of rival terrorist groups and led to an intensification and militarization of the intra-state conflict (Felbab-Brown 2004). From the early 1980s onwards,[7] the Fuerzas Armadas Revolucionarias de Colombia (FARC), the bigger of the country's two left-wing guerrilla groups,[8] embraced the drug industry as an important source of income. Initially, the FARC raised funds by taxing coca growers and drug traffickers operating in the regions they controlled (King 1997: 68).[9] The guerrilla group later – especially after the collapse of the Medellín and Cali cartels – expanded its activities in this business field and began to acquire plots, process coca leaf into cocaine, and to cooperate with regional mafia networks (Guáqueta 2003: 80). Estimates of the FARC's drug-related income vary considerably, ranging from US$269 million (King 1997: 68) to US$530 million (Guáqueta 2003: 81). FARC doubles its income with money earned from extortion and kidnapping (Guáqueta 2003; Rabasa *et al.* 2001: 126). The illegal right-wing paramilitary Autodefensas Unidas de Colombia (AUC) relies even more extensively on the drug business, which accounts for approximately 70 percent of its income, according to the own admission of the AUC's national chief (Guáqueta 2003: 82; Rabasa *et al.* 2001: 128).

The declared goal of narco-financed terrorist organizations is of an ideological nature,[10] but as the symbioses between these armed groups and the drugs industry strengthen over time, the distinction between goals (ideology) and means (drug-related profits) becomes increasingly

---

[6] Other examples include the Liberation Tigers of Tamil Eelam (LTTE) (see Rabasa *et al.* 2001: Part 2), the Shining Path (Sendero Luminoso) in Peru (Palmer 1992), and the Taliban in Afghanistan (Perl 2001).

[7] Rabasa *et al.* (2001: 125) name 1982 as the start date of the FARC's drug involvement.

[8] The smaller left-wing guerilla group is the Ejército de Liberación Nacional (ELN).

[9] Weinstein (2007: 290) reports how the FARC was initially ideologically opposed to getting involved in the drug business.

[10] E.g. the FARC was established as the military wing of the Moscow-line Colombian Communist Party and currently advocates land redistribution and the empowerment of the historically disenfranchised lower working and peasant classes (Rabasa *et al.* 2001).

blurred. While such a tendency to goal–means displacement is undeniable, one also needs to keep in mind that besieged governments have every incentive to exploit this drug–guerrilla nexus for their own propaganda purposes. They may find it a useful tool to deflect attention from the rebels' political agenda by depicting the fighters as driven by material self-enrichment alone.

These narco-funded conflicts often had and still have important repercussions on the international level, leading to a securitization of the drug problem even in countries that are not directly affected by large-scale drug-related violence. No country is more concerned about the national and international security implications of such drug-related spillover effects than the United States. In 1987, the US Senate held a hearing dedicated to "the threat posed by international narcotics networks as an increasing danger to the national security of the United States and its allies," and one year later, the US Congress Subcommittee on Terrorism, Narcotics, and International Operations published a special report in which it examined the security implications of the growing power of drug cartels (the Kerry report). William J. Bennett, then head of the Office of National Drug Control Policy, verbalized this growing fear when he declared in 1989 that "[t]he source of the most dangerous drugs threatening our nation is principally international. Few foreign threats are more costly to the US economy. None does more damage to our national values and institutions and destroys more American lives. While most international threats are potential, the damage and violence caused by the drug trade are actual and pervasive. Drugs are a major threat to our national security" (quoted in Bentham 1998: 35). In response to this perceived security threat, the United States launched its own "war on drugs,"[11] and sent off its Coast Guard to enforce American laws on the high seas and used military personnel to participate in a series of operations against Bolivian,[12] Colombian, and Peruvian drug manufacturers (Bogges 1992). Given the strong collusion between drug barons and political elites in many countries – as captured in the term "narcocracy" (Choiseul Praslin 1991) – such military-led

---

[11] The term was first used during the Nixon administration (Epstein 1977), but the use of military force against the drug industry became more widespread under the Reagan and the Bush administrations (Bogges 1992).

[12] E.g. the US Drug Enforcement Administration (DEA) operation "Blast Furnace" of 1986 (Labrousse 1991).

extraterritorial law enforcement operations started to resemble all elements of the classical understanding of "war"[13](see above 1.1.1).

Most of the above-mentioned examples of the association of drugs with crime and war are intimately linked to the criminalization of narcotic drugs. Their criminal status earns drugs a handsome premium, which makes it considerably harder for drug addicts compared to other substance abusers to finance their addiction through legally earned income.[14] At the same time, the prospect of exorbitant profits to be earned in the drug industry attracts terrorists and criminals alike.[15] The illegal status of drugs also forces drug gangs to settle their differences by guns rather than in court and compels drug producers and traffickers to protect their business interests through bribing and killing law enforcement agents rather than legal lobbying. Cases where the state tolerated or even actively endorsed the production of and trade in narcotics demonstrate that the drugs industry does not intrinsically have to stir up violence and can even strengthen the state by providing it with a lucrative tax base.[16]

4.1.2 International initiatives

The global nature of the drug business[17] and the transborder spillover effects of the associated problems led policymakers to realize early on that this issue required close international cooperation. They launched the first of such attempts in 1909, when thirteen states met in Shanghai

---

[13] The most telling example is the US campaign against Panama in 1989, when a 20,000-men (and women) strong commando seized control of the country and arrested its *de facto* ruler, General Manuel Noriega, on drug trafficking charges (Bogges 1992).

[14] A study by the UK Home Office found that only around 2 percent of surveyed arrestees reported the need for money to finance their alcohol addiction as the reason for their offenses, compared to 20 percent among drug addicts (Bennett 1998). It is thus not surprising that crime rates among chronic heroin addicts fell by 60 percent when they enrolled in a governmental pilot scheme of controlled heroin administration in Switzerland (Joyce 1999: 104).

[15] The most lucrative element in drugs' value chain is trafficking. Reuter and Greenfield (2001) calculate an implied value added between drug export and import markets of more than 2,000 percent, compared to 18 percent in coffee.

[16] For instance, McCoy (1992: 27) estimates that the French covered about half of the costs of their colonial government in Indochina through taxes levied on the production and trade in opium.

[17] Approximately four-fifths of all illicit drugs – and virtually all cocaine and heroin – consumed in the United States are of foreign origin (Perl 2006).

to discuss measures to curb opium addiction, which had reached alarming levels, especially in China[18] (US Senate Special Committee on Illegal Drugs 2003: 446). With the strong support of the United States and against initial reluctance of the British government,[19] the conference concluded with a call on all governments to ban opium smoking and to prohibit or otherwise regulate other forms of opium consumption. The Hague Convention of 1912 codified and expanded the agreement reached in Shanghai and regulated the trade in and abuse of opium, cocaine, and morphine. It represents the first truly multilateral agreement on drug control (Bassiouni and Thony 1999: 913) and the beginning of an era of treaties-based global coordination and convergence of domestic drug control policies. The 1925 Geneva Convention of the League of Nations (LoN) further expanded the scope of international drug control by including new substances (most importantly, cannabis) through the development of transnational (rather than just domestic) control mechanisms. For this purpose, the Geneva Convention established an eight-member Permanent Central Opium Board in charge of monitoring states' compliance and devised an import certification system to control the legal international trade in drugs. The last anti-drug treaty to be concluded under the auspices of the League of Nations was the 1936 Convention for the Suppression of Illicit Traffic in Dangerous Drugs. This convention established drug trafficking for the first time as a criminal offense and called upon governments to punish people involved in this activity regardless of their nationality and of the country where they committed this crime.

The post-World War Two international drug control framework rests predominantly upon three United Nations conventions, which are mutually supportive and complementary. They enjoy almost universal support – all three conventions count 183 parties[20] – and form

---

[18] At its apex, dependency on opium smoking affected 25 million Chinese, or more than 5 percent of the population – a drug addiction prevalence never reached by any country before or since (UNODC 2004: 26).

[19] The British government's endorsement of the Shanghai conference represented a massive U-turn. After all, the same government had not shied away from using its military might to force the Chinese to revoke their ban on the import and consumption of opium in the so-called Opium Wars of 1839–1842 and 1856–1858.

[20] As of July 2007.

the legal basis of what Nadelmann called the "global drug prohibition regime" (1990: 503).

The first pillar, the Single Convention on Narcotic Drugs of March 30, 1961 (the Single Convention or 1961 Convention,[21] henceforth), primarily consolidates into a single document the various drug treaties and protocols the UN had inherited from the League of Nations. The Single Convention continues the LoN treaties' prohibitionist leaning. In its preamble, the Convention recognizes the medical use of narcotics "to be indispensable for the relief of pain and suffering," while pointing out that "addiction to narcotic drugs constitutes a serious evil for the individual and is fraught with social and economic danger to mankind." The main purpose of the Single Convention is to limit the production and trade in these substances to the quantities required to meet legitimate medical and scientific needs. It calls upon parties to criminalize all activities related to the production, manufacturing, and distribution of narcotic substances outside defined medical and scientific purposes (Article 36). It introduces a categorization scheme in which drugs are listed in one of four schedules depending on their addictiveness, harmfulness, and therapeutic value which determines the rigidity of required control.[22] The second pillar of the UN drug treaty framework – the Convention on Psychotropic Substances of 1971 (hereafter, Psychotropic Substance Convention or 1971 Convention) – follows the Single Convention's prohibitionist orientation and supplements it by placing similarly stringent controls on a number of synthetic substances not previously covered. The 1971 Convention subjects synthetic mind-altering substances – namely stimulants (amphetamines), depressants (e.g. benzodiazepines and barbiturates), and hallucinogens (e.g. Lysergic Acid Diethylamide[23] and psilocybin) – to the same scheduling mechanism used for plant-derived drugs under the 1961 Convention.

The third and most recent cornerstone of the UN's anti-drug framework is the Convention against Illicit Traffic in Narcotic Drugs and Psychotropic Substances of 1988. This convention will be discussed in greater detail below.

---

[21] It was amended in 1972 by the Protocol Amending the Single Convention on Narcotic Drugs in light of the Psychotropic Substance Convention (see below) of 1971 mainly to demand reduction provisions.

[22] E.g. Schedule I includes the most dangerous drugs, including heroin, cocaine, and – controversially – cannabis.

[23] More commonly know under its acronym, LSD.

In addition to the international agreements of the UN, a great number of regional[24] and bilateral cooperation arrangements have been set up to strengthen cross-border drug control, but the UN remains the unchallenged leader in this field.

4.1.3 The 1988 UN Convention against Illicit Traffic in Narcotic Drugs and Psychotropic Substances

The Vienna Convention is a manifestation of the growing concern about the rapid increase in drug abuse[25] and about the wider crime and security implications of the drug business. Unlike the earlier conventions, the Vienna Convention does not primarily consider drugs from a health perspective, but places a greater emphasis on the problems arising from the association of drugs with organized crime. Its preamble refers to "the links between illicit traffic and other related organized criminal activities which undermine the legitimate economies and threaten the stability, security, and sovereignty of States" as the main justification for this effort to renew and strengthen the international fight against drugs. The drafters of the Vienna Convention recognized that the overwhelming bulk of narcotic drugs was produced by organized criminal groups and did not stem from a diversion of narcotic drugs from legal sources to illicit channels – the main concern addressed by the 1961 and the 1971 Conventions (Bayer and Ghodse 1999). An expanded toolbox was therefore needed, in particular with regard to the so far neglected trafficking stage. To combat drug trafficking, the Vienna Convention seeks to improve and strengthen international cooperation and coordination among all the relevant authorities, such as customs and police agencies, and judicial bodies (Bassiouni and Thony 1999: 922). As under the 1961 and 1971 Conventions, the key focus is on international legislative and judicial cooperation. The Convention seeks to harmonize the definition and scope of drug offenses (Article 3) and thereby to help states fulfill the double criminality

---

[24] E.g. the Pompidou Group of the Council of Europe established in 1971 and the Inter-American Drug Abuse Control Commission (CICAD) created in 1986.

[25] For instance, the number of cocaine abusers in the US rose from negligible levels in 1970 to over 1.2 million by 1988 (Bayer and Ghodse 1999). Already in 1981, the UNGA declared that drug abuse had reached "epidemic proportions in many parts of the world" (A/RES/36/168).

requirement[26] that had previously blocked many extradition requests (Article 6). It also includes the legal means to interdict drug trafficking.

The two most important innovations introduced by the Vienna Convention are provisions targeting the proceeds of the lucrative drug business and the legal substances used in the manufacturing of drugs. Article 5 on confiscation seeks to reduce the economic attractiveness of drug operations by "taking profits out of crime." It contains several provisions that address the question of how to deal with drug-related proceeds that have been transformed or converted into other property. In this respect, the Vienna Convention pioneered international efforts to combat money laundering even though the term itself does not appear in the Convention (see Chapter 5). The Vienna Convention's confiscation provisions attracted widespread praise for their innovative approach and precipitated the rash of asset confiscation legislation of the 1990s (Boister 2001: 390).

The 1988 Convention also stepped beyond the two earlier UN anti-drug conventions by subjecting precursors – i.e. legal chemicals and solvents used in the manufacture of narcotic drugs and psychotropic substances – to stricter monitoring (Article 12). The International Narcotics Control Board (INCB) is mandated to list such substances in Table I and Table II of the Convention and to update these tables regularly,[27] similarly to the scheduling procedure provided for by the Single Convention.

In sum, the Vienna Convention imposes "relatively extensive obligations to provide mutual legal assistance" (Donnelly 1992: 291), includes "the most comprehensive provisions for international penal cooperation" (Bassiouni and Thony 1999: 927), and represents "significant progress in establishing an international system of control over narcotic drugs and psychotropic substances" (Rolley 1992: 425).

4.2 Problem constellation

The Vienna Convention provides the first testing ground for the institutional design framework I presented in the two preceding chapters. In this section, I will assess the extent to which international cooperation

---

[26] This principle stipulates that the alleged crime for which extradition is being sought must be criminal in both the demanding and the requested countries.

[27] The current "red list" can be accessed at www.incb.org/pdf/e/list/red.pdf.

against drug trafficking is fraught with the risk of substantial damage
caused by shirking states who feel they have more to lose than to gain
from contributing to an effective anti-drug front – as is the case under
high asset specificity. I will also examine whether these states can defy
their treaty obligations without risking detection – as is the hallmark of
high behavioral uncertainty. This analysis will reveal that both of these
problem constellation variables are significant, while the third variable –
environmental uncertainty – is of minor relevance in the case of drug
trafficking.

4.2.1 Asset specificity

As developed above (see Chapter 3), asset specificity is higher the
greater the loss a party experiences when widespread non-compliance
causes the breakdown of a cooperative project and the greater the risk
that such a breakdown could occur. Both aspects of asset specificity
depend on the relative distribution of costs and benefits among the
parties. In the following, I will therefore qualitatively assess both costs
and benefits in the historic context of the late 1980s.

Costs
The Vienna Convention imposes on parties both direct implementation
costs and unintended indirect costs of an economic and political nature,
whereby the latter outweigh the former significantly.

The Vienna Convention was largely compatible with pre-existing
legal systems in North America and Western Europe, thus requiring
only minor changes in the legislation of these countries (Bentham 1998;
Donnelly 1992). For a number of other countries – especially those that
had not already ratified the 1961 and the 1971 Conventions[28] – the
Vienna Convention meant that they had to adjust their narcotics policies to the higher standards prevailing in such states as the US (Bewley-
Taylor 1999). One aspect of these "higher standards" is the share of
government revenues assigned to anti-drug law enforcement measures.
The unchallenged leader in this respect was and still is the United States.
The fast expansion of the United States federal budget for drug abuse

---

[28] Most coca-producing countries had become Party of the Single Convention prior
to the drafting process of the Vienna Convention, but none of the leading opium
producers.

control programs during the 1980s propelled this budget item to over US$10 billion a year[29] in the early 1990s (Celia Toro 1999). Almost 10 percent of this total – or US$1 billion – was spent on international programs, first and foremost on interdiction operations in Colombia, Peru, and Bolivia (Fuller 1996). It is therefore not surprising that the United States hoped to use the Vienna Convention as a vehicle for burden sharing, as a tool to shift part of its own law enforcement expenses on to other states, in particular on narcotics-producing and transhipment countries (McAllister 2000). In some countries like Colombia, the adoption of the Vienna Convention was indeed followed by a significant increase in public anti-drug expenditures. López estimates that Colombia's anti-drug expenditures rose from 0.6 percent of total public expenditures in the 1980s to 1.5 percent in 1993 (cited in Thoumi 2003: 195). Levels of public spending on anti-drug policies remain, however, disparate.[30]

For many drug-producing countries, concerns about these direct implementation costs were of secondary order compared to their fears about the potential repercussions a strong international anti-drug front might have on their economic and political stability.

In many narcotic-producing states, the illicit drug sector provides an indispensable source of income and employment which would be lost if effective anti-narcotic policies were implemented. The economic attractiveness of cultivating narcotic plants derives from the fact that these plants provide good yields in conditions that are unfavorable for many legal types of crops, and that no other crop is financially as rewarding.[31] According to Bewley-Taylor (1999), the gross income generated by a coca grower in Peru's Upper Huallaga Valley exceeded the income of a coffee producer by a factor of ten and that of a rice farmer by an even greater factor of twenty-one.[32] In Bolivia's Chapare region, coca is estimated to be between four and nineteen times more profitable than

[29] Which equaled 0.8 percent of the total federal budget or 0.17 percent of GDP.

[30] E.g. in 2002, the average EU country spent approximately 0.05 percent of its GDP on drug-related policies, i.e. less than a quarter of relative US expenditures (EMCDDA 2003).

[31] Growing narcotic plants is lucrative for farmers despite the fact that they only earn about 0.5 percent of the final retail value (Hopkinson 1991: 3). The illegal status of narcotic plants is a central reason for their higher profit margin.

[32] Palmer (1992) refers to a study that found that coca prices exceeded the price of leading alternative crops – namely cacao and corn – by factors of 4 and 34, respectively.

the next most profitable crop (Atkins 1998).[33] It is thus not surprising that the production of drugs formed (and to a lesser extent still forms) a strong pillar of both Peru and Bolivia's national economy. In Peru, which accounted for 55.1 percent of global coca production in 1988 (INCSR 1990, reprinted in Labrousse 1991), almost all of the 300,000 farmers in the Upper Huallaga Valley derived the lion's share of their income from this illicit crop (Palmer 1992). Though accounting for a smaller share in global coca production,[34] neighboring Bolivia was (and still is) the most drug-dependent economy in Latin America (Hopkinson 1991). The drug business employed at its peak in the 1980s between 6.7 and 13.5 percent of the country's workforce (Thoumi 2003: 154) and generated between 6 and 19 percent of Bolivia's gross domestic product.[35] With exports valued at about US$3 billion, coca leaves and their various derivatives earned half of the poor Andean country's inflow of foreign exchange (Kopp 2003). During the same period, the production, manufacturing, and trafficking of drugs created profits equaling 7 percent of Colombia's GDP.[36] In Myanmar, Afghanistan, and Laos – the world's leading poppy growers in the late 1980s[37] – opium production and trade played an equally significant economic role (see Table 4.1). Consequently, these states had strong economic incentives to resist international attempts to impose a rigorous drug control institution on them and to shirk their obligations to the greatest extent possible.

These narcotics-producing states feared international anti-drug efforts not only for their harmful impact on their country's economy but also for negative repercussions on their fragile political stability.[38] In many of these countries, the cultivation of narcotic drugs involved (and still involves) disenfranchised segments of society – often ethnic minorities[39] – whose non-existent allegiance toward national unity and

---

[33] This region's unique climatic conditions lead to a particularly high concentration of the psychoactive substance alkaloid (Clutterbuck 1995), and thus a quality premium.

[34] Bolivia contributed around 33.9 percent of global coca production in 1988 (INCSR 1990, reprinted in Labrousse 1991).

[35] And still around 2 percent of GDP in 2003 (UNODC 2004).

[36] 2.5 percent of GDP in 2003 (UNODC 2004).

[37] Accounting in 1988 for 44.7 percent, 26.1 percent, and 8.9 percent of the global opium output, respectively (INCSR 1990, reprinted in Labrousse 1991).

[38] The dilemma the international community faces today in stabilizing Afghanistan is the most prominent contemporary manifestation of the tensions between drug control efforts and security considerations (see, for instance, Felbab-Brown 2005).

[39] On Laos see Westermeyer (2004).

Table **4.1** *Output of leading opium and coca producers, 1988*

	Opium			Coca leaves	
Country	Production volume (t)	Share in global production (%)	Country	Production volume (t)	Share in global production (%)
Myanmar	1,282.5	44.7	Peru	110,500	55.1
Afghanistan	750	26.1	Bolivia	67,900	33.9
Iran	300	10.5	Colombia	21,600	10.8
Laos	255	8.9	Ecuador	400	0.2
Pakistan	205	7.1	**World, total**	200,400	100.0
Mexico	50	1.7			
Thailand	28	1.0			
World, total	2,870.5	100.0			

Source: INCSR (1990), reprinted in Labrousse (1991).

the central government can easily turn into outright hostility when their most important source of livelihood is threatened. For instance, in Myanmar, the central government's connivance with different ethnic rebel groups'[40] expanding involvement in the opium business was an indispensable part of an implicit ceasefire agreement between the government and the rebels. Peru's President Fujimori feared that militarization of coca eradication policies would only reinforce the Sendero Luminoso's grip over the peasants (Hopkinson 1991). In Bolivia, coca growers (or *cocaleros*) were and still are organized in strong unions and constitute a vital factor in maintaining the national unity in spite of strong tensions between the country's highland and lowland parts.[41]

---

[40] E.g. the United Wa State Army and the Myanmar National Democratic Alliance Army.

[41] These strong tensions manifested themselves, for instance, in the first years of this new century when pro-American president Gonzalo Sánchez de Lozada was forced to step down in 2003 by disgruntled peasants who had been hurt by a highly effective eradication campaign (Felbab-Brown 2004; The Economist 2005). Against this background, it is little surprise that his successor, Evo Morales – a former *cocaleros* leader – ordered a halt on all coca eradication programs.

Finally, some states feared that international anti-drug cooperation as envisaged by the Vienna Convention would result in significant political costs in the form of a loss of sovereignty. Latin American states, especially, were worried that the US would misuse the Convention to legitimize its interference in their domestic political life. This skepticism was based on the long and – as many Latin Americans would argue – infamous history of the US Drug Enforcement Administration and, to a lesser extent, the Central Intelligence Agency in enforcing US drug laws extraterritorially. Against this background, María Celia Toro argues that from a Latin American perspective, the encroachment of US law enforcement agents "represents as important a threat as losing the war against the traffickers themselves. It represents the 'loss of state control'" (quoted in Smith 1992: 248).

In sum, the greatest direct and indirect implementation costs of an international anti-drug agreement fell on a handful of producing countries which could thus be expected to oppose such an agreement or surreptitiously to shirk their obligation when they considered the costs of open defiance too high.

Benefits

Not only the costs, but also the benefits of a strengthened international drug control effort were highly unequally distributed among states in the late 1980s. This bias resulted from the fact that large differences existed in the extent to which countries suffered from substance abuse[42] and from drug-related violence.

No country placed greater importance on global drug elimination than the United States. Most US citizens agreed in the late 1980s that drugs posed the single most important problem the country faced (Hopkinson 1991: 15). This view is echoed by James Baker, the former Secretary of State, who declared that "[t]here is no foreign policy issue short of war and peace which has more direct bearing on the well-being of the American people" (quoted in US State Department 1991). In the late 1980s, the country counted approximately 35 million illicit drug users, including around 24 million marijuana users, almost 10 million cocaine users, and 1 million heroin users (Hopkinson 1991: 15). In

---

[42] Over the past decade, we have been witnessing an increasing global convergence both in terms of prevalence of drug abuse and of the relative "popularity" of different types of drugs.

1992, 5,660 Americans died from substance abuse (mainly cocaine or heroin, or a combination of both), and an estimated US\$60 billion were lost in productivity due to drug-related illnesses and accidents (Frischer, Green, and Goldberg 1994). On top of this concern about the national health consequences of growing addiction rates, the United States became increasingly worried about the foreign policy implications of a potential takeover of narcocracies in its backyard (see 4.1.1). At the height of the Colombian drug cartels' power, Charles Range, then-chairman of the US House Select Committee on Narcotics Abuse and Control, expressed his fear that the United States would one day find itself "an island of democracy in a sea of narco-political rule" (quoted in Andreas and Bertram 1992: 170).

Europe also experienced a rapid increase in drug abuse during the 1980s, with the key difference that its main problem drug was heroin, not cocaine.[43] In some European countries, the worsening drug situation caused as much alarm in political circles as in the United States. Switzerland suffered from a substance abuse-related death rate that was three times higher than in the United States, with heroin killing more than 400 addicts annually in the peak years of the late 1980s and early 1990s. Photos of hundreds of tattered abusers loitering in a public square in the country's commercial capital shook the self-image of the law-and-order loving country. Heroin produced an ever higher death toll in other European countries, most prominently in the United Kingdom, Luxembourg, Denmark, and Italy.

In contrast, drugs killed only a negligible number of people in narcotic-producing states as well as in other developing countries. While the traditional use of coca leaves is widespread in Latin America, it caused relatively little damage to individuals or to society because of the limited addictiveness of this form of consumption. Bolivia recorded three substance abuse-related deaths in 1991, whereby volatile solvents – not coca or cocaine – were the most important form of substance abuse (Frischer, Green, and Goldberg 1994). Similarly, the prevalence of traditional forms of drug abuse is also high in opium-producing countries, again with the effect that very few deaths are causally linked to drugs. The substance abuse-related death rate of

---

[43] Around 97 percent of all addicts in the then-European Community used heroin (Hopkinson 1991: 17).

Table 4.2 *Substance abuse-related death rates in most affected consumer states and in leading producer states in the early 1990s*

Country	Year	Population (in millions)	Number of substance abuse-related deaths	Substance abuse-related deaths per 1 million
Most affected states				
Switzerland	1992	6.7	419	62.54
United Kingdom	1990	57.561	2,356	40.93
Hong Kong	1991	5.8	170	29.31
Luxembourg	1990	0.3819	11	28.80
United States	1992	247.3	5,660	22.89
Denmark	1990	5.14	115	22.37
Italy	1990	56.719	1,161	20.47
Germany	1990	79.433	1,491	18.77
Norway	1990	4.2415	70	16.50
Russia	1992	148	2,036	13.76
Drug-producing states				
Bolivia	1991	7.2	3	0.42
Pakistan	1991	108.7	12	0.11
Myanmar	1992	40.8	2	0.05
Thailand	1990	55.4	1	0.02

Source: EMCDDA (2007); Frischer, Green, and Goldberg (1994); World Bank (2008); calculations by author.

Pakistan was, for instance, only 0.11 per 1 million people, and that of Myanmar only half of this already small number (Frischer, Green, and Goldberg 1994). These death rates are comparable to other developing countries that do not have a stake in the production of opium or coca. For instance, Senegal's substance abuse-related death rate was comparable to that of Pakistan's, while that of Algeria was in the range of Myanmar's.

Table 4.2 provides an overview of the substance abuse-related death rates of the most affected consumer states and contrasts these high rates with the very low rates of key drug-producing states around the time the Vienna Convention was drafted. These figures have to be treated with extreme caution because of serious definitional inconsistencies and reporting issues. Despite this qualification, most analysts would agree that in the late 1980s and early 1990s, high-potency drug abuse was primarily a scourge of developed consumer countries.[44]

Also, the extent to which states suffered under imminent or perceived drug-related threats to their national security varied considerably around the globe. As elaborated above, the Colombian drug industry – through the Medellín and the Cali cartels as well as the three terrorist groups FARC, AUC, and ELN – challenged the very foundations of the Colombian state. In contrast, drug cultivation in Bolivia, Laos, and Mexico[45] was much less a source of conflict or violence.

Asymmetry in the distribution of costs and benefits

This discussion of the cost and benefit structure allows us to distinguish four categories of countries.

A first category comprises countries wherein the expected benefits outweighed the costs of an effective global anti-drug regime form during the 1980s. The United States, Switzerland, Germany, the United Kingdom, and Italy fall within this category. They all suffered under a very high rate of substance abuse-related deaths,[46] while an effective repression of the global drug business would not have had any noticeably negative impact on these countries' economies or political stability. The United States, in particular, would have welcomed such a development as an important improvement of its national security situation. For this group of states, ensuring international compliance with a strong drug control agreement was a key concern as they sought to shift part of their drug control burden onto narcotics-producing countries.

In contrast, countries like Bolivia, Laos, and Myanmar form a second category, which feared very high costs from having to implement a rigorous international anti-drug agreement. Their main concern was thereby focused on the indirect implementation costs resulting from a loss in income and employment and from the unsettling of a very fragile power balance. At the same time, these states did not expect to reap any important benefits from the Convention, as they neither suffered from widespread drug abuse nor drug-related violence.

---

[44] The gap in drug-related deaths between consuming and producing states has been shrinking in the past decades.

[45] Mexico was the world's leading marijuana producer, accounting in the late 1980s for more than half of global production (Labrousse 1991).

[46] All with a substance abuse-related mortality rate of 0.02 or greater (per 1,000 population) (Frischer, Green, and Goldberg 1994).

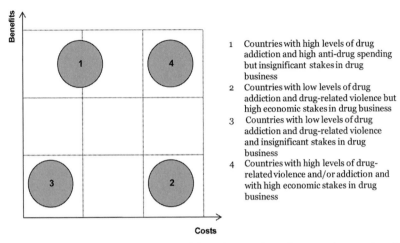

Benefits

Costs

1   Countries with high levels of drug addiction and high anti-drug spending but insignificant stakes in drug business

2   Countries with low levels of drug addiction and drug-related violence but high economic stakes in drug business

3   Countries with low levels of drug addiction and drug-related violence and insignificant stakes in drug business

4   Countries with high levels of drug-related violence and/or addiction and with high economic stakes in drug business

Figure 4.1 Distribution of costs and benefits resulting from an international anti-drug institution

The two remaining groups of states take the middle ground, with costs from implementing the Vienna Convention roughly equaling the benefits they derive from a functioning agreement. Category three comprises many African and developing states from other world regions which enjoyed low rates of narcotic drug abuse-related deaths and had no economic stakes in the production or trafficking of these drugs. The final category is formed by states which suffered severely from drug-related violence but simultaneously benefited economically from the drug industry, like Colombia and Mexico.[47] Figure 4.1 illustrates the distribution of costs and benefits among these four categories of states.

Figure 4.1 shows a very asymmetric distribution of the net effects of international drug control cooperation, with some countries expecting enormous benefits from an effective anti-drug institution, while others bear high costs. This constellation created strong incentives for the latter to shirk their obligations, while the former were eager to maximize compliance and thus the benefits they could reap from a functioning institution. As argued in Chapter 3, such a high degree of asset specificity calls for a high level of legalization, as only hard law can

---

[47] As mentioned, Mexico was the world's largest producer of cannabis and a major trafficking country in the 1980s. At the same time, the Mexican government explicitly recognized the security risk posed by narcotics in their national security doctrine (Krasner 1991).

reduce the risk of shirking and thereby preserve the benefits some states expect to derive from international cooperation.

4.2.2 Behavioral uncertainty

To what extent did the instigators of the Vienna Convention fear that key producer states not only had strong *incentives* to shirk (as seen above) but also many *opportunities* to do so without risking detection? This question is at the very heart of the behavioral uncertainty variable. In the following, I will assess this second dimension of the problem structure underlying international drug control efforts by first examining the governance capacity of states deemed pivotal to the success of an international anti-drug institution. This analysis will be followed by an assessment of the availability of reliable information on the drug problem from independent, non-state sources which would allow states to monitor other parties' compliance. Finally, I will examine the extent to which the opacity of the drug industry presented an obstacle for compliance monitoring. I will again base my analysis in the historic context of the late 1980s to capture the problem structure as it presented itself to the drafters of the Vienna Convention. As I will show, international efforts to curb drug trafficking were fraught with a high level of behavioral uncertainty stemming from a severe lack of governance capacity in key producer states, as well as from poor observability of actual state behavior resulting from the very limited availability of independent sources of information and a high degree of industry opacity.

Governance incapacity

The most striking commonality that source, and to a lesser extent, transit states around the world shared was the relative weakness of their central government's capacity to control the entirety of the country's territory.[48]

In 1996 – the earliest year for which the World Bank provides data on countries' governance capacity – most of the seven key source countries were placed below the median with regard to the three indicators, government effectiveness, rule of law, and control of corruption (see Table 4.3).

---

[48] This still holds largely true today, but amphetamine-type stimulants' growing share in the global drug business has given developed countries more prominence as source states.

Table 4.3 *Selected governance indicators for key drug producer states, 1996*

Country	Government effectiveness	Rule of law	Control of corruption	Average
Iran	−0.75	0.21	0.25	−0.10
Peru	−0.13	−0.58	−0.14	−0.28
Colombia	0.23	−0.65	−0.52	−0.31
Bolivia	0.07	−0.31	−0.94	−0.40
Laos	−0.06	−1.64	−1.00	−0.90
Myanmar	−1.28	−1.31	−1.21	−1.26
Afghanistan*	−2.27	−1.34	−1.91	−1.84

* Data are for 1998, as no earlier data are available for Afghanistan.
Source: World Bank (2007).

Only Iran, the fourth-largest opium producer in the late 1980s, scored above the median with regard to both rule of law (0.21)[49] and control of corruption (0.25), which helped the Islamic republic earn the highest average score among drug-producing states despite its relatively poor government effectiveness. It was followed by Peru – the world's leading coca grower – where all three governance indicators were below the median, but only marginally. The other two key coca producers, Colombia and Bolivia, both recorded an above-median government effectiveness score, but their significantly worse scoring in corruption and rule of law (Colombia) made them fall behind Peru's average. The capacity to govern was significantly worse in the top opium producer countries. While Laos' government effectiveness score was close to the median, its poor performance in the other two indicators earned it an average score that was 0.5 points lower that of Bolivia. Myanmar recorded consistently low scores across all three indicators. Afghanistan – the second biggest opium producer in the 1980s and the dominant producer today – claimed the infamous record as the country with the lowest level of government effectiveness and weakest control of corruption among all 212 states assessed by the World Bank.[50]

---

[49] On a scale from − 2.5 to + 2.5, with lower values reflecting weaker governance.
[50] Data are for 1998, as no earlier data are available for Afghanistan.

Consequently, instigators of a strengthened global drug control institution were concerned that the effectiveness of this institution might be undermined not only by willful non-compliance but also by the very weak capacity of the governments of key drug producer states to implement their policies, even if they were to be endorsed by them *bona fide*.

Relative reliance on governmental monitoring
Uncertainty about parties' behavior also arose from the fact that supporters of stronger global drug controls had – and still have – very limited information from independent sources that they can rely on in their assessment of other states' compliance. Unlike other types of crime,[51] drug trafficking produces victims that are highly unlikely to criticize a government for defiance of international obligations, as addicts benefit – at least from a myopic perspective – from lax implementation of prohibitionist policies through less harassment by law enforcement officers and lower street prices of drugs. Also, the pharmaceutical industry and scientific community which rely on narcotic and psychotropic substances for legitimate purposes have no direct incentive to ensure that states are living up to their international drug control obligations.

Furthermore, supporters of tighter international drug control were not able to counter their uncertainty about other states' compliance by relying on information and analysis provided by non-governmental organizations. In this respect, drug trafficking contrasts sharply with the illicit trade in conflict diamonds (Chapter 6) and small arms (Chapter 7). While there do exist a number of NGOs in support of a prohibitionist approach – e.g. Drug Free America Foundation, Europe against Drugs, Foundation for a Drug-Free Europe[52] – these organizations limit their efforts to advocacy rather than research. In contrast, civil society organizations (NGOs and think tanks) with a more skeptical perspective on drug prohibition have built up considerably stronger research capabilities.[53] However, given their anti-prohibitionist

---

[51] E.g. intellectual property violations.
[52] These NGOs formed an umbrella organization – the Vienna Non-Governmental Organization Committee – to which also a number of non-specialized civil society organizations, such as Rotary International, the Salvation Army, and Caritas belong.
[53] Among the most important research-oriented civil society organizations with an active interest in drug policies are the Drug Policy Alliance, the Open Society Institute's International Harm Reduction Program, the Beckley Foundation Drug Policy Program, and the Transnational Institute Drugs and Democracy Program.

leaning, these organizations tend to focus their research efforts on demonstrating the negative side effects of the international regulatory framework rather than on assessing states' compliance with these policies.

Industry opacity
Behavioral uncertainty was further aggravated by the fact that the global drug industry was highly non-transparent, and specialized in concealing its operations to the greatest extent possible. The nearly century-long history of criminalization of drugs had led to a total separation from the legal pharmaceutical industry, of which it had initially been a part.[54] Consequently, the drafters of the Vienna Convention could not rely on a strategy of responsibilization (Garland 1999), i.e. to shift part of the monitoring and enforcement burden on to a legal industry within easy reach of the regulator. In this respect, international drug control differs greatly from initiatives to stem the global flow of dirty money, conflict diamonds, and unlicensed small arms and light weapons, as I will show in later chapters.

In sum, efforts to strengthen international drug control faced a high degree of behavioral uncertainty resulting from the weak governance capacity of leading drug producer states, the non-transparency of the drug industry, and the absence of independent sources of information that would have allowed other parties to detect non-compliance.

4.2.3 Environmental uncertainty

A third and final aspect that drafters of the Vienna Convention had to take into account when designing the institutional architecture for their common anti-drug efforts was environmental uncertainty, i.e. the extent to which they felt confident that they had a sufficiently deep understanding of the nature of the problem and of the policy options at hand. I will argue in the following that policymakers indeed possessed a high degree of confidence thanks to collective experience on international drug control dating back to the dawn of the twentieth century, and the relatively low innovativeness of the criminal field.

---

[54] As mentioned above, the diversion of narcotics from licit into illicit channels was no longer a problem by the 1980s.

Novelty of policy issue

As elaborated above (4.1.2), the Shanghai Conference of 1909 launched a century of ever-expanding and intensifying international cooperation in the global war against drugs – in particular, the 1988 Drug Convention built directly on the Single Convention on Narcotic Drugs of 1961, the 1972 Protocol amending the Single Convention, the 1971 Convention on Psychotropic Substances, and the Comprehensive Multidisciplinary Outline of 1987. Apart from the provisions on the confiscation of drug-related proceeds (Article 5) and on precursors (Article 12), the Vienna Convention was largely drafted in a spirit of "more of the same," seeking to strengthen and expand the provisions of the two earlier UN anti-drug conventions. The environmental uncertainty stemming from insufficient experience in international drug control cooperation was thus very low for the drafters of the Vienna Convention.

Innovativeness of criminal field

The drafters of the Vienna Convention also felt that they commanded sufficient expertise on the nature of the drug industry, as the overall innovativeness of the industry was relatively constrained. From past experience, policymakers knew that the range of options drug barons had for marketing new drugs or changing production, trafficking, or retail methods was limited.

All the major drugs consumed at the time of the drafting of the Vienna Convention (and still today) had been developed several decades ago. Cocaine and heroin were first produced in the nineteenth century (Braithwaite and Drahos 2000: 362), while today's party drug Ecstasy (Methylenedioxymethamphetamine or MDMA) and its predecessor, LSD, were first synthesized in 1912 and 1938, respectively. Minor changes did occur in the processing of existing narcotics, for instance, the development of crack cocaine in the 1980s, or the breeding of cannabis varieties with significantly increased potency resulting from higher concentrations of the plant's psychoactive substance THC (terahydrocannabinol).

Overall, it is not so much the type of illicit drugs that has changed over time but rather the drugs' relative popularity among users. For instance, whereas the abuse of LSD was widespread in the 1960s, especially in the United States, the consumption of this hallucinogen has now stabilized at a very low level. While cocaine abuse in Europe was still marginal in the 1980s, it has now overtaken heroin as the number one drug in several European countries. The United States experienced the opposite development during the same period, with heroin now accounting for the greatest number of drug-related treatment cases (UNODC 2004: 32).

While the drug industry has largely failed to develop new types of drugs, it has shown slightly more creativity in protecting production and trafficking operations from the grip of law enforcement bodies. For instance, partly in response to massive US-led coca eradication programs, the Colombian drug industry "diversified" into the cultivation of opium, earning the country the infamous rank as the fourth-largest opium producer in 2004 (UNODC 2007).

Geographic displacement of production is the most famous type of balloon effect. The drug industry, like other criminal organizations, seeks to evade a hardening clampdown in one country by shifting production to another country with more lax law enforcement. Bewley-Taylor (1999), for instance, links the increase in illegal poppy cultivation in Mexico with the success of the Turkish government in eradicating opium in 1972. However, the scope for such displacement is limited – in particular with regard to coca. Coca bushes require a tropical climate and develop sufficient concentration of the psychoactive substance cocaine alkaloid only if grown in high altitudes – conditions that are only found in the Andes. Furthermore, it takes the plants between 12 and 24 months to reach a state at which the leaves can be harvested (US Department of Justice 1993), thus imposing a significant time-lag on geographic displacement.

Similarly, the drug industry also seeks to avoid detection by choosing trafficking routes through countries with weak law enforcement capacities and by responding to heightened anti-drug police efforts with a re-routing of cargo. Block (1992) reports how the crackdown on the traditional trafficking route Turkey–Marseilles–New York led to a breakup into more segments with an increased number of transhipment centers, thus making it more difficult to establish the link between the place of origin and the end destination. Large-scale drug trafficking, however, can only be diverted to places that have a minimum degree of legitimate interaction (tourism, trade, or diasporas) with the end destination, as it would otherwise be difficult to conceal drug shipments.

Finally, the drug business has also shown some flexibility with respect to smuggling methods. Whereas small private airplanes were the favored mode of coca smuggling into the United States in the 1970s and 1980s, this strategy was largely abandoned following the implementation of the United States National Air Interdiction Strategy in 1988 and substituted with ground transport via Mexico and shipping by sea (Block 1992). The industry has sought to conceal drugs in so-called "drug mules" by having a smuggler swallow a parcel of tightly sealed narcotics or by co-mingling it with all sorts of legitimate cargo. The Peruvian police made a most unlikely discovery when they found 700kg of cocaine hidden inside a frozen giant squid (The Economist 2005). The latest "transport innovation" includes a fiberglass submarine that the Colombian navy seized in a swampy mangrove close to the northernmost point of Colombia's Caribbean coast (International Herald Tribune 2007). As these examples show, the drug industry can exploit a set of tactics to evade law enforcement efforts, but these tactics are eventually limited, and to a considerable extent, predictable.

The combination of a low degree of novelty in the policy issue with the moderate degree of innovativeness in the criminal field makes it ambiguous – should the overall level of environmental uncertainty be considered low or moderate? A comparison, however, with the environmental uncertainty found in the three remaining case studies shows that the innovativeness of drug traffickers is more comparable to that of arms dealers, which I classify as low (see Chapter 7), than with the high innovativeness surrounding money laundering (see Chapter 5). Therefore, I consider it appropriate to round down the average of the low degree of novelty of the policy issue and the moderate degree of innovativeness of the criminal field to an overall low degree of environmental uncertainty. As a consequence, the instigators of the Vienna Convention had no strong reason to press for a soft law design solution, since flexibility was not an issue of particular concern to them.

4.2.4 Summary and implications for institutional design

Table 4.4 provides a summary of the assessment of this study's three explanatory variables and their sub-components in light of the Vienna Convention. As argued above, the drafters of the 1988 Convention faced a high degree of both asset specificity and behavioral uncertainty. Environmental uncertainty, in contrast, was relatively low. The combination of a high degree of asset specificity and behavioral uncertainty threatened to undermine the effectiveness of tighter international drug

Table 4.4 *Summary assessment of the problem constellation underlying the trafficking in narcotic drugs*

Problem attribute	Level	Argument
4. Asset specificity	**High**	
C. Potential loss	High	• Some net-consumer states suffer under very high rates of drug abuse and/or drug-related crime, and the issue ranks high on the political agenda. • Some producer and transit states suffer under large-scale drug-related violence.
D. Propensity to shirk	High	• The production of illicit drugs is an important economic factor in some source states. • Rigorous enforcement of anti-drug policies threatens to undermine a delicate political balance in some source states.
5. Behavioral uncertainty	**High**	
D. Governance incapacity	High	• Many source states have very weak governance capacity and often lack control over the entirety of their territory.
E. Reliance on governmental monitoring	High	• Individual victims of drug trafficking (i.e. addicts) are not organized and have no immediate interest in lobbying for tougher enforcement of anti-drug laws. • Pharmaceutical industry has no incentive to monitor states' drug control efforts. • NGOs in support of prohibitionist drug policies have weak research capabilities.
F. Industry opacity	High	• Illicit drug sector operates clandestinely to avoid detection. • Long-established dissociation between licit and illicit drug sector means that the former cannot be used as a tool to control the latter.
6. Environmental uncertainty	**Low**	
B. Novelty of policy issue	Low	• Countries have long experience in national drug control. • International drug control cooperation dates back to the beginning of twentieth century.

Table 4.4 (*cont.*)

Problem attribute	Level	Argument
C. Innovativeness of field	Moderate	• All illicit drugs that are being consumed have been known for several decades. • Production of some plant-based drugs (in particular coca) is limited to a few states, thus limiting the displacement potential. • Traffickers enjoy a moderate degree of flexibility in choosing trafficking routes, modes of transport, and concealment techniques.

control, since some states had strong incentives to shirk their obligations and many opportunities to do so without risking detection. The need for credibility therefore outweighed the need for flexibility, thus suggesting the adoption of a high degree of legalization as the best design solution to protect the hoped-for gains from an effective global anti-trafficking front.

4.3 Degree of legalization

The above analysis of the specific constellation underlying the drugs trafficking problem suggests a high level of legalization as the optimal design for an international institution created to tackle this global scourge. But does this theoretical expectation match the actual governance architecture chosen by drafters of the Vienna Convention to institutionalize their anti-drug cooperation? In this final section, I will argue that the Convention is indeed marked by an overall high degree of legalization, resulting from obligation and precision reaching relatively high levels, while the Convention's level of delegation can be classified as moderate.

4.3.1 Obligation

As elaborated in section 2.2.1, the extent to which an international institution imposes obligations on states is determined by two main criteria. First, the degree of obligation created by an international institution depends on whether this institution is built around an international agreement that is legally or only politically binding. Since the Vienna Convention is a legally binding agreement (as I will show in the next paragraph), I will also have to assess the extent to which its level of obligation is attenuated through provisions that allow states to unilaterally modify and sidestep the obligations the Convention outlines. Second, an international institution is considered to be more obliging when it provides for procedures and remedies to deal with non-compliance. I will argue that the level of obligation enshrined in the Vienna Convention can be considered as high as a result of its legal bindingness and compliance mechanisms.

Legal bindingness

There can be little doubt about the legal status of the Vienna Convention as a legally binding treaty. The Vienna Convention was explicitly established to give legal force to the illicit trafficking recommendations adopted at the International Conference on Drug Abuse and Illicit Trafficking in June 1987. It displays all the formal characteristics of a legally binding treaty. It uses language that suggests a legally binding character, exemplified by the name of the agreement – i.e. "Convention" – and by words such as "shall" and "obligations." It incorporates provisions on accession, entry into force, procedures for amending the Convention, and denunciations which are absent in agreements that are not meant to be legally binding. Also, the process through which signatories ratified the Convention indicates their intent to enter into a legally binding treaty.[55] Finally, the 1988 Drug Convention has been registered with the UN secretariat and published in the UN Treaty Series.[56] The Convention thus displays all characteristics of a legally binding treaty.

Like virtually all legally binding agreements, the Vienna Convention allows parties to modify and weaken their commitments through reservations, safeguard clauses, and withdrawal. In contrast to the 1961 and 1971 UN Drug Conventions,[57] the Vienna Convention does not contain a specific article dealing with reservations. The drafting committee

---

[55] In the United States, this required the advice and consent of the qualified majority of the Senate which was granted on November 22, 1989.
[56] The Vienna Convention was filed as Treaty Doc. No. 101–4 (1989).
[57] Article 49; Article 32.

deliberately decided against the inclusion of such an article – not intend-ing to invite states to make reservations, but rather out of the conviction that the issue was sufficiently well-governed by Article 19 of the 1969 Vienna Convention on the Law of Treaties (Boister 2001: 59). A total of forty-four parties filed reservations to modify the tenacity of some obligations.[58] Unsurprisingly, the reservations and declarations by two key source countries – namely Bolivia and Colombia – are the longest and most comprehensive. In addition to allowing states to modify some obligations through the deposit of reservations, the Vienna Convention contains three articles with specific safeguard provisions that states can use to relativize the degree of obligation established by these articles. These safeguards are standard in most international treaties and refer to the inviolability of state sovereignty,[59] the primacy of state "security, *order public* or other essential interests,"[60] and of national legal sys-tems.[61] Like virtually all international treaties, the Vienna Convention allows for denunciation. However, it imposes heavier constraints on this option than do most international treaties, as Article 30 requires the lapse of one year – a period much longer than that stipulated by most other conventions – before the denunciation submitted by a party takes effect.

Compliance mechanisms

The Vienna Convention – as well as the 1961 and the 1971 Conventions – is executory, i.e. it assigns responsibility for treaty implementation to the individual parties. In order to ensure that states do indeed implement the policies they have formally endorsed, the Vienna Convention relies on two main mechanisms: monitoring and sanctions.

The 1988 Convention contains a series of provisions[62] that require parties to furnish information on the legislative reforms they undertook in light of their treaty obligations (Article 20(1)(a)) and on "[p]articu-lars of cases of illicit traffic within their jurisdiction which they consider important because of new trends disclosed, the quantities involved, the sources from which the substances are obtained, or the methods employed by persons so engaged" (Article 20(1)(b)). The submission

---

[58] Compared to only six for the amended Single Convention.
[59] Article 2 Para 2.   [60] Article 7 Para 15, emphasis in original.
[61] Article 3 Paras 1, 2, and 10.
[62] E.g. Article 5 Para 4, Article 7 Para 9, Article 12 Para 2, and Article 17 Para 7.

of information pursuant to Article 20 is an indispensable prerequisite for the Commission on Narcotic Drugs (CND) to fulfill its oversight and supervisory mandate granted by Article 21. Article 20(2) therefore authorizes the CND to outline the modalities for the furnishing of information. Article 20 establishes a system that relies exclusively on self-reporting, which presents a relatively weak monitoring instrument.[63] To compensate for this shortcoming, the International Narcotics Control Board established the practice of reviewing states' compliance on a regular basis through country missions.[64] During these review missions, the INCB gathers information through interviews with state officials on "the functioning of national drug control administrations, the adequacy of national drug control legislation and policy, measures taken by Governments in combating drug abuse and illicit trafficking and Governments' fulfillment of their reporting obligations as required under the international drug control treaties" (INCB 2006: 23). The scope of these review missions thus goes beyond the information requirements under Article 20 as the INCB assesses not only the "law on the books" but also the "law in action."

Outside the direct scope of the Vienna Convention, but of significant importance for compliance with the treaty's key provisions, is the monitoring of treaty compliance undertaken by the US State Department. The Foreign Assistance Act of 1961, as amended (22 USC §2291) mandates the US State Department to evaluate within its annual International Narcotics Control Strategy Report whether countries are meeting the goals and objectives of the 1988 UN Drug Convention.

The provisions on dealing with a party's failure to comply with treaty obligations are less developed than these monitoring mechanisms. The Vienna Convention, in conjunction with the two earlier UN drug conventions, provides for two mechanisms to sanction non-compliance: the imposition of reputational costs through "naming and shaming" tactics and material costs through the imposition of an embargo on legal imports and exports of narcotic drugs to and from the non-complying state.

---

[63] Countries often fall short of compliance with the reporting obligation under Article 20. For instance, Papua New Guinea has failed to meet its reporting obligations under the international drug control treaties for the past decade (INCB 2006).

[64] Not explicitly provided for in the UN drug treaties.

Article 22 of the Vienna Convention provides the legal backbone of the formerly mentioned sanctioning mechanism. Article 22(1)(b)(iii) authorizes the INCB to bring a country's non-compliance to the attention of the parties, the Economic and Social Council (ECOSOC) of the UN General Assembly, and the Commission on Narcotic Drugs should the state fail to implement remedial measures the INCB had prescribed pursuant to Article 22(1)(b)(i). The INCB may also decide to publish its criticism in its annual report – a prerogative of which it makes frequent use. The effectiveness of this reputational sanctioning measure is disputed. On the one hand, its effectiveness is limited by the fact that it is only after a government has failed to convince the INCB of its compliance through a multi-stage process of hearings and discussions that the INCB is authorized to raise its concerns in public. Prior to this end point, the confidentiality requirement of Article 22(1)(b)(ii) applies. Furthermore, Article 22(1)(b)(iii) grants a non-complying party the right to have its views presented in the report in which it is criticized. On the other hand, some scholars have argued that the reputational costs of this sanctioning mechanism are high as the UN drug control bodies enjoy the "image of a benevolent movement whose mission it is to safeguard the well-being of all humankind," thus conferring upon them and their decisions "substantial moral influence and suasion" (Bewley-Taylor 1999: 172). In this respect, the UN anti-narcotics framework as established by the Vienna Convention represents what Donnelly (1992) referred to as a "promotional regime."

However, the sanctioning clout of the UN drug conventions is not confined to this promotional role. While the Vienna Convention itself does not contain specific provisions on imposing material sanctions on non-complying states, it can fall back on those provided by the earlier drug conventions. Article 14(2) of the Single Convention authorizes the INCB to "recommend to Parties that they stop the import of drugs, the export of drugs, or both, from or to the country or territory concerned, either for a designated period or until the Board shall be satisfied as to the situation in that country or territory." Similarly, Article 19 of the 1971 Convention allows the Board to recommend a drug embargo against a party when it has reason to believe that the aims of the Convention are being seriously endangered by the party's failure to implement the Convention's provisions. In practice, the effectiveness of these embargo provisions is rather limited – for two key reasons. First, the number of countries where the legal export and import of narcotics constitutes an important factor is limited. Legal production of poppy straw – the raw material from which palliative substances like morphine and thebaine are derived – is concentrated in just a handful of countries, namely Australia, Turkey, France, and Spain.[65] Legal demand for poppy straw is equally concentrated in Australia, France, the United Kingdom, and the United States – which account collectively for three-quarters of global utilization in 2003 (Fischer, Rehm, and Culbert 2005). Furthermore, in the forty years of the Single Convention's existence, no import or export embargo has ever been imposed. The INCB threatened sanctions on five occasions, but each time sanctions were avoided after the non-complying country implemented the INCB's recommendations (Bewley-Taylor and Trace 2006). Despite their rare evocation, Boister argues that these sanctioning mechanisms "represent potentially powerful instruments for enforcing observation of [treaty] obligations" (2001: 485).

Arguably more effective than the embargo provisions under the 1961 and 1971 Conventions are compliance mechanisms outside of the UN framework. The same Act that mandates the US State Department to monitor countries' compliance with the Vienna Convention also authorizes the US President to impose far-reaching sanctions on a country that is deemed, first, a major illicit drug producer or drug transit point and, secondly, fails in its efforts to cooperate with the US and to adhere to the UN drug conventions.[66] If a country is "decertified" as non-complying and non-cooperative, it will see all its foreign assistance from the US frozen and its applications for loans from a multilateral development bank vetoed by the US government (Perl 2001).[67] Referring to this unilateral enforcement of the UN drug conventions by the United States, Raustiala (1999: 111f.) argues that

---

[65] Accounting for 33.5, 32, 15, and 10 percent of worldwide production, respectively (Fischer, Rehm, and Culbert 2005).

[66] Of the twenty states currently on the so-called "majors list" – namely Afghanistan, the Bahamas, Bolivia, Brazil, Colombia, the Dominican Republic, Ecuador, Guatemala, Haiti, India, Jamaica, Laos, Mexico, Myanmar, Nigeria, Pakistan, Panama, Paraguay, Peru, and Venezuela – only Myanmar and Venezuela have been decertified (White House 2006).

[67] This unilateral enforcement mechanism has provoked widespread international criticism not at least because the (de)certification decision is based on technical as much as on political considerations.

as a formal matter, compliance with international drug law is largely managed rather than enforced by the UN system. That is to say, the UN system provides extensive assistance to parties in implementing their international commitments and solving problems of capacity, training, or technical expertise that might result in non-compliance with their treaty obligations. But managerial compliance efforts are, in the case of international drug control, in practice backed up by a large, if unofficial, enforcement stick.

For this reason Bewley-Taylor reaches the conclusion that given "[t]he moral voluntarism of the UN ... combined with the unilateral pressure exerted by ... Washington ... the international regime becomes more coercive than promotional" (1999: 172).

In sum, the Vienna Convention is of a legally binding nature and – in conjunction with the United States' unilateral enforcement of the Convention – establishes at least moderately strong mechanisms for detecting and sanctioning non-compliance. Although its compliance mechanisms do not quite reach the same high level as provided for by the FATF's Forty Recommendations (Chapter 5) or the Kimberley Process (Chapter 6), I still consider them strong enough to suggest a rounding up of the average of high degree of legal bindingness and the moderate level of compliance mechanisms. The Convention thus establishes an overall high degree of obligation.

4.3.2 Precision

The Vienna Convention is further strengthened by an overall high degree of precision. I will argue that provisions contained in the Vienna Convention are formulated in a moderately determinate way and are highly consistent in themselves and in relation to other international agreements.

Determinacy

A number of legal scholars and drug control experts have praised the Vienna Convention for its comprehensiveness and high level of detail. For instance, Bassiouni and Thony note that "the 1988 Drug Convention contains the most comprehensive provisions for international penal cooperation. More particularly, its provisions on extradition, mutual legal assistance, and money laundering are the most detailed of any other international criminal law convention"

(1999: 927).[68] The Vienna Convention earns this praise largely based on its relatively high degree of determinacy, which it achieves through three main mechanisms. First, in Article 1 the Vienna Convention meticulously defines twenty-one terms that are central to the proper interpretation of the Convention. Second, its categorization of precursors into different tables based on the substances' misuse potential could not be more specific. The so-called "Red List" of precursors includes the substances' French and Spanish names along with their full Chemical Abstracts Index name, Chemical Abstracts Service registry numbers, and Harmonized System codes.[69] The drafters of the Vienna Convention deliberately adopted this mechanism for identifying dangerous precursors in precise and narrow terms in order to enhance the legal strength against cases of illicit use and not to unduly inhibit or discourage legitimate chemical and pharmacological research and production (Bentham 1998: 47). Third, the degree of determinacy of the Vienna Convention has been strengthened further with the publication of an official commentary in 1998 which helps to preclude some interpretative disputes.

The effect of this determinacy-enhancing feature is mitigated by the Convention's reliance on standard-like provisions (Abbott and Snidal 2000) and the vagueness found in some articles. In recognition of states' sovereignty in domestic law enforcement, the Vienna Convention confines its role to obligating states to criminalize and punish certain acts that it enumerates in detail, while granting states the discretion to determine the exact level and type of punishment for these offenses. The Vienna Convention's degree of determinacy is also slightly reduced by the moderated use of the term "appropriate," which appears thirty times in the ninety-five-paragraph long document. In some cases, the vagueness of this term allows states to interpret a provision in different ways. For instance, Article 12 calls upon states to "take the measures they deem appropriate to prevent diversion of substances." Probably the most ambiguous of all provisions relates to the highly controversial question of a state's proper response to the personal consumption of narcotics.[70] All these instances of weak determinacy can be used by

---

[68] Similarly, Bayer and Ghodse (1999).
[69] The "Yellow List" on narcotic drugs and the "Green List" on psychotropic substances of the 1961 and the 1971 Conventions are equally determinate.
[70] The Vienna Convention can be seen as a step closer to the criminalization of personal drug consumption – a question that neither the 1961 nor the 1971

states to advocate an interpretation that best serves their purposes. This effect is partly counterbalanced by some other provisions where weak determinacy strengthens the discretion of the UN drug control bodies. Article 21 authorizes the Commission on Narcotic Drugs "to consider all matters pertaining to the aims of this Convention" and to "take such actions as it deems appropriate." Similarly, Article 22 grants the INCB the right to "call upon the Party concerned to adopt such remedial measures as shall seem under the circumstances to be necessary for the execution of the provisions of article 12, 13 and 16." The INCB in particular has used the weak determinacy of its mandate to expand its sphere of influence – for instance, with the above-mentioned decision to conduct in-country review missions.

Coherence

The Vienna Convention fulfills as a whole Franck's (1990) criteria for coherence, as its provisions relate to one another in a non-contradictory way, allowing for a coherent interpretation of an indefinite number of cases. As Bassiouni and Thony (1999) note, the evolutionary process of international drug control legislation has resulted in a system of mutually reinforcing and complementing treaties under the UN umbrella. To ensure coherence, the Vienna Convention makes explicit reference to the two earlier conventions and obliges all parties to implement the provisions of the 1961 and the 1971 Conventions. In the same vein, the UN General Assembly adopted a system-wide action plan on drug abuse control as an instrument to coordinate the anti-drug abuse activities of the UN drug control organs and to strengthen cooperation in this matter within the wider UN system (Boister 2001).[71] External coherence with other – not exclusively drug-related – international agreements is also relatively strong thanks to the fact that many of

---

Convention addressed explicitly. Article 3 Para 2 stipulates that "each Party shall adopt such measures as may be necessary to establish as a criminal offence under its domestic law, when committed intentionally, the possession, purchase or cultivation of narcotic drugs or psychotropic substances for personal consumption contrary to the provisions of the 1961 Convention, the 1961 Convention as amended or the 1971 Convention." However, this supposedly strong indication of the Convention's prohibitionist leaning is weakened by the qualifications contained in the opening of this provision, which posits that the criminalization of drug consumption is "[s]ubject to its constitutional principles and the basic concepts of its legal system."

[71] A/RES/44/141 of December 15, 1989.

these agreements – e.g. the Forty Recommendations of the Financial Action Task Force studied in more detail in the next chapter – make direct reference to the Vienna Convention and urge parties to ratify it.

The average of the Convention's moderate level of determinacy and its high level of coherence does not assign the overall level of precision to any of my three ordinal categories. To determine whether the overall level of precision should be considered moderate or high, I need to compare the Vienna Convention with international institutions that have the same constellation in their two precision sub-components. The Forty Recommendations studied in the next chapter present such a case. Although the level of determinacy is moderate in both cases, the Vienna Convention uses vague terms more sparingly and gives clearer indications of the preferred type of sanctions – i.e. penal measures – it expects states to impose against offenders. This suggests a rounding of the average of determinacy and coherence to an overall high degree of precision.

4.3.3 Delegation

The Vienna Convention does not create a new organization to which it delegates tasks, but builds upon a number of pre-existing UN bodies with non-drug specific mandates – namely, the International Court of Justice, as well as the anti-drug bodies that had been established by the earlier UN drug conventions – the UN Commission on Narcotic Drugs, the UN Office for Drug Control and Crime Prevention, which is known by its current name, the UN Office on Drugs and Crime,[72] and the International Narcotics Control Board. The Convention increases the administrative and policy powers of the Commission on Narcotic Drugs and of the International Narcotics Control Board to such an extent that they are now providing a "basis for an eventual direct control system" (Bassiouni and Thony 1999: 917). Despite these efforts to clarify, and to some extent strengthen, the role of the three UN anti-drug bodies, the overall level of delegation remains moderate.

---

[72] The new name was adopted on October 1, 2002. The UNODC also incorporates the UN International Drug Control Program (UNDCP) and administers the Fund of the UNDCP. To avoid unnecessary confusion, this study uses the agency's current name.

International Court of Justice

By far the weakest form of delegation provided for by the Vienna Convention relates to the settlement of disputes among parties. Article 32 Para 2 stipulates that disputes "shall be referred, at the request of any one of the State Parties to the dispute, to the International Court of Justice (ICJ) for decision" when parties fail to settle the dispute between them. This provision has had no practical impact, as many parties have submitted reservations against this article.[73] In the twenty-year history of the Convention, not a single case has been referred to international arbitration or judicial settlement (Boister 2001). In response to the weakness of the Vienna Convention's dispute-settlement mechanism, a number of Caribbean states called for the inclusion of drug trafficking offenses in the jurisdiction of the then still to be established International Criminal Court (ICC). Despite the backing of the INCB, this proposal was first watered down and ultimately relegated to a future review of the ICC's jurisdiction (Boister, 2001: 538f.).

United Nations Office on Drugs and Crime

Today's UNODC is the successor organization of the United Nations Drug Control Program, which the UN General Assembly created in the same year that the Vienna Convention came into force (1990) out of a merger of three formerly independent UN drug abuse control units: the Division of Narcotic Drugs, the Secretariat of the INCB, and the UN Fund for Drug Abuse Control. Its functional role is significantly larger than that of the CND and the INCB while its level of independence is smaller. It assumes a wide range of executive functions in supporting the secretary general, the CND, the INCB, and the parties in their respective duties under the drug conventions and UN resolutions (Bassiouni and Thony 1999). The UNODC's Legal Advisory Program fostered the wave of national legislative reform that followed the conclusion of the Vienna Convention. Its technical work includes the control of the UN Narcotics Laboratory which – *inter alia* – determines the origin of confiscated drugs, and field-based projects related to alternative development and law enforcement.[74] This latter aspect of the UNODC's

---

[73] Article 32 Para 4 explicitly allows reservations against the ICJ's jurisdiction – as is common practice in international law.

[74] E.g. the UNODC provides training to strengthen countries' freight container control capacities.

technical work has grown over the past years, leading to the opening of twenty field offices around the world and two liaison offices (in New York and Brussels).[75] Since 1997, the UNODC also compiles the annual World Drug Report in which it highlights important trends in the production, trafficking, and consumption of narcotic drugs and psychotropic substances.

The UNODC derives a moderate degree of independence from its unparalleled technical expertise and from the fact that it possesses a permanent body of staff recruited through regular UN hiring procedures and not appointed by member states.[76] Furthermore, the UNODC's executive director holds the rank of an under-secretary general, which grants the office some clout within the UN. A potential threat to the UNODC's independence is its heavy reliance on voluntary contributions by governments,[77] which entails the risk that large contributors may threaten to withhold their contributions as a tool for influencing the UNODC. So far, there are no direct indications that the UNODC's work has been affected by such a funding-related policy bias. On the contrary, the UNODC has proved astonishingly resistant to change. Harm reduction is still a largely taboo subject within the UNODC, despite the fact that it derives 70 percent of its funding from European sources, where this approach has become a central pillar of drugs policies (Bewley-Taylor 2002).

United Nations Commission on Narcotic Drugs
The United Nations Commission on Narcotic Drugs is the central policymaking body within the United Nations drug control system. The CND's operational role and level of independence are moderate. Article 21 of the Vienna Convention authorizes the CND to consider all matters pertaining to the aims of the Convention.[78] Against this broad supervisory role, Article 21 then specifies six areas of the CND's competence – namely to review the operations of the Convention

---

[75] The twenty-three field offices are found in Afghanistan, Austria, Belgium, Bolivia, Brazil, Colombia, Egypt, India, Iran, Kenya, Laos, Mexico, Myanmar, Nigeria, Pakistan, Peru, Russia, Senegal, South Africa, Thailand, United States of America, Uzbekistan, and Vietnam.
[76] Currently comprising around 500 employees worldwide.
[77] Only 10 percent of the UNODC's annual budget is directly funded by the UN.
[78] Similarly, Article 8 of the Single Convention and Article 17 of the Psychotropic Substance Convention.

(Article 21(a)); to make suggestions and general recommendations (Article 21(b)); to draw the attention of the Board to any matters which may be relevant to its functions (Article 21(c)); to take appropriate actions on any matter referred to it by the Board (Article 21(d)); to amend Table I and Table II of precursor chemicals requiring particular international control (Article 21(e)); and, finally, to draw the attention of non-parties to its decisions and recommendations (Article 21(f)). The CND has used this mandate to facilitate the implementation of the Vienna Convention in particular with respect to mutual legal assistance, money laundering, control of precursors, and illicit traffic by sea (Boister 2001). As the governing body of the Fund of the United Nations International Drug Control Program, the CND has also become increasingly involved in providing technical assistance to states with drug control problems.

The independence of the Commission on Narcotic Drugs is ambiguous. On one hand, the CND is dependent on the United Nations' Economic and Social Council, which established it in 1946 as a functional commission mandated to assist in carrying out its UN Charter functions (Boister 2001). The CND takes action through resolutions and decisions, which are generally adopted by consensus and prepared in the form of ECOSOC draft resolutions (Boister 2001). ECOSOC is also in charge of electing the CND's fifty-three (until 1991, only fifteen) members, whereby a formula guarantees equitable geographical distribution of seats.[79] Finally, the CND's level of independence is further limited by its heavy reliance on the administrative and technical support provided by the UNODC.

On the other hand, the CND derives some level of independence from explicit mandates assigned to it by the UN drug conventions, which entail that it falls outside ECOSOC's discretion to dissolve the CND. The CND's independence is further enhanced by the fact its members are elected by ECOSOC in a secret ballot and not directly appointed by member states as representatives. Furthermore, not all of the elected delegates are diplomats; many come with a professional background in health care and law enforcement. The four-year term of office is

---

[79] Eleven from African states, eleven from Asian states, ten from Latin American and Caribbean states, seven from Eastern European states, fourteen from Western European and other states, with an additional seat rotating every four years between the Asian and the Latin American/Caribbean states.

sufficiently long to allow for the emergence of an at least partly independent *esprit de corps*, especially during the annual three-week long
sessions held in Vienna. The CND's most far-reaching and independent
role lies in its authority to decide which substances shall be added to
Schedule I or Schedule II as the most harmful drugs or psychotropic substances[80] and to Table I or II as the precursor chemicals with the greatest
misuse potential.[81] Unlike other CND resolutions, decisions related to the
scheduling of drugs, psychotropic substances, and precursors do not require
unanimity but adoption by either a simple (narcotic drugs) or two-thirds
majority (psychotropic substances and precursors) (Boister 2001).

International Narcotics Control Board

The International Narcotics Control Board enjoys the greatest degree of
independence of all UN drug control organs, but its operational functions are more limited than that of the UNODC. The most important
role of the INCB is as a quasi-judicial control organ responsible for
promoting government compliance by identifying "weaknesses in
national and international control systems and [by contributing] to
correcting such situations" (INCB 2006). As discussed above (4.3.1),
the INCB is vested with the authority to invite parties to furnish information on efforts to implement the Vienna Convention, to recommend
remedial measures as it deems necessary (Article 22), and to put some
pressure on non-complying states through "naming and shaming"
practices or the imposition of a drugs embargo. The INCB also plays
an important role in the scheduling procedures envisaged by the three
UN drug conventions, as it is mandated to assess the health risks of
drugs and misuse potential of precursor substances and to recommend
to the CND how these substances should be categorized in the four
schedules or two tables.

   The Board enjoys a relatively high level of independence from member states. One important pillar of the INCB's independence is the fact
that it was established by treaty,[82] rather than created as an UN organ
by ECOSOC. Consequently, ECOSOC cannot abolish the INCB, even
though it is authorized to elect its members. It elects the thirteen

---

[80] Article 3 Single Convention and Article 2 1971 Convention.
[81] Article 12 Vienna Convention.
[82] In its present form by the Single Convention in 1968, but the INCB already had
    predecessors under the LoN anti-drug conventions.

members of the INCB in a secret ballot based on nominations by the World Health Organization (WHO) and by governments.[83] INCB members serve in their personal capacity with Article 9(2) of the Single Convention expressly providing that the INCB should consist of members who "by their competence, impartiality and disinterestedness, will command general confidence." In order to ensure such impartiality, this same article also prohibits INCB members from holding government posts during their term in office (Boister 2001: 483). The INCB's independence is also furthered by its relatively long term of office – five years, renewable. In contrast to the UNODC, the INCB relies entirely on UN funding, thus reducing the scope for pressure by individual states. Unlike the CND, the INCB takes all decisions not on consensus, but on a two-thirds majority basis.[84] The most serious impediment to its independence is the INCB's lack of technical and administrative capacity, which forces it to rely on statistical data of illicit traffic and governmental countermeasures provided by the parties and on analysis and research carried out by the UNODC.

Overall, the Vienna Convention reaches a moderate degree of delegation, as delegation to the three UN drug control bodies is characterized by an implicit trade-off between their degree of centralization and their relative independence. The UNODC surpasses the other two UN drug control bodies with regard to its operational role, while its independence is more curtailed. The inverse distribution of centralization versus independence is found in the CND and the INCB.

This overall moderate degree of delegation has sufficed to allow for a "lock-in" of the enacting coalitions' prohibitionist policy preference. Bewley-Taylor argues that delegation under the UN drug conventions "played an important role in creating and perpetuating a US-style international drug control regime" (Bewley-Taylor 1999: 170), while Walker notes that "in the first three decades of its existence the CND essentially accepted US antinarcotics objectives as its own" (1992: 19). Regarding the INCB, Bewley-Taylor and Trace (2006) argue that it has moved away from its initial role as a "watchdog" of the conventions – i.e. of describing the global drug situation and highlighting policy challenges and dilemmas – to become more of a "guardian" of the purity of the conventions, which it interprets as synonymous with drug prohibition.

---

[83] Three members are nominated by the WHO, ten by governments.
[84] Vienna Convention Article 22 Para. 4.

4.3.4 *Summary of actual institutional design and implications for model validity*

The above discussion reveals that the Vienna Convention is an example of an international institution based on hard law. The Convention's level of obligation and precision are high, while the level of delegation is moderate. The high level of obligation results from the Convention's legal bindingness and strong compliance mechanisms which are built into the Vienna Convention itself and into the two earlier UN drug conventions, as well as into the US Foreign Assistance Act of 1961. Furthermore, the provisions of the Vienna Convention are formulated in a highly precise manner. Finally, the Vienna Convention makes moderate use of delegation to three existing UN agencies to enhance implementation and ensure compliance. Table 4.5 summarizes these key features of the Vienna Convention. The overall degree of legalization enshrined in the Vienna Convention is thus high, which corresponds with the design solution my analysis of the underlying problem constellation suggests as optimal.

This high level of legalization found in the Vienna Convention corresponds with the design expectation derived from the preceding analysis of the problem constellation (section 4.2). I argued above that the problems associated with the production, trafficking, and consumption of illicit drugs required an international policy response with a high level of legalization in order to cater for the compliance hazards arising from a high degree of asset specificity and behavioral uncertainty. Some states benefit significantly from an effective international anti-drug institution, while others have strong incentives to shirk their obligations and many ways of concealing their non-compliance. The Vienna Convention addresses this risk of non-compliance primarily by endowing the Convention with a high degree of obligation and precision. The environmental uncertainty of the underlying policy problem is assessed to be low, as countries possess a great wealth of expertise in combating drugs, while the narcotics industry as a whole is not particularly innovative. Therefore, flexibility was not of major concern to the drafters of the 1988 Convention. They considered the inclusion of a few indeterminate provisions that grant states and the UN anti-drug bodies some level of discretion sufficient; a further softening beyond this point was not considered to be necessary.

In brief, the transaction cost economics model introduced in Chapter 3 provides a valuable analytic framework for explaining the specific

Table 4.5 *Summary assessment of the level of legalization of the Vienna Convention*

Design element	Level	Argument
1. Obligation	**High**	
A. Legal bindingness	High	
a. Language	High	• Agreement is called "Convention" and uses other expressions that indicate the legally binding character of the agreement (e.g. "shall," "obligations," etc.)
b. Procedural provisions	High	• Agreement is registered under UN Charter Article 102. • Agreement was subjected to domestic procedures employed when states intend to enter legally binding obligations.
c. Tenacity of obligation	Moderate	• Convention contains no explicit restriction of reservations. VCLT Article 19 applies. • Convention provides for longer denunciation period – one year – than most other international agreements.
B. Compliance mechanisms	Moderate	
a. Monitoring	High	• States are obliged to furnish annual information on their drug control efforts. • The UNODC plays an important role in data analysis and – to a lesser extent – data collection. • INCB detaches country missions to review implementation of drug control policies on-site. • The US State Department issues annual assessment of states' compliance with international anti-drug policies.
b. Enforcement	Moderate	• The INCB is authorized to bring a country's non-compliance to public attention but prefers confidential negotiations. • The INCB is authorized to impose an embargo on the legal trade in narcotic substances against non-complying states but has never availed itself of this prerogative.

Table 4.5 (*cont.*)

Design element	Level	Argument
		• The US government can sanction non-complying and non-cooperative states by suspending US assistance and blocking loans from multilateral development banks on which many drug-producing states depend.
2. Precision	**High**	
A. Determinacy	Moderate	• The Vienna Convention remains ambiguous on the highly controversial criminalization of drug possession for personal consumption. • The Vienna Convention uses vague expressions with a moderate degree of frequency – e.g. "appropriate" appears on average in every third paragraph. • An official commentary provides authoritative interpretation of the Convention. • The CND identifies unambiguously the narcotic drugs, psychotropic substances, and precursor chemicals that require special control measures.
B. Coherence	High	• Provisions related to one another in non-contradictory way. • The Vienna Convention complements earlier UN drug conventions in a non-contradictory way and bolsters external coherence by urging all parties to ratify the 1961 and 1971 Conventions.
3. Delegation	**Moderate**	
A. Independence	Moderate	
a. Human resources	High	• CND members are elected by ECOSOC, not directly appointed by member states. They serve a four-year term. • INCB members are elected by the ECOSOC in their personal capacity as experts, not as political representatives. They must not hold a government post during their – comparably long – five-year term in office. • The UNODC has a staff of over 500, recruited through the regular UN human resources process – not appointed by states.

Table 4.5 (*cont.*)

Design element	Level	Argument
b. Financial resources	Moderate	• UNODC relies to 90 percent on voluntary contributions, mainly from states, thus making it theoretically susceptible to political influence of the key donor states. • The INCB is funded through the UN and is thus not directly subject to financial pressure exerted by donor states.
c. Decision-making	Moderate	• The CND adopts decisions on a consensus basis, except for the important classification of narcotic drugs (simple majority) and psychotropic substances and precursor chemicals (two-thirds majority). • The INCB adopts decisions based on a two-thirds majority, no state possesses veto power. • Civil society representatives play no official role under the Vienna Convention.
B. Centralization	Moderate	
a. Rule-making	Moderate	• Both the CND and in particular the INCB have used the vagueness in the delegation articles to expand their mandate (mission creep). • CND is authorized to categorize drugs and precursor chemicals based on the danger they pose, which in turn determines the strictness of required control measures.
b. Implementation	High	• UNODC supports member states through legal advice and training, and through field-based technical projects. • UNODC supports the INBC, the CND, and the UN Secretary General in their respective drug control duties.
c. Dispute resolution	Low	• Article 32 provides for disputes to be taken to the ICJ, but this provision has never been invoked in praxis, and most states have made reservations against the ICJ's jurisdiction. • Attempts to transfer jurisdiction to ICC have so far been successfully resisted.

design the drafters of the Vienna Convention chose to facilitate their cooperative efforts to curb global drug trafficking.

Does this match between expected and actual design mean that all is well on the anti-drugs front? Few would feel confident to answer this question with a resounding "yes" (Gray 2001; Pew 2001). As I will explore in more detail in the concluding chapter of this book, the questionable effectiveness of the global anti-drug regime is to be attributed less to a poor choice in institutional design than to fundamental problems in the way policymakers framed the issue and the substantive remedies they focused on. While high degrees of legalization may induce states to undertake actions they would not otherwise consider, such a design does not guarantee that those actions are effective remedies for the problem at hand.

5 | Money laundering: the Financial Action Task Force and its Forty Recommendations

Unknown as a legal concept until the 1980s, money laundering developed from "one of the buzz phrases ... in the 1990s" (Gold and Levi 1994: 7) into a veritable "roar" in this decade (Beare 2001). Policymakers' growing interest in this phenomenon reflects their increasing disillusionment with the war against drug trafficking and other forms of organized crime and their hope that confiscation and anti-money laundering policies could provide them more effective – possibly even self-financing – tools for attacking the financial "soft belly" of criminal networks. It was immediately clear to policymakers that they had to join forces across borders to counter the fast advancing integration of financial markets and the many new and truly global opportunities this trend offered for criminals and terrorists to create a legitimate appearance for their "dirty" money. Less than a year after money laundering was first addressed in a legally binding international agreement – namely in the Vienna Convention studied in the previous chapter – the leaders of the then G-7 countries agreed to establish the so-called Financial Action Task Force as a platform for coordinating and strengthening their efforts to "follow the money" (Wechsler 2001) and to "take profit out of crime."

I will argue in the following that these cooperative anti-money laundering (AML) efforts are fraught with a paradoxical problem constellation, resulting in contradictory design expectations. On the one hand, the level of asset specificity is high, stemming from a rather asymmetric distribution of costs and benefits among states. Only a hard law institution can effectively mitigate the strong incentives net payers have to shirk under such conditions. On the other hand, policymakers faced great uncertainties about the nature of the problems, future trends, and about the effectiveness of different countermeasures. Such a high level of environmental uncertainty requires, in contrast, a flexible international institution and thus one that is designed in soft law terms. The examination of the actual design of the FATF's central agreement – the so-called Forty Recommendations – will reveal how policymakers have dealt with this contradiction.

5.1 Money laundering as an international policy problem

Before examining how policymakers solved this design paradox, I want to prepare the ground with a brief overview of how money laundering stretches across the full crime–war spectrum. I will begin with an introduction of the most important international anti-money laundering initiatives – in particular, the Forty Recommendations issued by the Financial Action Task Force in 2003.

5.1.1 From drug money to terrorist finance: the launderette's many different washing cycles

Money laundering is the child of crime's tremendous financial success. As revenues from the provision of illicit goods and services surged, drug kingpins and heads of other criminal networks found it increasingly difficult to use their illicit profits without attracting the suspicion of law enforcement agents. As a way around this problem, they developed mechanisms for converting illicit cash into other assets, thereby concealing the illicit source of these proceeds and creating a legitimate appearance for the money, and consequently, its owner. These three elements – conversion, concealment, and false legitimacy – form the quintessence of money laundering (Beare and Schneider 1990; FATF 2003; President's Commission on Organized Crime 2001). A full "washing cycle" typically runs through three stages and typically across many national borders (FATF 2003; Zagaris 1992).[1] During the first stage, the so-called placement stage, illicit cash proceeds are physically deposited into a bank account, usually in the same country where the illicit profits were generated. The purpose of the subsequent layering stage is to dissociate the "dirty" money from its source. Money launderers seek to achieve this through a complex series of financial transactions such as the wiring of funds through a globally scattered network of bank accounts or the purchasing and selling of investment instruments.

---

[1] E.g. 80 percent of the money laundering operations detected in Canada (Beare and Schneider 1990: 304) and 90 percent of those detected in Belgium (Stessens 2000, 90) involved money that had been brought in from abroad.

Finally, the launderer integrates the processed funds and inserts them into the legitimate economy in the form of, for example, investments in real estate, business ventures, or luxury assets. Throughout this layering and integration process, launderers move from countries with weak law enforcement to reputed international financial centers that provide an adequate financial infrastructure and great stability. The International Monetary Fund (IMF) estimated that an equivalent of 2–5 percent of the world's gross domestic product is laundered around the world annually (Camdessus 1998). In 2005, this corresponded to a money laundering stream ranging from US$893 billion to US$2.2 trillion.[2]

Criminals are not the only group of people contributing to this massive flow of dirty money. Every individual who has reason to fear that his or her financial assets might be frozen or confiscated will try to conceal the true origin of the money or the identity of its beneficial owner. As there are many reasons for such a fear, the group of potential clients of launderettes is very heterogeneous – including the insider trader, as well as the Mafioso, the government of a quarantined state,[3] or the corrupt president or guerrilla leader. For terrorist organizations, more than for any other group, proficiency in money laundering is paramount for organizational survival. First, as banned organizations, terrorists have to fear that their assets might be frozen or confiscated simply by association.[4] Second, as already discussed in the previous chapter, many terrorist networks raise their funds through illicit activities (e.g. FARC), which creates another legal ground for confiscation, and consequently, the need to engage in money laundering. Third and finally, in response to the terrorist attacks of September 11, 2001, international efforts have been stepped up to freeze or confiscate funds that might be of perfectly legitimate origin but are suspected of being intended to fund future terrorist acts (US General

---

[2] Other sources put the figure anywhere between US$500 billion (Schroeder 2001) and US$2.8 trillion (Walker 1999). The US General Accounting Office (2003a) quotes a UNODC estimate that quantifies annual money laundering volume as between US$500 billion and US$1 trillion. The IMF estimate is the most widely cited.

[3] E.g. the North Korean government allegedly laundered significant sums of money through the Macau-based Banco Delta Asia in order to circumvent financial sanctions imposed by the US (US State Department 2007).

[4] E.g. under the USA Patriot Act of 2001.

Accounting Office 2003b).[5] The diversity of customers that launderettes attract poses significant challenges to the creation and refinement of a global anti-money laundering regime, as I will show in the next section.

5.1.2 International initiatives dealing with money laundering

Money laundering is a recent legal concept whose initial internationalization is largely the result of a strong US-led campaign to enlist law enforcement agencies from around the world for this new front in the war on drugs (Sheptycki 2000a; Simmons 2000; Zagaris 1992). It was only in 1986, with the passing of the US Money Laundering Control Act that a national law was created exclusively to address the laundering of illicit proceeds. From the outset, the US government was keen to internationalize its AML offensive both through unilateral and multilateral channels. The Money Laundering Prosecution Improvement Act passed two years later provided the president with the power to sanction recalcitrant and non-complying foreign banks by denying them access to the US financial market. This same Act also called for the Department of the Treasury to conclude bilateral agreements with foreign governments to obtain access to information on all cash transactions in US dollars that occurred within that foreign country's jurisdiction. This unilateral attempt to impose US currency transaction laws on foreign governments and to isolate those who were not complying was crowned with little success (Simmons 2000: 249; Zagaris 1992: 22). The threat of unilateral enforcement worked, however, as an effective "stick" for compelling other states into supporting the United States' *multilateral* anti-money laundering initiatives.

A first US-led multilateral initiative was the inclusion of anti-money laundering provisions in the United Nations Convention against Illicit Traffic in Narcotic Drugs and Psychotropic Substances of 1988 covered in the previous chapter. This convention constituted the first binding

---

[5] A series of investigations revealed how innocuous companies as well as charities have helped finance terrorism: e.g. Naím (2005) reports how donations from a company that imported holy water from Mecca to Pakistan co-financed the original World Trade Center bombing in 1993 and a Saudi charity financially facilitated the strike against the US embassies in Kenya and Tanzania (see also Greenberg 2002; US General Accounting Office 2003b).

multilateral agreement that criminalized money laundering and the knowing participation of third parties in such activities (Article 3 Para 1). The Convention's emphasis on law enforcement contrasts with the Basel Statement of Principles for the Prevention of Criminal Use of the Banking System for the Purpose of Money Laundering, which was adopted a few days prior to the Vienna Convention, on December 12, 1988, by the then twelve members[6] of the Basel Committee on Banking Regulations and Supervisory Practices.[7] The United States was again the key driver behind this non-binding agreement,[8] with representatives of the US Federal Reserve drafting the whole statement by request of the Basel Committee (Zagaris 1992: 35f.).

Some states – namely the United States, Canada, Colombia, Australia, and some West European states – wanted to go beyond the anti-money laundering measures stipulated in the Vienna Convention (Zagaris 1992). Under the auspices of the Council of Europe (CoE), they formulated the Convention on Laundering, Search, Seizure, and Confiscation of the Proceeds of Crime in 1990,[9] which was the first legally binding agreement of international scope that focused exclusively on money laundering (Stessens 2000: 23). Unlike the Vienna Convention, it extended the crime of money laundering beyond drug-related cases to include the proceeds of all "serious crime" (Preamble). In 2005, the Council of Europe expanded its AML provisions with the adoption of the complementary Convention on Laundering, Search, Seizure, and Confiscation of the Proceeds from Crime and on the Financing of Terrorism.[10]

The European Community also became active in targeting money laundering since it feared that money launderers could misuse the single financial market for their own purposes (Savona 1999). For this reason, it

---

[6] G-7 plus Belgium, Luxembourg, the Netherlands, Sweden, and Switzerland.

[7] The Basel Committee addressed money laundering out of its concern with the potentially negative consequences for banks' stability if infiltrated with dirty money (Stessens 2000: 16; Sheptycki 2000b: 150).

[8] This statement spearheaded stringent customer identification requirements (commonly referred to as "know your customer" or KYC requirements), which the Basel Committee later elaborated in further detail in a separate statement on Customer Due Diligence for Banks in 2001.

[9] CETS No. 141. By March 2008, this convention had been ratified by all forty-seven member states of the Council of Europe plus Australia, but not by Canada, Colombia, or the United States.

[10] CETS No. 198 of May 16, 2005. The Convention entered into force on January 5, 2008, but only six member states of the Council of Europe had ratified this convention at the time of writing.

adopted the European Community Directive for the Prevention of the Use of the Financial System to Launder Suspect Funds on June 10, 1991.[11] Like the Vienna Convention, it criminalizes money laundering only in cases related to proceeds derived from drug-related offenses (Article 2), but it encourages member states in the preamble and in Article 1 to extend the definition of money laundering offenses to include the proceeds from other criminal activities as well. It also gives legal force to some of the standards developed in the Basel Statement, such as the "know your customer" maxim and the reporting of suspicious transactions (Articles 3–11). This directive was expanded and updated first in December 2001 and for a second time in October 2005.[12]

The pacesetter behind most of these AML initiatives was and still is the Financial Action Task Force. This intergovernmental body was established less than a year after the adoption of the Vienna Convention at the G-7 Summit of 1989. It initially included the G-7 member states, the European Commission, and eight other countries.[13] In nearly two decades of existence, the FATF expanded its membership to a total of thirty-one member states from every continent,[14] in addition to Hong Kong and two regional organizations.[15] It is a prototypical example of Slaughter's (2004a) concept of "government networks" that, in her view, increasingly supplant the old world order of formal international organizations and binding international agreements negotiated by career diplomats of foreign ministries. In contrast to this old world order, the FATF is set up as a loose policy forum – not a formal international organization (see 5.3) – in which government officials (typically from the finance ministry) deliberate on formally non-binding measures to counter money laundering. Despite being legally non-binding, however, the minimum AML standards defined by the FATF are – as I will argue below (5.3.1) – far from purely voluntary, though formulated under the title "Forty *Recommendations*" (emphasis added). The FATF published a first version of its Forty Recommendations in 1990 and has revised them twice since then: first in 1996 and again in

---

[11] 91/308/EEC.   [12] 2001/97/EC; 2005/60/EC.

[13] Namely Australia, Austria, Belgium, Luxembourg, the Netherlands, Spain, Sweden, and Switzerland.

[14] The countries that joined later are Argentina, Brazil, China, Denmark, Finland, Greece, Iceland, Ireland, Mexico, the Netherlands, New Zealand, Norway, Portugal, Russia, Singapore, South Africa, and Turkey. South Korea and India currently have observer status.

[15] The European Union and the Cooperation Council for the Arab States of the Gulf.

2003. Each revision expanded the scope of the money laundering offense, first from only drug-related crimes to all serious crimes, and most recently to include terrorist financing.[16] The FATF has consistently sought to expand the global reach of its standards through an expansion of its membership, the creation of so-called FATF-Style Regional Bodies (FSRBs),[17] and the direct imposition of its standards on individual non-member states through unique monitoring and sanctioning mechanisms.[18] The FATF's internationalization efforts have been extremely successful. Joseph Myers, acting deputy assistant secretary of the US Department of the Treasury estimated that "130 jurisdictions – representing about 85 percent of world population and about 90 to 95 percent of global economic output – have made political commitments to implementing the Forty Recommendations" (2001: 9). The "island of governance" (Keohane and Nye 2000) that the FATF initially presented has thus grown into a veritable archipelago (Simmons and de Jonge Oudraat 2001: 10).

5.1.3 Overview of the Forty Recommendations of the Financial Action Task Force

The remainder of this chapter will be centered on the most recent edition of the Forty Recommendations of the FATF. I will therefore examine the most important substantive provisions of these Recommendations issued in June 2003 before embarking on the theoretical discussion of whether this AML framework matches the particular constellation underlying the money laundering problem.

Like the Vienna Convention and the two earlier releases of the Forty Recommendations, the 2003 Recommendations emphasize the importance of international harmonization of domestic laws and practices

---

[16] Terrorist financing is covered in both the Forty Recommendations of 2003 and in the Nine Special Recommendations on Terrorist Financing of 2004.

[17] Namely the Asia/Pacific Group on Money Laundering (APG), the Caribbean Financial Action Task Force (CFATF), the Eastern and Southern African Anti-Money Laundering Group (ESAAMLG), the GAFISUD (covering South America), the Inter-Governmental Action Group against Money Laundering (GIABA) (covering West Africa), Moneyval (covering Central and Eastern Europe), and, most recently, the Eurasian Group (EAG) in Central Asia and the Financial Action Task Force for the Middle East and North Africa (MENAFATF) (FATF 2005).

[18] I will discuss this aspect in more detail below under 5.3.1.

Table 5.1 *Selected anti-money laundering chronology*

Date	Event
Oct 1970	US Bank Secrecy Act enacted
Oct 1986	US Money Laundering Control Act passed
Dec 1988	Basel Statement on Prevention of Criminal Use of the Banking System for the Purpose of Money Laundering
	Vienna Convention establishes multilateral legal framework for criminalization of laundering of drug-related proceeds
Jul 1989	US Financial Crimes Enforcement Network (FinCEN) created
Apr 1990	FATF releases original Forty Recommendations
Nov 1990	Council of Europe Convention on Laundering, Search, Seizure and Confiscation of the Proceeds from Crime
Jun 1991	First Money Laundering Directive of the European Community (EC) (91/308/EEC) is agreed
Jun 1996	FATF releases revised Forty Recommendations
Dec 1999	UNGA adopts International Convention for the Suppression of the Financing of Terrorism
Jun 2000	FATF publishes result of first review of non-cooperative countries and territories (NCCTs)
Oct 2000	Wolfsberg Group is formed as an association of twelve global banks and agrees on the Wolfsberg Anti-Money Laundering Principles for Private Banking
Nov 2000	UNGA adopts the United Nations Convention against Transnational Organized Crime
Oct 2001	FATF releases eight Special Recommendations on terrorist financing; US Patriot Act is enacted
Dec 2001	Second EC Money Laundering Directive (2001/97/EC) introduced
Jun 2003	FATF issues revised Forty Recommendations
Oct 2004	FATF adopts a ninth Special Recommendation on terrorist financing regarding cross-border cash movements
May 2005	Council of Europe adopts the Convention on Laundering, Search, Seizure and Confiscation of the Proceeds from Crime and on the Financing of Terrorism
Oct 2005	EC Third Money Laundering Directive (2005/50/EC) is adopted
Jan 2006	US Treasury issues first Money Laundering Threat Assessment
Mar 2006	Wolfsberg Group publishes "Guidance on a Risk-Based Approach for Managing Money Laundering Risks"
Dec 2007	Implementation deadline for EC Third Money Laundering Directive

Source: KPMG (2007: 13ff.)

with close cooperation in investigations and extraditions. With direct reference to the Vienna Convention and the UN Convention against Transnational Organized Crime of 2000 (Palermo Convention), the first three Recommendations define the scope of the criminal offense of money laundering to include money laundering related to "the widest range of predicated offenses"[19] and spells out legal countermeasures. The last part of the Forty Recommendations, namely Recommendations 35–40, stresses the importance of close international cooperation in the identification, freezing, seizing, and confiscation of laundered assets and addresses the legally thorny issue of extradition.

Unlike the UN Drug Convention and the CoE Money Laundering Convention, the Forty Recommendations do not rely on criminal law alone. The primary addressee of the Recommendations laid out in part B is not the legislator but the private sector. By making the private sector a primary agent in the surveillance of money movements, the anti-money laundering regime presents a prototypical example of "governance by distance" (Garland 1999), which seeks to shift the main responsibility for depriving criminals of their illicit proceeds to the private financial sector. Through regulatory requirements such as "customer due diligence" and record-keeping (Recommendations 5–12), as well as the reporting of suspicious transactions (Recommendations 13–16), the legislator imposes liability on the financial sector for cases where criminal liability seems neither possible nor desirable (Cuéllar 2004).

For the first time, the Forty Recommendations of 2003 also pay special attention to the problem of capital flight by politically exposed persons. Recommendation 6 urges financial institutions to tighten due diligence measures in their business relations with high ranking public officials, their family members, and close associates.[20] In response to the terrorist attacks of September 11, 2001, the Forty Recommendations of 2003 also

---

[19] The term "predicate offenses" refers to the fact that in most states with anti-money laundering legislation, evidence of a previous serious crime is required before anti-money laundering provisions become applicable. Unlike the Vienna Convention, these predicate offenses are not limited to drug-related offenses. A party's involvement in the predicate offense itself is not necessary to constitute a money laundering offense. It suffices that a party involved in money laundering activities knew or ought to have known that the money was the fruit of crime.

[20] Recommendation 6 targets primarily politically exposed persons of foreign countries, but the Interpretative Notes encourage countries to "extend the requirements of Recommendation 6 to individuals who hold prominent public functions in their own country."

introduce terrorism and terrorist financing as a predicate offense warranting particularly stringent measures. Despite the fact that the FATF dedicated Nine Special Recommendations exclusively to this problem,[21] the Forty Recommendations of 2003 refer to terrorism no less than twenty-two times, while this issue went completely unmentioned in the 1990 and 1996 versions. The most far-reaching innovation of the latest version of the Forty Recommendations is the expansion of the scope of addressees to non-financial businesses and professions such as casinos (Recommendation 12(a) and Recommendation 24(a)), real estate agents (Recommendation 12(b)), dealers in precious metals and stones (Recommendation 12(c)), lawyers and notaries (Recommendation 12(d)), and trusts and company service providers (Recommendation 12(e)). This extension is a direct response to an increasing displacement of money laundering activities away from the banking sector into other financial and near-financial sectors (more on this under 5.2.3).

5.2 Problem constellation

The testing of our institutional design model will again start with the analysis of the particular constellation underlying the money laundering problem along the three transaction cost economics dimensions: asset specificity, behavioral uncertainty, and environmental uncertainty. The following problem analysis will be based on data for the years nearest to draft date of the latest version of the Forty Recommendations. This analysis forms the basis for the formulation of specific expectations about the optimal design solution to cater to the governance problems arising from the specific structure of the problem, and ultimately, for the comparison of this expected design with the actual design of the international AML institution.

5.2.1 Asset specificity

As in the preceding case study, I will again assess the degree of asset specificity based on the extent to which costs and benefits are asymmetrically distributed, thereby creating strong incentives for net payers to

---

[21] Initially released in October 2001 as the "8 Special Recommendations on Terrorist Financing."

shirk their obligations, which in turn results in heavy losses for net benefiters. I will show that the overall level of asset specificity associated with anti-money laundering efforts is high because of the discrepancy between the countries that bear the brunt of direct and indirect implementation costs and those that benefit the most from an effective strategy against transnational organized crime and terrorist financing.

Costs

The Forty Recommendations resulted in direct implementation costs of varying magnitude. Virtually all states faced legislative costs as they had to reform their legal AML framework to a lesser or greater extent. Most states only had to adjust extant laws to account for the new elements introduced by the latest version of the Forty Recommendations (e.g. terrorist financing).[22] They already had laws in place that criminalized money laundering, typically even of non-drug-related offenses as required by the 1996 Forty Recommendations (US State Department 2004). However, for a handful of states – namely Liberia, Mauritius, Nauru, and Tunisia – the latest release of the Forty Recommendations resulted in a further widening of the gap between their weak domestic laws and tougher international norms, since they still had not criminalized money laundering at the time the latest Forty Recommendations were issued (US State Department 2004).

In contrast to the Vienna Convention, the Forty Recommendations contain many provisions that target the industry directly, thus creating operative implementation costs not only for governmental bodies but also – and *a fortiori* – for the industry. For instance, in the UK, the filing and handling of suspicious activity reports as required by Recommendations 5, 13, and 16 results in annual costs of more than US$20 million for the government and US$165 million for the private sector (Financial Times 2005) – and this AML obligation constitutes only a small part of the overall compliance costs. Similarly, in the United States, the requirement imposed on banks and other financial institutions to report currency transactions above US$10,000 resulted in the submission of over 12 million reports in 1997 (FinCEN 1998). Each of these reports costs banks between US$3 and US$15 to compile and the government around US$2 to process (Wray 1994),[23]

---

[22] Specifically, 53 out of 57 offshore centers reviewed by the US State Department (2004).

[23] Cost data are for 1992 based on estimates of the American Bankers Association and the Internal Revenue Service (IRS).

leading to costs of more than US$100 million for this particular AML measure alone. In 2003, the full array of AML requirements added up to implementation costs of around US$3.6 billion in the United States (up from US$700 million in 2000) and US$1.4 billion in Europe (The Economist 2004b). These direct implementation costs are not only significant but also expected to grow even further. A recent survey conducted by the international accounting firm KPMG found that the cost of AML compliance rose on average by 61 percent between 2001 and 2004, and by another 58 percent between 2004 and 2007 (KPMG 2004, 2007). Most of these costs are commensurate with the number of transactions so that countries with a stronger financial sector incur higher direct implementation costs in absolute terms than countries with only small or non-existent financial centers.

More important than the direct implementation costs associated with the FATF Recommendations are the potential indirect costs, which may result from a redirection of international financial flows and associated losses for a country's financial sector and the wider economy.

Part of such a decline in the demand for banking services is fully intended by money laundering regulators, as their goal is specifically to eliminate "dirty" money from the legal financial sector. If achieved without any unintended side-effects, this goal alone would already have had a noticeable impact on some financial centers. The US government estimates that approximately half of the global money laundering volume (i.e. US$250–500 billion [US General Accounting Office 2003b]) runs through US banks at one point or another (Schroeder 2001), and annually over US$45 billion in illegal cash is believed to be laundered through British accounts (Severin 2004). The loss of business related to assets of this magnitude would have been felt by the financial industry of any affected country, but in particular by those who strategically built the international competitiveness of the financial sector on light regulation. The most illuminating example in this regard is without doubt Nauru. This tiny island in the middle of the Indian Ocean placed all its hope on the establishment of a strong offshore sector to replace plummeting phosphate mining – its only traditional source of income (CIA 2004). In order to increase its attractiveness and to overcome the drawback of its remoteness, the Nauruvian government passed financial secrecy laws which granted banks and companies registered in Nauru protection against investigations and inquiries conducted by foreign law enforcement agencies. This strategy succeeded in prompting

Table 5.2 *International and domestic importance of leading banking centers, 2003*

Country	Banks' foreign liabilities to non-banks (US$billion), 2003	Gross value added[24] (% GDP), 2003	Share in total employment (%), 2003
United Kingdom	21.8	6.7	1.6
Cayman Islands	10.8	n/a	21.1[25]
United States	10.1	5.1	2.3
Germany	9.1	3.8	1.8
Switzerland	7.6	12.5	3.3
Luxembourg	4.4	26.3	11.5

Source: BIS (2004); Ortner and Geiger (2006).

around 400 banks (US State Department 2002) to open a legal (though only virtual) presence on Nauru's shores.[26] Nauru and other emerging offshore centers thus had strong reasons to fear that the implementation of stricter AML regulation would ruin their attempts to carve out a niche in the rapidly globalizing financial markets.

In contrast, established financial centers were less concerned about losing business in handling "dirty" money than about the risk that "clean" money would – for perfectly legal reasons – seek out other centers with less cumbersome and costly administrative procedures if they heightened AML standards. This worry was particularly acute in countries where the financial sector relies heavily on the management of international assets and where it constitutes a central pillar of the domestic economy.

Table 5.2 summarizes the relative importance of leading financial centers for global markets as well as for the domestic economy of their home country. It shows that the world's leading economies – namely the United Kingdom, the United States, and Germany – are also topping the list of states where banks registered in their territory control the largest share of

[24] Gross value added includes depreciation charges or consumption of fixed capital.
[25] Employment in all financial services, including insurance, in March 2004 (Economics and Statistics Office of the Government of the Cayman Islands 2004).
[26] Virtually all of these banks were shell banks, i.e. banks that exist on paper only for the purpose of transferring money through them in order to disrupt the paper trail leading back to the origin of this money. These Naruvian banks allegedly became involved in the laundering of about US$70 billion of illicit proceeds from Russian criminals.

foreign liabilities vis-à-vis the non-banks (BIS 2004). Additionally, however, a number of smaller economies – namely the Cayman Islands, Switzerland, and Luxembourg – are among the world's top financial players. For these smaller countries, the banking sector constitutes a considerably more important economic pillar, both in terms of the sector's contribution to the national income as well as employment.

Benefits

An effective instrument to curb money laundering is expected to create both social and economic benefits. First, the primary reason for the criminalization of money laundering activities was the hope that such a measure would reduce the economic attractiveness of organized crime. By expanding the list of predicate offenses in the two revisions of the original Forty Recommendations, the FATF has effectively broadened the circle of countries that can potentially benefit from the hoped-for crime reduction effect of AML measures.[27] While under the 1990 version of the Forty Recommendations, potential benefits were mainly limited to states suffering under high levels of drug-related violence or drug addiction, the 2003 version benefits all states that are affected by any form of serious organized crime. With the inclusion of Combating Terrorist Financing (CFT) provisions, states also confronted with imminent or potential terrorist threats have an incentive to press for global compliance with the FATF-sponsored global money laundering framework.

Since the extent to which states experience crime and terrorist threats varies considerably, the benefits they can obtain from the presumed counter-crime and counter-terrorism effects of AML measures differ from one country to another. A rough indicator of a country's suffering under serious crimes is the recorded rate of intentional homicides. While these statistics are fraught with reporting problems and to some extent measurement validity as well,[28] they still capture the basic idea that the crime-reducing properties of AML measures benefit some countries more than others, and more

---

[27] The effectiveness of money laundering measures in reducing crime is contested (Geiger and Wuensche 2007).

[28] Many homicides are not profit-driven or result in such small proceeds that they do not need to be laundered. A slightly more appropriate figure would be the number of more serious offenses recorded by police, but the range of offenses covered differs significantly between each country so that international comparisons based on these figures would be more misleading than the figures on homicides (Barclay and Tavares 2003).

Table 5.3 *Homicide rates in selected countries*

Country	Homicides recorded by police (per 100,000 population), 2003
Top 5	
Colombia	100.00[29]
South Africa	55.86[30]
Brazil	28.40[31]
Russia	22.05[30]
Suriname	15.10
Bottom 5	
Singapore	0.57
Brunei	0.56
Qatar	0.55
Morocco	0.50
Bahrain	0.43
Financial centers	
Cayman Islands	7.07[32]
USA	5.56[30]
Switzerland	2.59
England and Wales	1.61[30]
Germany	0.99
Luxembourg	0.77[33]

Source: UNODC (2006) (unless otherwise stated).

importantly, that those countries that bear the highest implementation costs (i.e. financial centers) typically do not suffer under particularly high crime rates. In fact, as shown in Table 5.3, two leading financial centers – namely Singapore[34] and Luxembourg – are among the states with the lowest homicide rates worldwide.

[29] Data are for 2000 from Cragin and Hoffman (2003: 8). This figure excludes the people killed in political violence.

[30] Annual average of 1999–2001 (Barclay and Tavares 2003).

[31] Data are for 2002 (CDC 2004).

[32] Data are for 2002. Source: Economics and Statistics Office of the Government of the Cayman Islands (2004).

[33] Annual average of 1999–2001; calculation by author based on homicide figures from Barclay and Tavares (2003) and population figure from the World Bank (2008).

[34] Singapore-based banks held 3 percent of all foreign liabilities in 2003 (BIS 2004).

The second type of benefit policymakers seek to realize through stringent anti-money laundering measures is even harder to gauge. It is of an economic rather than social nature and captures the idea that illicit profits and money laundering undermine the fairness and efficiency of market competition. In contrast to licit money, the cost of capital for dirty money is not set directly by banks and their interest rates, but indirectly by law enforcement bodies and their success in confiscating illicit profits. The greater the confiscation risk a drug kingpin, corrupt government official, or other well-off criminal faces, the higher their discount rate and the greater his or her willingness to direct the dirty money to front businesses and investment projects that would not be lucrative under the legal cost of capital. Examples of such front business and investment projects range from real estate to pizzerias[35] and airlines.[36] The existence of capital whose cost is not based on supply and demand undermines the allocative efficiency of the market with possibly serious consequences for a country's medium to long-term stability and international competitiveness. Countries with a higher prevalence of organized crime tend to be most affected by this negative economic impact of money laundering, thus reinforcing their incentive to ensure that the international institution in charge of combating money laundering is endowed with the necessary governance structure to make it effective.

Both the social and economic benefits of an effective AML institution are geographically more diffuse and less immediate than the benefits derived from an effective tool against drug trafficking. Both developed and developing countries have reason to hope that international efforts to combat money laundering will help reduce the crime rate and ensure a level playing field in domestic capital markets, but this hope appears more abstract than real because of the many intermediary stages between the actual crime and inefficient front businesses on the one hand and the process of money laundering on the other. The potential loss resulting from a breakdown of an international AML institution is thus considered to be moderate – not high as in the previous case.

---

[35] E.g. in connection with the contract killing of six Italians outside a pizzeria in Germany, it was revealed that many Italian restaurants in Germany are financed by the mafia (Frankfurter Allgemeine Zeitung 2007).

[36] Aero Continente, Peru's largest domestic airline company, was grounded in 2004 on drug trafficking and money laundering charges (Forero 2005).

Asymmetry in the distribution of costs and benefits

The above discussion of costs and benefits allows the grouping of countries into four categories. A first category is comprised of states that suffer considerably under organized crime or terrorism, and which do not have financial centers of international standing. South Africa and Colombia are prime representatives of this category. These states are net benefiters of an effective international AML institution, since joining the institution results in only low direct or indirect implementation costs, while they can hope that international efforts to combat money laundering support their domestic fight against crime or terrorism. These states can be expected to favor an international institution with a high level of legalization, since this governance architecture should foster compliance and thus the realization of the hoped-for benefits of an effective clampdown on money laundering.

The next two categories are formed by states whose costs roughly equal their expected benefits. States in which both costs and benefits are high fall into a second category, while those states that are barely affected by international efforts to curb money laundering are grouped in category number three. The United States and the United Kingdom are representatives of the former category, as they both have very strong financial sectors resulting in high implementation costs, and also face problems related to terrorist threats and organized crime. In contrast, many countries in the Middle East[37] and Northern Africa fall in the third category.

On the opposite end of the cost–benefit matrix are countries which have to shoulder high implementation costs that outweigh the benefits they can expect to derive from an effective international anti-money laundering institution. This category of states is composed of established financial centers like Luxembourg and Switzerland, as well as new or emerging offshore centers like the Cayman Islands. The states all have economies that rely heavily on the financial sector, and deal with neither high crime rates[38] nor acute terrorist threats. These states face a difficult dilemma in forming their design preferences. These states'

---

[37] At the time the latest version of the Forty Recommendations was drafted the financial centers in the Gulf (e.g. Dubai) were still largely in their infancy.

[38] When the latest FATF Recommendations were drafted the drug problem that had been of acute concern to the Swiss government in the run-up to the Vienna Convention (see Chapter 4), had lost much of its urgency thanks to a decade of falling drug-related death rates.

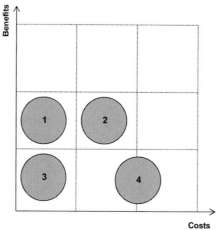

Figure 5.1 Distribution of costs and benefits resulting from an international anti-money laundering institution

initial impulse favors low levels of legalization since it would allow them to shirk their obligations. However, once they perceive the imposition of tough regulatory standards as inevitable, they may instead strategically lobby for an international institution designed with the necessary governance structure to ensure global compliance and thus prevent the redirection of money flows to centers with weak regulation. Figure 5.1 depicts these four groups of states and their relative position in the schematic cost–benefit diagram introduced in Chapter 3.

The figure shows an asymmetric distribution of costs and benefits among individual states, reflecting a high level of asset specificity. In our ordinal three-level assessment scheme, asset specificity associated with anti-money laundering measures thus falls in the same category as asset specificity associated with drug control policies. In reality, AML policies are charged with slightly less-pronounced asset specificity for two main reasons. First, benefits of an effective international AML institution are more diffused than in the case of narcotics, where in the 1980s, only a dozen countries were truly concerned about domestic drug addiction. Second, as seen in our analysis of costs, a partial disjunction exists between the global and domestic importance of a country's financial sector. In many countries the financial sector is critical for the domestic economy but of only secondary importance to global finance. This situation contrasts with the structure we found among narcotic drug producers, where there was a considerably stronger correlation between the drug sector's share in global markets and in its home country's economy,[39] which meant that the international community was most dependent on the compliance of those very states which had the weakest incentives to comply. Consequently, the risk that shirking will lead to the collapse of an international institution on money laundering is slightly smaller than that faced by an international anti-drug institution. However, in comparison with conflict diamonds and small arms, the cost–benefit asymmetry and asset specificity associated with money laundering are still very pronounced and closer to the degree of asset specificity found in drug trafficking, thus warranting the classification as a problem constellation with a high degree of asset specificity.

5.2.2 Behavioral uncertainty

The above analysis of the asset specificity of international anti-money laundering control efforts reveals that a number of countries have strong incentives to shirk their regulatory and supervisory obligations. These states are even more likely to dodge the AML obligations that others try to impose on them if they believe they can do so without risking detection. I will argue in the following that behavioral uncertainty understood in this way is of an overall moderate degree resulting from the combination of a low level of governance incapacity, a high reliance on governmental monitoring, and moderate industry opacity.

Governance incapacity

The comparison of the governance capacity in states with leading financial centers with the governance capacity of key drug-producing countries reveals a stark contrast. All countries with a financial sector of global importance measured well above the median with respect to government effectiveness, rule of law, and control of corruption in the year the latest version of the Forty Recommendations was released. As indicated in Table 5.4, Switzerland was among the top ten states worldwide in all three governance indicators. It was followed closely by Luxembourg and the United Kingdom, which scored an average of

---

[39] For coca and opium in particular.

Table 5.4 *Selected governance indicators for leading financial centers, 2003*

Country	Government effectiveness	Rule of law	Control of corruption	Average
Cayman Islands	1.33	1.20	1.30	1.28
Germany	1.48	1.71	2.01	1.73
Luxembourg	2.09	1.93	1.89	1.97
Switzerland	2.05	1.97	2.17	2.06
United Kingdom	1.94	1.75	2.08	1.92
United States	1.77	1.55	1.74	1.69

Source: World Bank (2007).

1.97 and 1.92, respectively. This difference between the case of drugs and money laundering is no coincidence. The production of narcotic drugs was criminalized many decades ago. As a result, the drug business moved to areas where the state lacked the ability (or will) to exert full control over its territory, as captured in the correspondingly low governance scores. In contrast, money laundering became illegal much more recently. Furthermore, it is in its very nature that money laundering is closely interwoven with the legal sector, since it is the only way criminals can create a legitimate appearance for dirty proceeds. The legal financial sector, however, requires strong regulation in order to thrive, as economic actors are only willing to entrust their money to a bank if they know that the bank is under strong governmental supervision and that legal redress can be sought in a dispute. Consequently, behavioral uncertainty stemming from governance incapacity is insignificant.

Relative reliance on governmental monitoring
The extent to which international anti-money laundering efforts can rely on private actors as watchdogs is limited and therefore comparable to the situation found in the drug trafficking case.

The most well-organized interest group affected by money laundering and AML measures is undoubtedly the financial sector. However, banks and other financial and near-financial institutions have little direct incentive to press the domestic government or a foreign government for the strict implementation of anti-money laundering policies, since such AML measures result in considerable costs without providing banks any immediate economic benefits (Quirk 1996). Quite to the contrary, they typically use their professional organization to lobby for less stringent laws and greater reliance on industry self-regulation.[40] In contrast, the beneficiaries of an effective fight against money laundering wield considerably less political clout. They are unable to form a united front to lobby the government for strict adherence to international AML obligations because of extreme heterogeneity and also since the link between money laundering and underlying crimes is indirect and obscure. Non-governmental organizations have thus far played a negligible role in supervising private actors' and states' compliance with anti-money laundering rules. The notable exception is Transparency International (TI), an international non-governmental organization devoted to combating corruption.[41] However, TI's interest in the issue is a rather recent phenomenon and not very sustained, which may be explained by the fact that corruption – Transparency International's core concern – was included in the list of predicate offenses for money laundering only in the 2003 Recommendations. TI's role in the global movement against money laundering is significantly weaker than that of NGOs working in other policy areas such as Global Witness and Partnership Africa Canada on conflict diamonds (see Chapter 6), the International Action Network on Small Arms (IANSA) on trafficking in small arms and light weapons (see Chapter 7), or End Child Prostitution in Asian Tourism (ECPAT) and the Global Survival Network (GSN) on the trafficking in women and children for the commercial sex trade (Williams 2001).

Industry opacity

It is the very hallmark of anti-money laundering strategies that they seek to enlist the "upper world" of well-regulated sectors in their difficult war against the "underworld" of organized crime and terrorism (Sheptycki 2000b). This strategy of responsibilization works particularly well vis-à-vis banks, as they have long been subject to comprehensive regulation and strong government oversight. Even before being granted a license to open their business, banks are required to furnish

---

[40] E.g. Swiss Bankers Association.
[41] This NGO was involved in the development of the Wolfsberg Principles mentioned above.

detailed proof of their organizational capacities to manage the entrusted assets properly, and they remain under stringent supervision afterwards. Opacity with regard to the banking industry is thus very low. Banks are, however, not the only sector in which money is laundered. In fact, it is estimated that only around half of all money laundering occurs in banks (The Economist 2004b). Probably the most important non-financial sector involved in money laundering is real estate, which is typically also subject to some – albeit weaker – reporting requirements. Money laundering also occurs in less transparent sectors such as casinos, galleries, and jewelers, but to a considerably smaller extent. The overall degree of industry opacity associated with money laundering is thus moderate.

With a low level of governance incapacity, moderate industry opacity, and strong reliance on government monitoring, the aggregate behavioral uncertainty associated with international anti-money laundering measures can thus be described as moderate.

5.2.3 Environmental uncertainty

Efforts to combat money laundering are fraught with an overall high level of environmental uncertainty resulting from a moderate degree of novelty of the policy issue and great innovativeness on the part of the money laundering industry.

Novelty of policy issue

When policymakers convened to revise the Forty Recommendations for the 2003 release, they were able to build upon a decade-long history of international efforts to combat money laundering and upon the practical experience they had gained with the two earlier versions of the Recommendations. However, the latest iteration of the Forty Recommendations addresses a number of new issues that had not or had only partly been covered previously (see 5.1.3). One important such change is the expansion of the scope of the money laundering offense. As mentioned, the Forty Recommendations of 2003 designated all types of serious crime as predicate offenses, including offenses that had become growing concerns in more recent years, such as the counterfeiting of products or insider trading and market manipulation. The latest version of the Forty Recommendations also responded to several high profile corruption scandals[42] by including corruption and bribery in its list of predicate offenses and by drafting a new recommendation – namely Recommendation 6, which explicitly addresses the problem of "politically exposed persons." In an attempt to prevent displacement, policymakers also expanded the reach of money laundering provisions into non-financial businesses and professions, thereby entering largely uncharted regulatory territory. The area of greatest uncertainty that policymakers embraced in 2003 was undoubtedly terrorist financing. In the wake of the terrorist attacks of September 11, 2001, they were keen to deploy the (supposedly) effective AML machinery in the global fight against terrorism despite the fact that the logic underlying terrorist financing is the inverse of that associated with money laundering. Whereas in the latter case the problem is the illicit input into the "launderette," i.e. money that is dirty because of its illicit origin, terrorist financing typically uses clean money for "dirty" purposes, thereby turning the required monitoring mechanisms on their head. All these changes in the Forty Recommendations of 2003 decreased the relevance of the policy experience gained from the previous versions of the Forty Recommendations, and thus increased the uncertainty policymakers faced on how best to address these new issues.

Innovativeness of criminal field

Environmental uncertainty related to the innovativeness of the criminal field is high, mostly resulting from the unlimited convertibility of money. Criminal organizations have developed many creative ways to bypass any advances by law enforcement agencies against money laundering. Some of these techniques are very simple, whereas others are more sophisticated and take advantage of technological progress.

The simplest and most predictable way that criminals or terrorists have tried to avoid attracting the attention of law enforcement agents is by breaking up larger sums of money into smaller amounts that fall below the threshold where special reporting requirements apply.[43] All they need for this so-called "smurfing" process is a number of people they trust who deposit less conspicuous sums in a designated bank account (Molander, Mussington, and Wilson 1998; Savona 1996).

---

[42] The billions of dollars that Nigeria's former President Sani Abacha stuffed away in overseas bank accounts provide one of the most glaring examples.

[43] E.g. US$10,000 in the case of the US Currency Transaction Reporting provisions.

This technique is particularly easy for terrorists, as their operations typically require relatively small sums of money.[44]

Anti-money laundering efforts give rise to a geographic displacement effect similar to the one found in the above-studied narcotics case, but with the difference that money launderers face fewer impediments in shifting their activities to countries with a more favorable "business climate" thanks to the virtuality of electronic money. The opportunities for criminal misuse of such instantaneous, low-cost transfers to obscure offshore havens are, however, decreasing as a result of increased surveillance of electronic transfers and an effective clampdown on the worst-regulated financial centers. Some criminals engaged in cash-intensive activities, therefore, have started to transfer their illicit proceeds to less-regulated places not electronically, but in bulk cash (US State Department 2005: 14).

Another low-tech evasion strategy popular among terrorists and criminals alike is to avoid transborder money transfers altogether. They do so, for instance, by engaging in barter trade as witnessed between US cocaine suppliers and Canadian marijuana producers (Labrousse and Laniel 2002). Another mechanism that has attracted the interest of policymakers is alternative remittance systems (ARS) (US State Department 2005). Such systems are traditionally rooted in Asia and the Middle East (Cao 2004), and are known by a variety of names, such as *hawala* or *hundi*. ARS are particularly popular among immigrant communities who want to transfer money to their respective native countries. They favor this transfer channel over the traditional financial sector since such avenues may be outside the reach of the traditional banking sector and also because ARS offer lower fees[45] and no paperwork.[46] The opacity of this system and its popularity in

---

[44] The National Commission on Terrorist Attacks Upon the United States (the so-called 9/11 Commission) (2004) estimated that the planning and execution of the attacks on the Twin Towers and the Pentagon cost no more than half a million dollars.

[45] According to the World Bank (2006), established financial institutions often charge up to 20 percent of the remitted money in fees.

[46] All it takes is a payment to the local ethnic banker in the desired sum for remittance in cash plus a small commission. The ethnic banker then contacts his corresponding ethnic banker in the recipient's country and advises him to pay the recipient the agreed amount. The two ethnic bankers often settle their debt through reciprocal remittances (Carroll 2002) so that no money actually crosses the border.

countries that have been deemed to pose a great terrorist threat[47] makes policymakers particularly worried about ARS' potential for misuse by terrorists. However, the strong desire of policymakers to exert greater control over these remittance channels contrasts starkly with the lack of information and understanding they possess with regard to the structure and operation of these systems (Carroll 2002).

Regulators' efforts to curb money laundering are lagging behind even further with respect to cyber-payments (Porteous 2000: 184). Cyber-payments are a new emerging class of instruments and payment systems that facilitate the electronic transfer of financial value (Molander, Mussington, and Wilson 1998: 1). They may occur via networks, such as the Internet, or via the use of stored value cards, or so-called "smart cards" (e.g. MONDEX) and are designed to replace cash for many retail and consumer level transactions. This technological development poses a substantial challenge for anti-money laundering agencies, since technology is now available "which could permit these systems to combine the speed of the present bank-based wire transfer systems with the anonymity of currency" (Molander, Mussington, and Wilson 1998: 1).

The combination of a high level of innovativeness in money laundering activities and a moderately novel international policy issue does not clearly assign the overall degree of environmental uncertainty to either the high or the moderate assessment category. To decide whether to round the average of policy novelty and innovativeness up or down, I will compare the money laundering case with other problems where policymakers face a similar degree of environmental uncertainty. The comparison with conflict diamonds is thereby most instructive. In the next chapter I will argue that international efforts to control the illicit flow of these precious stones are fraught with a moderate degree of environmental uncertainty stemming from a high degree of novelty of the issue and very low innovativeness of the criminal field. Assigning money laundering to this same category of moderate environmental uncertainty would gloss over the fact that the dynamism found in money laundering is far greater than in conflict diamonds. We therefore advocate a rounding up of the average of the two sub-components – novelty and innovativeness – to an overall high level of environmental uncertainty.

---

[47] For instance, it is estimated that more than US$7 billion flow into Pakistan through *hawala* channels each year (US Department of the Treasury n.d.).

Table 5.5 *Summary assessment of the problem constellation underlying money laundering*

Problem attribute	Level	Argument
1. Asset specificity	**High**	
A. Potential loss	Moderate	• Countries strongly affected by crime and terrorist threats hope that global AML and CFT cooperation strengthens their domestic law enforcement and intelligence efforts.
B. Propensity to shirk	High	• Financial sector constitutes important economic factor in some developed countries, and is perceived as great economic potential by some transition countries.
2. Behavioral uncertainty	**Moderate**	
A. Governance incapacity	Low	• The five leading financial centers are all located in countries with very strong governance capacity.
B. Reliance on governmental monitoring	High	• Victims of crimes encompassed by AML provisions are insufficiently organized to monitor states' efforts to combat money laundering. • NGOs are not directly involved in surveying and analyzing money laundering or states' AML policies.
C. Industry opacity	Moderate	• Financial service sector is well regulated with a long tradition of stringent record-keeping. • Some money laundering activities have recently migrated into less transparent industries (e.g. art dealers).
3. Environmental uncertainty	**High**	
A. Novelty of policy issue	Moderate	• International AML cooperation started in the late 1990s. • Desire to fight additional categories of crime (including terrorist financing) with AML provisions leads policymakers into uncharted waters.
B. Innovativeness of field	High	• Fungibility of money allows for almost unlimited diversion into other valuable assets. • Virtualization of money allows for immediate and global transfers at minimal costs.

5.2.4 *Summary and implications for institutional design*

Table 5.5 summarizes the above-developed assessment of the problem constellation underlying international anti-money laundering efforts. It shows that both asset specificity and environmental uncertainty are very significant, while behavioral uncertainty is of moderate degree. The design expectations derived from this type of problem constellation are ambiguous, as the two problem constellation elements exert a pull in opposite design directions. On the one hand, the high level of asset specificity increases the risk of opportunism which needs to be mitigated by institutions with hard legalization, while on the other hand great environmental uncertainty requires flexible institutions with soft legalization. Assuming that the relative impacts of asset specificity and of environmental uncertainty are equally strong, the former's pull to hard law neutralizes the latter's need for soft law. The moderate level of behavioral uncertainty then becomes the determining factor, thus suggesting moderately hard legalization as the optimal design solution.

It will be interesting to see in the following paragraphs how policymakers have actually addressed this inherent tension in the money laundering problem constellation and the architecture they have chosen to facilitate cooperative efforts to curb the global flow of dirty money.

5.3 Degree of legalization

How did policymakers handle the design dilemma found in the preceding analysis of the problem constellation underlying international money laundering? Did they indeed settle for the middle ground and decide that an institution with a moderate degree of legalization would be best equipped to handle the governance problems arising in cooperative AML efforts? In the following paragraphs, I will answer this question by systematically assessing the degree of obligation, precision, and delegation enshrined in the Forty Recommendations of 2003 and in the international praxis that evolved in the implementation of these recommendations. I will show that the overall degree of legalization of the Forty Recommendations does indeed fall in the medium range of the legalization spectrum as I predicted. However, below this apparently smooth match between expected and actual design emerges the more interesting story of evolutionary changes in the AML institution's architecture.

5.3.1 Obligation

"Obligation" is the most interesting design element of the international institution established to tackle global money laundering. While the FATF has always framed its guidelines as legally non-binding "recommendations," it developed strong compliance mechanisms that applied not only to its members but also – or even *a fortiori*, as many would argue (e.g. Broome 2005) – against non-members. Similar to the case on drug trafficking studied above, I will show that the international body officially established to lead and implement the international counter-efforts – here the Financial Action Task Force – is not the sole actor in monitoring states' compliance. In both cases, unilateral compliance mechanisms deployed by the United States also play an important role, but more so in the case of narcotic drugs than in money laundering.

Legal bindingness

The name of the FATF agreement – "Forty *Recommendations*" (emphasis added) – is very telling. It unambiguously reveals the legal nature of this document as a set of legally non-binding guidelines. This non-binding nature of the Forty Recommendations is reflected in several other terminological and procedural aspects. Official terminology and clauses typically associated with legally binding treaties or conventions are missing (Aust 2000). The Recommendations are formulated using "should" rather than "shall," the term "countries" substitutes "parties," and the Recommendations do not include any provisions on entry into force, reservations, or denunciation. Furthermore, the Recommendations were adopted by participating states without going through the procedures designated for the approval of treaties, such as the consent of parliaments. All these aspects support the legally non-binding character of the agreement, and suggest its categorization as a memorandum of understanding (Aust 2000).

Despite its legally non-binding nature, the Forty Recommendations contain some provisions that can be seen as safeguards allowing states to deviate from certain provisions. The most important type of safeguard is the reference to the supremacy of the "principles of domestic law" (Recommendations 1, 3, and 36), which echoes the domestic law safeguards found above in the Vienna Convention. Since the Forty Recommendations are not drafted as a legally binding convention, states cannot attenuate the degree of obligation of these Recommendations through the deposit of any formal reservations, nor can they escape its reach through formal denunciation.

Compliance mechanisms

The Forty Recommendations compensate for the legally non-binding design through a set of effective monitoring and sanctioning mechanisms. Similarly to the United Nations drug control organ studied above, I will show that the Financial Action Task Force is not the sole promoter of states' compliance with its standards. The Forty Recommendations also benefit from monitoring and – to a lesser extent, enforcement – by the United States, the World Bank, and the International Monetary Fund.

The FATF monitors compliance with its standards based on a two-pronged approach. First, from the very outset, the FATF adopted a mutual evaluation process in praxis without ever codifying it in any of the three versions of its Forty Recommendations. Through this process, the FATF seeks to assess whether a member has enacted the necessary laws, regulations, or other measures required by the Recommendations and whether it implements these provisions properly. Experts from different countries with professional backgrounds in financial, legal, and law enforcement areas team up with the FATF Secretariat to conduct these evaluations, which involve an on-site visit to the jurisdiction, along with comprehensive meetings with government officials and the private sector – not unlike the country missions carried out by the INCB (see 4.3.1 and 4.3.3).

Second, FATF members realized early on that their efforts to combat money laundering could be seriously undermined by non-members who sought to carve out a competitive niche for themselves as "regulatory havens" (FATF 1991) by resisting the call to criminalize money laundering and to impose stringent customer due diligence procedures. They agreed in 1998 to extend their monitoring activities to non-member states and to assess the comprehensiveness of these jurisdictions' legal framework and the adequacy of practical implementation.[48] Between 2000 and 2001, the FATF carried out two rounds of reviews to examine a total of forty-seven jurisdictions[49] that it suspected of non-compliance with its AML recommendations. These reviews found the money laundering

---

[48] See FATF (2000) for discussion of these criteria.   [49] N.B., non-members.

policies of half [50] of these jurisdictions seriously deficient, earning these states a mention on the newly created blacklist of "non-complying countries and territories."

The FATF's assessment of non-members' compliance stirred up considerable controversy as it basically meant that states were criticized for not implementing standards they had never been consulted on or even officially endorsed. Not only states that were branded by the FATF as NCCTs, but also independent scholars and ultimately the World Bank and the IMF voiced their concern that the FATF's practice lacked legitimacy because of its exclusive membership and inconsistency in assessment (Broome 2005).[51] In the light of this criticism, the FATF has held the NCCT process in abeyance since 2004, and has not reviewed any new non-members in the past three years despite its unbroken commitment to the NCCT approach.[52] Instead, the two international financial institutions, or IFIs, decided to assume a more active role in the promotion of AML policies among their almost universal membership base. The IMF integrated a set of AML-related assessment criteria in its standard Financial Sector Assessment Program (FSAP) and developed a detailed AML-specific assessment tool within its Report on the Observance of Standards and Codes (ROSC).

From the early 1990s onwards, the US government has also been directly engaged in monitoring states' compliance with anti-money laundering standards. The same Act mandating that the US State Department report annually on states' compliance with international drug control rules (see above 4.3.1) – namely section 489 of the amended Foreign Assistance Act of 1961[53] – also obliges the US State Department to identify major money laundering countries. It does so annually by publishing a separate list of jurisdictions which are considered of "primary concern" with respect to money laundering

---

[50] The Bahamas, Cayman Islands, Cook Islands, Dominica, Egypt, Grenada, Guatemala, Hungary, Indonesia, Israel, Lebanon, Liechtenstein, Marshall Islands, Myanmar, Nauru, Nigeria, Niue, Panama, Philippines, Russia, St. Kitts and Nevis, St. Vincent and the Grenadines, and Ukraine.

[51] The FATF has since developed a detailed evaluation handbook which provides guidance on how each assessment is to be carried out.

[52] Currently, the FATF argues that there is simply no need to launch a new sweeping review round thanks to the great success of the NCCT process in fostering global compliance with its standards.

[53] 22 USC §2291.

potential,[54] along with one listing all countries that are only "of concern." The former category includes all states that are deemed major money laundering countries because of the engagement of their financial institutions "in currency transactions involving significant amounts of proceeds from international narcotics trafficking" (US State Department 2007: 5).[55] A jurisdiction may fall in this category either because of its highly developed financial sector – which necessarily also attracts "dirty" money – or because of insufficient AML policies, or a combination of the two. Consequently, appearing on the State Department's list of "primary concern," unlike an appearance on the FATF NCCT list, is not necessarily a sign of poor compliance[56] and cannot in itself lead to declassification and aid cut-offs.

The main mechanism through which the FATF seeks to use monitoring to enhance compliance is through a "naming and shaming" strategy, with the NCCT blacklist as its backbone.[57] This measure in itself has already compelled many countries to align their AML policies with the FATF recommendations, as they feared negative consequences for their attractiveness to foreign investors.[58] In addition to this threat of reputational costs, the FATF also provides for material sanctions. Recommendation 21 stipulates that "[f]inancial institutions should give special attention to business relationships and transactions with persons, including companies and financial institutions, from countries which do not or insufficiently apply the FATF Recommendations." This Recommendation results in financial institutions facing higher due diligence costs and greater legal uncertainty in their business transactions with NCCTs. In most cases, blacklisting along with Recommendation 21-based measures have sufficed to induce non-complying states to align their AML policies with FATF recommendations.[59]

---

[54] Fifty-nine jurisdictions fell into this category in the International Narcotics Control Report of 2007.

[55] In practice, the State Department no longer differentiates between proceeds of narcotics trafficking and proceeds of other types of serious crime in its assessment of a country's vulnerability to money laundering.

[56] In fact, the US lists itself in this category.

[57] This blacklisting policy presented a drastic turnaround from FATF members' previous objections against such a radical measure.

[58] E.g. Russia (Pravda 2002).

[59] Five countries succeeded in aligning their AML policies with the FATF standards within the first year they were identified as an NCCT and seven within the first 24–30 months.

The FATF considered these sanctions too weak to effectuate the desired policy change in more stubborn cases. Recommendation 21 therefore concludes that "[w]here such a country [i.e. an NCCT] continues not to apply or insufficiently applies the FATF Recommendations, countries should be able to apply appropriate countermeasures." Such countermeasures are envisaged as enhanced surveillance and tightened reporting of financial transactions, including warnings to the non-financial sector that transactions with entities in NCCTs might run the risk of money laundering. The FATF indicated to six NCCTs (Nauru, Philippines, Russia, Nigeria, Myanmar, and Ukraine) that countermeasures would take effect if adequate reforms were not adopted within a deadline of either one or two months. Half of these NCCTs were able to satisfy FATF demands in a timely manner, whereas countermeasures went into effect against Nauru, Ukraine, and Myanmar (FATF 2008). Countermeasures against Ukraine were lifted after less than two months, while those against Myanmar and Nauru remained in place for almost one and three years, respectively. Since the withdrawal of countermeasures against Myanmar and Nauru in October 2004, no other jurisdiction has been subject to this type of tightened sanctioning. Furthermore, at the plenary meeting in October 2006, the FATF decided to remove Myanmar, the last remaining country, from the NCCT list.

It is worth noting that through its strategy of blacklisting and sanctioning of non-cooperative countries and territories, the FATF seeks to ensure *global* compliance with its anti-money laundering standards – among non-member as well as member states. Whereas legally binding conventions are typically based on wide-ranging consultations and only bind those states that have formally ratified them, the non-binding FATF Recommendations also oblige states that had never contributed to the formulation of these regulatory provisions and had never formally endorsed them. As Mitsilegas remarks critically, "[the FATF] is an ad hoc body consisting of rich countries, and not an international organization, which evaluates, on the basis of soft law, action taken by sovereign states" (2003: 205).

The sanctioning mechanisms the FATF deploys against jurisdictions with insufficient AML policies are more far-reaching – in theory and even more so in practice – than those enshrined in the UN drug control framework against states with a poor record in adopting and enforcing anti-drug laws. All states depend on a full integration into global financial markets whereas less than a dozen states would be materially

affected if they were refused access to the legal trade in narcotic substances. In practice, the difference is even larger because the FATF has
imposed such sanctions against a number of states on several occasions,
while the INCB has never used its prerogative to sanction non-
complying states. The UN drug control framework partly compensates
its inferiority vis-à-vis the FATF's stronger "in-house" sanctioning
weaponry with the "outsourced" threat of unilateral US sanctions
imposed by the Foreign Assistance Act. This threat of US sanctions is
greater for non-complying drug states than for money laundering centers, as no country has ever been decertified solely based on its AML
record.

In sum, the Forty Recommendations present an illustrative example
of how an international institution can compensate for the weak credibility stemming from its legal non-bindingness with rigorous monitoring and sanctioning mechanisms. In fact, Pieth and Aiolfi (2003: 360)
describe the original Forty Recommendations as "one of the most
rigorous enforcement mechanisms known thus far in international
law." The overall degree of obligation in the Forty Recommendations
can thus be categorized as moderate.

5.3.2 Precision

The overall degree of precision of the FATF's Forty Recommendations
is slightly lower than that of the Vienna Convention. The former is less
determinate as a result of a greater prevalence of vague formulations,
but both agreements share the status as the international standard
setters in their respective fields, thus leading to a high degree of coherence with other related international agreements.

Determinacy

As is typical for legally non-binding agreements, the FATF
Recommendations are couched in voluntary rather than mandatory
terms. For instance, the Recommendations consistently substitute
"shall" with "should." Other voluntary expressions like "may consider" and "are encouraged to [take a certain action]" also enjoy great
popularity in the Forty Recommendations. However, as seen in our
discussion on the Forty Recommendations' degree of obligation, this
promotional language should not detract from the fact that in reality

the Recommendations do not leave room for states to decide whether they wish to comply with them.

The Forty Recommendations are very similar to the Vienna Convention with respect to the reliance on "standard-like" – rather than "rule-like" – provisions (Abbott *et al.* 2000) which deliberately grant states some interpretative scope to "implement the details according to their particular circumstances and constitutional frameworks" (FATF 2003). Most importantly, the Recommendations deliberately abstain from specifying the type and severity of sanctions that states should impose against non-complying states (Recommendation 21) or against natural or legal persons who violate anti-money laundering requirements. For instance, Recommendation 17 contents itself with stating that "[c]ountries should ensure that effective, proportionate, and dissuasive sanctions, whether criminal, civil or administrative, are available."[60] The Vienna Convention, in contrast, shows a clearer preference for penal sanctions used against would-be offenders. The Forty Recommendations are also slightly less determinate than the Vienna Convention because of a more frequent use of ambiguous formulations such as "appropriate"[61] – which, on average, appears in every other Recommendation – "possible,"[62] or "unreasonable or unduly restrictive."[63]

Over the course of the Forty Recommendations' existence, many of the more ambiguous terms have been concretized by the FATF itself and by related bodies. The FATF clarified fifteen key terms in a glossary annexed to the Forty Recommendations, formulated interpretative notes for most Recommendations,[64] and published more detailed guidelines on cross-cutting issues.[65] The above-mentioned evaluation

---

[60] In contrast, the Vienna Convention favors more explicitly criminal sanctions such as imprisonment or other forms of deprivation of liberty, pecuniary sanctions, and confiscation (Article 3 Para 4).

[61] E.g. to "take any appropriate investigative measures" (Recommendation 3).

[62] In the combination of "as far as possible" in Recommendations 11, 21, 27, and 40 and "to the widest extent possible" in Recommendations 36, 37, and 40.

[63] Recommendations 36 and 40.

[64] The Forty Recommendations of 2003 include in their annex the interpretative notes that had already been developed at the time the latest version of the Recommendations was adopted. Interpretative notes that were formulated at a later point are published on the FATF website.

[65] E.g. "Guidance on the Risk-Based Approach to Combating Money Laundering and Terrorist Financing" (FATF 2007).

handbook has further enhanced the clarity of the Recommendations. Also, the Basel Committee on Banking Supervision[66] and the Wolfsberg Group[67] have been active in lending greater determinacy to some under-specified terms.

While the overall degree of determinacy of the Forty Recommendations remains lower than that of the Vienna Convention, most of the Recommendations are specific enough to differentiate between states' compliance with and breach of basic obligations.

Coherence

The Forty Recommendations in their entirety largely meet Franck's (1990) criterion of "coherence," as they create a non-contradictory framework which allows for consistency in case-by-case interpretations. The Recommendations are not only coherent in themselves, but with respect to other relevant international agreements as well. The Forty Recommendations explicitly acknowledge the importance of such external coherence in Recommendation 2, which calls on states to ensure that anti-money laundering regulation is consistent with the standards set forth in the Vienna Convention and the Palermo Convention. In the same spirit, Recommendation 35 urges states to "take immediate steps to become party to and implement fully the Vienna Convention, the Palermo Convention, and the 1999 United Nations International Convention for the Suppression of the Financing of Terrorism." Countries are also encouraged to ratify and implement other relevant international conventions, such as the 1990 Council of Europe Convention on Laundering, Search, Seizure and Confiscation of the Proceeds from Crime and the 2002 Inter-American Convention against Terrorism. Furthermore, regional and global agreements that address money laundering-related issues have all modeled their relevant provision closely – often word-for-word – on the FATF Recommendations, in a way that has given the Forty Recommendations a very high level of external coherence. Similarly, the FATF's Nine Special Recommendations on Terrorist Financing of 2001 (updated in 2004) call explicitly upon states to implement the UN's International Convention for the Suppression of the Financing of

---

[66] E.g. on customer due diligence procedures for banks (BIS 2001).
[67] E.g. on "politically exposed persons" (Wolfsberg Group 2007a) or "beneficial ownership" (Wolfsberg Group 2007b).

Terrorism and Resolution 1373 of the United Nations Security Council (UNSC) of September 2001 in order to ensure external coherence.

The slightly weaker determinacy of the Forty Recommendations compared to that of the Vienna Convention suggests a rounding down of the Recommendations' inconclusive average of the two subcomponents determinacy and coherence, resulting in an overall moderate degree of precision.

5.3.3 Delegation

As mentioned above, the FATF presents a prototypical example of Slaughter's concept of "government networks." The task force brings together government officials – typically from the treasury – "on a regular basis to exchange information, coordinate activity, and adopt policies to address common problems on a global scale" without relying either on legally binding agreements or on an international governmental organization (Slaughter 2004b).[68] Its overall degree of delegation is thus low, resulting from the combination of a low level of centralization and a moderate level of independence.

Centralization

The central policymaking body behind the Forty Recommendations is the plenary, which, as the name suggests, brings together all member states. The plenary simultaneously assumes the role of all three branches of government. First, the plenary acts as the legislative, setting the international anti-money laundering standards and specifying them through additional interpretation and guidelines. Through the annual "typologies exercise," the plenary examines the methods and trends of money laundering to ensure that its AML measures remain up-to-date with the evolving money laundering threat. Second, the plenary assumes an executive role by working toward an expanded reach of its standards through the establishment of FSRBs and the admission of new members. Finally, the FATF plenary is also the central judiciary as it is in charge of monitoring the compliance of its members and non-members and the identification of the NCCTs, as discussed above. However, neither the plenary nor any other body has a mandate to settle disputes among

---

[68] Although the FATF Secretariat is housed at the OECD headquarters in Paris, France, the FATF is an independent international body.

member states as the Forty Recommendations do not contain any provisions on dispute settlement.

The FATF secretariat assumes many support functions, some of which have the potential to develop their own policy dynamic. It organizes meetings of the plenary and of working groups, and offers administrative support to the president and the steering group. The secretariat prepares and produces the policy papers discussed in working groups and/or in the plenary, organizes the mutual evaluation missions, and produces the related assessment reports. Furthermore, the executive secretary and his or her staff are in charge of maintaining the external relations of the FATF with partner organizations (namely the FSRBs, the Offshore Group of Banking Supervisors, and IFIs) and with the media on a day-to-day basis.

Independence

The FATF functions primarily as an intergovernmental working party (Stessens 2000: 18) based on negotiations between representatives from member states. These negotiations are institutionalized in three plenary meetings per year, one annual meeting of governmental experts on typologies, and, depending on the focus of current work, meetings of various *ad hoc* groups (FATF 2005). All states are represented in the plenary, and all decisions within the FATF are taken on a consensus basis. Furthermore, the FATF presidency is assumed by a representative of a member state and rotates on an annual basis, which largely precludes the president from developing an independent agenda. The FATF's independence is further circumscribed by its limited lifespan. When the FATF was created in 1989, the founding members decided to limit its mandate to five years.[69] Only when all member governments agree that a continuation of the FATF is necessary is its mandate extended. Again, this measure is designed to bind the "agent" (i.e. the FATF) closely to its "principal" (i.e. the member states).

In comparison with the Kimberley Process Certification Scheme (Chapter 6), the FATF's independence is further weakened by its exclusive reliance on government officials at the expense of civil society representatives. FATF meetings are only open to delegations from FATF members and observers, but not to the general public or to

---

[69] In 2004, the participating states agreed to renew the FATF's mandate for an eight-year period (FATF 2004).

representatives from civil society organizations. In addition, the review missions are exclusively carried out by government representatives. The only element that lends a little bit of independence to the plenary is the comparably high frequency of plenary meetings, which allows the participants to develop some sort of *esprit de corps*. This limited source of independence is further amplified by the fact that the agenda is typically circulated at the last minute, thus leaving little time for ministers to consider the issue and formulate a unified national position. As Broome (2005: 555) notes, "[i]n many countries the determination of the national policy in relation to FATF activities seems to be left largely to those who attend the meetings." This mode of policymaking in the plenary exemplifies the inner workings under the new "disaggregated world order" (Slaughter 2004a) where national delegates from outside the traditional foreign service reach agreements with their foreign counterparts in discussions that are often less restricted by preordained national positions than is common under traditional diplomatic protocol.

The only centralized support structure in place is a small specialized secretariat housed in, but legally independent of, the Organization for Economic Cooperation and Development in Paris. This secretariat has experienced a significant increase in both personnel and budget over the past few years. While it had to rely on only three staff members in 1998 (FATF 2005), it can now count on the support of twelve employees (FATF 2006) and is set to expand even further. The secretariat's budget also experienced a fourfold increase during this same time period.[70] Despite this significant expansion of the secretariat's capacity, it remains under-resourced to fulfill its functions properly (Broome 2005) and is dwarfed by the UNODC, which is twenty times larger (4.3.3). The secretariat's only real source of independence is its funding mechanism that mitigates the extent to which individual states can yield the power of the purse. In analogy to the funding mechanism used for the OECD, member states' contribution to the FATF's budget is determined based on each member's national income and – unlike the funding of the UNODC – not on members' discretionary goodwill.

Overall, the FATF reaches a low level of delegation, both with respect to centralization and independence.

---

[70] US$2.5 million for the fiscal year 2006 (FATF 2006) – up from US$0.66 million in 1998 (Gilmore 1999).

5.3.4 Summary of actual institutional design and implications for model validity

Table 5.6 summarizes the assessment of the level of legalization of the Forty Recommendations of 2003. Looking purely at the text of the Forty Recommendations, one can easily be misled into believing that the level of legalization is low, but this picture changes once the FATF's practices and the legal environment are taken into account.

The legal bindingness of the FATF is low, as signatories did not intend to establish a legally binding treaty and are still opposed to such a move. However, in practice, the FATF has developed tough mechanisms for monitoring compliance and to sanction non-compliance – procedures which are only partly founded in the FATF's Forty Recommendations themselves. Similarly, many provisions in the Forty Recommendations seem ambiguous, but in conjunction with the annexed glossary and interpretative notes, they gain considerably in determinacy. The FATF's overall degree of delegation is low: the plenary possesses some powers with respect to rule-making, enforcement, and to a lesser extent, implementation, but it cannot use these powers independently from the member states, which are all represented in the plenary and must come to a consensus for decisions to be made.

The moderate level of legalization found in the Forty Recommendations and the evolving FATF praxis match the tentative design expectations I derived from the analysis of the particular constellation underlying the money laundering problem. In this second case study, I am more hesitant to formulate predictions about the optimal design solution for an international AML institution than in the case of drug trafficking. My caution results from the inherent contradiction between the hard law design expectation associated with the problem's high level of asset specificity and the soft law framework that seemed suitable given the pronounced environmental uncertainty. I conjectured above that the two opposite trends might neutralize each other, thus making the moderate level of behavioral uncertainty the pivotal factor for determining the optimal architecture of an international AML institution. This conjecture corresponds with the actual design of the Forty Recommendations.

Table 5.6 *Summary assessment of the level of legalization of the Forty Recommendations of 2003*

Design element	Level	Argument
1. Obligation	**Moderate**	
A. Legal bindingness	Low	
a. Language	Low	• The name of the agreement – i.e. "Forty Recommendations" – strongly suggests its legally non-binding character. • Other terms typically associated with legally binding conventions are missing, e.g. "shall" is substituted with "should," "parties" with "countries."
b. Procedural provisions	Low	• The Forty Recommendations were not subject to domestic procedures required for the ratification of legally binding international agreements. • The Forty Recommendations are not registered under UN Charter Article 102.
c. Tenacity of obligation	n/a	• As a legally non-binding agreement, the Forty Recommendations do not contain procedural provisions that allow states to unilaterally reduce an agreement's degree of obligation through reservations, withdrawal, etc.
B. Compliance mechanisms	High	
a. Monitoring	High	• Member states are required to complete an annual self-assessment exercise that is later analyzed by the FATF secretariat. • Each member state is subject to a mutual evaluation process, which involves on-site visits. • Candidate states' AML policies are assessed prior to their admission to FATF. • AML policies of non-member states are assessed based on criteria that initially went beyond those applied to member states. • US State Department assesses countries' AML policies in its annual International Narcotics Control Strategy Report.

b. Enforcement	High	• The FATF identifies NCCTs on a blacklist and requires financial institutions to employ enhanced due diligence in transactions with these countries. • Recommendation 21 requires further measures against persistent NCCTs, e.g. warnings to non-financial sectors about money laundering risk in business transactions with these states. • Poor compliance with AML policies increases a country's risk of being subjected to unilateral US sanctions under the Foreign Assistance Act.
2. Precision	**Moderate**	
A. Determinacy	Moderate	• Extensive use of ambiguous terms such as "appropriate," "unreasonable," "possible," etc. • Many imprecise terms can be interpreted based on the glossary and interpretative notes included in the annex of the Forty Recommendations and on clarifications developed later by the FATF. • Other AML agreements (e.g. Basel Committee) also clarify some vague terms.
B. Coherence	High	• High degree of internal coherence. • The Forty Recommendations explicitly acknowledge the importance of external coherence and call upon states to ratify related conventions (e.g. Vienna Convention, Palermo Convention, etc.). • AML provision in other international agreements closely modeled on the standards defined by the FATF.
3. Delegation	**Low**	
A. Independence	Moderate	
a. Human resources	Moderate	• The FATF maintains a permanent secretariat whose resources were significantly expanded prior to the adoption of the latest version of the Forty Recommendations. • FATF presidency rotates annually among member states.
b. Financial resources	High	• Funding for the FATF stems from a fixed formula based on a state's national income and is thus removed from the discretion and influence of individual states.

Table 5.6 (*cont.*)

Design element	Level	Argument
c. Decision-making	Low	• All member states are represented in the plenary where decisions are taken by consensus. • Civil society representatives play no official role in the FATF. • The FATF's mandate is limited to five (now eight) years, but renewable.
B. Centralization	Low	
a. Rule-making	Low	• Plenary makes all decisions; no rule-making powers have been delegated.
b. Implementation	Moderate	• Secretariat is in charge of organizing the mutual evaluation missions in which it participates directly. • Secretariat compiles, but plenary adopts NCCT list. • Secretariat prepares agenda for plenary meetings and annual reports.
c. Dispute resolution	Low	• No dispute mechanism provided for in the Forty Recommendations or by the FATF.

6 | Conflict diamonds: the Kimberley Process Certification Scheme

"Diamonds are a girl's best friend," Marilyn Monroe famously sang in the 1953 movie *Gentlemen Prefer Blondes*. Half a century later, the phrase took on a decidedly less romantic twist, as diamonds became a rebel's best friend, helping to fund bloody conflicts in western and central Africa. In response to these conflicts, officials of interested governments, together with non-governmental organizations and industry representatives met in the old South African diamond city Kimberley in May 2000 to hammer out an internationally coordinated effort to prevent rebels from turning diamonds into arms and payment for fighters. With great speed and creativity – at least in comparison with most other international initiatives – this diverse set of actors devised the so-called Kimberley Process Certification Scheme, which formulates a minimum set of trade control measures aimed at denying so-called "blood diamonds" or "conflict diamonds"[1] access to international markets.

This chapter examines whether the design of this scheme matches the particularities of the illicit trade in these tarnished stones. In contrast to the paradoxical problem constellation found in the previous chapter on money laundering, I will show that in this case all three problem attributes are of the same moderate degree, thus unanimously pointing toward a design solution in the mid-range of the soft–hard law spectrum. As I will argue below, the actual design adopted by the instigators of the Kimberley Process does indeed match this expectation. Like the FATF's Forty Recommendations, the Kimberley Process represents an international institution with a moderate degree of legalization. Like the Forty Recommendations, the KP deviates significantly from the "old world order" (Slaughter 2004a) dominated by a strong reliance on classic diplomacy, binding conventions, and international governmental organizations as epitomized in the Vienna

---

[1] The two terms are used interchangeably.

Convention. The Kimberley Process, unlike the Financial Action Task Force, incorporates the direct and significant involvement of civil society representatives from both the industry and the NGO community. The Kimberley Process thus typifies Reinicke's (1998) notion of a "global public policy network" or of a "multi-stakeholder process" (Hemmati 2002).

6.1 Conflict diamonds as an international policy problem

6.1.1 Diamonds between crime and war

Like drugs, diamonds are a high rents commodity that attracts gangsters and rebels alike. In both cases, the scale of associated violence, the – typically unofficial – implication of governments, and the motives of the central actors all contribute to the blurring of the demarcation line between crime and war. On one end of the spectrum, there are the clear-cut cases of crime that have proven an invaluable source of thrilling movie plots and sensationalist media headlines. The gangster quartet led by Robert Redford in *Hot Rock* (1972) and the equally unsuccessful gang behind the foiled half-billion-dollar heist at London's Millennium Dome in 2000 are just two of the more spectacular fictitious and real-world examples where criminal groups succumbed to the lure of these precious stones. These cases typically involve little or no violence and are carried out by private individuals or networks of more or less organized criminals who act purely out of selfishness. More widespread, but less often reported, is employee theft during mining operations or transit. Once stolen, these diamonds are typically smuggled into a neighboring country where they are reinserted into the legal market (Tailby 2002). Smuggling is also very popular among individuals and companies who seek to minimize their tax burden by smuggling diamonds into a country with low export levies, and then officially exporting the precious stones.[2] Government officials are often implicated in these cases of theft and smuggling – not only the corrupt police or customs officer but also, and more disturbingly, the highest echelon of the political establishment. Smillie (2005) reports

---

[2] Undervaluation of officially exported diamonds is another means to slash tax payments (see Oomes and Vocke 2003).

how Mobutu Sese Seko, Zaire's longtime dictator,[3] "informalized" the country's rich diamond industry and redirected the sector's profits to benefit himself and his political cronies. During his three decades in power, official diamond production shrank by almost two-thirds: from 18 million carats in 1961 to around 6.5 million carats in the 1990s. A very similar development occurred in Sierra Leone under President Siaka Stevens.[4] According to Gberie (2002: 2), Stevens "tacitly encouraged illicit mining" and became personally involved in "criminal or near-criminal activities," leading to an even more pronounced collapse of the official diamond sector than in the DRC.[5] Official diamond exports fell from over 2 million carats at the start of Stevens' presidency to less than a quarter at the end of his rule (Smillie, Gberie, and Hazleton 2000). This "informalization" of the sector resulted in an estimated loss of up to 70 percent of state revenues for "preferred (untaxed) concessions in diamond mining areas to political allies who were essential to [Stevens'] effort to resist local demands for greater revenue allocations" (Reno 1995: 18).[6]

The large-scale corruption and mismanagement in the exploitation of diamonds in many sub-Saharan African countries has been accompanied by and given rise to varying degrees of violence, politically motivated uprising, and interference of foreign states. In five cases, the combination of these three factors associates diamond-related violence more with crime than with war.

Angola provides a prototypical example of a diamond-related conflict. Right after gaining independence, the West African nation descended into a very bloody confrontation between the two liberation movements that had helped expel the former Portuguese colonial master.[7] During the first half of the nearly three-decades-long conflict, both the ruling Movimento Popular para a Libertação de Angola (MPLA)

---

[3] Mobutu ruled Zaire – today's Democratic Republic of Congo (DRC) – from 1965 to 1997.

[4] Prime minister (1967 and 1968–1971) and president (1971–1985).

[5] See Reno (1995, 2005) for a more theoretically underpinned discussion of how political elites shifted into violent clandestine rackets to control economic opportunity in order to exercise power and control people.

[6] United Nations University World Institute for Development Economics Research: Humanitarian emergencies and warlord economies in Liberia and Sierra Leone, Helsinki.

[7] Angola's civil war (1975–2002) killed up to 1.5 million people and displaced another 4 million.

and the rebel União Nacional para a Independência Total de Angola (UNITA) were able to sustain their fighting thanks to the military and financial support they received from the Soviet Union and Cuba and from the United States and South Africa, respectively. However, with the end of the Cold War, the two superpowers lost their strategic interest in this proxy war, leading to a localization of the conflict. To compensate for this loss of income, MPLA and UNITA alike intensified the exploitation of the country's natural resources. While the MPLA derived most of its income from the country's rich oil reserves, UNITA controlled 60–70 percent of Angola's diamond production (Le Billion 2001). Similar to FARC's involvement in the drug business, UNITA raised funds both by getting directly engaged in diamond mining and by taxing the many artisanal diggers who operated the fields under its control (Global Witness 1998). Though much lower than the MPLA's oil revenues, UNITA's diamond income still sufficed to withstand governmental offensives and to secure foreign support,[8] most importantly from Mobutu's Zaire[9] (S/2000/203).

Zaire was not only a catalyst of Angola's diamond-related conflict but itself suffered under a long history of natural resource-related violence. In the colonial period under the brutal rule of the Belgian King Léopold II, the country's immense wealth in natural resources had already provided the setting for "the vilest scramble for loot that ever disfigured the history of human conscious" (Joseph Conrad quoted in Hochschild 1999: 4). In contemporary times, the DRC's resource wealth played a central role in the massive eruption of violence that ravaged the country after Mobutu's forced departure.[10] The quest for control over lucrative commodities[11] not only inflamed inter-ethnic tensions but also motivated the intervention of troops from Uganda, Rwanda, Zimbabwe, Angola, and Namibia (S/2001/357).

The large number of victims and the involvement of foreign state actors also make Sierra Leone's diamond-related conflict more closely related with war than with crime. The conflict that ravaged the former British

---

[8] UNITA generated US$3–4 billion in diamond income between 1992 and 2000 (Le Billion 2001).

[9] Zaire was a primary export route for UNITA's diamonds and its main channel for the import of weapons and goods (Dietrich 2000).

[10] Leading to the death of more than 3.5 million people (Global Witness 2004b).

[11] In addition to diamonds, the DRC is also rich in gold, old-growth timber, Columbite-tantalite (Coltan), copper, and cobalt.

colony between 1991 and 2002 killed more than 50,000 people and displaced around one-third of the population. Like UNITA in Angola, Sierra Leone's Revolutionary United Front (RUF) managed to bring the lion's share of diamond production under its control[12] and to use these precious stones to buy the support of foreign states – most importantly, Charles Taylor's Liberia[13] (S/2000/1195). RUF's association with Taylor went so far that some saw Foday Sankoh's rebel group primarily as an instrument manipulated from Monrovia. The most prominent, though not disinterested, advocate of this thesis was Sierra Leone's President Ahmad Tejan Kabbah, who declared in 2001 that "[o]urs was not a civil war. It was not a war based on ideology, religion or ethnicity, nor was it a 'class war'… It was a war of proxy aimed at permanent rebel control of our rich diamond fields for the benefit of outsiders" (quoted in Gberie 2002: 1).

Côte d'Ivoire is the most recent case of a diamond-producing country undergoing a period of widespread violence. A failed coup attempt by discontented Muslim members of the military against President Laurent Gbagbo in September 2002 resulted in the *de facto* partition of the country with the southern half and the capital of Abidjan under government rule, and the northern half and its diamond mining sites controlled by rebel leader Guillaume Soro.

All four cases of these cases are recent civil wars[14] occurring in diamond-rich countries. Academics and policymakers agree that in all these cases, diamonds played an important role in the conflict, but no consensus has yet emerged on what exactly this role is and whether these cases share one and the same causal mechanism linking diamonds and conflict. Similar to the drug–terrorism nexus discussed above (4.1.1), the bone of contention is whether rebels primarily see in high rents sectors a motivation for staging an armed uprising or simply a factor that enables them to financially sustain their operations. Where on the crime–war spectrum should diamond-related conflicts be located analytically? The former assumption leads to an understanding of "rebellion as a quasi-criminal activity" (Collier 2000) where rebels are primarily

---

[12] A UN Panel of Experts estimated that the RUF annually generated between US $25 million and US$125 million in revenues (S/2000/1195).

[13] Liberia allegedly provided a safe haven for RUF troops and brokered several international arms deals on RUF's behalf, typically in exchange for diamonds (Africa Research Bulletin 2000).

[14] As mentioned, the common classification of these wars as "civil" or "internal" is problematic given the strong involvement of foreign forces.

profit-driven, while the latter leaves more room for political motives. The atrocities of these conflicts did not offer policymakers the luxury of waiting for this intricate question to be settled: they had to find a workable solution immediately to prevent further bloodshed.

6.1.2 Containing conflict diamonds: smart sanctions and their limits

In the case of narcotic drugs, the international community was primarily concerned about the issue because of its association with transnational organized crime. In contrast, the criminal aspects of the illicit trade in diamonds were of negligible importance compared to the severe security consequences diamonds had for the affected states and the region. When diamonds first started to emerge in international policy discussions in the second half of the 1990s, it was in combination with the terms "blood" or "conflict," not "theft" and "tax evasion." In January 2001, the United Nations General Assembly passed its first resolution dedicated exclusively to this topic, defining conflict diamonds as "rough diamonds that are used by rebel movements to finance their military activities, including attempts to undermine or overthrow legitimate Governments" (A/RES/55/56).[15] With conflicts in Angola and Sierra Leone still ongoing, the most widely accepted estimate put the share of conflict diamonds between 3 percent and 4 percent of global diamond production (in volume) (S/2000/1195),[16] or about a fifth of all illicitly traded diamonds.[17]

---

[15] This definition is clearly biased toward governments, since it fails to clarify the key term "legitimate governments," thereby protecting any government – democratically elected and accountable, or not. By the same token, it clearly assigns the sole responsibility for the outbreak and continuation of violence to rebels without acknowledging that governments' heavy hand against diamond diggers (e.g. Marques 2005) and failure to share diamond revenues equitably with local communities may also be contributing factors.

[16] After the cessation of hostilities in those two countries, that estimate has been revised down to less than 2 percent in 2003 (United Kingdom Parliament 2003) and around 0.2 percent today (McConnell 2007).

[17] As mentioned above, there are many "ordinary" criminal reasons why diamonds become illicit. Smillie (2005: 185) defines illicit diamonds as "diamonds that have been stolen, smuggled or used for the purposes of tax evasion and money laundering." Illicit diamonds include diamonds referred to as "conflict diamonds." The United Nations estimated that 20 percent of the world's rough diamond trade is illicit in nature (S/2000/1195).

As in the case of money laundering, conflict diamonds reveal an inclination of policymakers to stress the economic causes of transnational problems and to praise the effectiveness of financial countermeasures. Emphasizing the "greed" over the "grievance" dimension (Berdal and Malone 2000; Collier and Hoeffler 2004) of the complex and intractable ethnic and religious conflicts of the early 1990s allowed for a seemingly easier and less expensive solution than sending troops: the imposition of targeted economic sanctions, or "smart sanctions." While anti-money laundering measures seek to "take profit out of crime," the key rationale behind these sanctions was to "take profit out of rebellion" – to deprive rebel groups of their central source of income (and motivation), thus coercing them to the negotiation table or into full surrender. At the same time, the sanctions were intended to prevent damage either to the legitimate industries of the countries suffering resource-related conflicts or to conflict-free countries whose economies depended on those same resources.

In 1998, the United Nations Security Council employed this economic strategy for the first time to target conflict diamonds. Resolution 1173 (S/1998/1173) imposed an embargo on imports of all rough diamonds from Angola that were not certified by the central government and prohibited the export of mining equipment to UNITA-controlled territory. The Security Council took a similar step two years later against Sierra Leone's RUF (S/RES/1306). As the Liberian president Charles Taylor continued to lend military support to RUF (often in exchange for diamonds), the Security Council also imposed targeted sanctions against Freetown (S/RES/1343).[18] In 2001, the UN Panel of Experts on the Democratic Republic of the Congo declared illegitimate "[a]ll activities – extraction, production, commercialization, and exports – taking place in the Democratic Republic of the Congo without the consent of the legitimate government" (S/2001/357, 5), but fell short of calling for the imposition of official sanctions. Most recently, the UNSC passed resolution 1643 on December 15, 2005, which calls upon all states to prevent the import of rough diamonds from Côte d'Ivoire.

As the armed conflicts in both Angola and Sierra Leone were resolved in 2002, the sanctions on commodity exports from these two countries also ended. In the case of Sierra Leone, a United Nations Security

---

[18] This marked the first time in UN history that the Security Council imposed secondary sanctions against a sanctions buster.

Council Resolution (S/RES/1448) lifted the sanctions in December 2002, while those imposed on UNITA expired in June 2003. In April 2007, Liberia saw its diamond ban lifted by the Security Council (S/RES/1753). The only diamond-related sanctions currently in place are those imposed against Côte d'Ivoire.[19] Table 6.1 provides an overview of the key steps taken by the UNSC in response to diamond-fuelled conflicts in sub-Saharan Africa.

The effectiveness of the UN's targeted diamond sanctions is hard to gauge. In the two most prominent diamond-related conflicts – i.e. in Sierra Leone and Angola – peace was restored primarily through military means,[20] not commodities sanctions. Cortright and Lopez (2000) list three main reasons to substantiate the claim that the UN-imposed diamond sanctions were largely ineffective (see also Le Billion 2001). The first reason relates to the target state's weak governance capacity. Widespread corruption led to the fraudulent use of the diamond certification system by government officials (for Angola, see S/2000/203), and the government's inability to control the national borders allowed rebels to smuggle diamonds into neighboring states. Second, other states were often more than willing to condone this practice, and some openly collaborated with UNITA in its efforts to circumvent the sanctions. The UN panel of experts chaired by Canadian ambassador Robert Fowler denounced in unusually frank language the presidents of Togo and Burkina Faso as the main culprits. It also criticized other African[21] and some European[22] states for failing to prevent UNITA dealing diamonds within their territories (S/2000/203). As mentioned, the UN panel of experts on Sierra Leone exposed Charles Taylor's Liberia as the most important conduit for the RUF to circumvent the sanctions imposed against the rebel group. A third and final reason for the ineffectiveness of diamond embargoes was the reluctance of the Security Council to adopt measures to monitor and enforce the sanctions more effectively despite the widespread knowledge of the strategies adopted by UNITA and RUF to circumvent them (Cortright and Lopez 2000).

---

[19] These sanctions remain in effect until October 31, 2008, subject to renewal.

[20] In Angola, UNITA accepted a ceasefire after its leader, Jonas Savimbi, was killed in a gunfight with government forces in February 2002. In Sierra Leone, it was the arrest of Foday Sankoh in May 2000 that brought RUF back to the negotiating table.

[21] Namely Rwanda, Zambia, Côte d'Ivoire, and Gabon.

[22] Namely Portugal, France, Belgium, and Switzerland.

Table 6.1 *Diamond sanctions imposed by the United Nations Security Council*

Country	UNSC decision
Angola	S/RES/1173 (1998) prohibits the import of all rough diamonds not certified by the Angolan government and the export of mining equipment to areas outside government control.
	S/RES/1273 (1999) establishes an expert panel led by Ambassador Robert Fowler.
	S/RES/1295 (2000) establishes monitoring mechanism for sanctions.
	June 2003: All sanctions against UNITA expire.
Côte d'Ivoire	S/RES/1572 (2004) imposes an arms ban and establishes a panel of experts to study diamonds.
	S/RES/1643 (2005) bans the import of diamonds from Côte d'Ivoire.
	S/RES/1727 (2006) renews the arms and rough diamond bans until October 31, 2007.
	S/RES/ 1782 (2008) renews the arms and rough diamond bans until October 31, 2008.
DRC	S/PRST/2000/20 establishes a panel of experts to investigate the illegal exploitation of natural resources in the DRC.
	S/2001/357 publishes the report of the panel of experts with recommendations to impose a temporary embargo on natural resources exported from Rwanda, Uganda, and Burundi.
Liberia	S/RES/1306 (2000) bans the import of rough diamonds from Liberia and establishes a panel of experts.
	S/2005/176 publishes the report of the panel of experts and finds that illegal trade in diamonds persists.
	S/RES1647 (2005) renews the sanctions on diamonds.
	S/RES/1753 (2007) lifts the ban on Liberian diamonds.
Sierra Leone	S/RES/1306 (2000) prohibits the import of rough diamonds from Sierra Leone until governmental certification scheme is in place and establishes a panel of experts on the implementation of these sanctions.
	S/RES/11448 (2002) lifts sanctions against RUF.

When the fighting continued and even intensified in Angola and Sierra Leone in spite of UN sanctions, non-governmental organizations sought other means to prevent rough diamonds from financing these armed conflicts. Two NGOs, London-based Global Witness and

Partnership Africa Canada (PAC) from Ottawa, launched a campaign to put pressure on the diamond industry to establish procedures that would prevent conflict diamonds from entering legal distribution channels. In addition, they lobbied the governments of important consuming states – mainly the UK and the US – to spearhead international control efforts that went beyond the existing UN smart sanctions regime. Both NGOs also published highly influential, thoroughly researched reports on blood diamonds that presented the analytic backbone of a much larger network of more than one hundred NGOs – including the heavyweights Amnesty International, Oxfam, and Human Rights Watch – that used the media to generate significant public awareness of conflict diamonds.[23] This network considered launching a consumer boycott to exert additional pressure on the industry and on governments. Some NGOs[24] even demanded that diamond mining companies operating in the affected countries should pay compensation to the victims of civil wars.

6.1.3 The Kimberley Process Certification Scheme

Fearing a potential consumer boycott, the diamond industry and the governments of a number of diamond-producing and consuming countries decided to adopt a proactive policy to curb the illicit trade in conflict diamonds. Upon the invitation of the government of South Africa, the world's third-largest exporter of rough diamonds, representatives of governments, the industry, and NGOs gathered for a groundbreaking meeting in the old diamond mining city of Kimberley in May 2000. From the outset, the Kimberley Process – which adopted its name from the venue of its first meeting – sought to prevent rebel groups from selling rough diamonds to finance their activities, while also protecting the legitimate trade in rough diamonds from the adverse effects of a potential consumer boycott or a proliferation of uncoordinated UN embargoes on diamond exports from individual countries. Over the course of two years, the participants developed the Kimberley Process Certification Scheme and adopted it with a formal declaration at a ministerial meeting held in the Swiss resort of Interlaken in November

---

[23] E.g. in December 1998, Global Witness released a short report which highlighted the deadly role of diamonds in the Angolan conflict, and in 2000, PAC published a study elucidating the financial role sales of rough diamonds played in the civil war in Sierra Leone (Smillie, Gberie, and Hazleton 2000).

[24] E.g. the German NGO Medico International.

2002.[25] As the name Kimberley Process Certification Scheme suggests, the agreement provides a framework for certifying the legitimate, i.e. conflict-free, source of rough diamonds. For this purpose, the KPCS calls upon governments of diamond-producing states to establish an oversight mechanism that allows them to trace diamonds from the mine to the point of export. Upon export, diamonds are boxed in a sealed container and issued with a tamper-proof certificate specifying the precise content of the box, with a guarantee that all diamonds originate from rebel-free sources. This certificate must accompany rough diamonds on their way to trading and polishing centers. The KPCS asks all importing states of rough diamonds to insist on valid certificates, to seize any diamond shipments arriving without a certificate, and to mete out penalties to non-complying importers. Once diamonds are cut and polished, they fall outside the immediate regulatory scope of the Kimberley Process Certification Scheme and migrate into the realm of a voluntary industry regulation that the World Diamond Council[26] adopted just one week prior to the Interlaken meeting. This piece of industry self-regulation rests on a system of warranties that requires all buyers and sellers of both rough and polished diamonds to include in all invoices a written statement affirming that the delivered diamonds have been "purchased from legitimate sources not involved in funding conflict and in compliance with United Nations Resolutions" (World Diamond Council 2003: 2). In Section IV, the KPCS explicitly refers to this system of industry self-regulation and declares it a central part of the Kimberley Process' overriding goal of increasing the traceability of diamonds.

6.2 Problem constellation

After this brief overview of how conflict diamonds emerged on the international policy agenda, I will now address the theoretical puzzle of this study. In the following sub-section, I will examine in more detail the particular problem constellation of diamond-related conflicts. Specifically, I will again assess the degree of asset specificity, behavioral

---

[25] The representatives of forty-eight governments and of the European Community adopted the KPCS during the Interlaken meeting.

[26] This body was established in July 2000, i.e. two months after the first Kimberley meeting at the World Diamond Congress in Antwerp to act as a unified voice of the industry vis-à-vis governments and NGOs.

uncertainty, and environmental uncertainty associated with this problem, and ultimately reach the conclusion that all three dimensions are
moderately pronounced.

6.2.1 Asset specificity

International efforts to stem the flood in conflict diamonds result in
costs and benefits that both vary significantly among producing, trading, polishing, and consuming states. Unlike the two previously studied
cases, better controls of the illicit trade in conflict diamonds result in
a distribution of costs and benefits that leaves most countries with a
neutral – and no country with a strongly negative – balance. Consequently, the propensity of key states to shirk their obligations is only
moderate. Only a handful of states can expect to benefit strongly from a
well-functioning diamond trade control institution, as only very few
states are at risk of diamond-related conflicts or heavily dependent on
the diamond sector. For most countries with a stake in the mining,
trading, or polishing segment of the diamond business, the sector is of
moderate importance to the national economy and not a source of
conflict. The damage a shirking-induced collapse of the institution can
cause, therefore, is moderate for them. The degree of asset specificity
resulting from this moderate propensity to shirk and the high potential
loss a few states face is moderate as well. I will now proceed to develop
the backbones of this assessment by differentiating in more detail the
benefits and costs states expected to derive from an international diamond trade control institution.

Benefits
The drafters of the Kimberley Process Certification Scheme were motivated by the desire to produce two types of positive outcomes. First,
diamond mining states and – to a slightly lesser extent – countries
involved in diamond trading and polishing hoped to eliminate the
specter of a consumer boycott that was haunting them. Second, states
affected by diamond-related conflicts hoped that this new initiative
would provide a more effective tool for preventing rebels from funding
violent uprising through diamond sales. The relative importance individual participants attached to each of these two types of benefits varied
with their stake in the diamond business and the extent to which they
were threatened by diamond-related conflicts.

Table 6.2 *Economic importance of the diamond sector for leading producers in sub-Saharan Africa, 2000*

Country	Share of diamond exports in total exports (%)	Share of diamond production in GDP (%)
Botswana	85.0	41.9
DRC	45.5	11.1
Namibia	32.2	10.2
Sierra Leone	9.1	9.5
Angola	9.0	8.5
Guinea	7.0	4.3
South Africa	3.5	1.0

Source: Oomes and Vocke (2003).

The states most concerned about a potential consumer boycott were diamond mining states, as they are considerably more dependent on this sector than states involved in later stages of the production cycle. The most diamond-dependent economies are all found in sub-Saharan Africa, with Botswana leading the crowd by a wide margin. In 2000, this formerly poverty-ridden savannah state derived more than 40 percent of its GDP and a whopping 85 percent of all its exports from diamond mining and the diamond sector. In addition, the Democratic Republic of the Congo and Namibia each generated more than 10 percent of their national incomes and a third to almost half of export earnings from this sector. Table 6.2 provides an overview of the economic importance the diamond sector had for the leading sub-Saharan producers at the time the Kimberley Process was launched.

The relative importance of the diamond sector in terms of employment varies considerably across these countries, mainly depending on whether diamonds are mined in a corporate or artisanal way. The degree of industry professionalization and consolidation, in turn, strongly depends on the type of deposit from which most of a country's diamonds are mined. As the mining of kimberlite deposits is highly mechanized, it employs far less people than the much more labor-intensive mining of alluvial deposits. For instance, in kimberlite-rich Botswana only 6,000 people, or 1 percent of the country's labor force, find employment in the diamond sector, despite the sector's great economic preponderance (US General Accounting Office 2002). In contrast, around 300,000 people seek to support themselves and their families as

Table 6.3 *Industry structure in leading diamond producers in sub-Saharan Africa, 2000*

Country	Primary type of deposit	Share of artisanal production in total production (%)
Botswana	Kimberlite	0
DRC	Alluvial	70
Angola	Alluvial	66
South Africa	Kimberlite	0
Namibia	Kimberlite	0
Sierra Leone	Alluvial	100
Guinea	Alluvial	79

Source: Oomes and Vocke (2003); US General Accounting Office (2002).

freelance diamond diggers, or so-called *garimpeiros* in Angola, where alluvial diamonds are scattered over vast areas of the country (Goreux 2001). Table 6.3 provides a brief overview of the dominant industry structure in Africa's leading diamond mining states.

Some diamond mining states hoped that a global diamond trade scheme would not only avert a consumer boycott and thus a potential plunge in diamond-related revenues, but that such an international institution would even help them increase government revenues. They wanted the institution to be set up in a way that would make it harder for *all* illicitly traded diamonds – including those smuggled across borders to circumvent UN sanctions, parastatal buying cartels, or high export taxes – to enter the legitimate world market. Such a general anti-smuggling effect would be particularly significant for states that relied primarily on alluvial mining, as it is considerably harder to monitor this type of mining operation than it is for kimberlite mining. For instance, the Democratic Republic of the Congo claimed that it lost diamonds worth a total of US$800 million annually due to smuggling (Business Day 2002). Sierra Leone has also suffered under widespread illicit exports of diamonds – before (Reno 1995), during, and after the civil war.[27] Angolan officials estimated that the country lost US$375 million in annual revenue because of diamond smuggling (Afrol 2006).

---

[27] Even after the end of the civil war and the lifting of UN-imposed diamond sanctions, half to three-quarters of Sierra Leonean diamond production reportedly still left the West African nation illicitly (White 2005).

States involved in the downstream trading and polishing stage also had a strong interest in averting a consumer boycott. Even if the national economies for these states do not depend on diamonds to the same extent, the sector is often of great importance on a local level. In the world's largest trading center, the Belgian city of Antwerp, the diamond sector provides jobs for approximately 30,000 people (DPA 2006) and accounts for about 7 percent of the country's total exports (US General Accounting Office 2002). In India, the world leader in the processing of rough diamonds, the diamond sector in 2004 generated US$10.8 billion in exports and provided jobs for approximately 750,000 people (Kuriyan 2005).[28]

Consumer states, in contrast, had much less to fear from a potential diamond boycott, as the diamond industry is not a major economic force for any of these states.[29] However, some of them had a more indirect economic interest in the establishment of effective diamond trade controls. Such states were not so much concerned about the negative consequences a consumer boycott might have on their national economy, but rather, on that of developing states that they had close ties with. For instance, the British diplomat engaged in crafting the Kimberley Process worried that "if diamonds go the same way as fur [i.e. if they become the target of an effective consumer boycott campaign], we would have a big problem in many parts of Africa and India, where diamonds are key for economic development."[30]

Diamond mining states were also the main beneficiaries with regard to the hoped-for political benefits of an international institution controlling the trade in diamonds. After all, the main reason that diamonds had attracted so much attention on the international stage was precisely because of their role in some of the bloodiest conflicts ravaging Africa in the 1990s. However, only some diamond mining states were seriously threatened by diamond-related violence. As Table 6.4 indicates, of the top seven diamond producers in sub-Saharan Africa four – namely Angola, the Democratic Republic of the Congo, Sierra Leone, and

---

[28] This equals less than 0.2 percent of the country's total labor force, but the diamond sector geographically is highly concentrated and provides job opportunities for people with little formal education.

[29] For instance, in the United States, the world's largest consumer of diamond jewelry, the total value of retail sales amounted in 2005 to US$33.7 billion (Global Witness 2006), less than 0.3 percent of total GDP (World Bank 2008, calculations by author).

[30] Interview by author.

Table 6.4 *Occurrence of state failure in leading diamond-producing countries in sub-Saharan Africa, 1990–2000*

Country	State failure occurrence, 1990–2000	Diamond-related state failure
Angola	Yes	Yes
Botswana	No	n/a
DRC	Yes	Yes
Guinea	No	n/a
Namibia	No	n/a
Sierra Leone	Yes	Yes
South Africa	Yes	No

Source: State Failure Task Force (2000); author's assessment.

South Africa – experienced a period of state failure[31] during the last decade of the twentieth century, but only the first three cases can be linked to diamonds. As a number of recent academic papers argue, it may be no coincidence that all diamond-related conflicts occurred in countries where alluvial deposits are dominant, as these secondary deposits are more easily appropriated than kimberlite deposits (e.g. Lujala, Gleditsch, and Gilmore 2005; Snyder and Bhavnani 2005).

While diamond-related conflicts in sub-Saharan Africa were the trigger for international efforts to impose better trade controls on rough diamonds, an additional concern was added on to the agenda in the aftermath of the terrorist attacks on New York City and Washington, DC in September 2001. A number of media reports,[32] academic papers,[33] and policy briefs[34] emerged in the months after the attacks discussing the tactics of terrorist networks – in particular, Hezbollah and Al Qaeda – to generate income through direct involvement in the mining and trading of diamonds or the use of this precious commodity to launder money and store value (US General Accounting Office 2003b). Not surprisingly, this potential diamond–terrorism nexus received the greatest attention in US policy circles.[35]

---

[31] Based on the definition of the State Failure Task Force (2000).
[32] E.g. Farah (2001).   [33] Passas and Jones (2006).   [34] MEIB staff (2004).
[35] E.g. the US Congress held a hearing on February 13, 2002 on "Illicit Diamonds, Conflict, and Terrorism."

Table 6.5 *Output of major diamond producers, 2000*

Country	Production volume (trillion of carats)	Share of world production value (%)	Average price (US$)	Production value (million of US$)	Share of world production value (%)
Botswana	24.71	21.8	86	2,125.20	25.6
Russia	20.45	18.0	78	1,595.00	19.2
South Africa	10.57	9.3	105	1,109.51	13.4
Angola	4.00	3.5	185	739.66	8.9
DRC	16.71	14.8	35	585.00	7.0
China	3.58	3.2	131	469.34	5.7
Canada	2.62	2.3	173	453.55	5.5
Namibia	1.52	1.3	276	419.12	5.0
Australia	25.76	22.7	14	360.60	4.3
Guinea	0.45	0.4	230	103.50	1.2
World total/ average	113.31	100.0	73	8,303.00	100.0

Source: Rombouts 2001.

Costs

An international diamond trade control institution was expected to create implementation costs that would vary among countries depending on both the production stage they were involved in and on their share in the respective business segment. Mining states would necessarily face the highest costs, followed by countries with important trading and polishing sectors, and finally, consumer states. Implementation costs were also expected to increase with growing production and trade volumes, which vary considerably across countries (see Table 6.5). Botswana accounted for more than one quarter of diamond production in 2000 (by value), followed by Russia, South Africa, and Angola, which accounted for 19.2, 13.4, and 8.9 percent, respectively.

A second cost driver for mining countries is the establishment of effective controls over domestic production, which would come in addition to the implementation costs related to the regulation of exports. This second source of implementation costs was also expected to depend in part on the volume of production, but also – and more significantly – on the dominant type of mining operations. It was assumed that countries with predominantly artisanal, alluvial diamond digging operations would have to face higher control costs as these operations are harder to monitor, as already mentioned, because of their great geographic dispersion and low level of corporatization.

In contrast, implementation costs faced by diamond trading and polishing centers would only arise from border controls and be largely proportionate with each country's stake in that production stage. Some countries, e.g. Belgium, already had the necessary control structures largely in place when the Kimberly Process was launched, thus resulting in limited additional implementation costs. For most consumer states, direct implementation costs were minimal as they hardly ever imported or exported rough diamonds.

Concerns about potential indirect implementation costs of an economic or political nature were insignificant in the creation of the Kimberley Process. The combination of low direct implementation costs (relative to diamonds' value) and the price inelasticity of the demand for these precious stones meant that the instigators of the Kimberley Process did not need to worry about a potential economic fallout. Diversion of licit trade flows resulting from the adoption of more stringent trade control measures was therefore not a likely scenario. The only states that had to be concerned about negative repercussions were the "Naurus" of the diamond world, i.e. states that had placed a bet on gaining from activities that were criminalized elsewhere. Liberia was one such international "hub" for diamonds smuggled out of Sierra Leone. During the height of civil war in Sierra Leone, it is estimated that Liberia exported five times the value of diamonds that it produced domestically (US General Accounting Office 2002). The Republic of the Congo[36] is another notorious diamond smuggler, although the central government is less clearly implicated than was the Taylor regime in Liberia.

Asymmetry in the distribution of costs and benefits

As the above discussion has revealed, an international institution controlling the trade in rough diamonds can be expected to impose implementation costs of varying magnitude on mining, trading and polishing, and consuming states. Mining states – in particular those relying

---

[36] Also often referred to as Congo-Brazzaville. We will return to the Republic of the Congo under our discussion of the Kimberley Process' compliance mechanisms (see 6.3.1).

primarily on alluvial deposits – have to shoulder the greatest financial burden. However, these differences in costs roughly echo the asymmetric distribution of benefits that favors alluvial mining states over any other category of states. As alluvial diamond mining states face the greatest risk of (renewed) diamond-related conflicts, their gains from a functioning control scheme exceed their implementation costs. Free-riding on other states' control efforts is not a very attractive option for them because they benefit directly and immediately from better control of the diamond sector in the form of an increase in diamond revenues, in addition to the less-certain, long-term effect of better peace prospects. Conflict-prone diamond mining states with primarily alluvial diamonds form a first category which is characterized by high potential benefits and moderate costs.

Diamond mining states with primarily kimberlite deposits are grouped into a second category. They face slightly lower implementation costs, which are mirrored in lower potential benefits. Since these states are not as much at risk of diamond-related conflicts, the expected benefit is limited to the aversion of a consumer boycott and its negative economic consequences.

Diamond mining states share this benefit with states involved in the trading and polishing of diamonds, which form a third category. These states face still lower implementation costs because they only need to control trade and not domestic mining operations.

For the fourth category of states, consumer countries, implementation costs are negligible as are their direct benefits. However, depending on how far they are actively concerned about the economic development of diamond-producing countries or about the possible misuse of diamonds by terrorists, they may derive indirect benefits that outweigh their costs, placing them in the same cost–benefit quadrant as trading and polishing states.

Finally, only countries that benefit from exporting diamonds of illicit origin may feel compelled to shirk their obligations. However, these smuggling states' incentives to ignore their obligations under an international institution controlling the trade in diamonds is small compared to that of narcotic producers or of "dodgy" financial offshore centers. Furthermore, because of their geographic proximity to states that are threatened by diamond-related conflicts and their stake in the licit diamond sector, even these smuggling hubs have an interest in seeing the international diamond trade control institution succeed in preventing diamond-funded conflicts and a consumer boycott.

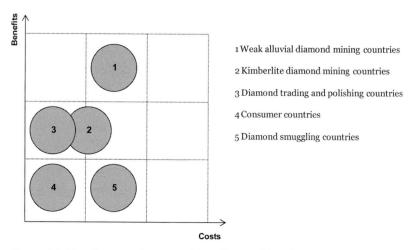

Figure 6.1 Distribution of costs and benefits resulting from an international anti-conflict diamond institution

Figure 6.1 summarizes the costs and benefits these different categories of states face under an international diamond trade control institution. It shows a rather symmetric distribution of costs and benefits. Weak states with primarily alluvial diamond deposits expect the highest net benefits and therefore face the greatest potential loss if international cooperation against the illicit trade in rough diamond breaks down because of widespread shirking. Consequently, they have an interest in designing an international institution in a way that lends the substantive provisions of that institution at least a moderate degree of credibility. This position is also endorsed by kimberlite mining states and countries with important diamond trading and polishing centers, since they too expect greater benefits than costs. In addition, consumer countries with an active interest in the development of diamond-dependent states or with a strong concern about diamonds as a source of terrorist financing may join this group of net benefiters. As the risk of shirking emanating from diamond smuggling hubs is only moderate, the overall level of asset specificity is also moderate.

6.2.2 Behavioral uncertainty

When policymakers set out to create an international institution to curb the illicit trade in rough diamonds, they had to be moderately worried about the risk that a participant could shirk obligations without being detected. While the overall moderate level of behavioral uncertainty in conflict diamonds is the same as in the money laundering case, I will argue in this section that the two cases differ from each other significantly with regard to the relative intensity of the three sub-components of behavioral uncertainty – namely governance incapacity, industry opacity, and reliance on governmental monitoring.

Governance incapacity

International diamond trade controls are only moderately reliant on full implementation by weak states. On the one hand, among the top five diamond producers are two states with very weak governance capacity, namely Angola and the Democratic Republic of the Congo. This weakness, as it existed in 2002 when policymakers created the KPCS and even today, results as much from the poor quality and lack of independence of the bureaucracy, as it does from insufficient efforts to establish the rule of law and to curb corruption. To put it into perspective, Angola's governance incapacity was as pronounced as Myanmar's at the time of drafting for the latest of the UN drug conventions, while the DRC fared slightly better than the worst-governed drug producer, Afghanistan. In contrast to the narcotics case, KP participants could also rely on important producer states that reached a positive score for the government's implementation capacity – namely Botswana and South Africa, which together controlled almost 40 percent of the global output of diamonds. Governance incapacity was further reduced by the great implementation capacity of leading trading centers and – to a slightly lesser extent – of states with a stake in diamond cutting and polishing. As a consequence, governance incapacity is of less concern for policymakers seeking to control the trade in diamonds than in narcotic drugs, but still greater than with regard to money laundering. Table 6.6 summarizes the government effectiveness scores of states with significant stakes in the mining, trading, or polishing of diamonds.

Industry opacity

Behavioral uncertainty related to conflict diamond policies is further accentuated by the opacity of the diamond industry. This element of behavioral uncertainty depends on the ease with which mining operations can be observed as well as on the transparency of the leading companies and market concentration.

Table 6.6 *Selected governance indicators for leading diamond mining, trading, and polishing states, 2002*

Country	Government effectiveness	Rule of law	Control of corruption	Average
Mining				
Angola	–1.14	–1.46	–1.2	–1.27
Botswana	0.74	0.59	0.7	0.68
DRC	–1.77	–1.82	–1.48	–1.69
Russia	–0.3	–0.88	–0.92	–0.70
South Africa	0.68	0.07	0.34	0.36
Trading				
Belgium	2.03	1.47	1.6	1.70
Israel	0.99	0.91	1.04	0.98
United Arab Emirates	0.8	0.93	1.16	0.96
United Kingdom	1.97	1.75	2.1	1.94
Cutting & polishing				
China	0.03	–0.36	–0.4	–0.24
India	–0.11	–0.02	–0.41	–0.18
Thailand	0.2	0.22	–0.34	0.03

Source: World Bank (2007).

The industry differences already discussed between the production of kimberlite versus alluvial diamonds in terms of mining states' costs and benefits (see above 6.2.1) also affect the observability of mining operations. As the mining of kimberlite diamonds involves the removal of large quantities of ore material by hydraulic shovels and trucks, these operations can be surveyed by air. Especially in the case of open pit mining, diamond outputs can be estimated based on the volume of removed materials. In contrast, air surveillance is less suited for the assessment of diamond mining activities in alluvial fields, because these secondary deposits are usually found ten to twenty feet below the surface (Leigh 2002), consequently requiring only minor digging. It is thus easier for other countries to assess whether the official export volume of a diamond mining state with primarily kimberlite deposits is in line with its domestic mining potential than it is to estimate production volumes of states with predominantly alluvial diamond deposits. The ability to estimate production volumes of alluvial diamonds is further limited by the fact that it is close to impossible to determine where an alluvial diamond was mined, as its inclusions are characteristic of the area where it was formed and not of where it was extracted.

Transparency of the industry as a whole is curtailed by a long tradition of secrecy (US General Accounting Office 2002). Deals are typically concluded on the basis of a handshake with little written documentation (Laitner 2005). Trust – often built on family ties or a shared ethnic background – rather than contracts forms the basis of most transactions. This situation contrasts starkly with the very well-documented, highly regulated financial sector I studied in the previous chapter. Industry transparency is further weakened by the fact that leading companies are not publicly traded and by decreasing market concentration.

In 2001, DeBeers was delisted, while the Russian diamond mining company Alrosa is state-owned, which absolves them from many disclosure requirements. DeBeers' greatest emerging challenger, the Lev Leviev Group, is not subject to shareholder oversight and listing requirements either, because it is solely owned by Lev Leviev, an Israeli billionaire.

Alrosa and the Lev Leviev Group, and also some non-specialized mining companies like Rio Tinto, have successfully undermined DeBeers' preponderance over the past few years. In just five years, DeBeers saw its share of global output drop from two-thirds in 1998 to 45 percent (The Economist 2004a),[37] and the Lev Leviev Group established itself as the world's largest diamond cutter and polisher (Berman and Goldman 2003). As more companies rush to carve out a position in the lucrative diamond business, monitoring becomes increasingly difficult, even though the global diamond market remains, for now, more concentrated than other commodity markets.

Reliance on governmental monitoring

The most important factor curtailing behavioral uncertainty in the diamond trade is the unusually strong capacity of NGOs in monitoring developments of the trade in rough diamonds and in government policies vis-à-vis this sector. Thanks to highly qualified staff working in many of the poorly governed diamond-producing states, Partnership Africa Canada, Global Witness, and other NGOs are well-positioned to

---

[37] Alrosa accounts for almost all of Russia's massive diamond production, which combined with the output of its Angolan operations, constitutes more than 20 percent of global supply.

serve as effective "fire alarms" surveying governments' trade control efforts. Consequently, states do not have to rely solely on the information provided by an individual government to judge whether or not that party is complying with its obligations. This relatively weak reliance on governmental self-reporting again contrasts starkly with our money laundering case, where civil society organizations played a negligible role.

In sum, behavioral uncertainty related to the illicit trade in diamonds reaches a moderate level. Governance incapacity poses a moderate challenge, and although industry opacity is pronounced, it is partly offset by the important role non-state actors play in monitoring compliance.

6.2.3 *Environmental uncertainty*

Policymakers were confronted with a moderate degree of environmental uncertainty when they started to hammer out a cooperative solution for the uncontrolled trade in conflict diamonds. On the one hand, they were uncertain about how to tackle an issue that was entirely new for most of them, while on the other hand they felt confident that the possibilities for the evasion of control measures by the illicit segment of the industry were limited.

Novelty of the policy issue
The novelty of conflict diamonds as a policy issue was comparably much higher than that of narcotic drugs. While the crafters of the Vienna Convention were able to build on a large body of expertise on drug trafficking and on decades of international drug control policies, most desk officers involved in devising the KPCS reported that the issue of conflict diamonds was "brand new" to them as individuals, to their ministry, and to the government as a whole.[38] Until the first meeting at Kimberley in May 2000, the link between armed conflicts and diamonds had received scant attention from academics, NGOs, the media, or policymakers. Moreover, at the time conflict diamonds began to attract international concern, no government-led commodity certification scheme existed for policymakers to use as a blueprint for the KPCS. The only pre-existing program that addressed a related concern was the Forest Stewardship Council Certification Scheme (FSC). However, the relevance of the FSC was limited by the fact that the FSC is managed by a private

---

[38] Interview by author.

non-profit organization and does not officially include government representatives.[39] This organizational structure was unacceptable to the leading NGOs behind the Kimberley Process who strongly demanded a central governmental role in the emerging international diamond trade control scheme. Thus the FSC's relevance for the Kimberley Process was greatly reduced as the NGO community insisted on a strong, active role from governments. Consequently, policymakers were forced to develop their common solution largely "from scratch."

Innovativeness of policy field

Although the novelty of trying to control conflict diamonds was fraught with significant environmental uncertainty, that uncertainty was mitigated in part by the inability of the targeted group to adapt expeditiously to new control measures. Unlike the production of some narcotic drugs, especially cannabis, diamond mining simply cannot switch to another country in order to avoid scrutiny. It is necessarily bound to a very limited number of states that happen to be endowed with rich diamond deposits.[40] Diamonds share with narcotic drugs a similar ease for smuggling, as both commodities present a highly concentrated form of wealth.[41] However, when compared with the virtuality and total fungibility of money, both of these physical commodities have a more limited set of options with which to evade law enforcement agents on their way to the consumer market.

A greater challenge to the scheme emerges from industry developments that could unintentionally render irrelevant controls of the international trade in rough diamonds. The most important of these trends is the current move to establish cutting and polishing centers in diamond mining countries. Some diamond-producing countries, namely Botswana, Namibia, Angola, and Sierra Leone, have recently embraced a "beneficiation strategy," seeking to create additional employment opportunities and wealth by compelling diamond mining companies to process the diamonds in the country where the diamonds are mined

---

[39] The only governmental bodies that can officially join the FSC are state-owned forestry companies.

[40] Rombouts (2001) estimates that commercially attractive mining is limited to roughly one dozen countries.

[41] Andrew Lamont of De Beers estimated that Sierra Leone's entire annual output – worth US$70 million – could fit in a single suitcase (Africa Research Bulletin 2000).

(Reed 2005). For instance, the Israeli diamond magnate Lev Leviev opened Namibia's biggest polishing factory in June 2004 (The Economist 2004a), and DeBeers had to succumb to the Botswanan government's insistence that all diamonds mined on its territory should be processed domestically (White 2005). This trend toward beneficiation could ultimately lead to a significant reduction in the volume of rough diamonds traded across borders. That in turn could reduce the relevance of the KPCS, which only covers international trade in rough diamonds, not in cut or polished diamonds.

Taken together, the high degree of novelty and the low innovativeness of the policy issue confronted policymakers with a moderately pronounced level of environmental uncertainty. It is higher than in the case of narcotic drugs, mainly because policymakers had little prior knowledge of the diamond industry or of conflict diamonds at the time the Kimberley Process was launched. In comparison to money laundering, the regulation of conflict diamonds involves less environmental uncertainty primarily because money launderers can easily switch to other carriers of value and financial centers, whereas diamond traffickers are ultimately bound to the limited set of existing diamond mining and, to a lesser extent, polishing states.

Summary and implications for institutional design

Conflict diamonds present a very coherent problem constellation that is moderate with regard to all three problem dimensions: asset specificity, behavioral uncertainty, and environmental uncertainty.

Table 6.7 summarizes the key elements that lead us to this assessment. This type of problem constellation suggests a moderate degree of legalization as the optimal design for an international institution that seeks to control the global trade in rough diamonds. Countries threatened by diamond-related conflicts can be expected to insist on at least a moderate degree of legalization to make it harder for states to defy their trade control obligations. A moderate – not high – degree of legalization should be sufficient to prevent shirking: for all key states, costs and benefits are approximately balanced, and the few net payers, i.e. diamond smuggling hubs, can be relatively easily detected and quarantined. Furthermore, a high degree of legalization would make it more difficult for policymakers to adjust to a newly created institution in response to the deeper understanding they gain in dealing with this novel policy problem.

Table 6.7 *Summary assessment of the problem constellation underlying conflict diamonds*

Problem attribute	Level	Argument
1. Asset specificity	Moderate	
A. Potential loss	High	• Countries threatened by diamond-related conflict hope that trade controls will help resolve conflict. • Diamond-producing and trading countries hope that political solution to "blood diamonds" will avert consumer boycott campaign and thus safeguard important economic interests.
B. Propensity to shirk	Moderate	• Individual countries' implementation costs are largely proportionate to their share in diamond production or trade, and thus to their benefits. • A few states profit from diamond smuggling and would forgo this source of revenue if international controls were effective.
2. Behavioral uncertainty	Moderate	
A. Governance incapacity	Moderate	• Almost half of global diamond output comes from countries with an above-median governance capacity. • Leading diamond trading centers are all very well governed.
B. Reliance on governmental monitoring	Low	• Well-organized NGOs with independent data access and expertise monitor states' compliance effectively.
C. Industry opacity	High	• It is easier for other states to estimate production volumes of a state with primarily kimberlite rather than alluvial deposits. • The identification of the origin of alluvial diamonds is almost impossible. • Diamond industry has traditionally been very secretive with greater reliance on ethnic bonds and trust than formal contracts. Non-listed companies dominate the industry.

Table 6.7 (*cont.*)

Problem attribute	Level	Argument
3. Environmental uncertainty	Moderate	
A. Novelty of policy issue	High	• Policymakers have virtually no knowledge of the trade in rough diamonds and the role of diamonds in conflicts.
B. Innovativeness of field	Low	• Displacement potential limited because commercial diamond deposits are limited to only a dozen countries. • Trend toward beneficiation reduces the international trade in *rough* diamonds.

6.3 Degree of legalization

The name "Kimberley Process" reflects an important characteristic of the international control scheme established to curb the trade in conflict diamonds: it is a process rather than a static agreement, with "learning-by-doing" and non-codified practice playing an important role in the scheme's development. To assess whether the degree of legalization incorporated in the Kimberley Process is indeed moderate as predicted by the analysis of the problem constellation, I will look beyond the scheme adopted with the Interlaken Declaration of November 2002. I will also take into account another series of documents, including final communiqués adopted at plenary meetings and annual reports of the chair and of working groups, as well as the more informal implementation praxis that has emerged over the years. My assessment of the "hardness" of the Kimberley Process will again be based on the detailed analysis of each of the three legalization components: obligation, precision, and delegation.

6.3.1 Obligation

Like the FATF's Forty Recommendations, the Kimberley Process presents a fascinating example of the way in which a legally non-binding agreement can still reach a moderate level of obligation thanks to strong compliance mechanisms.

Legal bindingness

The founders of the Kimberley Process did not intend to create a legally binding treaty. This becomes apparent from the very name of the central document, which is simply called the "Kimberley Process Certification Scheme," rather than a "treaty" or "convention." Although the KPCS never explicitly denies being a legally binding treaty, both its language and the process through which it was adopted on the national level indicate that the drafters did not intend to grant it formal legal power. For instance, the preamble concludes that participants "recommend the following provisions," and each provision states what participants "should" do, not what they "shall" do. Formulations such as "obligation" are also missing from the document which, moreover, refers to its signatories as "participants," not "parties." The official website of the Kimberley Process refers to the scheme as "an innovative, *voluntary* system" (emphasis added). Furthermore, the KPCS was not implemented in the participating states through the same procedures that would be required for a legally binding treaty. For these reasons, the KPCS cannot be considered a legally binding treaty; rather, it must be seen as a memorandum of understanding or a political agreement (Price 2003). Because the KPCS is not a legally binding agreement, its drafters did not see any need to incorporate obligation-attenuating provisions such as reservations, safeguards, or withdrawal procedures.

Compliance mechanisms

The non-binding nature of the Kimberley Process should not lead us to conclude that it creates an overall low level of obligation. The KPCS largely compensates for its weakness in legal obligation by means of rigorous mechanisms created over the course of its existence to detect and impose sanctions for non-compliance.

On a "learning-by-doing" basis, the Kimberley Process has developed unique mechanisms for monitoring the compliance of applicant states and existing participants. The first important development in this direction was the creation of a stringent admission policy. The first plenary meeting held after the KPCS came into effect established a participation committee and mandated it to assess which of the seventy-nine states that had officially endorsed the scheme could be considered "able and willing to fulfill the requirements of the Scheme" (Section VI paragraph 8 of the KPCS). After a three-month tolerance period, the participation committee declared itself satisfied with the

progress fifty-four states had made in "amend[ing] or enact[ing] appropriate laws or regulations to implement and enforce the Certification
Scheme and to maintain dissuasive and proportional penalties for
transgressions" (Section IV paragraph d). Based on the committee's
recommendation, the chair confirmed the admission of these states as
official KP participants.[42] After this initial "clean-up" of the list of
participants, the participation committee continued to assess the merits
of new applicant countries based on their legal reforms. In connection
with Liberia's application, the Kimberley Process even went a step further
and decided that the merits of the country's application would not be
assessed on Freetown's legal steps alone, but also on its bureaucratic
capacity to effectively implement diamond regulation (Martin 2004).
For this purpose, the Kimberley Process dispatched its first review
mission to an applicant state.

This pre-admission screening mechanism sets the Kimberley Process
apart from traditional, legally binding agreements like the Vienna
Convention. These multilateral conventions typically define only for-
malistic admission requirements such as the deposit of an instrument of
ratification, acceptance, or approval, without demanding any proof of
actual compliance with their substantive provisions.

In addition to strengthening the level of obligation through pre-
admission screening, the Kimberley Process also developed procedures
to ensure that even after official approval, participating states continue
to meet the minimum standards. The initial scheme established some
limited post-accession monitoring mechanisms. Paragraph 11 of Section VI
provides that "participants are to prepare, and make available to
other participants … information … outlining how the requirements
of the Certification Scheme are being implemented within their respective jurisdictions," while paragraph 13 in the same section specifies
that "[w]here further clarification is needed, participants at plenary
meetings … can decide on additional verification measures to be
undertaken … such as (a) requesting additional information and clarification from participants …" Up to this point, this provision is very
similar to the monitoring mechanism enshrined in Articles 20 and 22

---

[42] Most of the states removed from the list of official participants had no direct
involvement in the diamond trade; only two diamond producers – namely, Brazil
and Ghana – were excluded but they were readmitted four months later after
having passed the required amendments.

of the Vienna Convention (see 4.3.1). However, in the second part of this paragraph, the KPCS takes measures beyond those found in the Vienna Convention by suggesting the dispatch of "review missions by other participants or their representatives where there are credible indications of significant non-compliance with the Certification Scheme" (paragraph 14). Over the course of its first three years, the Kimberley Process sent out two review missions. The first was carried out in the Central African Republic (CAR) after a coup d'état in March 2003 cast serious doubt on the country's ability to honor its KPCS obligations. The Republic of the Congo became the second participant to receive a review mission after several participants expressed their suspicion that it served as a major export hub for smuggled diamonds.

The KP participants strengthened the review mechanism enshrined in the initial Kimberley Process Certification Scheme at the plenary meeting in Sun City, South Africa, in October 2003 by adding so-called "review visits."[43] In contrast to review missions, review visits are not initiated on the basis of suspected non-compliance. Instead, a participating state chooses voluntarily to invite a review team to gather a firsthand impression of its implementation efforts. The non-mandatory status of this measure has not prevented it from becoming highly effective. By the end of 2006, a total of twenty-eight states had undergone a review visit, and almost all remaining states have invited a review visit to take place in the near future. As with the FATF's mutual evaluations, a summary report of each review visit is published online.

The Kimberley Process compensates for its lack of legal bindingness not only through its monitoring mechanisms but also through stringent enforcement procedures. The initial agreement established *de facto* sanctions against all non-participating states. Section III (letter c) of the KPCS calls upon participants to "ensure that no shipment of rough diamonds is imported from or exported to a non-participant." This embargo provision provides the Kimberley Process with a highly effective instrument to compel all states with a stake in the trade of rough diamonds to join the process and to comply with its requirements since current KP participants cumulatively control 99.8 percent of the global trade in this commodity (Kimberley Process 2008). In this regard, the Kimberley Process employs a strategy to ensure global compliance similar to that

---

[43] The KP's review visits are similar to the FATF's mutual evaluation rounds and – to a lesser extent – the in-country reviews conducted by the INCB.

of the Financial Action Task Force, which also sanctions states for non-compliance independent of whether or not formal consent has been given to the standards.

Unlike the FATF,[44] the Kimberley Process has proved willing to suspend or cancel the membership of non-complying participants. Though not provided for in the KPCS of November 2002, membership sanctions have already been imposed on two occasions. In response to the above-mentioned military overthrow of the government of the Central African Republic, the Kimberley Process participants agreed to suspend the CAR's membership until they could establish that the new government had gained sufficient control over its territory to ensure compliance with the central requirements of the scheme.[45] The Republic of the Congo posed an even greater challenge to the willingness of the Kimberley Process to lend "teeth" to its requirements. The review mission carried out in Brazzaville confirmed that implementation of the core KPCS requirements was highly deficient, in particular with regard to the Republic of the Congo's system of internal controls.[46] On 9 July, 2004, in response to these serious compliance problems, the Kimberley chair decided to drop the ROC from the list of participants – the KPCS' euphemism for imposing membership sanctions (Global Witness 2004a).

The KP's compliance mechanisms are further strengthened by monitoring and sanctioning tools that have been adopted by the diamond industry. As mentioned above (6.1.3), the KPCS refers explicitly to the system of warranties developed by the World Diamond Council (WDC) as a central pillar of its efforts to bar conflict diamonds access to legal

---

[44] The FATF has often been criticized for being too lenient with its own members, e.g. Greece and Turkey (Broome 2005).

[45] For the CAR, this suspension had important economic ramifications, because diamonds account for more than 60 percent of the country's export revenues (Oomes and Vocke 2003). The suspension of the CAR's membership was lifted in June 2003 after the dispatched review mission was satisfied that the new government of the Central African Republic had met all the core requirements of the Kimberley Process.

[46] According to the 2003 KP chair, Abbey Chikane, the Republic of the Congo was found to have been exporting about 5.2 million carats of diamonds a year, one hundred times more than its estimated annual production potential (Fraser 2004). The only plausible explanation for this huge discrepancy was that the relatively diamond-poor Republic of the Congo exported diamonds that had been illicitly imported from its diamond-rich neighbors, the Democratic Republic of Congo and Angola.

markets. Under this piece of industry self-regulation, the International Diamond Manufacturers Association (IDMA) and the World Federation of Diamond Bourses (WFDB) – the two leading international trade bodies that created the WDC in 2000 to serve as a unified voice – agreed to monitor their members' compliance with the system of warranties and the KPCS. They also agreed to expel all members whose compliance was found unsatisfactory. This formal commitment by the diamond industry to assume responsibility for ensuring compliance exceeds the role of the Wolfsberg Group, the WDC counterpart in the realm of anti-money laundering, even though the diamond industry has not fully lived up to its pledges.[47]

Factoring in both the Kimberley Process' lack of legal bindingness and the great strength of monitoring and enforcement provisions, I find that the Kimberley Process imposes the same moderate level of obligation as does the Financial Action Task Force.

6.3.2 Precision

The Kimberley Process Certification Scheme is characterized by a high level of precision, which results as much from its high degree of determinacy as from its great internal and external coherence.

Determinacy

The KPCS is the only one of the four international institutions presented in this study that reaches a high level of determinacy. This very technical agreement starts out with an eighteen-item-long list of definitions, which is very extensive compared to the overall brevity of the document and its limited scope. Furthermore, the KPCS rarely uses formulations or language that are vague, and many of its more ambiguous terms, such as "*duly* validated Certificates" (emphasis added) become clear in the overall context of the document, particularly in light of the recommendations provided in the annexes. The term "appropriate" appears only in every seventh paragraph – compared to every other and every third paragraph in the Forty Recommendations and the Vienna Convention, respectively. The equally ambiguous term "possible" appears twice in the KPCS, whereas it appears seven times in the slightly longer Forty

---

[47] For a critical assessment of the industry's lackluster implementation of its self-regulation, see Global Witness (2007).

Recommendations. Annex I of the KPCS adds considerably to the degree of detail of the agreement. It spells out the minimum requirements of the diamond export certificates in terms of the information they must provide, specifying a great number of technical details – including the use of "unique numbering with the Alpha 2 country code, according to ISO 3166-1."

Finally, the Kimberley Process further increased its determinacy with the publication of a detailed checklist outlining the criteria for assessing a country's KP compliance in a review mission or a review visit.

Coherence

The internal coherence of the norms spelled out in the KPCS is high, as they form a non-contradictory whole in which all provisions serve one clear and overriding objective: to increase transparency in the international trade of rough diamonds. The drafters of the KPCS were also very concerned about the scheme's external coherence, and were keen to ensure that it did not contradict any of their other international obligations. The explicit backing they received from two unanimous UNGA decisions during the drafting process (and also since the adoption of the scheme) was therefore of central importance for driving the process forward.[48] By the same token, the potential incompatibility of the KPCS with World Trade Organization (WTO) obligations presented a serious roadblock,[49] which was only fully removed after the WTO Council granted a waiver on humanitarian grounds (WTO 2003).[50]

Combining the high degree of precision and a high level of coherence, I conclude that the Kimberley Process' overall level of precision is high – in fact, higher than in either of the two previously studied international institutions.

---

[48] UNGA Resolution, 55/56 on December 1, 2000; UNGA Resolution, 56/263 on March 13, 2002. In the month the KPCS became effective, the UNSC joined the UNGA in giving the Kimberley Process its explicit endorsement (S/RES/1385 of January 28, 2003).

[49] Namely, provisions in the General Agreement on Tariffs and Trade (GATT) on most-favored-nation treatment (Article I:1), elimination of quantitative restrictions (Article XI:1), and non-discriminatory administration of quantitative restrictions (Article XIII:1).

[50] This waiver is limited to four years and was last renewed by the Council on Trade in Goods in November 2006.

6.3.3 Delegation

Like the Forty Recommendations but unlike the Vienna Convention, the Kimberley Process Certification Scheme does not rely on a formal international governmental organization (IGO) with an independent legal identity. Instead of delegating authority to an IGO, the Kimberley Process, as well as the Financial Action Task Force, prefer the plenary to take all decisions, which – given their smaller membership base – is less cumbersome than for the universal Vienna Convention. While both the Kimberley Process and the FATF remain on a low level of delegation, they differ from each other with regard to the role they assign to civil society groups. I characterized the FATF as a prototypical example of Slaughter's concept of government networks, whereas the Kimberley Process epitomizes Reinicke's (1998) model of global public policy networks because of the latter's stronger inclusion of representatives from the diamond industry and the NGO community. In the following segment, I will examine in more detail the extent to which participants of the Kimberley Process centralized rule-making, implementation or dispute settlement functions, and the degree of independence for the bodies they established.

Centralization

In comparison with the Vienna Convention and the Forty Recommendations, the number of functions the Kimberley Process can assume is severely curtailed by the fact that it does not possess a permanent support structure. For this reason, it does not provide any legal or technical assistance to individual states,[51] and primarily limits its role to rule-making and rule enforcement. The plenary takes the lead on both functions. The KPCS mandates the plenary to "discuss the effectiveness of the Certification Scheme" (Section VI paragraph 1) and to amend the KPCS as deemed necessary (Section VI paragraph 19).

---

[51] Some KP states provide some KPCS-related assistance on a bilateral basis. For instance, the British government covered the costs for designing and printing the KP certificates of its former colony Sierra Leone. The United States allocated US $7.6 million dollars for diamond-related projects in Sierra Leone and Liberia (US General Accounting Office 2006). Also, the Diamond Development Initiative supports a number of diamond mining projects in a way that complements the efforts of the Kimberley Process. The DDI was launched in 2005 and brings together the World Bank's Communities and Small Scale Mining project and a number of NGOs and industry bodies.

The plenary is also authorized to dispatch review missions to countries suspected of breaching KPCS commitments – a prerogative it has already used twice. The plenary has exercised substantial freedom in shaping and advancing diamond trade controls, most notably by establishing the instrument of membership sanctions and peer reviews discussed above. The plenary is supported in these functions by three working groups[52] and two committees[53] that were established to study certain issues in greater depth and with greater continuity. The rule-making role of the chairman, typically assumed by a diplomat from a participating state, is limited to that of a moderator who facilitates and presides over meetings of the plenary and of working groups (KPCS Section VI paragraph 4) and helps to forge a consensus among disagreeing participants (Section VI paragraph 5). He or she supports rule enforcement by formulating recommendations regarding verification measures to be undertaken in cases of suspected non-compliance (paragraph 13) and by establishing review missions with the consent of the participants concerned (paragraph 14). The chairman is assisted by a secretariat that he or she has to provide and fund personally.

Independence

The level of independence for the bodies set up under the Kimberley Process is overall lower than that found under the Forty Recommendations and the Vienna Convention. The key difference among the three is that the latter two enjoy the support of a permanent secretariat with 12 and 500 employees, respectively, while the Kimberley Process simply relies on the secretariat of the chairperson. As the chairmanship rotates annually, the secretariat – often assumed by just one person – also moves from year to year. This frequent rotation makes it virtually impossible for the secretariat to develop independent expertise or authority, in contrast to the FATF, where the last executive secretary assumed his post for almost a decade.

Like the FATF, the Kimberley Process relies almost exclusively on the plenary. As all participants are represented in the plenary and decisions

---

[52] Namely, one working group on monitoring, one on statistics, and one on diamond expert issues.
[53] Namely, one participation committee and one selection committee.

are taken by consensus (Section VI paragraph 5 KPCS and Rule 42 of Rules and Procedures), the degree of independence for this body is nil. Also, the Kimberley Process is chaired by a president who is elected by the plenary for one year (as is the president of the FATF), thus severely limiting the extent to which he or she can leave a personal mark on the institution. The only area that grants the Kimberley Process a greater degree of independence in decision-making than in the FATF is the former's greater involvement of civil society groups (Section VI paragraph 10 KPCS). In fact, the KP is largely unparalleled by any other international institution in that respect. For one, the Kimberley Process grants delegates of the diamond industry and the NGO community – represented by members of Global Witness and Partnership Africa Canada – the right to participate in all meetings and to join government officials at the negotiations table. Even though they officially enjoy only observer status without a vote, they are full members for all practical purposes, since decisions are never taken by vote but negotiated until a tacit consensus emerges. Furthermore, civil society representatives participate in all working groups and committees, which, despite the absence of decision-making power in these bodies, yield considerable influence, thanks to the expertise they develop. Both industry and NGO representatives are also included in the review visits and review missions the KP dispatches. Finally, Section VI of the Kimberley Process Certification Scheme explicitly acknowledges the importance of the industry's system of warranties as a central pillar of effective internal control. While the financial sector has also sought to pre-empt FATF-initiated regulation through industry self-regulation,[54] the task force has never gone as far as the Kimberley Process in co-opting this form of private regulation. However, the greater independence in rule-making that the KP derives from the inclusion of non-state actors is insufficient to compensate for the independence boost the FATF gains from its permanent secretariat and its institutionalized financial basis.

In sum, with a low level of centralization and independence, the Kimberley Process remains at the low end of the delegation spectrum.

---

[54] The Wolfsberg Anti-Money Laundering Principles for Private Banking being a prime example (see Chapter 5).

Table 6.8 *Summary assessment of the level of legalization of the Kimberley Process Certification Scheme*

Design element	Level	Argument
1. Obligation	**Moderate**	
A. Legal bindingness	Low	
a. Language	Low	• Name of the core document – i.e. "Kimberley Process Certification Scheme" – strongly suggests its legally non-binding character. • Other terms typically associated with legally binding conventions are missing, e.g. "shall" is substituted with "should," "parties" with "participants."
b. Procedural provisions	Low	• The KPCS was not subject to domestic procedures required for the adoption of legally binding international agreements. • The KPCS is not registered under UN Charter Article 102.
c. Tenacity of obligation	n/a	• As a legally non-binding agreement, the KPCS does not contain procedural provisions that allow states to unilaterally reduce the document's degree of obligation through reservations, withdrawal, etc.
B. Compliance mechanisms	High	
a. Monitoring	High	• Participants are required to submit diamond production and trade statistics on an annual basis. States that fail to do so are publicly identified. • Mutual compliance evaluation is carried out in review visits dispatched to all participating states. Review missions are sent to participants suspected of non-compliance. • Applicants' diamond trade control policies are assessed prior to their admission to the Kimberley Process. • Independence of reviews is increased through the official inclusion of NGO and industry representatives.

Table 6.8 (*cont.*)

Design element	Level	Argument
b. Enforcement	High	• Applicant countries are only admitted after meeting all minimum KPCS requirements. • The KP can suspend or cancel the membership of participants whose compliance is found unsatisfactory. • Non-membership of the KP entails a global embargo on the country's import and export of rough diamonds.
2. Precision	**High**	
A. Determinacy	High	• All key terms are very precisely defined. • Vague terms (e.g. "appropriate," "possible") are used very sparingly. • Annexes to the KPCS specify requirements in more detail.
B. Coherence	High	• All provisions of the KPCS relate to each other in a non-contradictory way. • The KPCS is fully consistent with other international agreements thanks to a WTO waiver.
3. Delegation	**Low**	
A. Independence		
a. Human resources	Low	• The KP is not supported by a permanent secretariat, but by one that is attached to the annually rotating chairmanship.
b. Financial resources	Low	• Chairman covers costs of the small secretariat.
c. Decision-making	Moderate	• Decisions require unanimous endorsement by all participants. • Representatives of the diamond industry and of the NGO community are officially included in all KP bodies and yield significant influence over decisions, although without a formal vote.
B. Centralization		
a. Rule-making	Moderate	• Plenary takes all decisions, no rule-making powers have been delegated. • Plenary has expanded KP mandate by adopting formal and informal rules that go beyond initial agreement.

Table 6.8 (*cont.*)

Design element	Level	Argument
b. Implementation	Low	• The secretariat assumes only a limited support role. • The KP itself does not institutionalize capacity-building measures, but technical assistance has been granted on a bilateral basis.
c. Dispute resolution	Low	• The KPCS only provides for mediation by the chairperson on a confidential basis.

6.3.4 Summary of actual institutional design and implications for model validity

The Kimberley Process presents an international institution with an overall moderate level of obligation resulting from the combination of the legally non-binding status of its core agreement with strict compliance mechanisms developed in practice by the participants. The KPCS is characterized by an unusually high level of precision with provisions that are both highly determinate and coherent. In contrast, the level of delegation is low, despite the fact that it grants civil society representatives a much greater role than does either the Vienna Convention or the Forty Recommendations. Consequently, the Kimberley Process' overall level of legalization is moderate. Table 6.8 provides a detailed overview of the building blocks of this assessment.

The architecture of the Kimberley Process thus corresponds with the design expectations I derived from this study's transaction cost economics model. The above analysis of the problem constellation underlying the global trade in conflict diamonds revealed a moderate degree of asset specificity, behavioral uncertainty, and environmental uncertainty. The model suggested an international institution with moderately hard law best equipped for the governance challenges arising from a problem structured in this way. The Kimberley Process therefore presents a case supporting the explanatory power of our design model.

7 | *Small arms and light weapons: the United Nations Program of Action*

Small arms and diamonds have much in common. Both goods enjoy great popularity among criminals, rebels, and terrorists who often barter one for the other. The illicit trade in small arms, as in diamonds, emerged simultaneously on the international agenda against the backdrop of the post-Cold War rise in bloody intra-state conflicts. In contrast to negotiations aimed at curbing the trade in conflict diamonds, international attempts to impose better controls on transfers of small arms and light weapons have not yet resulted in a unified, global institution endowed with the form and substance necessary to reach the same degree of effectiveness as that of the Kimberley Process. Rather, small arms and light weapons became a matter for negotiations in a variety of regional and inter-regional policy forums, leading to the adoption of over a dozen agreements and protocols dedicated to this topic. The United Nations has been the driving agenda-setting and, to a lesser extent, norm-creating force in this process. The cornerstone of the UN's anti-SALW efforts is the legally non-binding Program of Action to Prevent, Combat, and Eradicate the Illicit Trade in Small Arms and Light Weapons in All Its Aspects (Program of Action or PoA, in brief), which was adopted at a special United Nations conference in July 2001.

This fourth and final case challenges the design hypotheses underlying this study more than any of the preceding empirical chapters so far. Specifically, the predicted institutional design does not match the actual design outcome. The analysis of the problem constellation suggests a moderate degree of legalization as the optimal design solution for an international institution created to tackle small arms transfers. In reality, the Program of Action remains weakly legalized, with governance structures that do not create a sufficient degree of obligation, precision, and delegation to ensure compliance of net payers. As in the previous case studies, this chapter tests this study's design model by formulating expectations of an institution's optimal design based on the analysis of the underlying problem constellations along the three transaction costs economics variables – asset specificity, behavioral

221

uncertainty, and environmental uncertainty. Based on these variables, an expected design outcome is derived, then compared to the actual governance architecture that policymakers adopted in reality. Again, this two-step analysis is preceded by an opening section which provides a brief overview of the problems arising from the proliferation and diffusion of small arms and light weapons and also introduces the most important policy initiatives that have been launched to tackle it.

7.1 Small arms and light weapons as an international policy problem

This first section prepares the ground for the later testing of my design hypotheses by first positioning the trafficking of small arms and light weapons in its global context, as well as showing how interconnected it is with the illicit flows in narcotic drugs, dirty money, and conflict diamonds already studied in the previous chapters. The following section provides an overview of the most important global, inter-regional, and regional initiatives that policymakers launched to tackle this problem, whereby special attention is paid to the United Nations' Program of Action of 2001.

7.1.1 Small arms and light weapons between crime and war

Small arms kill almost as many people in homicides and suicides as in armed conflicts. Annually, approximately 200,000 people die from small arms-inflicted homicides and suicides (UN Department of Disarmament Affairs 2005). Another 300,000 deaths can be attributed directly to the misuse of small arms and light weapons in violent conflicts, even after the most deadly civil wars of the 1990s abated (UN Department of Disarmament Affairs 2005).[1] Attributing cases of gun violence to either crime or war is often more complicated than these figures reveal, since the already-discussed blurring between these two categories also affects the misuse of small arms and light weapons. The positioning of this fourth case study on the crime–war continuum is in part complicated by the broadness of the definitional category of small arms and light weapons, and also by the growing diversity of actors who have access to these weapons.

---

[1] In 95 percent of the cases of major violent conflict in the 1990s, small arms and light weapons were the most important or even the sole weapons category deployed.

No single universally agreed-upon definition exists to define small arms and light weapons. According to the working definition of the Organization for Security and Cooperation in Europe – the definition most widely referred to in international policy circles – these two weapon categories include weapons that are "man-portable, made or modified to military specifications for use as lethal instruments of war" (OSCE 2000, Preamble, paragraph 3). The distinction between small arms and light weapons is based on the number of people typically operating such a weapon. The category of small arms comprises "those weapons intended for use by individual members of armed or security forces," such as revolvers and self-loading pistols, rifles and carbines, sub-machine guns, assault rifles, and light machine guns (European Union 1999; OSCE 2000). Light weapons, in contrast, are designed for use by a small team or crew of armed or security forces (OSCE 2000). This second category includes heavy machine guns, handheld under-barrel and mounted grenade launchers, portable anti-aircraft guns,[2] portable anti-tank guns, recoilless rifles, portable launchers of anti-tank missile and rocket systems, portable launchers of anti-aircraft missile systems, and mortars of calibers less than 100 mm.[3] In general, "ordinary criminals" mainly use small arms, while terrorists and rebel groups also use light weapons. However, the already-discussed problem of the quasi-criminal nature of some rebel groups complicates this neat binary attribution of small arms to the crime end of the spectrum and light arms to war.

A second element in the increasing blur between the criminal and the military side of the small arms and light weapons problem is the growing diversion of these arms to a variety of state and non-state actors. While the proliferation of small arms and light weapons is not a new phenomenon, the diffusion, for the most part, is (Klare 1995). During the Cold War, the United States and the Soviet Union had already equipped their allied states and rebel groups with small arms and light weapons in great abundance.

---

[2] Man-portable air defense systems, so-called MANPADs, have recently gained considerable attention from the international community and are now often debated separately from other SALW (e.g. the "Elements for Export Controls of Man-Portable Air Defense Systems" adopted by the participating states of the Wassenaar Arrangement in December 2003).

[3] Anti-personnel landmines, which according to the above definition would fall within the category of small arms, have been addressed by separate international initiatives and are usually not included in the international negotiations focused on SALW.

The end of the superpower confrontation led simultaneously to a significant drop in SALW proliferation and an increase in the uncontrolled dispersal within societies and across borders. Diversion, i.e. "the movement of a weapon from legal origins to the illicit realm" (Small Arms Survey 2002: 128) mostly occurs through two main channels: purchase and theft.

Small arms and light weapons are diverted in the above sense when they are sold across borders "contrary to the laws of states and/or international law" (UN Guidelines for International Arms Transfers of 1991; A/RES/46/36H para 7). Such a transaction is illegal when the buyer is a non-state party and transfers occur without official approval of the recipient state's government. In that case, the transfer constitutes an interference in the internal affairs of the state to which the weapons are shipped, and is therefore an illegal act (UN Panel of Governmental Experts on Small Arms 1997: 51). A contemporary example of this type of illicit transfer is Venezuela's alleged military support of FARC in Colombia (Wezeman 2003). Even with the approval of the recipient state, a SALW transfer can become illicit when it violates a regional or international arms embargo targeted against the recipient state. The Fowler report on compliance with the international sanctions imposed against UNITA (S/2000/203 of March 10, 2000) and the UN Panel of Experts on Liberia (S/2002/1115 of October 25, 2002) – both mentioned in the previous chapter – provide a rich reading on the ingenious methods a great number of exporting and transhipment states developed to circumvent the UN arms embargoes. According to the Small Arms Survey (2002), more than fifty-four countries can directly or indirectly be linked to SALW transfers in violation of international arms embargoes. While some of these states engage in illicit SALW transactions primarily for political reasons, a growing number of states are primarily driven by economic motives. As Lumpe, Meek, and Naylor (2000) note, with the end of the Cold War and shrinking defense budgets, many states became increasingly willing to sell weapons for profit, whereas political considerations had previously prevailed.

A second important source of diversion consists of weapons that may disappear from government and military weapons stockpiles as a result of mismanagement, corruption among soldiers or other personnel with legal access to government-owned weapons, or theft or raid by criminal organizations or rebel groups.[4] The Small Arms Survey estimates that

---

[4] Theft from legitimate private owners is also an important diversion mechanism (see 7.1.3)

annually over 1 million light weapons are stolen or lost around all the world's regions in this way (Small Arms Survey 2004). For instance, Soviet troops are reported to have "lost" 81,000 tons of ammunition during the withdrawal from East Germany (Smith 1999). Even in today's Russia, the problem of unexplained losses of arms and weapons from military stockpiles is still prevalent: the Russian Office of the Chief Military Prosecutor claimed that up to 54,000 firearms disappeared in 2004 (IANSA 2006). Albania's collapse in 1997 was accompanied by raids of government arsenals with more than half a million weapons flowing into the hands of individual and gang looters (Stohl 2005). Cragin and Hoffman (2003) show how most SALW trafficked into Colombia from Ecuador and Peru originate from stolen military stocks or supplies that have been illegally resold by members of private security firms. Allegations also emerged accusing Guinean troops participating in the United Nations Mission in Sierra Leone (UNAMSIL) of selling UN weapons to Liberian rebels (Vines 2005). Iraq provides the most recent – and the most glaring – example of arms diversion. The think tank Small Arms Survey argues that "[t]he collapse of Saddam Hussein's regime led to the single most significant small arms stockpile transfer the world has known" (Small Arms Survey 2004). Iraqi civilians may have brought 7 to 8 million small arms into their possession (Small Arms Survey 2004), and between 2004 and 2005, the Pentagon lost track of about 190,000 AK-47 assault rifles and pistols given to Iraqi security forces (Kessler 2007).

Though accounting for only 10–20 percent of the global trade in SALW (Small Arms Survey 2002), this illicit segment is of greatest concern. It is not the prevalence of small arms and light weapons as such that is causally linked to high rates of gun crime[5] or armed conflict,[6] but rather, the weakness of governance structures to control

[5] For instance, the rate of gun-related homicides is almost 600 times higher in South Africa than in Germany, despite the fact that gun ownership is much more widespread in the latter than in the former country.

[6] See for instance Sislin and Pearson (2001), who argue that an excessive accumulation of weapons is neither necessary nor sufficient to start violent conflict. This view contrasts with the argument often forwarded by NGOs but also by some branches of the UN which see in the presence of weapons a trigger of conflicts. For instance, Mervyn Patterson, the UN chief representative in northern Afghanistan argued that "[t]here is a universal understanding that if weapons are present it will lead to conflict" (quoted in Oxfam and Amnesty International 2003: 11).

access to and misuse of these arms. In fact, private gun ownership[7] tends to be more widespread and military stockpiles larger in affluent countries where armed violence does not pose a significant threat. In contrast, conflict-prone sub-Saharan Africa accounts for less than 5 percent of the world total in firearms, including those in the possession of civilians, insurgents, and government forces (Small Arms Survey 2003: 80). Thus the challenge faced by the international community was to devise a solution that helped weak states cope with the accumulation and diffusion of small arms and light weapons without unduly restricting the legal trade (worth an estimated US$4 billion per year) (Small Arms Survey 2002).

7.1.2 *International initiatives*

The association of small arms and light weapons with both crime and war is further mirrored in the way that policymakers have sought to address the problem. While some international initiatives conceptualize the problem primarily from a law enforcement perspective, a greater number of recent agreements focus more on SALWs' consequences in terms of human security.

In April 1998, the Vienna-based ECOSOC Commission on Crime Prevention and Criminal Justice started negotiations on a draft Protocol against the Illicit Manufacturing of and Trafficking in Firearms, Their Parts and Components and Ammunition (or, in brief, the Firearms Protocol (A/RES/55/255)). This protocol built directly on the Inter-American Convention against the Illicit Manufacturing of and Trafficking of Firearms, Ammunition, Explosives and other Related Materials (CIFTA)[8] of 1997, and was eventually adopted as a legally binding supplement to the United Nations Convention against Transnational Organized Crime of November 2000. It urges parties to adopt a series of crime-control measures, to criminalize the illicit manufacture and trade of firearms, to strengthen government licensing procedures for firearms manufacturers, and to establish effective means of marking and tracing firearms. The protocol entered into force on July 3, 2005, and by March 2008, it

---

[7] E.g. in the United States between 238 and 276 million firearms are privately owned, which equals almost one firearm per person.

[8] (AG/RES. 1800 (XXXI-O/01). By March 2008, twenty-seven of the thirty-four OAS states had ratified the Convention. The most notable absentees are the United States and Canada (Organization of American States 2007).

counted a total of ninety-four parties. Among the bystanders who have neither ratified nor signed are a number of states with major stakes in the manufacturing and trade of firearms – most notably the Russian Federation and the United States (UNODC 2007).

The human security implications of the misuse of small arms and light weapons have set off a veritable flurry of activities on the global, inter-regional, and regional level. The first and most conventional type of initiative to reduce SALW-inflicted violence in post-Cold War conflicts are mandatory arms embargoes imposed by the United Nations Security Council on rebel groups, governmental forces, or both warring parties. During the 1990s, the UNSC adopted arms embargoes against a total of thirteen different parties (Lumpe, Meek, and Naylor 2000). As already noted above, the effectiveness of such arms embargoes is often limited. In response to the ineffectiveness of these embargoes and their *ex post facto* adoption, the UN started to look for other policy tools which would tackle the problem at an earlier stage – possibly before the actual outbreak of armed conflict. The United National General Assembly pioneered this new thinking in its resolution of December 12, 1995.[9] This resolution asked the secretary general to establish a Panel of Governmental Experts on Small Arms mandated to scrutinize the small arms problem and to assess possible cures. This panel published a first report on August 27, 1997 in which it presented twenty-four specific recommendations on SALW reduction and the prevention of their spread.[10] One of these recommendations suggested convening a UN conference to address the issues raised in the report.[11] Pursuant to this recommendation, the United Nations held a special conference in New York from July 9–20 in 2001. This conference culminated in the adoption of a Program of Action to Prevent, Combat, and Eradicate the Illicit Trade in Small Arms and Light Weapons in All Its Aspects,[12] which I will discuss in more detail in the next subsection. The most recent SALW-related development under the auspices of the United Nations is the development of an international instrument on the mark-ing and tracing of small arms and light weapons, along with the UNGA's decision in December 2006[13] to examine the necessity for and viability of an international legally binding arms trade treaty covering all

[9] A/RES/50/70B.   [10] A/52/298.
[11] Report of the Panel of Governmental Experts on Small Arms, Recommendation k.
[12] A/CONF. 192/15.   [13] A/61/89.

conventional arms and weapons, including SALW. These latest developments follow up on recommendations presented by the High-Level Panel on Threats, Challenges, and Change, which recommended in its 2004 report that "States should expedite and conclude negotiations on legally binding agreements on the marking and tracing, as well as the brokering and transfer, of small arms and light weapons" (2004: 36).

The awareness created through the UN Panel of Governmental Experts on Small Arms also gave rise to a large number of inter-regional and regional agreements – but marked differences exist between different world regions. On the inter-regional level, the Organization for Security and Cooperation in Europe and the Wassenaar Arrangement have been the most important for the development of norms with regard to small arms and light weapons. The OSCE adopted in November 2000 the politically binding Document on Small Arms and Light Weapons as a confidence- and security-building measure among its fifty-six participating states. In 2003, the OSCE complemented this document with the publication of its "Handbook of Best Practices on Small Arms and Light Weapons" which discusses in more detail issues surrounding the marking and tracing of small arms and light weapons, record-keeping, stockpile management, brokering, and the licensing of exports. On December 12, 2002, the smaller but geographically more diverse[14] Wassenaar Arrangement on Export Controls for Conventional Arms and Dual-Use Goods and Technologies adopted the non-binding Best Practice Guidelines for Exports of Small Arms and Light Weapons, which refers directly to the UN PoA and the 2000 OSCE Document. In its 2003 plenary, the Wassenaar participants also agreed on a set of export standards for man-portable air defense systems (MANPADS) and on brokering.

On the regional level, SALW-related activities are very unequally distributed, with Africa and the European Union as the most active and Asia and the Middle East the least active regions.

The African continent is home to the greatest number of agreements that are specifically targeted against the illicit trade in small arms and light weapons. The most far-reaching agreement is the Convention on Small Arms and Light Weapons, Their Ammunition, and Other Related Material, adopted by the Economic Community of West African States

---

[14] The Wassenaar Arrangement counts a total of thirty-four member states from the Americas, Asia, Europe, and Oceania.

on June 14, 2006. This Convention is essentially the transformation of the non-binding Moratorium on the Importation, Exportation, and Manufacture of Small Arms and Light Weapons in West Africa of 1998 into a legally binding institution. The Moratorium and the Convention are the only international agreements banning all transfers of SALW into member states' territory – unless they requested a prior exemption for a specific transfer (Article 3 Para 1). The Moratorium was also the first international agreement that explicitly prohibited SALW transfers to non-state actors unless these transfers had been explicitly authorized by the importing state (Article 3 Para 2 ECOWAS Convention).[15] In an attempt to address some of the Moratorium's shortcomings, the 2006 Convention grants the ECOWAS Executive Secretary and a Group of Independent Experts an explicit mandate to monitor states' compliance (Article 28). Less ambitious in their substantive scope are the African Union's Bamako Declaration on an African Common Position on the Illicit Proliferation, Circulation, and Trafficking of Small Arms and Light Weapons of December 1, 2000, and the legally binding Protocol on Control of Fire Arms, Ammunition, and Other Related Materials adopted by the Southern African Development Community (SADC) on August 14, 2001, as well as the Nairobi Protocol for the Prevention, Control, and Reduction of Small Arms and Light Weapons in the Great Lakes Region and the Horn of Africa of April 21, 2004.[16] The Nairobi Protocol is one of the most specific agreements on the regulation of guns in the hands of civilians, prohibiting, among other things, the unrestricted civilian possession of small arms (Centre for Humanitarian Dialogue 2006).

Within the European Union, the core agreement with respect to SALW is the EU Joint Action on Small Arms which was adopted on December 17, 1998. In this legally non-binding agreement, the Council of the European Union pledges to work toward the realization of a series of principles and measures aimed at providing security assistance to regions emerging from conflict. The most important provision in the Joint Action for furthering this goal is the commitment by exporting countries to supply arms only to governments (Article 3(b)), which is

---

[15] For an assessment of the Moratorium and the Convention, see Vines (2005) and Berkol (2007).

[16] The Nairobi Protocol, signed by the governments of Burundi, the DRC, Djibouti, Ethiopia, Eritrea, Kenya, Rwanda, the Seychelles, Sudan, Tanzania, and Uganda, will be legally binding once ratified by two-thirds of signatory states, which has not occurred at the time of writing.

similar to the ECOWAS Moratorium's ban of SALW transfers to non-state actors. This joint action is firmly embedded in the EU Code of Conduct for Arms Exports, which the General Affairs Council adopted half a year earlier (8675/2/98 Rev. 2, of June 8, 1998). Unlike the African SALW agreements, both the Joint Action and the Code of Conduct refer explicitly to human rights and declare the human rights record of a recipient state an important criterion in exporting countries' decisions on whether or not to authorize SALW exports.

In Latin America, the most important agreement that addresses the human security side of small arms and light weapons is the legally non-binding Andean Plan to Prevent, Combat, and Eradicate the Illicit Trade in Small Arms and Light Weapons in All Its Aspects, which the Andean Community adopted on June 25, 2003. In Australasia, the Nadi Framework provides a legal platform for harmonizing weapons controls in the Pacific region. The Association of Southeast Asian Nations (ASEAN) has shown some willingness to discuss small arms, but the strong reluctance against any agreement that could potentially sanction outside interference in internal matters has limited the scope of these initiatives (Small Arms Survey 2001). Conspicuous in the absence of any coordinated efforts to address transfers of small arms and light weapons is the Middle East.

7.1.3 The UN Program of Action

The United Nations Program of Action to Prevent, Combat, and Eradicate the Illicit Trade in Small Arms and Light Weapons in All Its Aspects is the central global agreement on preventing and reducing the trafficking and proliferation of SALW. It presents a compromise forged by the high-level representatives of over 150 countries in the final hours of the UN SALW Conference in July 2001 in a desperate attempt to save the heated negotiations of two weeks from ending without any tangible result. Three aspects proved to be particularly controversial.

First, the EU, Canada, Costa Rica, and some African states lobbied for a mention in the Program's preamble of the link between small arms and light weapons and human rights violations (Small Arms Survey 2002). They sought to redress the long history of governments misusing SALW as a tool of internal repression either directly or by allowing irregular troops to commit small arms-aided human rights abuses with impunity (Wezeman 2003). This position deviated from the perspective underlying the Report of the Panel of *Governmental* Experts of 1997 (emphasis

added), which clearly distinguishes between governmental forces conceived as disciplined troops respecting established norms of international
law and irregular forces that are assumed to make no distinction between
combatants and non-combatants. As a logical extension of this thinking,
the 1999 SALW Report (A/54/404 of September 24, 1999) identifies the
following categories as recipients of illicit small arms trafficking: armed
groups, criminal organizations, terrorists, individual criminals, private
security services, mercenaries, and private citizens – with governments
conspicuously absent in this enumeration. China and a number of other
countries lobbied hard for the continuation of this perspective and threatened to boycott any SALW document that mentioned human rights.
This position eventually prevailed, with the PoA shunning any references
to human rights. The only consolation for the supporters of an inclusion
of human rights-related provisions was the promise – not codified in the
PoA – that an independent United Nations Special Rapporteur on the
Prevention of Human Rights Violations Committed with Small Arms and
Light Weapons would be appointed to study the issue.[17]

The second bone of contention was the issue of civilian possession of
small arms and light weapons. This issue is of great significance, since an
estimated 59 percent of the firearms around the world are owned by
civilians (Small Arms Survey 2003) and diversion from legal possession
to illicit trade and misuse is a common phenomenon. In the US, approximately 500,000 small arms enter the black market as a result of theft from
legitimate private owners each year (Small Arms Survey 2004). In South
Africa, the equivalent figure amounts to almost 25,000 firearms (Swart
2005). However, the regulatory harmonization of civilian possession was
extremely sensitive politically, especially for the United States, where
private gun ownership is not only very widespread, but also guaranteed
by the US Constitution's Second Amendment[18] and strongly defended by
the National Rifle Association (NRA), a powerful lobby group. Well
before the start of the UN Conference, the US pro-gun lobby had thrown
down the gauntlet to the UN's efforts to control SALW transfers. The
NRA stirred up its supporters with warnings like the following: "The UN
is after Americans' Second Amendment gun rights – it wants gun

---

[17] Professor Barbara Frey, the Special Rapporteur, submitted her final report on
July 27, 2006.
[18] The Second Amendment of the US Constitution stipulates that "[a] well regulated
Militia, being necessary to the security of a free State, the right of the people to
keep and bear Arms, shall not be infringed."

ownership banned in the US, and it's not going to stop until it gets its way" (cited in Browne 2005). The US government adopted the NRA's position that any provisions that could potentially circumscribe the possession of small arms by civilians were unacceptable. As Herbert L. Calhoun, one of the US negotiators at the UN SALW conference and the then-deputy division chief in the Office of Policy, Plans, and Analysis at the State Department's Bureau of Political-Military Affairs made plain: "We had warned the international community as far as nine months out of the conference that we could not accept any controls on civilian possession of firearms, because we consider that beyond the UN mandate for the conference" (cited in Kellerhals 2001). In the end, the opponents prevailed, and the UN Program of Action does not even mention the issue of civilian possession.

A third and final point that stirred up considerable controversy was the question of whether or not to ban arms sales to all non-state groups, as provided for by the EU Joint Action and the ECOWAS Memorandum. Again, the United States was the strongest opponent against such a far-reaching measure. Herbert Calhoun explained his country's opposition to a general ban on SALW transfers to non-state parties in the following words: "We thought it would preclude being able to give arms to oppressed groups, such as victims of genocide, and it violated traditions of the American Constitution. We were sort of a non-state actor group when we founded this country" (cited in Kellerhals 2001). Again, the opponents gained the upper hand, with the result that the PoA does not touch upon this controversial point.

What remained was an eighty-seven-paragraph long legally non-binding document that spells out national, regional, and global measures to prevent, combat, and eradicate the illicit trade in small arms and light weapons. On the domestic level, these measures include record keeping on the manufacture, holding, and transfer of small arms, and the marking of all weapons by manufacturers for identification and tracing. Furthermore, states are asked to adopt and thoroughly implement laws and regulations criminalizing the illegal manufacture and trafficking in small arms – echoing similar provisions in the UN Firearms Protocol. States are also urged to establish strict controls over the export[19] and transit of small

---

[19] In contrast to the UN Disarmament Commission's 1996 Guidelines for International Transfers or the EU Code of Conduct, the Program of Action does not specify the criteria based on which states should take their decision to authorize an arms export deal. It contents itself with referring in Article 11 to an already established body of international law that should guide states' export regulations.

arms and light weapons, including the issuing of end-user certificates for exports and transit, and the notification of the original supplier nation in the case of re-export. Surplus, confiscated, or collected weapons are to be destroyed, and a national agency is to be mandated to coordinate the efforts of all relevant governmental agencies working to reduce gun violence. To foster international cooperation, the Program of Action calls upon states to establish a single Point of Contact through which information can be shared internationally, to harmonize policies through the development or ratification of legally binding instruments on a regional level, and to meet regularly to report on the progress they have made.

7.2 Problem constellation

After this overview of the nature and scope of the SALW problem and of the most important international initiatives launched to tackle it, I will now embark on a systematic analysis of the particular constellation underlying this issue and formulate specific expectations about the optimal design of an international institution created to tackle this problem. I will show in the following section that at the time the PoA was hammered out, both asset specificity and behavioral uncertainty were moderately pronounced, while environmental uncertainty was not of particular concern to the drafters of the Program of Action. Consequently, I postulate a moderate degree of legalization to present the optimal institutional design for tackling the problematic accumulation of small arms and light weapons in weak states.

7.2.1 Asset specificity

Which states had reason to expect important benefits from a strong international SALW institution, and how important to them were these hoped-for benefits? Which states feared ending up as net payers? The following section assesses the asymmetry between benefits and costs and shows that international efforts to impose tighter controls on small arms transfers were associated with a moderate degree of asset specificity. It will further reveal that states had moderately strong incentives to shirk their SALW control obligations, as they could expect their opportunity costs of compliance to be lower than in the drug and money laundering cases. However, the potential damage of such shirking could be significant, because countries suffering from armed violence strongly depend on international support in their own efforts to curb the uncontrolled influx of weapons into their territory. This distribution of costs and benefits is highly comparable to that found in the conflict diamonds case and results in an overall moderate degree of asset specificity.

Costs

As in the previous case studies, direct implementation costs were not the major concern of the negotiators of the global SALW institution. All leading SALW exporters already had legislation in place regulating the export of major conventional weapons systems, and often also of SALW, with varying degrees of stringency. They had previously mandated governmental bodies with the monitoring and approval of weapons exports. It was clear from the outset that overseeing a tightening of SALW export controls would fall within the domain of that pre-existing body, and would typically be manageable with existing resources. Policymakers were more concerned about the harder-to-gauge indirect costs resulting from an effective mechanism for preventing the diffusion of small arms. Some states – namely leading weapons exporters – were primarily concerned about potential economic opportunity costs, while others most feared an attack on their sovereign prerogative to use SALW exports or imports as they deemed appropriate from their foreign policy or national security perspective.

Potential economic repercussions of a tougher SALW export regime were of greatest concern to states for which SALW exports presented an important source of income. These SALW-exporting states were particularly concerned if an important share of sales went to the developing world, as trade with these countries was the main target of the PoA.

No reliable data on SALW exports to developing countries are available. I am therefore using data on exports of all conventional arms and weapons to developing countries as a proxy for identifying states with the strongest economic interest. Table 7.1 lists the seven leading exporters of conventional arms to developing countries and provides data on three different metrics. It shows each country's average value of conventional arms exports to developing countries in US dollars. Table 7.1 also indicates the global importance of each producer measured as the average market share each exporter claimed over the 1997–2001 period. The final column of Table 7.1 displays the relative domestic importance of this sector measured as the share of conventional arms exports in a country's total merchandise exports. This third indicator reveals that conventional arms exports to developing countries were not a major currency earner in any of these seven states. The country most dependent

Table 7.1 *Transfers of conventional arms to developing countries, average 1997–2001*

Country	Value of arms exports (million US$)	Share in global arms exports (%)	Share of arms exports in merchandise exports (%)
China	700	2.83	0.34
France	3,880	14.35	1.23
Germany	380	1.47	0.07
Italy	260	0.99	0.11
Russia	2,980	12.85	3.31
United Kingdom	4,520	18.15	1.63
United States	9,370	36.95	1.32

Source: Gimmett (2005); World Bank (2008); calculations by author.

on conventional arms exports – Russia – earned less than 4 percent of its export revenues from this export category. Dependency on SALW exports to developing countries was logically even smaller, as SALW constitute only a sub-group within the category of conventional arms.

All states listed in Table 7.1 are major[20] or medium[21] producers and exporters of small arms and light weapons. Other medium-sized SALW producers for which data on arms exports to developing countries are often not available include four other Western European states,[22] five Central European[23] and Asian[24] states, and five from other world regions[25] (Small Arms Survey 2001). Figure 7.1 shows the world's legal small arms producers of major (in black) or medium (in gray) size.

For most of the major or medium SALW-producing states, the economic importance of this sector was relatively small in terms of export share and contribution to domestic employment[26] and GDP.[27] The weak

[20] Namely China, Russia, and the United States.
[21] Namely France, Germany, Italy, and the United Kingdom.
[22] Austria, Belgium, Spain, and Switzerland.
[23] Bulgaria, the Czech Republic, Hungary, Poland, and Romania.
[24] India, Pakistan, Singapore, South Korea, and Taiwan.
[25] Brazil, Egypt, Israel, South Africa, and Turkey.
[26] E.g. in the United States, small arms manufacturers employed only 9,907 people in 1997 (US Census Bureau 1999).
[27] US small arms manufacturers added less than 0.008 percent to the country's GDP (US Census Bureau 1999).

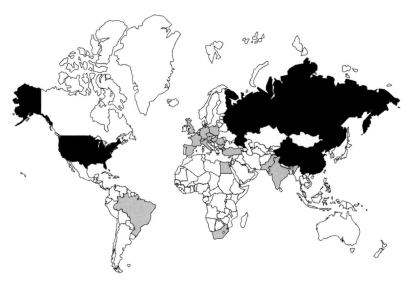

Figure 7.1 The world's legal small arms producers
Source: Small Arms Survey (2001); major SALW producers in black; medium producers in gray

national importance of the sector contrasts with the local prominence that small arms and light weapons manufacturers have in some of these countries. For instance, Germany's leading small arms manufacturers, Heckler & Koch and Carl Walther, absorb almost the entire workforce of the small towns in which they are located. The local importance of small arms manufacturers was (and still is) even more pronounced in formerly socialist states that had specialized in this segment under the international labor division devised under the Warsaw Pact. At the end of the twentieth century, these countries' SALW manufacturers were still struggling to become internationally competitive. In Kazanlak, a Bulgarian city of 81,000 inhabitants, this transformation process cost more than 20,000 jobs at the local small arms manufacturer Arsenal Co. (Center for the Study of Democracy and Saferworld 2004). Russian SALW manufacturers made slower progress in increasing their efficiency, so that the leading company – JSC Izhmash – still employed more than twice as many people (that is, 25,400) than the entire US firearms industry as a whole (Small Arms Survey 2001; US Census Bureau 1999). Because of their competitive disadvantage, former socialist countries had good reason to reject international obligations that imposed additional restrictions on an industry that was already fighting for survival.

While concerns of local SALW manufacturers had some bearing on the formulation of a national position on international SALW controls,[28] it is clear that these companies yielded considerably less lobbying power than, for instance, Luxembourg's financial sector or Botswana's diamond industry, which account for an incomparably larger share of their country's income.

States with a strong stake in the production of small arms and light weapons were, however, not the only countries with an economic interest in unfettered SALW trade. Equally important, and with respect to the armed conflicts of the 1990s even more significant, were states that dumped their surplus weapons stockpiles on the international market. Only some of these states were also significant SALW producers.

One way of working around the lack of data on SALW exports stemming from national stockpiles rather than production is by identifying the countries with the greatest surplus of small arms and light weapons in their military arsenal. No common agreement exists on the optimal level of stockpiles. However, it seems reasonable to assume that countries with a firearms-to-soldier ratio many times higher than that of the United States may have many more arms than actually needed and may therefore be more inclined to sell off some of their SALW. Table 7.2 lists the twelve countries with the greatest relative stockpiles. The United States is also listed as a reference point. Though many former Warsaw Pact states engaged in the large-scale sale of firearm stockpiles right after the end of the Cold War, many of these states still topped the list of SALW surplus states. Countries with excessive stockpiles had even stronger reasons to oppose tighter export control measures than SALW producers. The most likely buyers of secondhand weapons are poorer states which lack the funds to buy the latest technology. It is precisely this same category of states that is most at risk for armed conflict, and thus, the logical focus of the Program of Action and any other international agreement that addresses SALW from a human security perspective. Stockpile sales were less important for the national economy of these surplus states, but they presented one of the few options defense ministries had to counteract massively shrinking budgets.

Indirect economic costs are not the only reason states may be disinclined to support and comply with stronger restrictions on SALW

---

[28] The German desk officer argued that economic considerations played a negligible role in his country's stance on SALW (interview by author).

Table 7.2 *Selected countries with potential surplus stockpiles, 2003–2005*

Country	Total military personnel	Total firearms	Ratio (arms per soldier)
Russia	988,100	30,000,000	30.4
Ukraine	302,300	7,000,000	23.2
Vietnam	484,000	9,800,000	20.2
China	2,270,000	41,000,000	18.1
Korea, North	1,082,000	14,000,000	12.9
Korea, South	686,000	7,100,000	10.3
Taiwan	370,000	3,800,000	10.3
Czech Republic	49,450	500,000	10.1
Albania	21,500	148,742	6.9
Estonia	15,300	83,550	5.5
Bosnia-Herzegovina	84,600	450,000	5.3
Bulgaria	100,000	504,096	5.0
United States	2,515,300	3,054,553	1.2

Source: Small Arms Survey (2006); IISS (2004); calculations by author.

transfers. Political considerations were at least of equal importance, whereby exporting states followed a different logic than importing states.

A number of leading SALW exporters – most prominently the United States, Russia, and China – feared that they would lose an important foreign policy instrument if they were restricted in their right to (covertly) transfer arms and weapons to governments or non-state actors they supported for ideological or strategic reasons. While such transfers experienced a pronounced drop with the end of the Cold War, they remain an option in the toolbox for many governments. For instance, Russia has been accused of supporting insurgents in Georgia and Moldova as a means to convince the governments of those countries that it is not in their interest to act against Moscow's will (Mathiak and Lumpe 2000), while the United States directed an important share of its post-Cold War arms transfers to opposition groups in Iraq (Mathiak and Lumpe 2000).[29] For the United States, fierce opposition by the

---

[29] With the passage of the Iraq Liberation Act by the US Congress in 1998, arms transfers to Iraq were elevated to an official national policy but they had allegedly already begun earlier.

National Rifle Association was of even greater concern than the possible impact UN standards could have on the government's discretion over international arms transfers. As mentioned above (7.1.3), the NRA skillfully married the defense of citizens' right to bear arms with widespread hostility toward the United Nations and held great sway over the formulation of the official US position.

In addition, importing states had political reasons to oppose the establishment of an effective international SALW control institution. States with records of political terror were especially concerned because they were the most likely targets of tougher trade restrictions. From this perspective, the EU Code of Conduct for Arms Exports of 1998 had set an unwelcome precedent in infringing upon national sovereignty by defining a destination state's human rights situation as a central criterion in the assessment of whether an export license should be granted. These states feared that access to legal, competitive international markets would be diminished, forcing them to accept fewer purchasing options at a black-market premium. Table 7.3 identifies the twenty countries with the worst record of political terror in the decade prior to the UN SALW Conference. It is based on Gibney's Political Terror Scale (2006) which assigns states an ordinal score between one (best) and five (worst) based on the prevalence of torture, disappearances, and political murder. Two of the states listed in Table 7.3 not only claimed a top position as countries with a high level of political terror, but also figured as prominent importers of SALW. In 2003, Colombia and Sudan spent approximately US$34 million and US$18 million on official SALW imports, respectively (Small Arms Survey 2006: 75), which meant that they would have been strongly affected by an international institution that limited SALW transfers on human rights grounds.

Benefits

As mentioned above, the main goal pursued by the drafters of the Program of Action was to assist weak, conflict-prone states in their efforts to stem the uncontrolled influx of small arms and light weapons into their territory. The main beneficiaries, therefore, are countries threatened by the outbreak or continuation of armed conflict. One of the strongest predictors of an outbreak of armed conflict in any given country is that country's experience of conflict in the recent past. Figure 7.2 lists all countries that experienced at least one year of armed conflict in the decade prior to the UN SALW conference. Any given year that

Table 7.3 *Average political terror score of countries with worst human rights record, 1991–2000*

Country	Average political terror score, 1991–2000
DRC	5.0
Iraq	5.0
Korea, North	5.0
Colombia	4.9
Afghanistan	4.8
Burundi	4.8
Sudan	4.8
Algeria	4.6
Rwanda	4.6
Myanmar	4.6
Angola	4.5
Liberia	4.4
Sierra Leone	4.4
Somalia	4.4
India	4.3
Sri Lanka	4.3
Yugoslavia (Serbia-Montenegro)	4.2
Turkey	4.2

Source: Gibney (2006).

these countries suffered under major conflict, i.e. a conflict resulting in at least one thousand battle-related deaths, is indicated with a black rectangle. It shows that between 1991 and 2000, a total of thirty-one states were affected by major conflicts. The African continent accounts for more than half of all cases. Asia was the second most affected world region, with seven countries suffering under at least one year of major armed conflict in the 1990s. All these conflicts were of an intra-state nature,[30] with the majority involving rebel groups that sought not secession, but an overthrow of the incumbent government. Years of intermediate armed conflict are marked in gray, while years of minor armed conflict are indicated by white boxes.

[30] The sole exception was the still-simmering border dispute between Eritrea and Ethiopia.

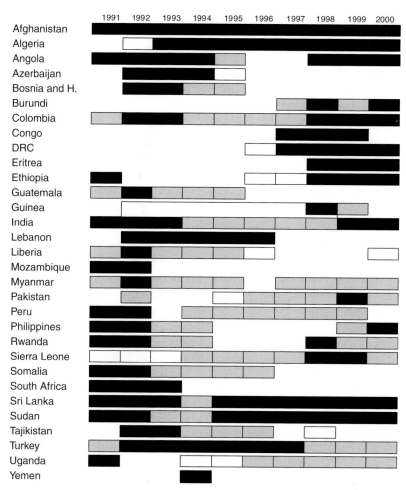

Figure 7.2 Countries affected by armed conflicts, 1991–2000
Source: Wallensteen and Sollenberg (2000); legend: black cell = major armed conflict; gray cell = intermediate armed conflict[31]; white cell = minor armed conflict.[32]

States suffering under an ongoing or recently concluded armed conflict had strong incentives to press the international community to adopt

---

[31] With more than one thousand battle-related deaths recorded during the course of the conflict, but fewer than one thousand in any given year.
[32] The number of battle-related deaths during the course of the conflict is below one thousand.

global control measures that would help curb the uncontrolled influx of small arms and light weapons.

Asymmetry in the distribution of costs and benefits

The above analysis of costs and benefits allows for a classification of states into four categories.

Exporting states that expected to end up as net payers form a first group. These states feared that tighter international SALW controls could curtail their ability to export small arms and light weapons from domestic production and, in particular, from surplus stockpiles. This concern was particularly acute if the pre-existing SALW regime was more lax than the measures proposed under the Program of Action. However, in none of these countries did small arms manufacturing account for an important share in national income or employment – very much in contrast to the strong dependency some drug or diamond-producing states experienced vis-à-vis the respective commodity. Some of these states, most notably the United States, Russia, and China, also weighed the potential political costs resulting from the loss in their sovereignty to transfer small arms to states and non-state actors at their discretion and often without public scrutiny. At the same time, they had little to gain directly from an effective international institution as they were spared high levels of political or private armed violence. In addition to the United States, Russia, and China, this first category also includes Central European arms exporters like Bulgaria, the Czech Republic, and Romania, along with Asian exporters such as India, Pakistan, South Korea, and Taiwan.

A second category is comprised of importing states which had reason to fear the restriction of the ability to import small arms and light weapons from sellers of their choice. Countries with a record of political terror, including many African states (e.g. Algeria, Liberia, Sudan) and a few Middle Eastern (e.g. Iraq) and Asian states (e.g. Myanmar, Sri Lanka), fall within this second category.

The third category includes states that expected a relatively neutral outcome from the establishment of a global SALW institution. They share three characteristics: first, these states were typically not directly affected by armed violence. Second, SALW transfers did not figure as an important tool for furthering foreign policy interests. Third, they were either not actively engaged in the manufacturing and export of small arms and light weapons or their extant SALW regulation was more stringent than global standards were likely to be. SALW producers with stringent regulation could even expect to emerge as net winners from a global SALW framework as it helped to level the playing field for their exporters. Many Western European states fall within this category as do a number of states in the Americas (e.g. Canada, Mexico), Asia (e.g. Japan), and Oceania (e.g. New Zealand and Australia).

The fourth and final category is made up of states that expected higher benefits than costs from an international institution to control the transfers of small arms and light weapons. These states are not significantly involved in the manufacturing of small arms and light weapons and rarely or never use SALW transfers as a tool for furthering foreign policy interests. They all suffer under recent or ongoing armed conflicts. For instance, Colombia advocated the creation of a strong global SALW institution hoping that this institution would make it harder for rebel groups like FARC and the AUC to obtain small arms and to misuse them in political acts of violence. For Bogotá, this expected benefit outweighed the potential cost that a strong international institution on SALW transfer controls might curtail the country's access to the global small arms market as a result of its poor human rights record. Other Latin American countries – for instance, Guatemala – were in a similar position, as were a large number of African states. Figure 7.3 illustrates the distribution of costs and benefits among these different categories of states.

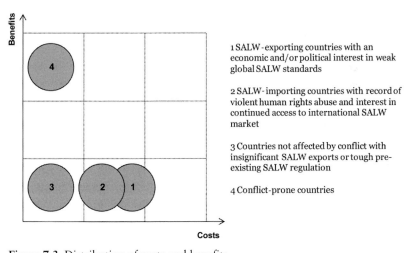

1 SALW-exporting countries with an economic and/or political interest in weak global SALW standards

2 SALW-importing countries with record of violent human rights abuse and interest in continued access to international SALW market

3 Countries not affected by conflict with insignificant SALW exports or tough pre-existing SALW regulation

4 Conflict-prone countries

Figure 7.3 Distribution of costs and benefits

Figure 7.3 reveals a moderate degree of cost–benefit asymmetry and thus asset specificity. The incentives for SALW-exporting states to dodge global SALW transfer controls were only moderate. Not a single one of them was strongly dependent on these exports for economic reasons – certainly not in comparison with the dependency some drug or diamond producers experienced. Foreign policy reasons for defending sovereignty over transfers in small arms and light weapons were probably of greater (but still not major) importance. States affected by intra-state wars hoped that the creation of a strong international SALW institution would help to curtail rebel groups' access to small arms and light weapons and thus to increase the prospects for peace. For these states, a potential shirking-induced breakdown of an international institution would have resulted in a great loss as their very existence was threatened by the uncontrolled influx of small arms and light weapons.

The case of small arms and light weapons is therefore highly comparable to that of conflict diamonds, which was also characterized by a moderate propensity of states to shirk and the high potential damage such shirking would entail. As in the previous chapter, the resulting overall degree of asset specificity is to be categorized as moderate.

7.2.2 Behavioral uncertainty

States suffering under armed conflicts were particularly worried about the moderate risk that a net payer might defy obligations if they were uncertain about their ability to detect acts of non-compliance. In the following section, I will argue that the drafters of the Program of Action faced an overall moderate degree of behavioral uncertainty resulting from moderately pronounced governance incapacity of key states, weak reliance on governmental monitoring, and moderate industry opacity.

Governance incapacity

The first element of behavioral uncertainty – governance incapacity – refers to non-compliance resulting from a state's insufficient capacity to implement a policy, even one that is genuinely endorsed. The question, therefore, arises: to what extent does the success of a global institution rely on substantive contributions by states with weak governance capacities? The success of international controls of small arms transfers depends on more than two dozen leading producer states which vary considerably with regard to the effectiveness of government and ability to uphold the rule of law and control corruption. Of the three leading small arms producers, only the United States in the year prior to the UN SALW Conference earned a positive average with regard to these three governance indicators. In the same year, China's average was slightly negative and Russia's more strongly negative, in that in both countries the rule of law was the weakest point. Among the SALW producers of medium importance, sixteen out of twenty-three received positive scores, and none underbid Russia's average score of –0.86. This situation contrasts starkly with that of narcotic drugs and money laundering. In the former case, all leading producer states suffered from an extremely limited governance capacity (reflected in their negative average scores), with Afghanistan and Myanmar being among the worst-governed countries in the world. In contrast, in the case of money laundering, countries with key financial centers competed for the top scores in governance capacity. The governance incapacity surrounding international SALW transfer controls compares best to that of conflict diamonds, which also depended on the compliance of some very well-governed states and some with poor implementation records. The SALW case, like that of conflict diamonds, therefore, presents a moderate degree of governance incapacity.

Relative reliance on governmental monitoring
The second element of behavioral uncertainty captures the idea that the risk of surreptitious shirking is reduced when civil society organizations are actively monitoring states' implementation efforts in the policy field in question. With regard to small arms transfers, low reliance on governmental self-reporting is particularly important as the deliberate misreporting by both importing and exporting states is more widespread than in any of the previously studied cases. For instance, the Small Arms Survey revealed a huge discrepancy between official figures on the size of many African countries' SALW stockpiles and its own estimates, with the former surpassing the latter by a wide margin (Small Arms Survey 2001). This discrepancy can largely be attributed to the desire of importing states to exaggerate their military capacities in order to deter potential attackers. Exporting states, on the other hand, may have strong incentives to under-report arms transfers, as some of these transfers might violate international embargoes or stir up political controversy at home. The US Iran–Contra affair of the mid-1980s is such a case in point.

Table 7.4 *Selected governance indicators for leading SALW producers, 2000*

Country	Government effectiveness	Rule of law	Control of corruption	Average
Major SALW producers				
China	−0.03	−0.44	−0.36	−0.27
Russia	−0.61	−1.04	−0.94	−0.86
United States	1.88	1.66	1.77	1.77
Medium SALW producers				
Austria	1.92	1.83	1.93	1.90
Belgium	1.70	1.40	1.54	1.55
Brazil	0.03	−0.28	0.09	−0.05
Bulgaria	0.11	−0.15	−0.24	−0.09
Czech Republic	0.77	0.68	0.26	0.57
Egypt	−0.24	−0.04	−0.37	−0.22
France	1.60	1.35	1.50	1.48
Germany	1.91	1.69	2.00	1.86
Hungary	0.94	0.81	0.69	0.81
India	−0.14	0.19	−0.33	−0.10
Israel	1.06	0.99	0.98	1.01
Italy	0.86	0.86	0.98	0.90
Korea, South	0.77	0.74	0.14	0.85
Pakistan	−0.65	−0.80	−0.76	−0.74
Poland	0.59	0.59	0.48	0.55
Romania	−0.38	−0.20	−0.34	−0.31
Singapore	2.28	1.43	2.25	1.98
South Africa	0.64	0.12	0.57	1.51
Spain	1.75	1.36	1.43	1.51
Switzerland	2.16	1.95	2.13	2.08
Taiwan	0.91	0.86	0.79	0.85
Turkey	−0.06	−0.06	−0.19	−0.10
United Kingdom	1.90	1.72	2.13	1.92

Source: World Bank (2008); Small Arms Survey (2001).

Given the incentives governments have to misreport SALW transfers, an important aspect of behavioral uncertainty was reduced in the late 1990s, when a number of think tanks, NGOs, and activist networks specializing in the small arms and light weapons *problématique* were established. The most respected among these specialized SALW civil society groups is undoubtedly the Small Arms Survey, founded in 1999 as an independent research project at the Graduate Institute of International Studies in Geneva, Switzerland. Its annual yearbook and working papers, as well as its database on SALW-related governmental position papers and voting and implementation records constitute one of the most important sources of information for the media, researchers, and government officials alike. Other leading think tanks in the field include the Norwegian Initiative on Small Arms (NISAT), the Belgian Groupe de recherche et d'information sur la paix et la sécurité (GRIP), the South African Institute for Security Studies (ISS), the Bonn International Center for Conversion (BICC), and the US American Center for Defense Information (CDI). Motivated by the success they achieved with the ban of anti-personnel landmines, a wide range of NGOs with broader agendas turned to small arms and light weapons as the new battle ground. Based on the model of the International Campaign to Ban Landmines, the International Action Network on Small Arms was launched in 1998 to serve as an umbrella organization to coordinate and synergize anti-SALW work. Today, IANSA counts more than 500 member organizations, including the heavyweights Oxfam, Amnesty International, and Human Rights Watch, and smaller NGOs like Saferworld and International Alert. Many of these NGOs are not only active as lobbyists, but often also conduct credible research on SALW-related topics.[33]

The strong role SALW-oriented NGOs and think tanks assume in collecting data on states' efforts to curb the uncontrolled proliferation and diversion of small arms and light weapons contrasts starkly with the situation found in the case of drugs or money laundering. Instead, the strong monitoring role of civil society organizations in the SALW-related issues strongly compares with the conflict diamonds case. Reliance on self-reporting is further reduced by information compiled in the United Nations Comtrade database.[34] While this database depends entirely on self-reported data, the fact that it publishes the

---

[33] E.g. under the catchy name "Biting the Bullet Project" (2001). Saferworld, International Alert, and the Department of Peace Studies at the University of Bradford have authored many assessment reports on states' SALW transfer controls.

[34] This database differentiates between seven different harmonized categories of arms and weapons.

data submitted by the importing and exporting state separately allows for the detection of discrepancies which may result from deliberate misreporting by either the importer or the exporter.[35]

The drafters of the PoA, like the instigators of the Kimberley Process, knew from the start that they could count on civil society monitoring and, to a lesser extent, on information provided by the UN Comtrade database. This low reliance on governmental monitoring significantly reduced the behavioral uncertainty they faced.

Industry opacity

Industry opacity is the third element that determines the risk of detection faced by a shirking state. Unlike the case of narcotic drugs, small arms and light weapons are characterized by the great importance of diversion from the legal to the illegal sector. Even the 10–20 percent of all small arms and light weapons traded illicitly originated in the plants of a legal manufacturer. In contrast to the diamond sector, governments had already taken a strong interest in controlling the production and trade in small arms and light weapons long before trafficking in these commodities was problematized in international policy circles. Governments' concern about the potential bearing of this sector on national security and foreign policy interests has had both positive and negative consequences for the transparency of this industry. On the one hand, it meant that governments had already subjected small arms and light weapons manufacturers to licensing and reporting requirements, which meant that at least vis-à-vis their home government these companies could not operate in total obscurity. On the other hand, governments' desire to control the sector often went so far that private ownership in SALW manufacturing companies was restricted. This, in turn, reduces industry transparency, since state-owned enterprises are not subject to the same disclosure requirements as are publicly

---

[35] The same logic holds true for the UN Register of Conventional Arms of 1991. This register compiles the data states submit on the imports and exports of conventional arms. The register does not include small arms, but Togo, which had previously attracted serious international criticism for its arms policy (Fowler report) decided to use its 2001 submission to the UN Register as an opportunity to demonstrate exemplary transparency and included voluntarily detailed data on its small arms holding in its report (Wezeman 2003). The possibility of institutionalizing such a disclosure of SALW transfers through the extension of the scope of this register to include SALW has been raised, but no definite decision has yet been reached (A/55/281 of August 9, 2000).

listed companies. For instance, China's entire defense industry, including small arms production, is government-controlled (Brem 2006). In Russia, the share of fully state-owned, partly state-owned,[36] and privately owned arms and weapons manufacturing companies is almost equally split (Brem 2006).

The resulting degree of industry opacity is therefore lower than in the case of narcotic drugs and diamonds, and comparable to the moderate transparency we found in the financial and near-financial sector.

In sum, the behavioral uncertainty associated with a global institution regulating SALW transfers is moderate, resulting from a moderate degree of governance incapacity and industry opacity and a weak reliance on governmental monitoring.

7.2.3 Environmental uncertainty

Environmental uncertainty was not of particular concern to the drafters of the Program of Action. When policymakers gathered at the UN SALW Conference in 2001 to agree on a common platform, the issue was no longer novel to them nor was it fraught with a high degree of uncertainty stemming from fast innovation cycles in the industry.

Novelty of policy issue

When the diffusion of small arms and light weapons was first raised within the UN in 1995 as a factor undermining human and national security, the topic was perceived as new and unfamiliar terrain by the overwhelming majority of policymakers. However, by the time the final version of the UN Program of Action was negotiated and adopted in July 2001, policymakers felt that they had gained sufficient experience and confidence in this matter. In only six years, this considerable reduction in the novelty of the issue can be attributed to three major reasons.

First, the SALW initiative was able to build upon the experience gained from disarmament and transfer control measures related to major conventional weapons. Unlike SALW, major conventional weapons had already become the topic of international negotiations during the Cold War. In the 1970s, the United States and the Soviet Union held four rounds of Conventional Arms Transfer (CAT) talks to agree on

---

[36] Typically in the form of joint-stock companies.

ways to limit the growing conventional arms trade. These talks prepared the ground for a number of bilateral and multilateral agreements that followed in subsequent years, the most important of which was the Treaty on Conventional Armed Forces in Europe, signed in 1990. The experience gained in relation to these initiatives on conventional weapons systems provided an important starting point for governments' SALW-related learning process. This knowledge transfer was facilitated by the fact that many of the desk officers who were assigned to work on the SALW dossier had previously worked on major conventional weapons issues.

A second building block for governments' SALW expertise was the movement to ban landmines, which had culminated in the signing of the Convention on the Prohibition of the Use, Stockpiling, Production, and Transfer of Anti-Personnel Mines and on their Destruction (Ottawa Convention) in 1997. Many government officials followed NGO representatives' migration path from the landmines issue to that of small arms and light weapons. The experienced gathered in the anti-landmine campaign was very relevant for desk officers later working on SALW, not only because landmines fall, technically speaking, in the small arms category but also – and *a fortiori* – because they had learned firsthand how to negotiate security-related issues with a great number of civil society representatives, including NGOs and industry officials.[37] Furthermore, desk officers working on SALW already knew many of the civil society representatives as the former drivers of the landmine campaign and therefore understood the new game's dynamic.

Third, by the time the PoA was concluded in July 2001, six major intergovernmental SALW initiatives outside the UN framework had already been implemented (see 7.1.2), thus providing practical experience in regulating small arms and light weapons transfers. Furthermore, in the three years preceding the UN SALW Conference, more than fifty high-level seminars and conferences had been held (Krause 2002: 253), giving policymakers a chance both to build up substantive expertise and to get to know their counterparts in person.

---

[37] The involvement of civil society representatives in policy discussions related to security issues was still largely uncharted territory in the 1990s and remains considerably less developed praxis than, for instance, in environmental policymaking. The above-mentioned Treaty on Conventional Armed Forces in Europe was a "governments only" affair.

Given the considerable experience government officials brought to the negotiation table of the UN SALW Conference in 2001, environmental uncertainty stemming from the novelty of the issue could be categorized as minor.

Innovativeness of criminal field

Fast-paced innovations are not the hallmark of small arms and light weapons development. The technology applied in the manufacturing of small arms and light weapons has barely changed over the past fifty years (Small Arms Survey 2003),[38] and there are few indications that the industry will find ways in the near future to move beyond the technological plateau on which it is currently stuck (Small Arms Survey 2003: 34). The few technological developments that have taken place simultaneously increase the necessity for state control and the potential effectiveness of such measures. The past decades witnessed the increase in the overall lethality of military small arms, resulting from improved laser aiming devices, penetration, and rate of fire. The industry also developed technological means to make gun control more effective for the future, such as so-called intelligent firearms, which can be discharged only by a given individual identified by, for instance, fingerprints. However, both these fronts of product innovation are only of subordinate relevance with respect to the core problems international initiatives on small arms and light weapons seek to solve, i.e. the misuse of these weapons in conflict regions. As the UN Panel of Governmental Experts on SALW noted in its 1997 report, the "majority of the small arms and light weapons being used in conflicts ... are not newly produced" (p. 14), but rather the "oldest and cheapest" (Small Arms Survey 2004).

The gray and black segments of the small arms and light weapons sector are slightly more dynamic, but the options they have at hand are largely limited to geographic displacement of production and trafficking routes. In response to tighter SALW transfer controls, criminals, rebels, or governments who see their access to the legal international arms market diminished can seek to boost domestic production. A

---

[38] For instance, the design of the 0.50 caliber Browning heavy machine gun, a staple in the inventories of military forces around the world, has largely remained untouched since it was first introduced early in the twentieth century (Hart Ezell 2002).

government may try to promote industrial production, but this strategy is likely to be very expensive. A new manufacturer will find it difficult to break into the highly competitive and largely saturated international market, and domestic demand is likely to be insufficient to allow the company to scale up production to cost-efficient levels. Consequently, domestic industrial production in countries without a pre-existing competitive player is unlikely to be sustainable without heavy subsidies. Domestic craft production, in contrast, is an option that governments, but also criminals and rebels, can turn to as a strategy of last resort. Although almost negligible in terms of global market share, craft production is a relevant factor in the problematic aspects of small arms and light weapons as this type of production predominantly takes place without regulatory oversight and in close proximity to countries threatened by armed conflict.[39]

SALW traffickers can seek to circumvent tighter regulation and control by rerouting shipments through weaker jurisdictions. Geographic displacement of trafficking routes is facilitated by the fact that small arms and light weapons can easily be disassembled, reassembled, and transported. However, in comparison to drugs and diamonds, they are harder to conceal, and their lower price-per-volume ratio makes it economically less attractive to adopt highly sophisticated concealment techniques.

The level of innovation associated with the small arms and light weapons issue is therefore comparable to the low level found in the case of conflict diamonds.

7.2.4 *Summary and implications for institutional design*

The above analysis reveals a moderate degree of asset specificity and of behavioral uncertainty for problems arising from an uncontrolled diffusion of small arms and light weapons. Consequently, these two variables point toward a moderate level of legalization as the optimal institutional design, as soft legalization would be insufficient to prevent

---

[39] Ghana, for instance, is an important artisan manufacturer. The West African nation allegedly produces up to 200,000 firearms annually (Vines 2005). Other countries with illicit craft production are Pakistan, South Africa, Chile, and the Philippines. Growing craft production is also reported from Senegal, Guinea, and Nigeria.

shirking by net payers, i.e. by states with a strong economic or political interest in unrestricted export opportunities for small arms and light weapons. The low level of environmental uncertainty found in the previous section does not counteract this pull toward the midsection of the soft–hard law continuum. Policymakers had sufficient knowledge about the SALW issue and experience in dealing with it on a national and regional basis at the time they gathered to draft the Program of Action, so there was no overriding need for a more flexible (thus softer) institution. Based on the analysis of all three problem constellation variables, an institution vested with a moderate degree of legalization seems to be most appropriate in catering for the governance problems arising from international cooperation on curbing the proliferation and diversion of small arms and light weapons.

Table 7.5 summarizes the core findings of the above analysis of the problem constellation underlying the small arms and light weapons issue. The remainder of this chapter sets out to determine whether the expected moderate level of legalization corresponds with the actual design of the United Nations Program of Action of 2001.

Table 7.5 *Summary assessment of the problem constellation underlying the trafficking in small arms and light weapons*

Problem attribute	Level	Argument
1. Asset specificity	**Moderate**	
A. Potential loss	Moderate	• Weak states hope that international controls of SALW trade will prevent the outbreak of new violence or make it easier and less fatal to curtail. • Some developed states hope that SALW controls will help prevent human catastrophe in developing countries that are the focus of their development assistance.
B. Propensity to shirk	Moderate	• Some import or export countries prefer opaque SALW transfers on national security or foreign policy grounds. • Some countries – in particular the US – oppose tighter controls for domestic politics reasons.

Table 7.5 (*cont.*)

Problem attribute	Level	Argument
2. Behavioral uncertainty	Moderate	
A. Governance incapacity	Moderate	• Countries with the largest SALW production are well governed. • Craft production takes place in poorly governed states.
B. Reliance on governmental monitoring	Low	• Several UN agencies compile data on SALW transfers in publicly available databases. • A large number of NGOs take an active interest in the topic, and a handful of NGOs and research centers engage in data collection and analysis.
C. Industry opacity	Moderate	• The most important production of SALW – in volume and value – takes place in countries where the SALW manufacturing and trading sector is regulated. • The industry leaders' role in the reselling of older SALWs is limited, with the main actors being established, less-regulated states.
3. Environmental uncertainty	Low	
A. Novelty of policy issue	Low	• Policymakers were able to build directly on the long international experience in regulating transfers of other types of weapons. • Policymakers can build directly on extant regional SALW initiatives.
B. Innovativeness of field	Low	• Technology applied in SALW production has not changed significantly over the past half century. • SALW used in most armed conflicts are of an older generation. • Increasing domestic production could potentially reduce the relevance of control measures targeting international trade.

7.3 Degree of legalization

I have just shown why a moderate degree of legalization would be the optimal design for an international SALW institution. But does the actual design of the UN Program of Action on Small Arms and Light Weapons of 2001 match this expectation? I will argue in the following section that it does not – in fact, the PoA remains consistently on the low end of the legalization spectrum. This mismatch challenges the validity of the framework put forward in this study and provides rich food for thought in the concluding chapter.

7.3.1 Obligation

The Program of Action is considerably less obliging than any of the three previously studied international institutions. It is not only non-binding, but also falls short of adopting compliance mechanisms for monitoring and enforcing the appropriate behavior of states.

Legal bindingness

The question of whether the final document should be legally or only politically binding was subject to considerable controversy among the negotiating parties. EU member states, Canada, Switzerland, and, to a lesser extent, member states of the Southern African Development Community lobbied hard in favor of a legally binding small arms treaty, in particular with regard to arms brokering and the marking and tracing of weapons. They were backed by the overwhelming majority of NGOs. However, this position was fiercely opposed by the United States, Russia, China, the Arab group, and a few other countries from the South (Small Arms Survey 2002). Eventually, the latter group prevailed, and the final agreement was designed to be solely of a politically binding nature. The legally non-binding nature of the agreement is reflected in its name "Program" rather than "Convention" or "Treaty." Binding formulations such as "shall" are carefully avoided. Quite tellingly, the sole exception where "shall" rather than "should" was used is in paragraph 11 of the preamble, which posits that the "territorial integrity or political unity of sovereign and independent States" *shall* be respected. In the rest of the document, considerably weaker formulations prevail, such as the declaratory, "We, the States participating in this Conference ... undertake the following measures" (e.g. section II paragraph 1), or the hortatory "States are encouraged to ..." (e.g. section III paragraph 12) and recommendation for action "on a voluntary basis." Also, the procedural aspects of the PoA point clearly in the direction of a non-binding agreement. It was adopted by consensus among the states participating at the conference and did not require a formal signing procedure. The PoA was formally welcomed by the UN General Assembly in its resolution A/RES/56/24 V of December 24, 2001. No ratification process followed on the national level. Furthermore, no provisions on procedural issues such as accession, ratification, reservations, and withdrawal typically included in legally binding treaties exist in the PoA, which confirms the non-binding character of the agreement. Finally, the PoA is not registered under Article 102 of the UN Charter.

Although the agreement presents nothing but a declaration of intent, it still includes a number of formulations that can be seen as safeguards, which states can use to excuse a certain behavior that seems to violate the recommendations contained in the PoA. For instance, the introduction of section II explicitly acknowledges the "different situations, capacities and priorities of States and regions," thus allowing for a non-uniform application of the forty-one measures suggested thereafter. Paragraph 23 of the national recommendations of section II points in the same direction when relativizing the call for international information exchange with the reference "in accordance with national practices." All these formulations weaken the tenacity of obligations.

Compliance mechanisms

The PoA also remains weakly legalized with respect to the second element of obligation, i.e. compliance mechanisms. It does not contain any reference to potential consequences of non-compliance, nor has the praxis that has developed around the PoA since its adoption made any progress on this issue.

Monitoring mechanisms are not developed much further either. All monitoring rests strictly upon government self-reporting.[40] All recommendations regarding the sharing of information come with considerable qualifications such as in paragraph 23 of section II, which asks states "to submit, *on a voluntary basis*, to relevant regional and

---

[40] This has, for instance, led to complaints that the list of National Points of Contacts compiled by the UN Department of Disarmament Affairs (DDA) based on information submitted by states contains a large number of National Points of Contact (NPCs) that are not yet operational or already defunct (IANSA 2006).

international organizations and *in accordance with their national practices*, information on *inter alia*, (a) small arms and light weapons confiscated or destroyed within their jurisdiction" (emphasis added) or in section III paragraph 13, which posits that "States are encouraged to exchange information *on a voluntary basis* on their national marking systems on small arms and light weapons" (emphasis added). These provisions contrast starkly with the Vienna Convention which requests that "Parties shall furnish ... information on ... particulars of cases of illicit traffic within their jurisdiction" (Article 20 Para 1).

The only legally binding instrument that in part compensates for the PoA's lack of monitoring and enforcement mechanisms are the arms embargoes enacted by the UNSC under Chapter 7 of the UN Charter. However, this option is rarely evoked and typically does not provide for effective monitoring and enforcement either.[41] UN arms embargoes are therefore not comparable to the extra-institutional monitoring and enforcement by the US Department of State from which international drug control (see 4.3.1) and – to a lesser extent – anti-money laundering measures (see 5.3.1) benefit.

In sum, the degree of obligation created by the Program of Action is very modest, as it is only politically binding, contains several safeguard-like clauses, and lacks real monitoring and enforcement mechanisms.

7.3.2 Precision

The UN Program of Action also remains at the lower end of the legalization spectrum with respect to the second dimension – precision. I will argue in the next two sections that the weak degree of determinacy in the agreement's formulations renders it almost impossible to assess its degree of coherence.

Determinacy
The PoA leaves wide margins for states to exercise discretion both as a result of a failure to provide definitions of central terms and the frequent use of ambiguous expressions.

---

[41] Among the few exceptions are the investigations into UNITA's unbroken ability to purchase arms (despite existing UN embargoes), the imposition of secondary sanctions against Liberia (both discussed in Chapter 6), and the inquiry into the parties "aiding and abetting the illegal acquisition of arms" in Rwanda's civil war.

The definition of small arms and light weapons is conspicuously absent. This non-inclusion of a definition for these two central terms resulted from unbridgeable differences among the participants of the UN SALW Conference on the scope of the definition. Whereas some states including India, Sri Lanka, and some African states lobbied in favor of using the definition developed by the 1997 Panel of Experts,[42] the United States – adopting the NRA's concern about any UN infringement on civilian possession of arms – advocated a more narrow definition focused on weapons of strictly military types. A third camp was against the inclusion of any definition altogether, arguing that precision was not necessary as the document was of a non-legally binding nature (Small Arms Survey 2002: 221). As these differences could not be settled by the end of the conference, the participating states adopted a Program of Action which evades defining its very object – small arms and light weapons. Since the UN Conference deliberately rejected the inclusion of a definition of these terms, the definitions provided in pre-existing agreements (e.g. OSCE) cannot be used to help to fill this lacuna. Similarly, the Program of Action fails to clarify terms that are fundamental to the stated motivation of the agreement. Like the UNGA resolution establishing the UN Register of Conventional Arms,[43] the PoA identifies in its preamble the "excessive and destabilizing accumulation of small arms and light weapons" in fragile regions (para 22(c)) as one of its key concerns. Again in full accord with the earlier UNGA resolution, the PoA refrains from specifying how in praxis it should be established whether a country is suffering under an excessive and destabilizing SALW accumulation.[44]

The second source of indeterminacy stems from the liberal use of vague clauses such as "where applicable," "as appropriate," or "where needed." The second formulation, "as appropriate," appears no less than thirty-eight times, which is on average in almost every other paragraph, with a disproportionate, but telling, accumulation in section II on steps to be undertaken by states on the national, regional, and global level.[45]

An illustrative example of the vague and non-obliging spirit of the Program of Action is paragraph 35 of section II, which declares that

---

[42] A/52/298 Section III.   [43] A/46/36L of December 9, 1991.

[44] Laurance, Wagenmakers, and Wulf (2005) provide an interesting argument as to why, in contrast, the Wassenaar Arrangement succeeded in agreeing on such a definition in December 1995 (Wassenaar Arrangement 1995).

[45] See also Krause (2002) on the vagueness of the PoA.

participating states will undertake measures "[t]o *encourage* the United Nations Security Council to *consider, on a case-by-case basis,* the inclusion, *where applicable,* of *relevant* provisions for disarmament, demobilization and re-integration in the mandates and budgets of peacekeeping operations" (emphases added).

Coherence

The PoA's degree of coherence is challenging to assess. The Program does not contain any paragraphs that are necessarily in contradiction with each other or with any other existing international agreement on small arms and light weapons. However, this seemingly high degree of coherence can largely be attributed to the PoA's low precision, as many formulations are vague enough to allow for both an interpretation which is in line, for instance, with the considerably more precise OSCE document on SALW as well as for an interpretation which deviates from it. The Program of Action seeks to ensure external coherence with the Firearms Protocol[46] and other "international legal instruments against terrorism and transnational organized crime" which states are encouraged "to consider ratifying or acceding" (section II para 38). These provisions are considerably weaker than the Forty Recommendations' call that "Countries should take immediate steps to become party to and implement fully the Vienna Convention, the Palermo Convention, and the 1999 United Nations International Convention for the Suppression of the Financing of Terrorism" (Recommendation 35).

Combining this assessment of determinacy and coherence, I conclude that the overall degree of precision adopted in the Program of Action is low.

7.3.3 Delegation

The Program of Action also makes few advances to strengthen the third legalization dimension, i.e. delegation. Section III paragraph 1 emphasizes explicitly that "the primary responsibility for solving the problems

---

[46] "[R]ecognizing that the Protocol against the Illicit Manufacturing of and Trafficking in Firearms, Their Parts and Components and Ammunition, supplementing the United Nations Convention against Transnational Organized Crime, establishes standards and procedures that complement and reinforce efforts to prevent, combat and eradicate the illicit trade in small arms and light weapons in all its aspects" (Preamble para 20).

associated with the illicit trade in small arms and light weapons in all its aspects falls on all States." This emphasis on states' individual responsibility contrasts with the equally non-self-executory Vienna Convention, which creates more of a shared commitment by stressing in its preamble "that eradication of illicit traffic is a *collective* responsibility of all States and that, to that end, coordinated action within the framework of international cooperation is necessary" (emphasis added). The two agreements have in common, however, that neither creates new entities with the mandate to control SALW and drugs, respectively, but rather build on pre-existing UN bodies. Specifically, the Program of Action refers to the UNGA (section IV para 1) and the UN Secretary General and the UN Department of Disarmament Affairs (DDA)[47] (section II para 33), but the functional role and independence is very limited.

Independence

Like the Vienna Convention, the UN body entrusted with an – albeit considerably more limited – executive function holds the status of an office (the Department of Disarmament Affairs)[48] headed by a director of the rank of an undersecretary general. Like the UNODC, the DDA derives some independence from the fact that its personnel is recruited through regular UN hiring procedures and is not appointed by states. However, in both cases, this independence-enhancing procedure is offset by the fact that the two offices largely depend on voluntary contributions by member states.[49] The two policy issues differ from each other with respect to the relative prominence they claim in the respective UN office's mandate. While drug control is at the center stage of the UNODC's work, small arms and light weapons constitute a minor part of the DDA's overall mission.[50] The relatively weak status of SALW on the DDA's agenda is a direct function of policymakers' limited willingness to support the further development and implementation of

---

[47] Also referred to as the UN Office of Disarmament Affairs.

[48] This office was re-established on January 1, 1998, six years after it had been dissolved.

[49] E.g. the government of the Czech Republic, which has often been accused of irresponsible arms transfers, donated US$102 million to the DDA in 2004 (IANSA 2006).

[50] The DDA also has a mandate vis-à-vis landmines and weapons of mass destruction. SALW fall in the domain of the DDA's Conventional Arms Branch, which, *inter alia*, is also overseeing the UN Register of Conventional Arms.

SALW control measures. In fact, the Program of Action states explicitly that the DDA has to assume its SALW related functions "within existing resources" (section II para 33). This provision is particularly constraining given the fact that the DDA is the smallest of all offices under the Secretariat.

The Disarmament Commission, the counterpart of the Commission on Narcotic Drugs, assumes no official role vis-à-vis small arms and light weapons, and no equivalent to the INCB exists in the SALW domain. The sole policymaking body on SALW is the UNGA sponsored conference of 2001 and the review conference of 2006, where all nations have a vote and decisions are adopted if supported by a two-thirds majority.

As in the case of conflict diamonds, the prominence of small arms and light weapons on the international policy agenda was largely driven by NGOs' persistent lobbying efforts. While recognizing the desirability of close cooperation with civil society organizations,[51] the UN Program of Action does not assign an official role in decision-making. Krause (2002) argues, in fact, that many policymakers pressed successfully for a curtailing of NGOs' direct involvement in the Conference, wary that the Ottawa process (resulting in a legally binding treaty banning anti-personnel landmines) had set a problematic precedent. Participation and access rights of NGOs, therefore, were defined along more traditional UN lines. For instance, civil society representatives were granted access only to open sessions – and then confined to separated galleries – but not to "negotiation sessions." Because of this weak mechanism for officially including NGO and industry representatives in SALW-related decision-making, civil society cannot be seen as a source of independence under the PoA. In this regard, the Program of Action contrasts significantly with the Kimberley Process which boosts its overall low level of delegation by assigning important and direct functions to civil society.

The Program of Action – or more specifically, its failure to address a number of key areas – motivated a dozen states and NGOs to deepen their cooperation on selected issues outside the PoA framework. Four major initiatives have been launched since the 2001 Conference addressing issues that proved too controversial to be included in the Program

---

[51] Preamble para 16, section II para 20, section II para 40, section III para 2, section III para 18, section IV para 2(c).

of Action. These initiatives vary with regard to their official association with the UN and the role assigned to NGOs. Directly under the UN umbrella and with greater constraints on NGO involvement is the Group of Governmental Experts on Tracing Illicit Small Arms and Light Weapons, established pursuant to the General Assembly resolution 56/24 V of December 24, 2001. Simultaneously, the UK government sponsored the Transfer Control Initiative,[52] while NGOs, governments,[53] the UN, and several regional organizations teamed up in January 2003 to form the Consultative Group Process.[54] The NGO community plays the strongest role in the fourth initiative, which seeks to establish a binding International Arms Trade Treaty. The Control Arms Campaign, an umbrella organization of more than 600 civil society organizations, is the motor of this process, which also enjoys the official backing of the governments of the United Kingdom, Tanzania, and Finland (Saavedra 2007). However, none of these initiatives – with perhaps the sole exception of the earlier mentioned Group of Governmental Experts[55] – derives its mandate from the PoA. Thus they cannot be seen as examples of delegation.

Centralization
The DDA is the only body that assumes some practical functions in the implementation of the Program of Action. Before the adoption of the PoA, the DDA's Conventional Arms Branch had already assumed the role as the lead agency of the Coordinating Action on Small Arms (CASA) mechanism,[56] which seeks to coordinate action by the various UN agencies working in this field. The PoA explicitly mandates the DDA to "collect and circulate data and information provided by States" on their implementation efforts. The DDA with regard to this function has been referred to as a "post office," as it does barely more than pass on the implementation

---

[52] This initiative works with governments on the regional level to build a consensus on the need to strengthen control on SALW transfers (Saavedra 2007).

[53] Over thirty governments (Saavedra 2007).

[54] The focus of this process is to develop common ground on the restrictions on transfers of SALW to non-state actors and to develop a set of decision criteria for states in their decision on whether to authorize SALW transfers (IANSA 2006).

[55] Section II paras 10 and 11 of the PoA make explicit reference to the need to strengthen "international cooperation and assistance to examine technologies that would improve the tracing and detection of illicit trade in small arms and light weapons."

[56] Established by the secretary general in 1998.

reports it receives from governments. While the UNODC compiles voluminous annual reports exclusively dedicated to the latest trends in illicit drugs based on its own analysis of data information received from member states and field offices, the DDA dedicates only ten pages of its 500-page long annual report to SALW. Outside the mandate directly defined by the PoA, the DDA has also been engaged in organizing biennial meetings and the review conference that the PoA called for as well as regional meetings (DDA 2007).[57] Given the DDA's constraint in assuming its SALW mandate "within existing resources," it is not too surprising that the scope of its functions has remained very limited.

As mentioned previously, the only rule-making body under the PoA is the Conference of 2001 and the Review Conference of 2006. Such an infrequent meeting schedule already limits the PoA's decision-making capacity severely, but the actual outcome of the 2006 Review Conference fell even below these already-low expectations. The Program of Action does not contain any provisions on dispute settlement.

In sum, the Program of Action remains at the very low end of delegation both with respect to the centralization of functions and the independence of the bodies involved.

7.3.4 Summary of actual institutional design and implications for model validity

The above analysis has shown that the overall degree of legalization enshrined in the UN Program of Action on Small Arms and Light Weapons must be qualified as low. The PoA remains a soft law agreement with respect to all three dimensions – obligation, precision, and delegation. The agreement's failure to establish stronger forms of legalization, more so than the exclusion of particularly controversial issues, was the main reason for the widespread dissatisfaction among NGO representatives who had lobbied hard for a legally binding agreement and who decried the outcome of the UN Conference on Small Arms and Light Weapons as a Program of *Inaction*. This view is shared by the UN High-Level Panel on Threat, Challenges, and Change, which argues that "efforts to limit the widespread availability of small arms and light weapons have barely moved beyond rhetoric to action" (2004: 36). Table 7.6 summarizes this assessment and its argumentative building blocks.

---

[57] Section IV para 1(b) and section IV para 1(a), respectively.

Table 7.6 *Summary assessment of the level of legalization of the UN Program of Action on Small Arms and Light Weapons*

Design Element	Level	Argument
1. Obligation	**Low**	
A. Legal bindingness	Low	
a. Language	Low	• The name of the agreement – i.e. "Program of Action" – strongly suggest its legally non-binding character. • The PoA relies exclusively on voluntary, hortatory formulations.
b. Procedural provisions	Low	• The PoA was not subject to domestic procedures required for the adoption of legally binding international agreements. • The PoA is not registered under UN Charter Article 102.
c. Tenacity of obligation	n/a	• As a legally non-binding agreement, the PoA does not contain procedural provisions that allow states to reduce unilaterally an agreement's degree of obligation through reservations, withdrawal, etc.
B. Compliance mechanisms	Low	
a. Monitoring	Low	• The submission of information on implementation efforts is encouraged but expressly voluntary.
b. Enforcement	Low	• Neither the PoA nor subsequent praxis has developed mechanisms for addressing non-compliance.
2. Precision	**Low**	
A. Determinacy	Low	• Key terms (notably "small arms," "light weapons") are not defined in the PoA. • Vague terms are frequently used, e.g. "appropriate" appears in half of all paragraphs. • The UN does not provide an official interpretation commentary to the PoA.
B. Coherence	Low	• Internal and external coherence cannot be assessed because of insufficient determinacy.

Table 7.6 (*cont.*)

Design Element	Level	Argument
3. Delegation	**Low**	
A. Independence	Low	
a. Human resources	Low	• DDA assumes a very limited SALW-related role, and the PoA states explicitly that the DDA has to carry out its SALW-related functions "within existing resources."
b. Financial resources	Low	• Same as above.
c. Decision-making	Moderate	• Decisions are taken by a two-thirds majority. All UN member states have a vote.
B. Centralization	Low	
a. Rule-making	Low	• SALW norms are developed at infrequent, dedicated conferences convened by the UNGA, namely the 2001 SALW Conference and the 2006 Review Conference.
b. Implementation	Low	• The DDA's role is limited to the collation and circulation of information which states provide voluntarily.
c. Dispute resolution	Low	• Neither the PoA nor subsequent praxis provides for mechanisms for resolving disputes among participating states.

The PoA's reliance on soft legalization contrasts with the design expectations I derived from the analysis of the problem constellation underlying the global diffusion of SALW. The moderate level of asset specificity and behavioral uncertainty combined with a low level of environmental uncertainty suggested a moderate degree of legalization as the optimal institutional design to cater for the specific governance risks associated with a problem of this type. The expected design is thus more strongly legalized than the actual architecture of the Program of Action. This mismatch between design prediction and outcome casts serious doubt on the explanatory power of the transaction cost economics model adopted in this study. The most likely explanation of this apparent failure of the design model is the as yet overlooked power factor. As mentioned in the introduction to this chapter, many of the most powerful states were fiercely opposed to the creation of a global institution regulating the transfer of small arms and light weapons. They felt that the resulting indirect costs far outweighed the benefits they could expect from an effective SALW institution. These states lobbied as hard against the inclusion of substantive provisions touching upon the issues most sensitive for them (e.g. human rights, civilian possession) as they did against the design of an institution with a sufficient degree of legalization to compel compliance. If – and how – power can be integrated in this study's problem-oriented design model will be the subject of the Conclusion, which explores in greater detail the model's promises and limitations as revealed in its application in the four case studies.

8 | Conclusion

This study set out to test the power of a transaction cost economics based model in explaining the observed variance in the design of international institutions. In three of the four cases examined in the previous chapters, the analysis of the particular constellation underlying a trafficking-related problem did indeed lead to the right design prediction. This apparent success gives little reason for complacency. In the three cases where the expected design corresponded with the actual design the impact of problem constellation variables on design outcomes may be spurious, and the case where the model's prediction failed gives us even stronger reasons to re-examine the validity of the model's underlying assumptions.

Transaction cost economics theory, like other functionalist design theories, rests on the assumption that rational actors endow an international institution with the substance and form that are most pertinent for dealing with the governance challenges arising from a particular problem constellation, so that the institution can effectively solve the problem for which it was created. This assumption rests on two fundamental premises. First, the crafters of an international institution are rational, purposeful actors. Second, they establish an institution as a means to facilitate effective international cooperation on a policy problem. Both of these assumptions have been criticized for various reasons. The goal of this concluding chapter is therefore to examine the robustness of this study's problem-oriented design model in the light of this criticism and to explore how its reach may be expanded by accommodating elements of alternative design theories. Before entering this new territory, I will recapitulate the results of the four cases studied in the preceding chapters and show how much explanatory power we were able to get with this study's problem-tailored design model in its original specifications.

8.1 Summary of results

8.1.1 Degree of legalization

As discussed in the Introduction, the cases covered in this study were purposefully selected to span the full spectrum from high to low levels of legalization.

The Vienna Convention on narcotics trafficking represents an example of a highly legalized international institution with a high degree of obligation and precision coupled with a moderate degree of delegation. It is legally binding and does not make excessive use of escape clauses, reservations, or other types of procedural provisions to weaken the agreement's degree of obligation. Its compliance mechanisms do not share the same level of stringency. The Vienna Convention's sanctioning capacity relies to a considerable extent on the "stick" wielded by the US decertification process. The Vienna Convention attains such an overall high level of precision because of its strong emphasis on coherence with pre-existing international institutions and as a result of explicit recognition from subsequently created international institutions. This strong coherence compensates for the fact that the Vienna Convention makes moderately frequent use of imprecise terms. Finally, the Convention delegates some executive and, to a lesser extent, rule-making tasks to a number of pre-existing anti-drug bodies within the UN family.

The Forty Recommendations on money laundering and the Kimberley Process on rough diamonds both display a moderate level of legalization. These two international institutions deviate from the traditional international law model typified by the Vienna Convention in two important respects. First, both the Forty Recommendations and the Kimberley Process do without the support of a legally binding agreement. They compensate for this weakening effect on obligation through unusually stringent monitoring and sanctioning mechanisms which go beyond those provided by the Vienna Convention. Second, neither the Forty Recommendations nor the Kimberley Process relies on an intergovernmental organization for rule-making, implementation, or dispute settlement. Instead, they content themselves with the mainly administrative support offered by a small secretariat that lacks an independent legal personality. They prefer to handle most matters in plenary meetings – an option that is viable thanks to the circumscribed number of members.

This combination of legal non-bindingness, strong compliance mechanisms, and low levels of delegation presents a design configuration that has been gaining popularity in recent years. Some scholars praise the design innovation as a promising way to foster effective international cooperation in an era when it is has become increasingly hard to ratify legally binding conventions because of paralyzed parliaments and growing distrust in international "mega-bureaucracies" (Klabbers 2001; Shelton 2000). The Kimberley Process deviates from the traditional institutional architecture even further by granting non-state actors a prominent role in monitoring, rule-making, and implementation.

The Program of Action on Small Arms and Light Weapons, finally, falls back into the traditional design mold international policymakers prefer whenever they try to mask fundamental disagreements. It embodies the low end of the legalization spectrum, with obligation, precision, and delegation all remaining at low levels, thus allowing governments to continue their business as usual.

Table 8.1 summarizes the detailed assessment of the degree of legalization found in the four international institutions on global trafficking studied in the previous chapters.

8.1.2 Problem constellation

The level of legalization found in three out of the four international institutions summarized above corresponds with the design predictions I reached based on the analysis of the constellations underlying the respective policy problem (see Table 8.2).

In the case of drugs, the postulated high degree of legalization is matched by the actual hard law design of the Vienna Convention. Because of the high degree of asset specificity and behavioral uncertainty, I postulated that hard law would be best suited for mitigating the governance challenges arising from states' strong incentives to shirk and their ability to do so with little risk of detection. I also classified money laundering as having a high degree of asset specificity even though the threat posed by money laundering is perceived as less existential than the drug menace. However, the degree of behavioral uncertainty is only moderate, reducing the necessity of hard law, and the high degree of environmental uncertainty also makes hard law less desirable. The moderate degree of legalization found in the Forty Recommendations presents the best design response for this type of problem constellation.

Table 8.1 *Summary of legalization of four international institutions against global trafficking*

Indicator	Drugs	Money laundering	Diamonds	SALW
1. Obligation	**High**	**Moderate**	**Moderate**	**Low**
A. Legal bindingness	High	Low	Low	Low
a. Language	High	Low	Low	Low
b. Procedural provisions	High	Low	Low	Low
B. Tenacity of obligation	Moderate	n/a	n/a	n/a
C. Compliance mechanisms	Moderate	High	High	Low
a. Monitoring	High	High	High	Low
b. Sanctions	Moderate	High	High	Low
2. Precision	**High**	**Moderate**	**High**	**Low**
A. Determinacy	Moderate	Moderate	High	Low
B. Coherence	High	High	High	n/a
3. Delegation	**Moderate**	**Low**	**Low**	**Low**
A. Independence	Moderate	Moderate	Low	Low
a. Human resources	High	Moderate	Low	Low
b. Financial resources	Moderate	High	Low	Low
c. Decision-making	Moderate	Low	Moderate	Moderate
B. Centralization	Moderate	Low	Low	Low
a. Rule-making	Moderate	Low	Moderate	Low
b. Implementation	High	Moderate	Low	Low
c. Dispute resolution	Low	Low	Low	Low
Overall legalization	**High**	**Moderate**	**Moderate**	**Low**

The hybrid design of the Kimberley Process also matches the design expectation derived from a problem constellation marked by a moderate degree of asset specificity, behavioral uncertainty, and environmental uncertainty. The only deviant case is the international institution on small arms and light weapons, which turned out to be less legalized than the problem constellation analysis suggested as optimal. Instead of the proposed moderate degree of legalization, the PoA remains firmly rooted in the soft law tradition.

Table 8.2 *Summary assessment of problem constellation underlying four cases of global trafficking*

Indicator	Drugs	Money laundering	Diamonds	SALW
1. Asset specificity	**High**	**High**	**Moderate**	**Moderate**
A. Potential loss	High	Moderate	High	Moderate
B. Propensity to shirk	High	High	Moderate	Moderate
2. Behavioral uncertainty	**High**	**Moderate**	**Moderate**	**Moderate**
A. Governance incapacity	High	Low	Moderate	Moderate
B. Relative reliance on governmental monitoring	High	High	Low	Moderate
C. Industry opacity	High	Moderate	High	Moderate
3. Environmental uncertainty	**Low**	**High**	**Moderate**	**Low**
A. Novelty of policy issue	Low	Moderate	High	Low
B. Innovativeness	Moderate	High	Low	Low
Expected level of legalization	**High**	**Moderate**	**Moderate**	**Moderate**
Match between expected and actual design?	**Yes**	**Yes**	**Yes**	**No**

8.2 Rationality

In the next two sections, I will revisit the two central assumptions of this study's problem-tailored design model – rationality and instrumentality – and subject them to the various forms of criticism that the theoretical literature has to offer. My goal thereby is not to provide a comprehensive account of these alternative explanations or to test them in a systematic way. Rather, I want to explore if and how this study's problem-tailored design model can be reconciled with seemingly contradictory theories and also to show how subjecting it to this scrutiny reveals promising ways for expanding the model's explanatory reach. I will start with the re-examination of the rationality assumption and then move on to scrutinize the instrumentality assumption (see 8.3).

8.2.1 Bounded rationality

The first group of critics share with the theory underlying this study's problem-tailored design model the assumption that policymakers do indeed strive to design international institutions that are effective in solving the problems they were created to tackle. They deviate from the theory advanced here mainly by questioning the rationality assumption.

Herbert Simon was among the first scholars to counter the growing popularity of rational theories on policymaking with reference to the limitations of human intelligence. He pointed out that people (and by extension, states) intend to behave rationally but the "capacity of the human mind for formulating and solving complex problems is very small compared with the size of the problems whose solution is required for objectively rational behavior in the real world – or even for a reasonable approximation to such objective rationality" (Simon 1957: 198). To describe these intellectual limitations Simon coined the term "bounded rationality." Bounded rationality can affect policymakers' ability to properly frame the problem, to identify the most effective and efficient solutions, and to anticipate institutional effects (Pierson 2004).

However, the fact that human rationality is bounded rather than absolute does not deal a fatal blow to the rational design argument presented in this study. In fact, transaction cost economics theory (e.g. Williamson 1996) and many functionalist theories in international relations explicitly endorse this proposition (e.g. Allison and Zelikow 1999; Hart, Stern, and Sundelius 1997; Janis 1983; Jervis 1975; Keohane 1984; Steinbruner 1974; Vertzberger 1990). As David Lake (1999: 41) argues, bounded rationality does not fundamentally undermine rational design models as long as misperceptions are not systematically biased.

Furthermore, this study's problem-tailored design model and many other functionalist approaches explicitly build bounded rationality into their model by including a variable that captures policymakers' uncertainty about the causal mechanisms underlying a problem they seek to tackle and about the range of feasible instruments ("environmental uncertainty"). This variable suggests that a low level of legalization is the best design solution for institutions dealing with poorly understood problems. Soft law arrangements provide the institution with the necessary flexibility to adjust to new insights that policymakers gain on a learning-by-doing basis or from scientific progress. Bounded rationality may, of course, also affect policymakers' ability to properly assess the degree of environmental uncertainty they are facing. Policymakers may, for instance, assume that they have a much better grasp of a problem and its solution than they in fact do. Consequently, they may propagate a design solution that is harder than a correct analysis of the underlying problem constellation would suggest. However, Lake's argument about the presumed lack of bias in the policymakers' miscalculations also applies to this particular type of bounded rationality.

The negative consequences of imperfect rationality are in part mitigated by a process that can be described as evolutionary rationality. Williamson (1985: 236) and others argue that even if some institutions are poorly designed at their inception, they will eventually be reformed or supplanted by more effective institutions. Thelen (2004; also Pierson 2000) criticizes this assumption, pointing out that the competitive force guaranteeing the survival of the "fittest" (or "best designed") institution in the marketplace does not exist in the political sphere, allowing non-functional institutions to persist indefinitely. Thelen is certainly right in her observation that institutional competition is stronger in the market-place than in international politics, but as the growing body of literature on regime complexes (Alter and Meunier 2007; Raustiala and Victor 2004) and "forum shopping" (Drezner 2006; Hafner-Burton 2005; Helfer 1999) highlights, the difference between the two spheres may be smaller than she acknowledges. When a new policy problem has emerged on the international agenda requiring an institutionalized solution, policymakers have chosen to assign the new problem to a pre-existing institution or to use a pre-existing institution as the blue-print for a new institution (see the discussion on isomorphism below). It does not seem too far-fetched to assume that the track record of pre-existing institutions in solving the problems they were created to tackle is a factor in policymakers' institutional choice. This selection process provides a positive feedback mechanism for well-designed, effective institutions, even if the elimination of non-functional[1] institutions may take longer than in the marketplace. Bounded rationality and the "stickiness" of institutions can therefore be reconciled with the problem-tailored design model presented here without requiring any major revisions of the model's underlying assumptions.

---

[1] I will later discuss the various functions an institution may serve that are not related to its official purpose, i.e. to the solving of a particular policy problem. As long as the institution continues to fulfill its unofficial mandate and the power and interest structure of the enacting coalition remains unchanged, the institution will persist even if it is not particularly apt in solving the policy problem for which it was officially created.

8.2.2 Isomorphism

A more fundamental critique of rational design models comes from scholars who question not only the *ability* of humans to think rationally but even their *inclination* to try to devise a rational solution. They argue along with March and Olsen (1989) that actors may be guided more by a logic of appropriateness, i.e. by considerations that emphasize the importance of a choice's congruence with preconceived notions of identity rather than interests, or by a logic of consequences, i.e. a rational calculation based on anticipated effects and prior preferences. For instance, Hall and Taylor (1996: 946–947) argue against the instrumentality assumption in the following words:

Many of the institutional forms and procedures used by modern organizations were not adopted simply because they were most efficient for the tasks at hand, in line with some transcendent "rationality". Instead, they ... should be seen as culturally-specific practices, akin to the myths and ceremonies devised by many societies, and assimilated into organizations, not necessarily to enhance their formal means-end efficiency, but as a result of the kind of processes associated with the transmission of cultural practices more generally.

Within "new institutionalism," this line of reasoning is particularly popular among sociological and historic institutionalists. They highlight the importance of "institutional isomorphism," which DiMaggio and Powell (1983: 149) define as a "constraining process that forces one unit in a population to resemble other units that face the same set of environmental conditions." Lodge (2002) differentiates between two different directions in which policymakers can turn for isomorphic inspiration: they may emulate the design of institutions within the same sector as established in other countries, of other levels of government (global, regional, national, sub-national), or of previous periods of time. He captures this form of design emulation with the term "domain-oriented isomorphism." Alternatively, policymakers may absorb contemporary debates on governance structures in general and seek to implement these ideas in the design of a new institution (paradigm-oriented isomorphism). The cases studied here provide examples of both types of isomorphism at work.

The Vienna Convention presents a prototypical example of domain-oriented isomorphism. It builds directly on the long design tradition within international drug control that The Hague Convention spearheaded in 1912. This tradition relies heavily on binding international

law and on the support of a formal international governmental organization (first the League of Nations and later the UN). Also, in terms of
substance, the Vienna Convention largely follows a "more of the same"
approach, with many of its provisions almost verbal transcripts of the
1961 and 1971 Conventions.

In contrast, the Kimberley Process epitomizes the concept of
"paradigm-oriented isomorphism." It is unprecedented in the way it
operates without relying on a legally binding convention or international governmental organization and includes both government
representatives and non-state actors. All these features make the
Kimberley Process look like a 1:1 implementation of governance ideas
that emerged in the 1990s under the headings "global governance,"[2]
"global public policy,"[3] and "multistakeholder process."[4]

The design of the Forty Recommendations of the Financial Action
Task Force on money laundering and the UN Program of Action on
Small Arms and Light Weapons are harder to explain from an isomorphist perspective. The FATF was established almost before the ink
of the signatures under the Vienna Convention had dried. Despite this
temporal proximity, the governance structure of the Financial Action
Task Force presents a stark deviation from the Vienna Convention's
unbroken continuation of the classic twentieth-century design approach
with its strong reliance on formal (i.e. legally binding) conventions and
on intergovernmental organizations. The FATF presents a blueprint of
what Slaughter sees in both empirical and normative terms as the "New
World Order" – a world governed by government networks. Her
definition of such governance arrangements as "networks of national
government officials who come together on a regular basis to exchange
information, coordinate activity, and adopt policies to address common
problems on a global scale" (2004b) could hardly capture the essence of
the FATF's set-up more pointedly. The institutional design difference
between the Vienna Convention and the FATF can in part be explained

---

[2] E.g. the report of the United Nations Commission on Global Governance of 1994.

[3] Which Reinicke (1999: 44) defines as "loose alliances of government agencies,
international organizations, corporations, and elements of civil society, such as
nongovernmental organizations, professional associations, or religious groups,
that join together to achieve what none can accomplish on its own."

[4] E.g. defined by Hemmati (2002: 19) as a process that "aim[s] to bring together all
major stakeholders in a new form of common decision finding (and possibly
decision-making) on a particular issue."

by domain-oriented isomorphism. The FATF's set-up as a government network largely resembles the design of the Basel Committee, a relatively informal[5] platform for regular exchange and discussion among governors of the central banks of G-10 countries. The Basel Committee presented itself as a plausible design model, not least because it was one of the few international bodies with expertise in money laundering.[6] While the Basel Committee did indeed present a plausible design model, it was not the only one the instigators of the FATF had at hand. It would not have been far-fetched either to associate the new AML institution with the UN drug control organs – after all, it was the Vienna Convention that first introduced money laundering as a criminal offense in international law.[7] It would also make sense to connect the new AML institution with the Council of Europe Convention on Laundering, Search, Seizure, and Confiscation of the Proceeds of Crime, which was already well advanced in its drafting process when the FATF was established, or to associate the FATF with Interpol's specialized branch for "Funds Derived from Criminal Activities"[8] which had been established in 1986. All of these rejected alternative arrangements fall within the mold of classical international law design. We can therefore speculate that the choice of the only non-formalistic (Klabbers 2001) design model, i.e. the Basel Committee, was at least as much determined by paradigm-oriented isomorphism as by domain-oriented isomorphism. It may also be seen as an example of evolutionary rationality at work, as discussed in the previous section.

Isomorphism does not have to be incompatible with the (bounded) rationality and instrumentality assumption upon which this problem-tailored design model is based. Only relatively modest assumptions, therefore, are required to align design expectations derived from

---

[5] Like the FATF, the Basel Committee is not an intergovernmental organization, and it does not draft its decisions as legally binding conventions.

[6] N.B.: the Basel Committee had published the Basel Statement of Principles for the Prevention of Criminal Use of the Banking System for the Purpose of Money Laundering just days before the adoption of the Vienna Convention (see Chapter 5).

[7] As mentioned in Chapter 5, anti-money laundering is a child of the global war on drugs. This affiliation is still reflected in the organizational structure of the US State Department where the same unit is responsible for assessing countries' compliance with international drug control norms and evaluating their vulnerability to money laundering activities.

[8] This branch is commonly referred to by its French acronym FOPAC.

institutional isomorphism with those formulated based on the problem-tailored design model developed here or in other functionalist theories.

Domain-oriented isomorphism results in optimal design solutions if we assume a sufficient degree of similarity among the constellation of problems within a certain domain. For instance, policymakers' decision to replicate the architecture of the 1961 and the 1971 UN Drug Conventions in the Vienna Convention may well have been an intellectual shortcut based on ideas about appropriateness. However, given the fulfillment of two conditions, the outcome would have been the same had they engaged in instrumental means–end calculations. First, the design of the two earlier conventions has to be assumed to be appropriate for solving the problems targeted by each of these two conventions. Second, the problem constellation of the Vienna Convention is sufficiently similar to the problem constellation underlying the 1961 Convention and the 1971 Convention. This study's problem-tailored design model is well positioned to assess whether a sufficient degree of problem congruency existed to justify such a design transfer.

Similarly, it seems reasonable to assume that new paradigms emerge in response to fundamental shifts in the constellation of problems. It has become commonplace to argue that globalization has radically changed the nature of the policy problems facing the world today (e.g. Reinicke 1997; Slaughter 2004a). If this is the case, paradigm-oriented isomorphism can well lead to institutional designs that are appropriate for dealing with the particular governance challenges arising from these new types of problems. As Slaughter argues, "international institutions created in the late 1940s ... are outdated and inadequate to meet contemporary challenges" (2004a: 8). Today's increasing anti-formalism and move away from big government and comprehensive grand schemes as observed by Klabbers (2001) may thus not simply be the product of an irrational fashion whim but present a rational response to changing circumstances.

Isomorphist scholars highlight an additional reason explaining why policymakers may copy the design of existing institutions: "economies of scale." The homogenization of institutional designs offers an important advantage in that it reduces design costs and enhances the interoperability of these institutions. For instance, Blais and Massicotte (1997) found in their global survey of legislative electoral institutions that most former British colonies adopted electoral systems and rules rooted in their colonial culture rather than designed to meet the specific requirements of the local setting. Pierson (2004) sees in these findings a vindication of his argument that in many cases, designs do not act instrumentally. However, it seems equally plausible to argue that this design decision was perfectly rational as few former colonial states could call on local experts of electoral systems design, and that the development of a completely new system would have been costly, time-consuming, and risky. Furthermore, copying the design of a pre-existing institution may also have helped to save political capital since politicians were able to piggyback on the perceived legitimacy and effectiveness of the copied model. Perhaps the adopted electoral system was not best equipped for dealing with the particular cleavages of the individual society, but it may well have been the best viable choice given important constraints in human and political capital.

In sum, isomorphist reasoning may lead to the same design expectations as derived from the problem-tailored design model provided that the institution that policymakers decide to copy has a sufficiently similar problem constellation as the one to which the design is transferred, and that such a transfer generates important economies of scale.

8.3 Instrumentality

The second category of criticism presents a considerably greater challenge to this study's problem-oriented design model. It shares the rationality assumption with this model, but questions the instrumentality assumption in such a way that I feel compelled to loosen the restriction that says institutions serve exclusively or predominantly the purpose of solving the stated policy problem.

As argued throughout this book, policymakers create institutions because they are committed to finding an effective solution to a problem that requires international cooperation. This line of reasoning corresponds with Pierson's (2004) notion of societal functionalism.[9] In contrast, many other rational design theories – especially, but not exclusively, those studying domestic institutions – are rooted in an actor-centered variant of functionalism (Pierson 2004). They show how particular institutions may be "functional for powerful actors but quite *dysfunctional* for society as a whole" (Pierson 2004: 106;

---

[9] Koremenos, Lipson, and Snidal's (2001) design model implicitly rests on the same assumption.

see also Miller 2000b).[10] This difference between societal and actor-centered functionalism suggests two important and interrelated qualifications of the instrumentality assumption upon which this study's problem-tailored model is based. First, the design preference of some states may reflect goals other than the creation of an effective solution of a shared policy problem. Second, the dysfunctional design preferences of these states may take the upper hand if they are more powerful than those states which are truly committed to an effective solution. Consequently, we can only expect an international institution to be endowed with the governance structure that is most pertinent for dealing with the policy problem at hand if the most powerful state or coalition of states is indeed actively interested in a solution of that problem and thus in the creation of an effective international institution. It is therefore indispensable to take a closer look at the impact of power on design outcomes and on the formation of powerful states' institutional preferences.

8.3.1 Power

Pierson's observation of the possibly pathological outcomes from actor-centered functionalism highlights the importance of power in the creation and design of institutions. The power aspect is of particular relevance in the cases studied here, as international institutions created to curb illicit flows through cooperative law enforcement and other measures result in an unequal distribution of costs and benefits among states, intentionally or unintentionally leaving some states better and others worse off than under the *status quo ante*. The creation of these institutions does not therefore result in Pareto efficiency gains as envisaged by the classical neo-liberal theories (Keohane 1984) and has to rely to a lesser or greater extent on coercion by powerful states (Knight 1992; Krasner 1993; Moe 2005; Young 1983). Such coercive institutions may still facilitate the generation of Kaldor–Hicks efficiency gains and be optimal from a societal functionalism perspective depending on whether powerful states are actively interested in the creation of an effective international institution. In this case, the most powerful state or coalition of states will press for the adoption of an international

---

[10] Miller (2000b: 542) even goes a step further, arguing that from a rational choice perspective a socially effective institution is in fact an exotic exception rather than the rule.

institution that is vested with both the substance and the form that is most pertinent for dealing with the problem at hand.[11] But what happens if these powerful states are opposed to an effective institution? How does such opposition affect institutional design outcomes? Two opposite archetypical scenarios are possible which I summarize as "shallow and weak" versus "wrong and strong."

Under the "shallow and weak" scenario, an opposing state initially seeks to obstruct the creation of any sort of institution related to the problem at hand.[12] If this state realizes that it cannot prevent the creation of an international institution altogether, it will advocate the adoption of shallow substantive provisions that do not require a significant deviation from the *status quo ante*. Often in combination with this second strategy, the opposing state will also seek to weaken the impact of an international institution by insisting on inappropriately low levels of legalization to ensure that no monitoring and enforcement mechanisms are included, provisions are formulated in vague terms, and that no authority is delegated to an independent body. Consequently, I expect that whenever the most powerful state or coalition of states is opposed to an effective institution, it will dictate soft law arrangements independent of the actual problem constellation.

The small arms and light weapons case examined in the empirical part of this study provides an illustrative example of this form of interaction between power and design. As argued above, the low level of legalization enshrined in the UN Program of Action of 2001 is too weak for dealing with the governance challenges arising from a problem constellation marked by a moderate degree of asset specificity and behavioral uncertainty. A number of powerful states, namely the United States, Russia, and China, threw as much weight behind their fight against far-reaching substantive provisions as against the adoption of a hard law structure. China lobbied fiercely against the mentioning of SALW-related human rights violations in the UN Program of Action, while the United States fought against the inclusion of provisions on civilian possession. They collectively opposed the proposal put forth by the European Union and Canada to draft provisions on marking, tracing, and brokering in legally

---

[11] Raustiala (2005) provides a thought-provoking discussion on the interplay between form and substance in international agreements.

[12] E.g. the United States voted in 2006 against the launch of a process that would examine the feasibility of a UN Arms Trade Treaty.

binding terms. Given the PoA's shallow substance and weak legalization, it is not surprising that most observers criticize it as a program of *in*action (Human Rights Watch 2001, emphasis added) – as an international institution with a very limited impact on the problematic proliferation and diffusion of small arms and light weapons in poorly governed parts of the world (e.g. Berkol and Gramizzi 2006).

More intriguing is the case of the UN Drug Convention of 1988. The analysis of the underlying problem constellation revealed a high degree of asset specificity and behavioral uncertainty and only low environmental uncertainty. This type of problem constellation suggested a high degree of legalization as the most adequate design solution, which corresponded with the actual design of the Vienna Convention. Despite this apparent match between expected and actual design, few observers would praise the Convention as a highly effective international institution.[13] In stark contrast to the Program of Action, the Vienna Convention and the UN drug control institutions in general are typically criticized neither for being too shallow in substance nor too weak in form but for codifying and enforcing policies that are substantially flawed. An increasing number of scholars point out that the prohibitionist approach underlying the UN drug conventions results in serious avoidable health and social problems for drug addicts (e.g. the infection with HIV viruses through the use of infected syringes and prostitution) (Csete and Wolfe 2007; Human Rights Watch 2004) and in political problems for drug-producing states (Buiter 2007). In their view, these negative consequences by far outweigh the benefit of upholding the (illusionary) hope of ever eradicating drug abuse in society. The growing skepticism about the effectiveness of the Vienna Convention has not yet resulted in a redirection of international drug control cooperation. Instead, Bertram (1996: ix) notes that "when policies seeking to address social problems through the exercise of fear, coercion, and force reaped failure and further problems, the response was often to 'get tougher' ... It seemed to be conventional wisdom that the reason force had not worked was that not enough had been applied and that the logical response to failure, therefore, was escalation – not reevaluation." It might be added that this logic has been upheld more strongly by the United States than by any other country.

---

[13] Among the most convincing critics are Human Rights Watch (2004); Nadelmann (2007); Thoumi (2004).

The United States was as much a driving force behind the 2001 Program of Action on Small Arms and Light Weapons as behind the UN drug trafficking convention of 1988. To a large extent, both the substance and the design of these two institutions reflect US preferences. While realist theories help explain why the United States succeeded in making its institutional preferences prevail, this school of thought is less well-equipped to explain why the most powerful actor at the international table was opposed to the creation of an effective institution, and why it preferred a "shallow and weak" institution in the former case and a "wrong and strong" institution in the latter. In order to better understand the formation of the institutional preferences of powerful states, I will now turn to domestic politics approaches.[14]

8.3.2 *Domestic politics*

From an actor-centered functionalist perspective, there are a number of reasons explaining why a powerful state might oppose the creation of an effective international institution. The backbone of these different explanations is the shared assumption that a government's principal goal is to remain in power. The most important stumbling block for the creation of effective international institutions is therefore the fact that the attainment of this goal depends exclusively on securing the support of influential domestic groups and not of the world community. Consequently, it can be assumed that a government will advocate an effective international institution only if the interests of the key domestic players are consistent with those of the states suffering most under the transnational problem at hand. Such a congruence of interests occurs when key players in the powerful state are directly and intensely threatened by an international policy problem. For instance, since September 11, 2001, the United States has advocated strong international measures against terrorist financing because a large and influential segment of the population felt directly threatened by terrorist networks and demanded tough action.

---

[14] Some scholars assume that a state's relative power position in itself affects its design preference. While a strong correlation between a state's power and its design preference might indeed exist, the empirical verdict on this assumption is still pending – domestic politics presents the most likely transmission channel linking power and design preferences (see Chapter 2).

The extent to which strong domestic support is required to move a government toward supporting an international institution depends on the relative strength of the expected domestic opposition. If an international institution provokes little domestic opposition in a state, relatively weak domestic support may suffice to turn the government into a (passive) supporter of that institution. The Kimberley Process presents an important demonstration of this point. In this case, the United States was not immediately affected by diamond-related conflicts. Rather, it endorsed the normative arguments put forward by NGOs and affected African governments,[15] despite the fact that neither group was able to establish conflict diamonds as a topic of similar concern to the US public as, for instance, narcotic drugs enjoyed throughout the 1980s.

Congruency of the societal interests and norms of a powerful state with those in the states most affected by a transnational problem is a necessary but insufficient condition. The domestic politics literature has focused most of its attention on examining the reasons why a government, even in a democratic state, might fail to represent the preferences of the majority of its citizens.[16]

Of greatest relevance to the cases studied here is the unequal degree to which interests and norms can be organized and subsequently succeed in imposing their preferences on the government. Schattschneider (1935) pioneered this branch of research and demonstrated how a concentrated interest defeats diffuse ones – an idea developed further in Olson's (1982) account of collective action problems in economic policy. Constructivist scholars pay particular attention to the process through which moral entrepreneurs frame a particular policy problem to align it with widespread norms (Keck and Sikkink 1998).

It is beyond the scope of this study to provide a thorough account of the various domestic politics factors at work in the preference formation of the US government or of any other key state. All I can do at this point is to offer a speculative re-examination of the two policy areas wherein Washington lobbied for the establishment of an international

---

[15] This preference formation mechanism is very much in line with the argument advanced by constructivist scholars who emphasize the importance of norms in the creation of international institutions (e.g. Klotz 1995; Kratochwil and Ruggie 1986) and the normative power of transnational civil society (Lipschutz 1996; Price 1998).

[16] For an overview of the various strands within domestic politics see Gourevitch (2002).

institution whose effectiveness was undermined both by its substance and/or form: small arms and narcotic drugs.

The small arms and light weapons case provides the most convincing example of dysfunctional interest group influence. As argued in Chapter 7, the main reason for the intransigence of the United States delegation at the UN SALW Conference of 2001 was the strong political influence wielded at home by the National Rifle Association. Just a month prior to the UN conference, the NRA took the crown in *Fortune* magazine's "Power 25" survey of lobbying groups (Sarasohn 2001). With almost 4.5 million members and an annual budget of more than US$200 million (Birnbaum 2001), the NRA possesses an immense organizational strength, and its skillful interpretation of the Second Amendment of the US Constitution endows it with a strong normative argument in support of its cause.[17] The considerable growth the NRA experienced over the 1990s was a counter-reaction against the momentum the pro-gun control lobby had drawn from a number of headline-catching firearms incidents (e.g. the Columbine High School shooting of April 1999). The NRA skillfully stirred up and capitalized on gun owners' fear of a legislative backlash. As Birnbaum, the author of the Power 25 survey of 2001 argued: "Nothing inspires zealotry like a threat, and few people feel more threatened than gun owners, more and more of whom are finding comfort in the NRA" (quoted in Sarasohn 2001: A21). In contrast, the rallying power emanating from the fear of becoming a gun victim or from the solidarity with those who faced such a risk was much more short-lived. Despite the fact that national surveys show consistently high levels of public support (over 70 percent) for tougher restrictions on the manufacture, sale, and ownership of guns (Teret *et al.* 1998), the NRA maintained the upper hand and convinced the US delegation to the UN conference that civilian ownership was a "no-go" area. The discrepancy between societal preferences and governmental preferences seems highly compatible with the collective action problem argument developed by domestic politics scholars. As a consequence of this discrepancy, the NRA's strong

---

[17] The NRA repeatedly associated the right to bear arms with other fundamental rights guaranteed by the US Constitution such as the right to free speech. For instance, in his annual presidential address to the NRA convention in 1999, Charlton Heston maintained that "[t]he Founding Fathers guaranteed this freedom because they knew no tyranny can ever arise among a people endowed with the right to keep and bear arms" (quoted in Brem 2006).

influence on the drafting of the UN Program of Action led to an institutional outcome that was sub-optimal from both a (US) domestic and international perspective.

Explaining the United States' insistence on the continuation of a prohibitionist anti-drug tradition on the national and global level is less straightforward. No single, unified organization exists in support of this position which can command a stature comparable to that of the NRA. However, the weaker organizational strength of the proponents of tough anti-drug laws may reflect the fact that their stance is more secure than that of free gun ownership. A strong majority of the population is still opposed to the legalization of marijuana (let alone harder drugs), and tough law enforcement at the national border and in the streets is still favored over education and treatment programs (Polling Report 2002). The comfortable position of drug prohibition results in part from the important argumentative advantage it enjoys over the pro-gun lobby. Drug addicts suffering from the indirect health and social consequences of punishment rather than treatment-oriented policies can be easily stigmatized as "sinners" who suffer the consequences of their own wrongful actions. In contrast, the victims of the ever more deadly high school shooting incidents could barely present more innocent victims with which the nation could easily sympathize. Drug prohibition supporters may therefore represent the sleeping dog that no government dares to wake up, while the NRA is already wide awake and barking loudly.

Despite these differences, both cases demonstrate the importance of complementing the analysis of the problem under the (global) effectiveness presumption – as developed in the problem-tailored design model – with an examination of the dominant interest structures in the most powerful states. Only when the latter-mentioned examination reveals that the most influential groups within the most powerful states are not actively opposed to an effective international solution to a shared problem can the problem-tailored design model yield accurate design predictions.

8.4 The step beyond: bounded rationality and multi-purpose instrumentality

The critical discussion above regarding the assumptions underlying this study's design model clarified the theoretical claims it can justifiably make and highlighted areas where its explanatory power can be expanded through the analysis of power-related and domestic politics-based considerations. While upholding the assumption that the enactors of an international institution are boundedly rational and instrumental in their design choice, I need to review, but not discard, the problem-oriented design model's second assumption.

This study presents a three-stage analytic approach for institutional design predictions. The problem-tailored design model developed here first analyzes the particular constellation of a policy problem for which international cooperation is sought. This analysis then allows for the identification of the optimal governance structure for an international institution created to solve that problem. Finally, the actual design of that institution is assessed along the three legalization dimensions and compared with the design prediction reached after stage two of the analysis.

All three steps remain highly relevant even when the assumption that policymakers are necessarily interested in designing an effective solution is relaxed. The detection of institutional design "matches" and "mismatches" can guide future research into the power-related and domestic politics-based causes that help explain why in some cases the actual design of an institution deviates more or less from what is optimal for dealing with the particular problem at hand. Realist theories can enhance this model's explanatory reach by identifying the sources of power (e.g. economic or military strength, legal capabilities, moral standing, etc.) most important to a state's bargaining position and by highlighting the design preferences that will eventually prevail. This study's design model can benefit from domestic politics scholars' expertise on how preferences are formed in individual states and on the conditions under which a powerful state adopts a stance on a transnational problem that is consistent with the requirements for an effective solution of that problem.

Even if we acknowledge the many strong reasons explaining why international institutions may often be designed in ways that are suboptimal for tackling policy problems, it remains important to understand what an optimal design would look like – for analytical reasons as well as to nurture our hope that the world community will eventually find ways to overcome these obstacles and move toward effective international cooperation.

References

Abbott, Frederick. 2000. The NAFTA and the Legalization of World Politics: A Case Study. *International Organization* **54** (3): 519–548.

Abbott, Kenneth W. and Duncan Snidal. 1998. Why States Act through Formal International Organizations. *Journal of Conflict Resolution* **42** (1): 3–32.

2000. Hard and Soft Law in International Governance. *International Organization* **54** (3): 421–456.

2004. Pathways to International Cooperation. In *The Impact of International Law on International Cooperation: Theoretical Perspectives*, ed. E. Benvenisti and M. Hirsch. Cambridge: Cambridge University Press.

Abbott, Kenneth W., Robert O. Keohane, Andrew Moravcsik, Anne-Marie Slaughter, and Duncan Snidal. 2000. The Concept of Legalization. *International Organization* **54** (3): 401–419.

Africa Research Bulletin. 2000. Sierra Leone: UK Promises to "Go the Distance." *Africa Research Bulletin* **37** (6): 14019–14021.

Afrol. 2006. Angola to double diamond production in 2006. *Afrol News*, March 14. www.afrol.com/articles/15888 (accessed March 26, 2008).

Alesina, Alberto and Guido Tabellini. 2005. *Why do Politicians Delegate?* Harvard Institute of Economic Research, Discussion Paper No. 2079. http://post.economics.harvard.edu/hier/2005papers/2005list.html.

Allison, Graham and Philip Zelikow. 1999. *Essence of Decision: Explaining the Cuban Missile Crisis*. 2nd ed. New York: Longman.

Alter, Karen J. 1998. Who Are the Masters of the Treaty? European Governments and the European Court of Justice. *International Organization* **52** (1): 121–147.

Alter, Karen J. and Sophie Meunier. 2006. Nested and Overlapping Regimes in the Transatlantic Banana Trade Dispute. *Journal of European Public Policy* **13** (3): 362–382.

2007. The Politics of International Regime Complexity. Introduction to the symposium "The Politics of International Regime Complexity," currently under submission at *Perspectives on Politics*.

Anderson, Erin and David C. Schmittlein. 1984. Integration of the Sales Force: An Empirical Examination. *Rand Journal of Economics* **15** (3): 385–395.

Andreas, Peter and Eva Bertram. 1992. From Cold War to Drug War. In *Paradigms Lost: The Post Cold War Era*, ed. C. Hartman and P. Vilanova. London: Pluto Press.

Annan, Kofi A. 1999. *Facing the Humanitarian Challenge: Towards a Culture of Prevention* (Unis/Sg/2358).

Apter, David Ernest. 1997. Political Violence in Analytical Perspective. In *The Legitimization of Violence*, ed. D. E. Apter. New York: New York University Press.

Ashworth, Andrew. 2003. *Principles of Criminal Law*. 4th ed. Oxford: Oxford University Press.

Atkins, Andy. 1998. The Economic and Political Impact of the Drug Trade and Drug Control Policies in Bolivia. In *Latin America and the Multinational Drug Trade*, ed. Elizabeth Joyce and Carlos Malamud. Basingstoke: Macmillan.

Aust, Anthony. 2000. *Modern Treaty Law and Practice*. New York: Cambridge University Press.

Bagley, Bruce M. 1988. Colombia and the War on Drugs. *Foreign Affairs* **67**: 70–92.

Balakrishnan, S. and B. Wernerfelt. 1986. Asset Specificity, Firm Heterogeneity, and Capital Structure. *Strategic Management Journal* **7**: 347–359.

Ballman, Alexander, David Epstein, and Sharyn O'Halloran. 2002. Delegation, Comitology, and the Separation of Powers in the European Union. *International Organization* **56** (3): 551–574.

Barclay, Gordon and Cynthia Tavares. 2003. International Comparisons of Criminal Justice Statistics 2001. www.csdp.org/research/hosb1203.pdf (accessed January 15, 2008).

Barnard, Chester. 1938. *The Functions of the Executive*. Cambridge, MA: Harvard University Press.

Barro, Robert and David Gordon. 1983. A Positive Theory of Modern Policy in a Natural Rate Model. *Journal of Political Economy* **91**: 589–610.

Bassiouni, M. C. and François Thony. 1999. The International Drug Control System. In *International Criminal Law*, ed. M. C. Bassiouni. Ardsley, NY: Transnational Publishers.

Bawn, Kathleen. 1995. Political Control versus Expertise: Congressional Choices about Administrative Procedures. *American Political Science Review* **89** (1): 62–73.

Bayart, Jean-François, Stephen Ellis, and Béatrice Hibou. 1999. *The Criminalization of the State in Africa*. Oxford, Bloomington, and Indianapolis: James Currey and Indiana University Press.

Bayer, I. and Ghodse, H. 1999. Evolution of international drug control, 1945–1995. *UNODC Bulletin on Narcotics* LI (1–2): 1–12. www.unodc.org/unodc/en/data-and-analysis/bulletin/bulletin_1999–01–01_1_page003.html (accessed March 23, 2008).

Beare, Margaret E. 2001. Critique of a Compliance-Driven Enforcement Strategy: Money Laundering and the Financial Sector. Paper presented at the Transparency International Conference, Toronto, ON.

Beare, Margaret E. and Stephen Schneider. 1990. *Tracing of Illicit Funds: Money Laundering in Canada*. Ottawa: Ministry of the Solicitor General of Canada.

Bennett, Trevor. 1998. Drugs and Crime: The Results of Research on Drug Testing and Interviewing Arrestees. London: Home Office. www.home-office.gov.uk/rds/pdfs/hors183.pdf (accessed March 1, 2008).

Bentham, Mandy. 1998. *The Politics of Drug Control*. Basingstoke: Macmillan.

Berdal, Mats and David M. Malone. 2000. *Greed and Grievance: Economic Agendas and Civil Wars*. Boulder, CO: Lynne Rienner.

Berkol, Ilhan. 2007. Analysis of the ECOWAS Convention on Small Arms and Light Weapons and Recommendations for the Development of an Action Plan. GRIP: Groupe de recherche et d'information sur la paix et la sécurité. www.grip.org/bdg/g1071en.pdf.

Berkol, Ilhan and Claudia Gramizzi. 2006. La Conférence d'évaluation du Programme d'action des Nations Unies sur les armes légeres (26 juin–7 juillet 2006): Un non-résultat logique. Brussels, Belgium: Groupe de recherché et d'information sur la paix et la sécurité. www.grip.org/bdg/g4604.html (accessed April 1, 2008).

Berman, Phyllis and Lea Goldman. 2003. Cracked De Beers: Lev Leviev Is Taking on the Most Successful Cartel in the World. *Forbes*, September 15. www.forbes.com/global/2003/0915/046.html (accessed March 22, 2008).

Bertram, Eva. 1996. *Drug War Politics: The Price of Denial*. Berkeley, CA: University of California Press.

Bewley-Taylor, David R. 1999. *The United States and International Drug Control, 1907–1997*. London and New York: Pinter.

2002. Habits of a Hegemon: The United States and the Future of the Global Drug Prohibition Regime. *Transnational Institute*. http://drugtext.org/library/articles/tni002.htm (accessed March 23, 2008).

Bewley-Taylor, David and Mike Trace. 2006. *The International Narcotics Control Board: Watchdog or Guardian of the UN Drug Conventions?* Witley, Surrey, UK: Beckley Foundation. www.internationaldrugpolicy.net/reports/BeckleyFoundation_Report_07.pdf (accessed March 22, 2008).

Birnbaum, Jeffrey H. 2001. Washington Power 25: Fat and Happy in DC. *Fortune*, May 14.

BIS. 2001. Customer Due Diligence for Banks. Basel Committee on Banking Supervision. October. www.bis.org/publ/bcbs85.pdf (accessed March 25, 2008).

——— 2004. External Positions of Banks in Individual Reporting Countries, Table 2B. *BIS Quarterly Review*. December. www.bis.org/statistics/bankstats.htm (accessed March 20, 2008).

Biting the Bullet. 2001. International Alert and Saferworld. www.basicint.org/WT/smallarms/UN2001/BTB_Recommendations.pdf (accessed March 27, 2008).

Blais, Andre and Louis Massicotte. 1997. Electoral Formulas: A Macroscopic Perspective. *European Journal of Political Research* **32**: 107–129.

Block, Alan A. 1992. Failures at Home and Abroad: Studies in the Implementation of US Drug Policy. In *War on Drugs: Studies in the Failure of US Narcotic Policy*, ed. A. W. McCoy and A. A. Block. Boulder, CO: Westview Press.

Boaz, David. 1991. The Consequences of Prohibition. In *The Crisis in Drug Prohibition*, ed. D. Boaz. Washington, DC: Cato Institute.

Bobrow, David B. and John S. Dryzek. 1987. *Policy Analysis by Design*. Pittsburgh: University of Pittsburgh Press.

Boerner, Christopher S. and Jeffrey T. Macher. 2001. Transaction Cost Economics: An Assessment of Empirical Research in the Social Sciences. Georgetown University Working Paper.

Bogges, D. Brian. 1992. Exporting United States Drug Law: An Example of the International Ramifications of the "War on Drugs." *Brigham Young University Law Review*: 165–190.

Boister, Neil. 2001. *The Penal Aspects of the UN Drug Convention*. The Hague and Boston: Kluwer Law International.

Bradley, Curtis A. and Judith G. Kelley. 2006. *The Concept of International Delegation*. Duke Law School Legal Studies Paper No. 141. http://ssrn.com/abstract=943044 (accessed March 29, 2008).

Braithwaite, John and Peter Drahos. 2000. *Global Business Regulation*. Cambridge: Cambridge University Press.

Brem, Stefan M. 2006. Regulating Small Arms: The Role of NGOs and Private Companies Negotiating an International Action Framework. Ph.D. Thesis, University of Zurich.

Brierly, James L. 1963. *Law of Nations: An Introduction to the International Law of Peace*. 6th ed. Oxford: Oxford University Press.

Broome, John. 2005. *Anti-Money Laundering: International Practice and Policies*. Causeway Bay, Hong Kong: Sweet & Maxwell Asia.

Browne, Marjorie Ann. 2005. *The United Nations and "Gun Control."* April 7. Order Code RS22108. Washington, DC: Congressional

Research Service. www.italy.usembassy.gov/pdf/other/RS22108.pdf (accessed March 18, 2008).

Brütsch, Christian and Dirk Lehmkuhl, eds. 2007. *Law and Legalization in Transnational Relations*. London and New York: Routledge.

Bueno de Mesquita, Bruce, James D. Morrow, Randolph M. Siverson, and Alastair Smith. 1999. Policy Failure and Political Survival. *Journal of Conflict Resolution* 43: 147–161.

Buiter, Willem. 2007. Legalise Drugs to Beat Terrorists. *Financial Times*, August 7.

Burchell, Graham, Colin Gordon, and Peter Miller, eds. 1991. *The Foucault Effect: Studies in Governmentality*. Chicago: University of Chicago Press.

Business Day. 2002. DRC Loses $800m to Diamond Fraud. *Business Day*, 28 October. http://globalpolicy.igc.org/security/issues/congo/2002/1028loses.htm.

Buzan, Barry, Ole Wæver, and Jaap de Wilde. 1998. *Security: A New Framework for Analysis*. Boulder, CO: Lynne Rienner.

Camdessus, Michel. 1998. Money Laundering: The Importance of International Countermeasures. Address given on February 10 in Paris at the Plenary Meeting of the FATF on Money Laundering. www.imf.org/external/np/speeches/1998/021098.htm (accessed August 20, 2007).

Cao, Lan. 2004. International Money Laundering: From Latin America to Asia, Who Pays? The Transnational and Sub-National in Global Crimes. *Berkeley Journal of International Law* 59: 59–97. www.wm.edu/law/publications/online/cao-653-6684.pdf.

Carey, John M. 2000. Parchment, Equilibria, and Institutions. *Comparative Political Studies* 33 (6/7): 735–761.

Carr, Edward Hallett. 1946. *The Twenty Years' Crisis: 1919–1939*. 2nd ed. London: Macmillan.

Carroll, Lisa C. 2002. Alternative Remittance Systems: Distinguishing Sub-Systems of Ethnic Money Laundering in Interpol Member Countries on the Asian Continent. Interpol, March 6, pp. 26–27.

Celia Toro, María. 1999. The Internationalization of Police: The DEA in Mexico. In *Journal of American History*, ed. David Thelen. Special Issue, *Rethinking History and the Nation State: Mexico and the United States*. www.indiana.edu/~jah/mexico/mtoro.html.

Center for the Study of Democracy and Saferworld. 2004. *Weapons under Scrutiny: Implementing Arms Export Controls and Combating Small Arms Proliferation in Bulgaria*. Sofia, Bulgaria: Center for the Study of Democracy.

Centers for Disease Control and Prevention (CDC). 2004. Homicide Trends and Characteristics: Brazil, 1980–2002. *Morbidity and Mortality Report Weekly*, 53(08): 169–171. www.cdc.gov/mmwR/preview/mmwrhtml/mm5308a1.htm (accessed March 1, 2008).

Centre for Humanitarian Dialogue. 2006. Putting Guns in Their Place: A Resource Pack for Two Years of Action by Humanitarian Agencies. www.hdcentre.org/files/PuttingGunsInTheirPlace.pdf (accessed March 14, 2008).

Chayes, Abram and Antonia Handler Chayes. 1993. On Compliance. *International Organization* **47**: 175–205.

1995. *New Sovereignty: Compliance with International Regulatory Agreements*. Cambridge, MA: Harvard University Press.

Chinkin, Christine. 2003. Normative Development in the International Legal System. In *Commitment and Compliance: The Role of Non-Binding Norms in the International Legal System*, ed. D. Shelton. Oxford: Oxford University Press.

Choiseul Praslin, Charles-Henri de. 1991. *La drogue: une economie dynamisée par la repression: la marée blanche*. Paris: Presses du CNRS.

CIA. 2004. *Nauru*. The World Factbook. www.cia.gov/cia/publications/factbook/index.html (accessed January 11, 2005).

Clutterbuck, Richard. 1995. *Drugs, Crime and Corruption: Think the Unthinkable*. Basingstoke: Macmillan.

Coase, Ronald H. 1937. The Nature of the Firm. *Economica* **4**: 386–405.

Collier, Paul. 2000. Rebellion as a Quasi-Criminal Activity. *Journal of Conflict Resolution* **44** (6): 839–853.

Collier, Paul and Anke Hoeffler. 2004. Greed and Grievance and Civil War. *Oxford Economic Papers* **56**: 563–595.

Cortell, Andrew P. and Susan Peterson. 2006. Dutiful Agents, Rogue Actors, or Both? Staffing, Voting Rules, and Slack in the WHO and WTO. In *Delegation and Agency in International Organizations*, ed. D. G. Hawkins *et al.* Cambridge: Cambridge University Press.

Cortright, David and George A. Lopez, eds. 2000. *The Sanctions Decade: Assessing UN Strategies in the 1990s*. Boulder, CO: Lynne Rienner.

Cragin, Kim and Bruce Hoffman. 2003. *Arms Trafficking and Colombia*. Santa Monica, CA: RAND.

Csete, Joanne and Daniel Wolfe. 2007. The International Narcotics Control Board and HIV/AIDS. *Treatment Issues (GMHC)* **21** (1): 4–7.

CTBTO. 2001. The Global Verification Regime and the International Monitoring System. Preparatory Commission. www.ctbto.org/reference/outreach/booklet3.pdf.

Cuéllar, Mariano-Florentino. 2004. The Mismatch between State Power and State Capacity in Transnational Law Enforcement. *Berkeley Journal of International Law* **22** (1): 15–58.

DDA. 2007. Small Arms and Light Weapons. UN Department of Disarmament Affairs. http://disarmament.un.org/cab/salw.html (accessed August 30, 2007).

DeSombre, Elizabeth. 1995. Baptists and Bootleggers for the Environment: The Origins of United States Unilateral Sanctions. *Journal of Environment and Development* 4 (1): 53–75.

Dietrich, Christian. 2000. Porous borders and diamonds. In *Angola's War Economy: The Role of Oil and Diamonds*, ed. Jakkie Gilliers and Christian Dietrich. Pretoria: Institute for Security Studies.

DiMaggio, Paul J. and Walter W. Powell. 1983. The Iron Cage Revisited: Institutional Isomorphism and Collective Organizational Fields. *American Sociological Review* 28 (2): 147–160.

Diver, Colin S. 1983. The Optimal Precision of Administrative Rules. *Yale Law Journal* 93 (1): 65–109.

Dixit, Avinash K. 1996. *The Making of Economic Policy. A Transaction-Cost Politics Perspective*. Cambridge, MA: MIT Press.

Donnelly, Jack. 1992. The United Nations and the Global Drug Control Regime. In *Drug Policy in the Americas*, ed. P. H. Smith. Boulder, CO: Westview Press.

Downs, George W., David M. Rocke, and Peter N. Barsoom. 1996. Is the Good News About Compliance Good News About Cooperation? *International Organization* 50 (3): 379–406.

DPA. 2006. Antwerp diamond faces Asian competition. www.indian-muslims.info/news/2006/may/07/economy/antwerp_diamond_faces_asian_competition.html (accessed March 27, 2008).

Drezner, Daniel W. 2001. Sovereignty for Sale: Why It's Never Been More Profitable to Be a Nation-State than in Today's Non-Nation-State World. *Foreign Policy* (September/October): 76–77.

2006. The Viscosity of Global Governance: When Is Forum-Shopping Expensive? Paper presented at the International Political Economy Society Conference, Princeton University. www.princeton.edu/~pcglobal/conferences/IPES/papers/drezner_S1100_16.pdf (accessed March 28, 2008).

Dworkin, Ronald. 1986. *Law's Empire*. Cambridge, MA: Belknap Press of Harvard University Press.

Dyer, Jeffrey H. 1996. Does Governance Matter? Keiretsu Alliances and Asset Specificity as Sources of Japanese Competitive Advantage. *Organization Science* 7 (6): 649–666.

Economics and Statistics Office of the Government of the Cayman Islands. 2004. Employment Report. www.eso.ky/pages1.php?page=employment.

Edwards, Adam and Peter Gill. 2003. After Transnational Organised Crime? The Politics of Public Safety. In *Transnational Organised Crime: Perspectives on Global Security*, ed. A. Edwards and P. Gill. London and New York: Routledge.

Eggertsson, Thrainn. 1990. *Economic Behavior and Institutions*. Cambridge: Cambridge University Press.

Einhorn, Jessica. 2001. The World Bank's Mission Creep. *Foreign Affairs* **80** (5): 22–35.

Elgie, Robert and Iain McMenamin. 2005. Credible Commitment, Political Uncertainty or Policy Complexity? Explaining Variations in the Independence of Non-Majoritarian Institutions in France. *British Journal of Political Science* **35**: 531–548.

EMCDDA. 2003. Public Spending on Drugs in the European Union during the 1990s. Lisbon: European Monitoring Centre for Drugs and Drug Addiction. www.emcdda.eu.int/?nnodeid=1345 (accessed April 2, 2008).

   2007. Annual Report on the State of the Drugs Problem in Europe. Lisbon: European Monitoring Centre for Drugs and Drug Addiction. www.emcdda.europa.eu (accessed March 28, 2008).

Epstein, David and Sharyn O'Halloran. 1999. *Delegating Powers: A Transaction Cost Politics Approach to Policy Making under Separate Powers*. Cambridge: Cambridge University Press.

Epstein, Edward Jay. 1977. *Agency of Fear: Opiates and Political Power in America*. New York: G. P. Putnam's Sons.

European Union. 1999. Joint Action of 17 December 1998. *Official Journal of the European Communities* (1999/34/CFSP), January 15.

Evans, Peter. 1997. The Eclipse of the State? Reflections on Stateness in an Era of Globalization. *World Politics* **50** (1): 62–87.

Farah, Douglas. 2001. Al Qaeda Cash Tied to Diamond Trade. *Washington Post*, November 2. www.globalpolicy.org/security/issues/diamond/2001/1102qaeda.htm (accessed March 26, 2008).

Farer, Tom. 2000. Shaping Agendas in Civil Wars. In *Greed and Grievance: Economic Agendas in Civil Wars*, ed. M. Berdal and D. M. Malone. Boulder, CO and London: Lynne Rienner.

FATF. 1991. *Financial Action Task Force on Money Laundering 1990–1991*. Paris: Financial Action Task Force.

   2000. *FATF Annual Report 1999–2000*. Paris: FATF. www.fatf-gafi.org/dataoecd/13/42/34328015.pdf (accessed March 12, 2008).

   2003. *The Forty Recommendations*. Paris: FATF.

   2004. *Mandate for the Future of the FATF (September 2004–December 2012)*. Paris: FATF. www.fatf-gafi.org/dataoecd/14/60/36309648.pdf (accessed March 25, 2008).

   2005. *FATF Annual Report 2004–2005*. Paris: FATF. www.fatf-gafi.org/dataoecd/41/25/34988062.pdf.

   2006. *FATF Annual Report 2005–2006*. Paris: FATF. www.fatf-gafi.org/dataoecd/38/56/37041969.pdf (accessed March 25, 2008).

   2007. *Guidance on the Risk-Based Approach to Combating Money Laundering and Terrorist Financing*. Paris: FATF. www.fatf-gafi.org/dataoecd/43/46/38960576.pdf (accessed March 25, 2008).

2008. *Non-Cooperative Countries and Territories: Timeline*. www.fatf-gafi. org/document/54/0,3343,en_32250379_32236992_33919542_1_1_1_1,00. html (accessed March 10, 2008).

Fearon, James D. 1997. Signaling Foreign Policy Interest: Tying Hands Versus Sinking Costs. *Journal of Conflict Resolution* **41** (1): 68–90.

Felbab-Brown, Vanda. 2004. The Coca Connection: The Impacts of Illicit Substances on Militarized Conflicts. Paper presented at the annual meeting of the American Political Science Association.

2005. Afghanistan: When Counternarcotics Undermines Counterterrorism. *Washington Quarterly* **28** (4): 55–72.

Financial Times. 2005. Compliance Costs of Following the Money. *Financial Times*, June 10.

FinCEN. 1998. *Fincen Further Streamlines Exemption Process*. Washington, DC: Financial Crimes Enforcement Network (FinCEN).

Finnemore, Martha and Toope, Stephen J. 2001. Alternatives to "Legalization": Richer Views of Law and Politics. *International Organization* **44** (3): 743–758.

Fiorina, Morris P. 1982. Legislative Choice of Regulatory Forms: Legal Process or Administrative Process? *Public Choice* **39**: 33–66.

Fischer, Benedikt, J. Rehm, and T. Culbert. 2005. *Opium-Based Medicines: A Mapping of Global Demand, Supply and the Pharmaceutical Industry*. The Centre for Addiction and Mental Health, University of Toronto.

Forero, Juan. 2005. Ex-Airline Chief Gets 20 Years For Ferrying Cocaine. *The New York Times*, December 21.

Franck, Thomas M. 1990. *The Power of Legitimacy among Nations*. New York: Oxford University Press.

Frankfurter Allgemeine Zeitung. 2007. Morde in Duisburg: Wo es Pizza gibt, ist auch die Mafia zu Hause. FAZ.net, August 16.

Fraser, John. 2004. Congo Seeks to Regain Role in Gem Trade. *Business Day*, July 20.

Friman, H. Richard and Peter Andreas. 1999. Introduction: International Relations and the Illicit Global Economy. In *The Illicit Global Economy and State Power*, ed. H. R. Friman and P. Andreas. Lanham, Maryland and Oxford: Rowman & Littlefield.

Frischer, Martin, Stephen T. Green, and David Goldberg, eds. 1994. *Substance Abuse Related Mortality: A Worldwide Review*. Scotland, UK: Scottish Centre for Infection and Environmental Health.

Fuller, Jim. 1996. Global Cooperation Vital in Addressing Drug Concerns. *Global Issues* **1**(7): 1–5. http://usinfo.state.gov/journals/itgic/0796/ijge/ ijge0796.pdf (accessed March 23, 2008).

Galeotti, Mark. 2001. Underworld and Upperworld: Transnational Organized Crime and Global Society. In *Non-State Actors in World*

Politics, ed. D. Josselin and W. Wallace. Basingstoke: Palgrave Macmillan.

Garland, D. 1999. Governmentability and the Problem of Crime. In *Governable Places: Reading on Governmentability and Crime Control*, ed. R. Smandych. Aldershot: Ashgate.

Gberie, Lansana. 2002. *War and Peace in Sierra Leone: Diamonds, Corruption and the Lebanese Connection*. Ottawa: Partnership Africa Canada.

    2004. *Diamonds without Maps: Liberia, the UN, Sanctions and the Kimberley Process*. Ottawa: Partnership Africa Canada.

Geiger, Hans and Oliver Wuensche. 2007. The Fight against Money Laundering – An Economic Analysis of a Cost–Benefit Paradoxon. *Journal of Money Laundering Control* 10 (1): 91–105. www.solami. com/geiger.pdf (accessed March 22, 2008).

Gely, Rafael and Pablo T. Spiller. 1990. A Rational Choice Theory of Supreme Court Statutory Decisions with Applications to the State Farm and Grove City Cases. *Journal of Law, Economics and Organization* 6 (2): 263–300.

George, Alexander L. and Timothy J. McKeown. 1985. Case Studies and Theories of Organizational Decision Making. *Advances in Information Processing in Organizations* 2: 21–58.

Georgiev, Dencho. 1993. Politics or Rule of Law: Deconstruction and Legitimacy in International Law. *European Journal of International Law* 4 (1): 1–14.

Gibney, Mark. 2006. Political Terror Scale. www.unca.edu/politicalscience/ DOCS/Gibney/Political%20Terror%20Scale%201980-2005.pdf (accessed March 18, 2008).

Gilardi, Fabrizio. 2002. Policy Credibility and Delegation to Independent Regulatory Agencies: A Comparative Empirical Analysis. *Journal of European Public Policy* 9 (6): 873–893.

Gilardi, Fabrizio, Jacint Jordana, and David Levi-Faur. 2006. Regulation in the Age of Globalization: The Diffusion of Regulatory Agencies across Europe and Latin America. Institut Barcelona d'Estudis Internacionals (IBEI) Working Papers 2006/1. http://papers.ssrn.com/sol3/papers.cfm? abstract_id=960739.

Gilmore, William C. 1999. *Dirty Money: The Evolution of Money Laundering Countermeasures*. Strasbourg: Council of Europe Publishing.

Gimmett, Richard F. 2005. *Conventional Arms Transfers to Developing Nations, 1997–2004. Order Code RL33051.* Washington, DC: Congressional Research Service.

Global Witness. 1998. *A Rough Trade: The Role of Companies and Governments in the Angolan Conflict*. London: Global Witness.

2004a. *The Kimberley Process Gets Some Teeth: The Republic of Congo Is Removed from the Kimberley Process for Failing to Combat the Trade in Conflict Diamonds.* London: Global Witness. www.globalwitness.org/ press_releases/display2.php?id=248 (accessed May 30, 2005).

2004b. *Same Old Story: Natural Resources in the Democratic Republic of Congo.* London: Global Witness.

2006. *The US Diamond Sector.* London: Global Witness. www.global witness.org/data/files/media_library/8/en/the_us_diamond_sector.pdf (accessed March 26, 2008).

2007. *Combating Conflict Diamonds.* London: Global Witness. www. globalwitness.org/pages/en/the_diamond_industry.html (accessed March 26, 2008.)

Gold, M. and M. Levi. 1994. *Money Laundering in the UK: An Appraisal of Suspicion-Based Reporting.* London: The Police Foundation.

Goldstein, Judith. 1996. International Law and Domestic Institutions: Reconciling North American "Unfair" Trade Laws. *International Organization* 50 (4): 541–564.

Goldstein, Judith and Lisa L. Martin. 2000. Legalization, Trade Liberalization, and Domestic Politics: A Cautionary Note. *International Organization* 54 (3): 603–632.

Goldstein, Judith, Miles Kahler, Robert O. Keohane, and Anne-Marie Slaughter. 2000. Introduction: Legalization and World Politics. *International Organization* 54 (3): 385–399.

Goodin, Robert E. 1996. Institutions and Their Design. In *Theories of Institutional Design*, ed. R.E. Goodin. Cambridge and New York: Cambridge University Press.

Goreux, Louis. 2001. *Conflict Diamonds.* Africa Region Working Paper Series No. 13. Washington, DC: World Bank.

Gourevitch, Peter. 2002. Domestic Politics and International Relations. In *Handbook of International Relations*, ed. Walter Carlsnaes, Thomas Risse, and Beth Simmons. London: Sage.

Gray, James P. 2001. *Why Our Drug Laws Have Failed and What We Can Do About It: A Judicial Indictment of the War on Drugs.* Philadelphia: Temple University Press.

Green, Peter S. 1997. Use of Banknotes Aids Criminals: Launderers Cash in On Eastern Europe. *International Herald Tribune*, February 17.

Greenberg, Maurice R. 2002. *Terrorist Financing: Report of an Independent Task Force.* New York: Council on Foreign Relations.

Gruber, Lloyd. 2000. *Ruling the World: Power Politics and the Rise of Supranational Institutions.* Princeton, NJ: Princeton University Press.

Guáqueta, Alexandra. 2003. The Colombian Conflict: Political and Economic Dimensions. In *The Political Economy of Armed Conflict: Beyond Greed and Grievance*, ed. K. Ballentine and J. Sherman. Boulder, CO: Lynne Rienner.

Gulati, Ranjay and Harbir Singh. 1998. The Architecture of Cooperation: Managing Cooperation Costs and Appropriation Concerns in Strategic Alliances. *Administrative Science Quarterly* **43**: 781–814.

Guzman, Andrew T. 2004. *The Design of International Agreements.* International Legal Studies Working Papers Series, No. 8. Berkeley: University of California at Berkeley. http://repositories.cdlib.org/ils/wp/8.

Haas, Peter M. 2003. Choosing to Comply: Theorizing from International Relations and Comparative Politics. In *Commitment and Compliance: The Role of Non-Binding Norms in the International Legal System*, ed. D. Shelton. Oxford: Oxford University Press.

Hafner-Burton, Emilie. 2005. Forum Shopping for Human Rights: Trade Arrangements For Sale. Paper presented at the American Political Science Association, Annual Meeting, September 1–4, Washington, DC. www.princeton.edu/~smeunier/Hafner-Burton.pdf (accessed March 30, 2008).

Hall, Peter and Rosemary Taylor. 1996. Political Science and the Three New Institutionalisms. *Political Studies* **44**: 936–958.

Handl, Gunther F., W. Michael Reisman, Bruno Simma, Pierre Marie Dupuy, Christine Chinkin *et al.* 1988. A Hard Look at Soft Law. *American Society of International Law Proceedings* **82**: 371–395.

Hart Ezell, Virginia. 2002. Small Arms: Dominating Conflict in the Twenty-First Century. *Brown Journal of World Affairs* **9** (1): 305–310.

Hart, Paul 't, Eric K. Stern, and Bengt Sundelius. 1997. *Beyond Groupthink: Political Group Dynamics and Foreign Policy-Making.* Ann Arbor: University of Michigan Press.

Hasenclever, Andreas, Peter Mayer, and Volker Rittberger. 1997. *Theories of International Regimes.* Cambridge: Cambridge University Press.

Hawkins, Darren, David A. Lake, Daniel Nielson, and Michael J. Tierney. 2006. Delegation Under Anarchy: States, International Organizations, and Principal Agent Theory. In *Delegation and Agency in International Organizations*, ed. D. Hawkins *et al.* Cambridge: Cambridge University Press.

Helfer, Laurence R. 1999. Forum Shopping for Human Rights. *University of Pennsylvania Law Review* **148** (285): 288–289.

Helfer, Laurence R. and Anne-Marie Slaughter. 1997. Toward a Theory of Effective Supranational Adjudication. *Yale Law Journal* **107** (2): 273–391.

Helmke, Gretchen and Steven Levitsky. 2004. Informal Institutions and Comparative Politics: A Research Agenda. *Perspectives on Politics* **2** (4): 724–740.

Hemmati, Minu. 2002. *Multi-Stakeholder Processes for Governance and Sustainability: Beyond Deadlock and Conflict.* London: Earthscan.

Henisz. 2000. The Institutional Environment for Multinational Investment. *Journal of Law, Economics and Organization* 16 (2): 334–364.

High-Level Panel on Threats, Challenges, and Change. 2004. *A More Secure World: Our Shared Responsibility.* New York: United Nations. www. un.org/secureworld/ (accessed March 18, 2008).

Hirsch, Moshe. 2004. Compliance with International Norms. In *The Impact of International Law on International Cooperation: Theoretical Perspectives,* ed. E. Benvenisti and M. Hirsch. Cambridge: Cambridge University Press.

Hochschild, Adam. 1999. *King Leopold's Ghost: A Story of Greed, Terror, and Heroism in Colonial Africa.* Boston, MA: Houghton Mifflin.

Hoekman, Bernard M. and Michel M. Kostecki. 2001. *The Political Economy of the World Trading System: The WTO and Beyond.* Oxford: Oxford University Press.

Hoffmann, Stanley. 1968. International Law and the Control of Force. In *The Relevance of International Law,* ed. K. W. Deutsch and S. Hoffmann. Cambridge, MA: Schenkman Publishers.

Hopkinson, Nicholas. 1991. *Fighting Drugs Trafficking in the Americas and Europe.* London: HMSO.

Horn, Murray. 1995. *The Political Economy of Public Administration: Institutional Choice in the Public Sector.* Cambridge: Cambridge University Press.

Horn, Murray J. and Kenneth A. Shepsle. 1989. Commentary on "Administrative Arrangements and the Political Control of Agencies": Administrative Process and Organizational Form as Legislative Responses to Agency Costs. *Virginia Law Review* 75: 499–508.

Horvitz, Leslie Alan. 1994. FBI Enters Global Battle on Organized Crime. *Washington Times,* July 19.

Huber, John D. and Charles R. Shipan. 2002. *Deliberate Discretion? The Institutional Foundations of Bureaucratic Autonomy.* Cambridge: Cambridge University Press.

Human Rights Watch, 2001. UN: "Program of Inaction" on Small Arms. July 19. http://hrw.org/english/docs/2001/07/19/global308_txt.htm (accessed April 1, 2008).

2004. Written Statement Submitted by Human Rights Watch to the UN Economic and Social Council. Asserting the Human Rights of Injection Drug Users in the Era of HIV/AIDS, March 11. www.unhchr.ch/ Huridocda/Huridoca.nsf/0/366b8a2202edf69cc1256e600057a025? Opendocument (accessed April 1, 2008).

IANSA. 2006. Reviewing Action on Small Arms 2006: Assessing the First Five Years of the UN Programme of Action. Biting the Bullet Project.

IISS. 2004. *Military Balance 2004–5*. London: International Institute for Strategic Studies.

Iklé, Fred Charles. 1964. *How Nations Negotiate*. New York, Evanston, and London: Harper & Row.

International Herald Tribune. 2007. Colombia Navy Seizes Submarine Suspected of Hauling Cocaine. August 7.

International Narcotics Control Board (INCB). 2006. *Report of the International Narcotics Control Board*. Vienna: International Narcotics Control Board.

Janis, Irving Lester. 1983. *Groupthink: Psychological Studies of Policy Decisions and Fiascoes*. 2nd ed. Boston: Houghton Mifflin.

Jervis, Robert. 1975. *Perception and Misperception in International Politics*. Princeton, NJ: Princeton University Press.

Johnston, Douglas M. 1997. *Consent and Commitment in the World Community: The Classification and Analysis of International Instruments*. New York: Transnational Publishers.

Jojarth, Christine. 2007. The Birth of a New World Order. Parliamentary Brief, November 2–3. www.thepolitician.org/articles/the-birth-of-a-new-602.html.

Joyce, Elizabeth. 1999. Transnational Criminal Enterprise: The European Perspective. In *Transnational Crime in the Americas*, ed. T. Farer. London: Routledge.

Kahler, Miles. 2000. Legalization as Strategy: The Asia-Pacific Case. *International Organization* 54 (3): 549–571.

Kaldor, Mary. 1999. *New and Old Wars: Organised Violence in the Global Era*. Cambridge: Polity Press.

Keck, Margaret E. and Kathryn Sikkink. 1998. *Activists Beyond Borders: Advocacy Networks in International Politics*. Ithaca, NY: Cornell University Press.

Keck, Otto. 1993. The New Institutionalism and the Relative Gains Debate. In *International Relations and Pan-Europe: Theoretical Approaches and Empirical Findings*, ed. F. R. Pfetsch. Münster: Lit Verlag.

Keefer, Philip and David Stasavage. 1998. *When Does Delegation Improve Credibility? Central Bank Independence and the Separation of Powers*. Working Papers Series 98–18. Oxford: Centre for the Study of African Economies.

Keegan, John. 1993. *A History of Warfare*. New York: Knopf.

Keen, David. 1998. *The Economic Functions of Violence in Civil Wars*, Adelphi Paper 320. Oxford: Oxford University Press for the International Institute of Security Studies.

Kellerhals, Merle D. Jr. 2001. UN Small Arms Conference a Success, US Official Says. August 21. www.fas.org/asmp/campaigns/smallarms/UNConf_US_success.htm (accessed March 18, 2008).

Keohane, Robert O. 1982. The Demand for International Regimes. *International Organization* **36** (2): 325–355.

1984. *After Hegemony: Cooperation and Discord in the World Political Economy*. Princeton, NJ: Princeton University Press.

1988. International Institutions: Two Approaches. *International Studies Quarterly* **32** (4): 379–396.

1989. *International Institutions and State Power: Essays in International Relations Theory*. Boulder, CO: Westview Press.

Keohane, Robert O. and Joseph S. Nye, eds. 1971. *Transnational Relations and World Politics*. Cambridge, MA: Harvard University Press.

1989. *Power and Interdependence: World Politics in Transition*. 2nd ed. Boston: Little, Brown.

2000. Introduction. In *Governance in a Globalizing World*, ed. J. Nye and J. Donahue. Washington, DC: Brookings Institution.

Keohane, Robert O., Andrew Moravcsik, and Anne-Marie Slaughter. 2000. Legalized Dispute Resolution: Interstate and Transnational. *International Organization* **54** (3): 457–488.

Kessler, Glenn. 2007. Weapons Given to Iraq Are Missing. *Washington Post*, August 6. www.washingtonpost.com/wp-dyn/content/article/2007/08/05/AR2007080501299.html (accessed March 28, 2008).

Kimberley Process. 2008. Background. www.kimberleyprocess.com/background/index_en.html (accessed March 14, 2008).

King, Charles. 1997. *Ending Civil Wars*. Adelphi Paper 308. Oxford and New York: Oxford University Press for the International Institute of Security Studies.

King, Gary, Robert O. Keohane, and Sidney Verba. 1994. *Designing Social Inquiry*. Princeton, NJ: Princeton University Press.

Klabbers, Jan. 2001. The Changing Image of International Organizations. In *The Legitimacy of International Organizations*, ed. Jean-Marc Coicaud and Veijo Heiskanen. Tokyo and New York: United Nations University Press.

2002. *An Introduction to International Institutional Law*. Cambridge: Cambridge University Press.

Klare, M. T. 1995. Light Weapons Diffusion and Global Violence in the Post-Cold War Era. In *Light Weapons and International Security*, ed. J. Singh. New Delhi: Pugwash and the Institute for Defence Studies and Analysis.

Klein, Benjamin, Robert G. Crawford, and Armen A. Alchian. 1978. Vertical Integration, Appropriable Rents and the Competitive Contracting Process. *Journal of Law and Economics* **21** (2): 297–326.

Klein, Eckart. 1997. Die Internationalen Organisationen Als Völkerrechtssubjekte. In *Völkerrecht*, ed. W. Graf Vitzhum. Berlin and New York: Walter de Gruyter.

Klotz, Audie. 1995. *Norms in International Relations: The Struggle against Apartheid*. Ithaca, NY: Cornell University Press.

Knight, Frank H. 1921. *Risk, Uncertainty and Profit*. 1st ed. Boston and New York: Houghton Mifflin.

Knight, Jack. 1992. *Institutions and Social Conflict*. Cambridge and New York: Cambridge University Press.

Koh, Harold H. 1995. A World Transformed. *Yale Law Journal* 20: ix–xiii.

1996. Transnational Legal Process. *Nebraska Law Review* 75 (1): 181–206.

Kopp, Pierre. 2003. *Political Economy of Illegal Drugs, Studies in Crime and Economics*. London and New York: Routledge.

Koremenos, Barbara. 2001. Loosening the Ties That Bind: A Learning Model of Agreement Flexibility. *International Organization* 55 (2): 289–325.

Koremenos, Barbara, Charles Lipson, and Duncan Snidal. 2001. The Rational Design of International Institutions. *International Organization* 55 (4): 761–799.

KPMG 2004. Global Anti-Money Laundering Survey 2007: How Banks Are Facing Up to the Challenge. www.kpmg.se/download/102716/123054/Global%20Anti-Money%20Laundering%20Survey%202004.pdf (accessed March 30, 2008).

2007. Global Anti-Money Laundering Survey 2007 – Appendices. www.kpmg.com/Services/Advisory/Other/AML2007.htm (accessed March 30, 2008).

Krasner, Stephen D. 1983. Structural Causes and Regime Consequences: Regimes as Intervening Variables. In *International Regimes*, ed. S. D. Krasner. Ithaca, NY: Cornell University Press.

1985. *Structural Conflict: The Third World against Global Liberalism*. Berkeley, CA: University of California Press.

1991. Global Communications and National Power: Life on the Pareto Frontier. *World Politics* 43: 336–366.

1993. Sovereignty, Regimes, and Human Rights. In *Regime Theory and International Relations*, ed. V. Rittberger. Oxford: Clarendon Press.

Kratochwil, Friedrich V. and John Gerard Ruggie. 1986. International Organization: A State of the Art on an Art of the State. *International Organization* 40: 753–775.

Krause, Keith. 2002. Multilateral Diplomacy, Norm Building, and UN Conferences: The Case of Small Arms and Light Weapons. *Global Governance* 8: 247–263.

Kuriyan, Vinod. 2005. Botswana Won't Force Beneficiation Said Pres. Mogae. *Rapaport News*, May 24. www.diamonds.net/news/newsitem.asp?num=12314 (accessed May 30, 2005).

Labrousse, A. 1991. *La drogue, l'argent et les armes*. Paris: Fayard.

Labrousse, A. and Laurent Laniel. 2002. *The World Geopolitics of Drugs, 1998/1999*. Dordrecht, Boston, and London: Kluwer Academic Publishers.

Laitner, Sarah. 2005. New Diamond Centres Seek to Take Shine off Antwerp. *Financial Times*, May 26: 20.

Lake, David A. 1996. Anarchy, Hierarchy, and the Variety of International Relations. *International Organization* 50 (1): 1–33.

1999. *Entangling Relations: American Foreign Policy in Its Century*. Princeton, NJ: Princeton University Press.

2000. Global Governance: A Relational Contracting Approach. In *Globalization and Governance*, ed. A. Prakash and J. A. Hart. London and New York: Routledge.

Lake, David A. and Mathew D. McCubbins. 2006. Delegation to International Agencies. In *Delegation Under Anarchy: Principals, Agents, and International Organizations*, ed. D. Hawkins *et al.* Cambridge: Cambridge University Press.

Lambert, Edouard. 1921. *Le Gouvernement des juges et la lutte contre la legislation sociale aux Etats-Unis*. Paris: Giard & Cie.

Landes, William M. and Richard A. Posner. 1975. The Independent Judiciary in an Interest-Group Perspective. *Journal of Law and Economics* 18 (3): 875–901.

Lane, C. and R. Bachmann. 1996. The Social Constitution of Trust: Supplier Relations in Britain and Germany. *Organization Studies* 17: 365–395.

Laurance, Edward J., Hendrik Wagenmakers, and Herbert Wulf. Managing the Global Problems Created by the Conventional Arms Trade: An Assessment of the United Nations Register of Conventional Arms. *Global Governance* 11: 225–246.

Lawrence, Thomas Joseph. 1910. *The Principles of International Law*. Boston, New York, and Chicago: D. C. Heath and Co.

Le Billion, Phillippe. 2001. Angola's Political Economy of War: The Role of Oil and Diamonds, 1975–2000. *African Affairs* 100: 54–80.

Lee, Rensselaer W. III. 1999. Transnational Organized Crime: An Overview. In *Transnational Crime in the Americas: An Inter-American Dialogue Book*, ed. T. Farer. New York and London: Routledge.

Lee, Rensselaer W. III and Raphael Perl. 2002. *Drug Control: International Policy and Options. March. Order Code IB88093*. Washington, DC: Congressional Research Service. http://fpc.state.gov/documents/organization/8975.pdf (accessed January 10, 2008).

Leigh, John E. 2002. Testimony before US Congress. Senate Committee on Governmental Affairs. Illicit Diamonds, Conflict and Terrorism: The Role of US Agencies in Fighting the Conflict Diamonds Trade. February 13.

Levy, Brian and Pablo T. Spiller. 1996. A Framework for Resolving the Regulatory Problem. In *Regulations, Institutions, and Commitment: Comparative Studies of Telecommunications*, ed. B. Levy and P. T. Spiller. Cambridge: Cambridge University Press.

Levy, Marc A. 1993. European Acid Rain: The Power of Tote-Board Diplomacy. In *Institutions for the Earth: Sources of Effective International Environmental Protection*, ed. P. M. Haas, R. O. Keohane, and M. A. Levy. Cambridge, MA: MIT Press.

Lijphart, Arend. 1971. Comparative Politics and the Comparative Method. *American Political Science Review* 65 (3): 682–693.

Lipschutz, R. 1996. *Global Civil Society and Global Environmental Governance: The Politics of Nature from Place to Planet*. Albany, NY: State University of New York Press.

Lipson, Charles. 1991. Why Are Some International Agreements Informal? *International Organization* 45 (4): 495–538.

Lodge, Martin. 2002. *On Different Tracks: Designing Railway Regulation in Britain and Germany*. Westport, CT: Greenwood Press.

Lujala, Päivi, Nils Petter Gleditsch, and Elisabeth Gilmore. 2005. A Diamond Curse? Civil War and a Lootable Resource. *Journal of Conflict Resolution* 49 (4): 538–562.

Lumpe, Lora, Sarah Meek, and R. T. Naylor. 2000. Introduction to Gun-Running. In *Running Guns: The Global Black Market in Small Arms*, ed. L. Lumpe. London and New York: Zed Books.

Luttwak, Edward N. and Stuart Koehl. 1991. *The Dictionary of Modern War*. New York: HarperCollins.

Lutz, Ellen and Kathryn Sikkink. 2000. International Human Rights Law and Practice in Latin America. *International Organization* 54 (3): 633–659.

Macao Trade and Investment Promotion Institute. 2006. Monetary Authority of Macao Improves By-Laws and Regulations and Introduced an Efficient Mechanism to Combat Money-Laundering. www.ipim.gov.mo/en/publication/macauimage/cover/no38_06.htm (accessed March 28, 2008).

Majone, Giandomenico. 1997. Independent Agencies and the Delegation Problem: Theoretical and Normative Dimensions. In *Political Institutions and Public Policy*, ed. B. Steunberg and F. van Vught. Dordrecht: Kluwer Academic Publishers.

Malamud-Goti, Jaime. 1992. Reinforcing Poverty: The Bolivian War on Cocaine. In *The War on Drugs: Studies in the Failure of US Narcotics Policy*, ed. A. W. McCoy and A. A. Block. Boulder, CO: Westview Press.

Malanczuk, Peter. 1997. *Akehurst's Modern Introduction to International Law*. 7th revised ed. London and New York: Routledge.

Malone, David M. ed. 2004. *The UN Security Council: From the Cold War to the 21st Century*. Boulder, CO: Lynne Rienner.

Manger, William. 1968. Reform of the OAS: The 1967 Buenos Aires Protocol of Amendment to the 1948 Charter of Bogotá: An Appraisal. *Journal of Inter-American Studies*, **10** (1): 1–14.

March, James G. and Johan P. Olsen. 1989. *Rediscovering Institutions: The Organizational Basis of Politics*. New York: Free Press.

1990. Rediscovering Institutions: The Organizational Basis of Politics. *Canadian Journal of Political Science* **23** (4): 843–844.

1998. The Institutional Dynamics of International Political Orders. *International Organization* **52** (4): 943–969.

Marques, Rafael. 2005. Lundas – The Stones of Death – Angola's Deadly Diamonds: Human Rights Abuses in the Lunda Provinces, 2004. Amsterdam: NIZA. www.niza.nl/docs/200605151104305565.pdf?&username=guest@niza.nl&password=9999&groups=NIZA&workgroup= (accessed March 26, 2008).

Martin, Lisa L. 1993. *Coercive Cooperation: Explaining Multilateral Economic Sanctions*. Princeton, NJ: Princeton University Press.

Martin, Tim. 2004. Chair Report – Fourth Quarter. December. www.kimberleyprocess.com:8080/site/www_docs/chairs1/chair4quarterreport.pdf (accessed May 30, 2005).

Masten, Scott E., James W. Meehan Jr., and Edward A. Snyder. 1991. The Costs of Organization. *Journal of Law, Economics and Organization* **7** (1): 1–25.

Mathiak, Lucy and Lora Lumpe. 2000. Government Gun-Running to Guerrillas. In *Running Guns: The Global Black Market in Small Arms*, ed. L. Lumpe. London and New York: Zed Books.

McAllister, William B. 2000. *Drug Diplomacy in the Twentieth Century: An International History*. London and New York: Routledge.

McCall Smith, James. 2000. The Politics of Dispute Settlement Design: Explaining Legalism in Regional Trade Pacts. *International Organization* **54** (1): 137–180.

McConnell, Tristan. 2007. Fighting diamond smuggling in Africa. *Christian Science Monitor*, July 30. http://csmonitor.com/2007–0730-p07s02-woaf.html (accessed March 26, 2008).

McCoy, Alfred W. 1992. Heroin as a Global Commodity: A History of the Southeast Asia Drug Trade. In *War on Drugs: Studies in the Failure of US Narcotics Policy*, ed. Alfred W. McCoy and Alan A. Block. Boulder, CO: Westview Press.

McCubbins, Mathew D. and Talbot Page. 1993. A Theory of Congressional Delegation. In *Congress: Structure and Policy*, ed. M. D. McCubbins and T. Sullivan. Cambridge: Cambridge University Press.

McCubbins, Mathew D. and Thomas Schwartz. 1984. Congressional Oversight Overlooked: Police Patrols Versus Fire Alarms. *American Journal of Political Science* **28**: 165–179.

McCubbins, Mathew D., Roger Noll, and Barry Weingast. 1987. Administrative Procedures as Instruments of Political Control. *Journal of Law, Economics and Organization* **3** (2): 243–277.

1989. Structure and Process, Politics and Policy: Administrative Arrangements and the Political Control of Agencies. *Virginia Law Review* **75**: 431–482.

McFarlane, John and Karen McLennan. 1996. *Transnational Crime: The New Security Paradigm*, Working Paper No. 294, Strategic and Defence Studies Centre, Australian National University, Canberra.

Mearsheimer, John J. 1994–1995. The False Promise of Institutions. *International Security* **19** (3): 5–49.

MEIB staff. 2004. Hezbollah and the West African Diamond Trade. *Middle East Intelligence Bulletin* **6** (6–7).

Miller, Gary. 2000a. Above Politics: Credible Commitment and Efficiency in the Design of Public Agencies. *Journal of Public Administration Research and Theory* **10**: 289–327.

2000b. Rational Choice and Dysfunctional Institutions. *Governance: An International Journal of Policy and Administration* **13** (4): 535–547.

Milner, Helen V. 1997. *Interests, Institutions and Information: Domestic Politics and International Relations*. Princeton, NJ: Princeton University Press.

2006. Why Multilateralism? Foreign Aid and Domestic Principal-Agent Problems. In *Delegation and Agency in International Organizations*, ed. D. G. Hawkins *et al.* Cambridge: Cambridge University Press.

Milner, Helen V., B. Peter Rosendorff and Edward D. Mansfield. 2004. International Trade and Domestic Politics: The Domestic Sources of International Trade Agreements and Institutions. In *The Impact of International Law on International Cooperation: Theoretical Perspectives*, ed. E. Benvenisti and M. Hirsch. Cambridge: Cambridge University Press.

Mitchell, Ronald B. 2006. Relative Effectiveness of International Environmental Agreements. *Global Environmental Politics* **6** (3): 72–89.

Mitchell, Ronald B. and Patricia M. Keilbach. 2001. Situation Structure and Institutional Design: Reciprocity, Coercion, and Exchange. *International Organization* **55** (4): 891–917.

Mitsilegas, Valsamis. 2003. Countering the Chameleon Threat of Dirty Money: "Hard" and "Soft" Law in the Emergence of a Global Regime against Money Laundering and Terrorist Financing. In *Transnational Organized Crime: Perspectives on Global Security*, ed. A. Edwards and P. Gill. London and New York: Routledge.

Moe, Terry M. 1990a. Political Institutions: The Neglected Side of the Story. *Journal of Law, Economics and Organization* **6** (Special issue): 213–254.

1990b. The Politics of Structural Choice: Toward a Theory of Public Bureaucracy. In *Organization Theory*, ed. O. E. Williamson. New York: Oxford University Press.

1991. Politics and the Theory of Organization. *Journal of Law, Economics and Organization* 7 (Special issue): 106–129.

2005. Power and Political Institutions. *Perspectives on Politics* 3 (2): 215–233.

Molander, Roger C., David A. Mussington, and Peter A. Wilson. 1998. *Cybercrime and Money Laundering: Problems and Promise*, ed. C. T. Institute. Santa Monica, CA: RAND Corporation.

Monteverde, Kirk and David Teece. 1982. Supplier Switching Costs and Vertical Integration in the Automobile Industry. *Bell Journal of Economics* 13: 206–213.

Moravcsik, Andrew. 1993. Preferences and Power in the European Community: A Liberal Intergovernmentalist Perspective. *Journal of Common Market Studies* 31 (4): 473–524.

Morgenthau, Hans J. 1953. *Politics among Nations: The Struggle for Power and Peace*. New York: Alfred A. Knopf.

Morrill, Cameron and Janet Morrill. 2003. Internal Auditors and the External Audit: A Transaction Cost Perspective. *Managerial Auditing Journal* 18 (6): 490–504.

Morrow, James D. 2000. Alliances: Why Write Them Down? *Annual Review of Political Science* 3: 63–83.

Munck, Gerardo L. 2004. Tools for Qualitative Research. In *Rethinking Social Inquiry: Diverse Tools, Shared Standards*, ed. H. E. Brady and D. Collier. Lanham, MD: Rowman & Littlefield Publishers.

Myers, Joseph. 2001. International Standards and Cooperation in the Fight against Money Laundering. In *Economic Perspectives*, ed. US Department of State. Washington, DC: US Department of State.

Nadelmann, Ethan A. 1990. Global Prohibition Regimes: The Evolution of Norms in International Society. *International Organization* 44 (4): 503–526.

2007. Think Again: Drugs. *Foreign Policy* (September): 24.

Naím, Moisés. 2005. *Illicit: How Smugglers, Traffickers, and Copycats Are Hijacking the Global Economy*. New York: Doubleday.

National Commission on Terrorist Attacks Upon the United States. 2004. *The 9/11 Commission Report*. Washington, DC: US Government Printing Office.

National Security Council. 2000. *International Crime Threat Assessment*. Washington, DC: US Government.

Naylor, R. T. 1995a. From Cold War to Crime War: The Search for a New "National Security" Threat. *Transnational Organized Crime* 1 (4): 37–56.

1995b. The Structure and Operation of the Modern Arms Black Market. In *Lethal Commerce: The Global Trade in Small Arms and Light Weapons*, ed. J. Boutwell *et al.* Cambridge, MA: American Academy of Arts and Sciences.

New York Times. 1995. Colombian Press Feels Heat for Linking President to Drug Lords. April 5. http://query.nytimes.com/gst/fullpage.html?res=990CE2D91538F936A35757C0A963958260&sec=&spon=&pagewanted=print (accessed March 31, 2008).

Nielson, Daniel L. and Michael J. Tierney. 2003. Delegation to International Organizations: Agency Theory and World Bank Environmental Reform. *International Organization* 57 (Spring): 241–276.

North, Douglass C. and Barry Weingast. 1989. Constitutions and Commitment: The Evolution of Institutions Governing Public Choice in Seventeenth-Century England. *Journal of Economic History* 49 (4): 803–832.

Office of the President of the Republic. 1989. *The Fight against the Drug Traffic in Colombia*. Bogotá: Imprenta Nacional De Colombia.

Olson, Mancur. 1971. *The Logic of Collective Action*. Cambridge, MA: Harvard University Press.

1982. *The Rise and Fall of Nations: Economic Growth, Stagflation, and Social Rigidities*. New Haven: Yale University Press.

ONDCP. 2000. Drug-Related Crime. Washington, DC: Executive Office of the President. Office of National Drug Control Policy. www.whitehousedrugpolicy.gov/publications/factsht/crime/index.html (accessed March 10, 2008).

Oomes, Nienke and Matthias Vocke. 2003. *Diamond Smuggling and Taxation in Sub-Saharan Africa*. IMF Working Paper No. 03/167. Washington, DC: International Monetary Fund. www.imf.org/external/pubs/cat/longres.cfm?sk=16812 (accessed March 15, 2008).

Ortner, Alessia and Hans Geiger. 2006. *Comparing Financial Centers by Using Gross Value Added as Main Indicator*. Zurich, Switzerland: Universität Zürich/ Institut für schweizerisches Bankwesen, Working Paper No. 4, 44. www.isb.uzh.ch/publikationen/pdf/workingpapernr44.pdf.

OSCE. 2000. OSCE Document on Small Arms and Light Weapons. Vienna: Organization for Security and Co-operation in Europe. www.fas.org/asmp/campaigns/smallarms/osce-sa.pdf (accessed March 27, 2008).

Oxfam and Amnesty International. 2003. *Shattered Lives: The Case for Tough International Arms Control* 2003. www.oxfam.org.uk/what_we_do/issues/conflict_disasters/downloads/shattered_eng_full.pdf (accessed October 10, 2005).

Oye, Kenneth. 1986. Explaining Cooperation Under Anarchy: Hypotheses and Strategies. In *Cooperation Under Anarchy*, ed. K. Oye. Princeton: Princeton University Press.

Palmer, David Scott. 1992. Peru, the Drug Business and Shining Path: Between Scylla and Charybdis? *Journal of Interamerican Studies and World Affairs* **34** (3): 65–88. http://links.jstor.org/sici?sici=0022-1937%28199223%2934%3A3%3C65%3APTDBAS%3E2.0.CO%3B2-P (accessed March 22, 2008).

Passas, Nikos and Kimberly Jones. 2006. Commodities and Terrorist Financing: Focus on Diamonds. *European Journal on Criminal Policy and Research*, **12**(1): 1–33.

Perl, Raphael Francis. 1992. The United States. In *International Handbook on Drug Control*, ed. S. B. MacDonald and B. Zagaris. Westport, CT and London: Greenwood Press.

2001. *Taliban and the Drug Trade. Order Code RS21041*. Washington, DC: Congressional Research Service.

2006. *Drug Control: International Policy and Approaches. Order Code: IB88093*. Washington, DC: Congressional Research Service.

Permanent Court of International Justice. 1927. S.S. "Lotus" (France v. Turkey). P.C.I.J. Series A, No. 10.

Pessin, Al. 2006. *Pentagon Prepares to Help Control US–Mexico Border*. Pentagon. May 15.

Pew. 2001. Interdiction and Incarceration Still Top Remedies: 74% Say Drug War Being Lost. Washington, DC: Pew Research Center for the People and the Press. http://people-press.org/reports/print.php3?ReportID=16 (accessed April 2, 2008).

Pierson, Paul. 2000. Returns, Path Dependence and the Study of Politics. *American Political Science Review* **94** (2): 251–267.

2004. *Politics in Time: History, Institutions, and Social Analysis*. Princeton, NJ: Princeton University Press.

Pieth, Mark and Gemma Aiolfi. 2003. The Private Sector Becomes Active: The Wolfsberg Process. *Journal of Financial Crime* **10** (4): 359–365.

Polling Report. 2002. *Illegal Drugs*. CNN Time Poll. www.pollingreport.com/drugs.htm.

Porteous, Samuel D. 2000. Targeted Financial Sanctions. In *Greed & Grievance: Economic Agendas in Civil Wars*, ed. M. R. Berdal and D. Malone. Boulder, CO: Lynne Rienner Publishers.

Pravda. 2002. Russia's Deletion from FATF "Black List" to Raise Its Credibility. June 13. http://english.pravda.ru/economics/2002/06/13/30302.html (accessed January 17, 2005).

President's Commission on Organized Crime. 2001. *The Cash Connection: Organized Crime, Financial Institutions, and Money Laundering*. New York: Books for Business.

Price, Richard. 1998. Reversing the Gun Sights: Transnational Civil Society Targets Land Mines. *International Organization* **52** (3): 613–644.

Price, Tracey Mitchell. 2003. The Kimberley Process: Conflict Diamonds, WTO Obligations, and the Universality Debate. *Minnesota Journal of Global Trade* **12** (1): 1–69.

Przeworski, Adam and Henry Teune. 1970. *The Logic of Comparative Social Inquiry*. Malabar, FL: Krieger Publishing.

Quirk, Peter J. 1996. *Macroeconomic Implications of Money Laundering*. IMF Working Paper. Washington, DC: International Monetary Fund.

Rabasa, A. *et al.* 2001. *Beyond al-Qaeda: The Outer Rings of the Terrorist Universe, Part 2*. RAND Corporation. http://rand.org/pubs/monographs/2006/RAND_MG430.pdf.

Ragin, Charles C., Dirk Berg-Schlosser, and Gisèle de Meur. 1998. Political Methodology: Qualitative Methods. In *A New Handbook of Political Science*, ed. R. E. Goodin and H.-D. Klingemann. Oxford: Oxford University Press.

Raine, Linnea P. and Frank J. Cilluffo, eds. 1994. *Global Organized Crime: The New Evil Empire*. Washington, DC: Center for Strategic and International Studies (CSIS).

Raustiala, Kal. 1999. Law, Liberalization and International Narcotics Trafficking. *International Law and Politics* **32**: 89–145.

   2004. Police Patrols & Fire Alarms in the NAAEC. UCLA School of Law Research Paper No. 05–14. Los Angeles, CA: University of California.

   2005. Form and Substance in International Agreements. *American Journal of International Law* **99**: 581–614.

Raustiala, Kal and David G. Victor. 2004. The Regime Complex for Plant Genetic Resources. *International Organization* **58** (Spring): 277–309.

Reed, John. 2005. Real Diamonds May Not Be Forever. *Financial Times* (May 6): 28.

Reinicke, Wolfgang H. 1997. Global Public Policy. *Foreign Affairs* **76** (6): 127–138.

   1998. *Global Public Policy: Governing without Government?* Washington, DC: Brookings Institution.

   1999. The Other World Wide Web: Global Public Policy Networks. *Foreign Policy* **117** (Winter): 44–57.

Reinicke, Wolfgang H. and Jan Martin Witte. 2000. Independence, Globalization, and Sovereignty: The Role of Non-Binding International Legal Accords. In *Commitment and Compliance: The Role of Non-Binding Norms in the International Legal System*, ed. D. Shelton. Oxford: Oxford University Press.

Reno, William. 1995. *Corruption and State Politics in Sierra Leone*. Cambridge: Cambridge University Press.

   2005. The Politics of Violent Opposition in Collapsing States. *Government and Opposition* **40** (2): 127–151.

Reuter, Peter and Victoria Greenfield. 2001. Measuring Global Drug Markets: How Good Are the Numbers and Why Should We Care About Them? *World Economics* **2** (4): 155–173.

Risse-Kappen, Thomas. 1991. Public Opinion, Domestic Structure, and Foreign Policy in Liberal Democracies. *World Politics* **43** (4): 479–512.

Rittberger, Volker and Bernhard Zangl. 2004. *International Organization: Polity, Policy and Politics*. Basingstoke: Palgrave Macmillan.

Rogowsky, Robert A. 2001. WTO Disputes: Building International Law on Safeguards. *Virginia Lawyer* (June/July): 1–7.

Rolley, Robin. 1992. United Nations' Activities in International Drug Control. In *International Handbook on Drug Control*, ed. S. B. MacDonald and B. Zagaris. Westport, CT and London: Greenwood Press.

Rombouts, Luc. 2001. Diamond Annual Review – 2000. www.terraconsult. be/overview.htm.

Root, Hilton L. 1994. *The Foundation of Privilege: Political Foundations of Markets in Old Regime France and England*. Berkeley, CA: University of California Press.

Rosendorff, B. Peter and Helen V. Milner. 2001. The Optimal Design of International Trade Institutions: Uncertainty and Escape. *International Organization* **55** (4): 829–857.

Saavedra, Boris. 2007. Balkan Trafficking in Historical Perspective. In *Transnational Threats: Smuggling and Trafficking in Arms, Drugs, and Human Life*, ed. Kimberley L. Thachuk. Westport, CT: Praeger Security International.

Sarasohn, Judy. 2001. Fortune: NRA Lobby is No. 1 on Capitol Hill. *Washington Post*, May 18: A21.

Savona, Ernesto. 1996. Money Laundering, the Developed Countries and Drug Control: The New Agenda. In *European Drug Policies and Enforcement*, ed. N. Dorn, J. Jepsen, and E. Savona. Basingstoke: Macmillan.

1999. *European Money Trails*. Amsterdam: Harwood Academic Publishers.

Schachter, Oscar. 1977. The Twilight Existence of Nonbinding International Agreements. *American Journal of International Law* **71** (2): 296–304.

Schattschneider, Elmer E. 1935. *Politics, Pressures and the Tariff: A Study of Free Private Enterprise in Pressure Politics, as Shown in the 1929–1930 Revision of the Tariff*. New York: Prentice-Hall.

Schelling, Thomas C. 1960. *The Strategy of Conflict*. Cambridge, MA: Harvard University Press.

Schermers, Henry G. and Niels M. Blokker. 1995. *International Institutional Law: Unity within Diversity*. 3rd ed. Cambridge, MA: Kluwer Law International.

Schroeder, William R. 2001. Money Laundering. *FBI Law Enforcement Journal* **70** (5): 1–9.

Severin, Christin. 2004. Doppelmoral Londons in Der Geldwäscherei. *Neue Zürcher Zeitung*. November 22. www.nzz.ch/2004/11/24/wi/page-articleA0EMM.html (accessed January 2, 2005).

Shannon, Vaughn P. 2000. Norms Are What States Make Them: The Political Psychology of Norm Violation. *International Studies Quarterly* **44** (2): 293–316.

Shelton, Dinah, ed. 2000. *Commitment and Compliance: The Role of Non-Binding Norms in the International Legal System*. Oxford and New York: Oxford University Press.

Shepsle, Kenneth A. 1991. Discretion, Institutions, and the Problem of Government Commitment. In *Social Theory for a Changing Society*, ed. P. Bourdieu and J. S. Coleman. Boulder, CO: Westview Press.

Sheptycki, James William Edward. 2000a. The "Drug War": Learning from the Paradigm Example of Transnational Policing. In *Issues in Transnational Policing*, ed. J. W. E. Sheptycki. London and New York: Routledge.

2000b. Policing the Virtual Launderette: Money Laundering and Global Governance. In *Issues in Transnational Policing*, ed. J. W. E. Sheptycki. London and New York: Routledge.

2003. Global Law Enforcement as a Protection Racket: Some Sceptical Notes on Transnational Organised Crime as an Object of Global Governance. In *Transnational Organised Crime: Perspectives on Global Security*, ed. A. Edwards and P. Gill. London and New York: Routledge.

Simmons, Beth A. 2000. International Efforts against Money Laundering. In *Commitment and Compliance: The Role of Non-Binding Norms in the International Legal System*, ed. D. Shelton. Oxford: Oxford University Press.

2002. Capacity, Commitment, and Compliance: International Institutions and Territorial Disputes. *Journal of Conflict Resolution* **46** (6): 829–856.

Simmons, Beth and Lisa L. Martin. 2002. International Organizations and Institutions. In *Handbook of International Relations*, ed. W. Carlsnaes, T. Risse, and B. A. Simmons. Thousand Oaks, CA: Sage Publications.

Simmons, P. J. and C. de Jonge Oudraat. 2001. Managing Global Issues: An Introduction. In *Managing Global Issues: Lessons Learned*. Washington, DC: Carnegie Endowment for Peace.

Simon, Herbert Alexander. 1957. *Models of Man: Social and Rational*. New York: John Wiley.

1976. *Administrative Behavior: A Study of Decision-Making Processes in Administrative Organization*. 3rd ed. New York: Free Press.

Sislin, John and Frederic S. Pearson. 2001. *Arms and Ethnic Conflict*. Lanham, MD: Rowman and Littlefield.

Slaughter, Anne-Marie. 2004a. *A New World Order*. Princeton and Oxford: Princeton University Press.

2004b. Power and Legitimacy of Government Networks. In *Governance in the 21st Century: The Partnership Principle*. Berlin, Germany: Alfred Herrhausen Society. www.princeton.edu/~slaughtr/Articles/GovtNetworks.pdf.

Small Arms Survey. 2001. *Small Arms Survey 2001: Profiling the Problem*. Oxford: Oxford University Press.

2002. *Small Arms Survey 2002: Counting the Human Cost*. Oxford: Oxford University Press.

2003. *Small Arms Survey 2003: Development Denied*. Oxford: Oxford University Press.

2004. *Small Arms Survey 2004: Rights at Risk*. Oxford: Oxford University Press.

2006. *Small Arms Survey 2004: Unfinished Business*. Oxford: Oxford University Press.

Smandych, Russell, ed. 1999. *Governable Places: Readings on Governmentality and Crime*. Aldershot: Ashgate.

Smillie, Ian. 2005. *Comparative Case Study 1: The Kimberley Process Certification Scheme for Rough Diamonds*. VERIFOR Case Study. www.verifor.org/resources/case-studies/kimberley-process.pdf (accessed March 26, 2008).

Smillie, Ian, Lansana Gberie, and Ralph Hazleton. 2000. *The Heart of the Matter: Sierra Leone, Diamonds & Human Security*. Ottawa: Partnership Africa Canada.

Smith, Alastair. 1998. International Crises and Domestic Politics. *American Political Science Review* **92** (3): 623–638.

Smith, Chris. 1999. Areas of Major Concentration in the Use and Traffic of Small Arms. In *Small Arms Control: Old Weapons, New Issues*, ed. J. Dhanapala. Aldershot: Ashgate.

Smith, Peter H., ed. 1992. *Drug Policy in the Americas*. Boulder, CO: Westview Press.

Snidal, Duncan. 1985. Coordination Versus Prisoners' Dilemma: Implications for International Cooperation and Regimes. *American Political Science Review* **79**: 923–942.

Snyder, R. and R. Bhavnani. 2005. Diamonds, Blood and Taxes: A Revenue-Centered Framework for Explaining Social Order. *Journal of Conflict Resolution* **49**: 563–597.

State Failure Task Force. 2000. State Failure Task Force Report: Phase III Findings. http://globalpolicy.gmu.edu/pitf/SFTF%20Phase%20III%20Report%20Final.pdf.

Stein, Arthur A. 1983. Coordination and Collaboration: Regimes in an Anarchic World. In *International Regimes*, ed. S. D. Krasner. Ithaca, NY: Cornell University Press.

Steinbruner, John. 1974. *The Cybernetic Theory of Decision: New Dimensions of Political Analysis*. Princeton, NJ: Princeton University Press.

Stessens, Guy. 2000. *Money Laundering: A New International Law Enforcement Model*. Cambridge: Cambridge University Press.

Stohl, Rachel. 2005. Fighting the Illicit Trafficking of Small Arms. *SAIS Review* 25 (1): 59–68.

Stone, Randall. 2002. *Lending Credibility: The International Monetary Fund and the Post-Communist Transition*. Princeton, NJ: Princeton University Press.

Strange, Susan. 1983. Cave! Hic Dragones: A Critique of Regime Analysis. In *International Regimes*, ed. S. D. Krasner. Ithaca, NY: Cornell University Press.

Swart, Lucia. 2005. Illegal Gun Pool Growing, News24, October 26. www.news24.com/News24/South_Africa/News/0,,2-7-1442_1823434,00.html (accessed October 30, 2005).

Tailby, Rebecca. 2002. The Illicit Market in Diamonds. *Australian Institute of Criminology*, 218 (January). www.aic.gov.au/publications/tandi/ti218.pdf (accessed March 26, 2008).

Teret, Stephen P. *et al.* 1998. Support for New Policies to Regulate Firearms: Results of Two National Surveys. *New England Journal of Medicine* 339 (12): 813–818. http://content.nejm.org/cgi/content/full/339/12/813.

Thatcher, Mark. 2002. Delegation to Independent Regulatory Agencies: Pressures, Functions and Contextual Mediation. *West European Politics* 25 (1): 125–147.

The Economist. 2004a. The Cartel Isn't for Ever. *The Economist*, July 17: 67–69.

2004b. Coming Clean: Money-Laundering. *The Economist* 373 (8397): 95.

2005. Drugs in Latin America: Battles Won, a War Still Lost. *The Economist*, February 12: 49–50.

2008. Rumours of War: Ecuador, Venezuela Confront Colombia. *The Economist*, March 4. www.economist.com/daily/news/displaystory.cfm?story_id=10794694&top_story=1 (accessed March 10, 2008).

Thelen, Kathleen. 2004. *How Institutions Evolve: The Political Economy of Skills in Germany, Britain, the United States, and Japan*. Cambridge: Cambridge University Press.

Thoumi, Francisco E. 1999. The Impact of the Illegal Drug Industry on Colombia. In *Transnational Crime in the Americas: An Inter-American Dialogue Book*, ed. T. Farer. New York and London: Routledge.

2003. *Illegal Drugs, Economy and Society in the Andes.* Washington, DC: Woodrow Wilson Center Press.

2004. A Modest Proposal to Clarify the Status of Coca in the United Nations Conventions. *Crime, Law, and Social Change* **42**: 297–307.

United Kingdom Parliament. 2003. *Conflict Diamonds.* House of Commons Hansard Written Answers for May 8 (21). www.publications.parliament.uk/pa/cm200203/cmhansrd/vo030508/text/30508w21.htm (accessed March 28, 2008).

UN Department of Disarmament Affairs. 2005. *Small Arms and Light Weapons.* http://disarmament.un.org/cab/salw.html (accessed October 10, 2005).

UNODC. 2004. *World Drug Report 2004.* Vienna: United Nations Office on Drugs and Crime.

2006. *Ninth United Nations Survey of Crime Trends and Operations of Criminal Justice Systems.* Vienna: United Nations Office on Drugs and Crime.

2007. *World Drug Report 2007.* Vienna: United Nations Office on Drugs and Crime.

UN Panel of Governmental Experts. 1997. *Report of the Panel of Governmental Experts on Small Arms.* August 27. A/52/298.

US Census Bureau. 1999. *1997 Economic Census: Manufacturing–Industry Series: Small Arms Manufacturing.* EC97M-3329H. Washington, DC: US Department of Commerce.

US Congress. Senate Committee on Foreign Relations: Subcommittee on Terrorism, Narcotics and International Operations. 1988. *Drugs, Law Enforcement and Foreign Policy.* 100th Cong., 2nd sess. S. Prt. 100–165 ("Kerry Report").

US Department of Justice, Drug Enforcement Administration. 1993. *Coca Cultivation and Cocaine Processing.* Washington, DC: US Department of Justice.

US Department of the Treasury. *Hawala and Alternative Remittance Systems.* US Treasury Office of Terrorism and Financial Intelligence. www.ustreas.gov/offices/enforcement/key-issues/hawala (accessed August 17, 2007).

US General Accounting Office (GAO). 1992. *International Environment: International Agreements Are Not Well Monitored.* Report to Congressional Requesters GAO/RCED-92-43. http://archive.gao.gov/d31t10/145711.pdf (accessed March 28, 2008).

2002. *International Trade: Critical Issues Remain in Deterring Conflict Diamond Trade.* Report to Congressional Requesters GAO-02-678. Washington, DC: US General Accounting Office.

2003a. *Combating Money Laundering: Opportunities Exist to Improve the National Strategy.* Report to Congressional Requesters GAO-03-813. Washington, DC: US General Accounting Office.

2003b. *Terrorist Financing: US Agencies Should Systematically Assess Terrorists' Use of Alternative Financing Mechanisms.* Report to Congressional Requesters GAO-04-163. Washington, DC: US General Accounting Office.

2006. *Conflict Diamonds: Agency Actions Needed to Enhance Implementation of Clean Diamond Trade Act.* Report to Congressional Committees (GAO-06-978). Washington, DC: US Government Accounting Office.

US Senate Special Committee on Illegal Drugs. 2003. *Cannabis: Report of the Special Committee on Illegal Drugs.* Toronto: University of Toronto Press.

US State Department. 1991. International Narcotics Control. *US Department of State Dispatch* 2(28). http://dosfan.lib.uic.edu/ERC/briefing/dispatch/1991/html/Dispatchv2no28.html.

US State Department. 2002. *International Narcotics Control Strategy Report of 2001.* www.state.gov/p/inl/rls/nrcrpt/2001/c6085.htm (accessed March 27, 2008).

2004. *International Narcotics Control Strategy Report.* Bureau for International Narcotics and Law Enforcement Affairs. http://state.gov/p/inl/rls/nrcrpt/2003/vol2/html/29918.htm.

2005. *International Narcotics Control Strategy Report.* Bureau for International Narcotics and Law Enforcement Affairs. http://state.gov/documents/organization/42881.pdf.

2007. *International Narcotics Control Strategy Report.* Bureau for International Narcotics and Law Enforcement Affairs. www.state.gov/documents/organization/81446.pdf (accessed March 25, 2008).

Vertzberger, Yaacov. 1990. *The World in Their Minds: Information Processing, Cognition, and Perception in Foreign Policy Decisionmaking.* Stanford: Stanford University Press.

Victor, David G., Kal Raustiala, and Eugene Skolnikoff, eds. 1998. *The Implementation and Effectiveness of International Environmental Commitments: Theory and Practice.* Boston: MIT Press.

Vines, Alex. 2005. Combating Light Weapons Proliferation in West Africa. *International Affairs* **81** (2): 341–360.

von Clausewitz, Carl. 1992. *Vom Kriege.* Hamburg: Rowohlt.

Walker, Gordon and David Weber. 1984. A Transaction Cost Approach to Make-or-Buy Decisions. *Administrative Science Quarterly* **29**: 373–391.

Walker, John. 1999. Measuring the Extent of International Crime and Money Laundering. Paper prepared for the Kriminal Expo, a conference held in Budapest, Hungary on June 9. www.ozemail.com.au/~born1820/Budapest.html (accessed June 16, 2005).

Walker, William O. III. 1992. International Collaboration in Historical Perspective. In *Drug Policy in the Americas*, ed. P.H. Smith. Boulder, CO: Westview Press.

Wallensteen, Peter and Margareta Sollenberg. 1995. After the Cold War: Emerging Patterns of Armed Conflict. *Journal of Peace Research* **32** (3): 345–360.

2000. Armed Conflict, 1989–99. *Journal of Peace Research* **37** (5): 635–649.

Wassenaar Arrangement. 1995. The Wassenaar Arrangement on Export Controls for Conventional Arms and Dual-Use Goods and Technologies (successor to COCOM). Vienna, Austria. www.wassenaar.org/.

Weber, Katja. 1997. Hierarchy Amidst Anarchy: A Transaction Costs Approach to International Security Cooperation. *International Studies Quarterly* **41** (2): 321–340.

2000. *Hierarchy Amidst Anarchy: Transaction Costs and Institutional Choice*. Albany: State University of New York Press.

Wechsler, William F. 2001. Follow the Money. *Foreign Affairs* **80** (4): 40–57.

Weil, Prosper. 1983. Towards Relative Normativity in International Law? *American Journal of International Law* **77** (3): 413–442.

Weinstein, Jeremy M. 2007. *Inside Rebellion: The Politics of Insurgent Violence*. Cambridge and New York: Cambridge University Press.

Westermeyer, Joseph. 2004. Opium and the People of Laos. In *Dangerous Harvest: Drug Plants and the Transformation of Indigenous Landscapes*, ed. Michael K. Steinberg, Joseph J. Hobbs, and Kent Mathewson. New York: Oxford University Press.

Wezeman, Pieter D. 2003. *Conflicts and Transfers of Small Arms*. Stockholm: Stockholm International Peace Research Institute.

White, David. 2005. A Test Case for the Recovery of Failed States. *Financial Times*, February 14: 1–2.

White House. 1997. *International Organized Crime*. Presidential Decision Directive No. 42. www.fas.org/irp/offdocs/pdd42.htm (accessed March 31, 2008).

2006. *Memorandum for the Secretary of State: Presidential Determination on Major Drug Transit or Major Drug Producing Countries for Fiscal Year 2007*. Washington, DC: White House Press Release. www.state.gov/p/inl/rls/prsrl/ps/72379.htm (accessed April 1, 2008).

Widener, S.K. and F.H. Selto. 1999. Managment Control Systsems and Boundaries of the Firm: Why Do Firms Outsource Internal Auditing Activities? *Journal of Management Accounting Research* **11**: 45–73.

Williams, Phil. 2001. Crime, Illicit Markets, and Money Laundering. In *Managing Global Issues: Lessons Learned*, ed. P. J. Simmons and C. de Jonge Oudraat. Washington, DC: Carnegie Endowment for International Peace.

Williamson, Oliver Eaton. 1975. *Markets and Hierarchies: Analysis and Antitrust Implications*. New York: Free Press.

1985. *Economic Institutions of Capitalism.* New York: Free Press.

1996. *The Mechanisms of Governance.* New York: Oxford University Press.

Wolfsberg Group. 2007a. Wolfsberg FAQ's on Politically Exposed Persons. www.wolfsberg-principles.com/faq.html (accessed March 3, 2008).

2007b. Wolfsberg FAQ's on Beneficial Ownership. www.wolfsberg-principles.com/faq.html (accessed March 3, 2008).

World Bank. 2006. *Global Economic Prospects: Economic Implications of Remittances and Migration.* Washington, DC: World Bank.

2007. *Governance Matters VI: Aggregate and Individual Governance Indicators 1996–2006.* World Bank Policy Research Working Paper 4280. www.govindicators.org (accessed March 25, 2008).

2008. World Development Indicators database. http://go.worldbank.org/SI5SSGAVZ0 (accessed June 28, 2007).

World Diamond Council. 2003. *The Essential Guide to Implementing the Kimberley Process.* New York: World Diamond Council.

Wray, Henry R. 1994. *Money Laundering: The Volume of Currency Transaction Reports Filed Can and Should be Reduced.* Washington, DC: US General Accounting Office.

WTO. 2003. Agreement Reached on WTO Waiver for "Conflict Diamonds." February 26. www.wto.org/english/news_e/news03_e/goods_council_26fev03_e.htm (accessed March 26, 2008).

WWF. 2006. Mahogany Position Paper, March 31. www.worldwildlife.org/trade/pubs/wwfmahoganyposition.pdf (accessed March 29, 2008).

Yarbrough, Beth V. and Robert M. Yarbrough. 1990. International Institutions and the New Economics of Organization. *International Organization* **44** (2): 235–259.

1992. *Cooperation and Governance in International Trade: The Strategic Organizational Approach.* Princeton, NJ: Princeton University Press.

Yin, Robert K. 1994. *Case Study Research: Design and Methods.* Thousand Oaks, CA: Sage.

Young, Oran R. 1983. Regime Dynamics: The Rise and Fall of International Regime. In *International Regimes*, ed. S. D. Krasner. Ithaca, NY: Cornell University Press.

Zagaris, Bruce. 1992. Money Laundering: An International Control Problem. In *International Handbook on Drug Control*, ed. S. B. MacDonald and B. Zagaris. Westport, CT and London: Greenwood Press.

Index

Afghanistan
  political terror score of, 240
  selected governance indicators
    for, 112
Africa
  asset specificity, 148–157
  drug-related deaths in, 110–111
Albania
  potential stockpiles in, 238
Algeria
  political terror score of, 240
Amnesty International, 247–248
Angola
  governance indicators for, 202
  political terror score of, 240
Annan, Kofi (quoted), 5
arms
  defined, 223
  potential stockpiles of, 238
  trafficking summary assessment,
    254, 267
  transfers to developing nations, 235
  unexplained loss of, 224–225
asset specificity, 72–80, 148–157, 192,
  233–244
  benefits and, 106–109, 239–242
  costs and, 102–106, 234–239
Association of Southeast Asian
  Nations (ASEAN), 230
Austria
  governance indicators for, 246
Autodefensas Unidas de Colombia
  (AUC), 95

Bahrain
  homicide rate in, 153
banking centers
  international and domestic
    importance of, 152

Basel Statement of Principles for the
  Prevention of Criminal Use of the
  Banking System, 143
behavioral uncertainty, 80–84,
  157–160, 200–204, 244–249
  conceptualization and, 80–82
  governance incapacity and, 111–114,
    244–248
  industry opacity and, 114
  operationalization and, 82–84
Belgian Groupe de recherche et
  d'information sur la paix et la
  sécurité (GRIP), 247–248
Belgium
  governance indicators for,
    202, 246
benefits, 192–196
  asset specificity and, 106–109,
    239–242
Bennett, William J., 96
blood diamonds. *See* Kimberly Process
  Certification Scheme (KPCS)
Bolivia
  drug-related deaths in, 106–109
  selected governance indicators
    for, 112
Bonilla, Rodrigo Lara, 94
Bonn International Center for
  Conversion (BICC), 247–248
Bosnia-Herzegovina
  potential stockpiles in, 238
Botswana
  governance indicators for, 202
bounded rationality, 271–273
  multi-purpose instrumentality and,
    285–286
Brazil
  governance indicators for, 246
  homicide rate in, 153

319

Brunei
  homicide rate in, 153
Bulgaria
  governance indicators for, 246
  potential stockpiles in, 238
Burundi
  political terror score of, 240

Cayman Islands
  homicide rate in, 153
centralization
  as second element of delegation, 51
  delegation and, 215–216,
    262–263
China
  governance indicators for,
    202, 246
  potential stockpiles in, 238
  transfers of arms to, 235
Clinton, Bill (quoted), 5
coca
  leading producers, 105
coherence
  concept of, 45–46
  precision and, 259
Cold War, 223–224
collateral damage, 4
Colombia
  homicide rate in, 153
  political terror score of, 240
  selected governance indicators
    for, 112
compliance mechanisms, 55
  obligation and, 208–213
conceptualization
  asset specificity and, 73–75
  behavioral uncertainty,
    80–82
  environmental uncertainty and,
    85–86
Conciliation and Good Offices
    Commission, 53
conflict diamonds. See Kimberly
    Process Certification Scheme
    (KPCS)
Convention against the Illicit Traffic in
    Narcotic Drugs and Psychotropic
    Substances, 99–100
Conventional Arms Transfer
    (CAT), 249

costs, 197–198
  asset specificity and, 102–106,
    234–239
Council of the International
    Organization for Migration, 51
credibility
  domestic, 23–24
  international, 24–26
  state and, 22–23
crime
  drugs and, 93–97
  push towards securitization, 5–6
  small arms and, 222–226
  transnationalization of, 7–8
Czech Republic
  governance indicators for, 246
  potential stockpiles in, 238

deaths
  substance abuse-related, 108
decision-making procedures
  delegation and, 50–51
delegation, 128–133, 174–176,
    215–217, 259–263
  as third dimension of legalization, 46
  centralization and, 215–216
  decision-making procedures,
    50–51
  independence and, 216–217,
    260–262
  obligation and, 56–57
  precision and, 57–58
Denmark
  heroin in, 107
design
  defined, 59–60
determinacy
  precision and, 213–214, 257–259
diamonds. See also Kimberly
    Process Certification Scheme
    (KPCS)
  crime and war and, 182–186
  economic importance of, 193
  industry structure of, 181–194
  output of major producers, 197
  problem constellation of,
    207–208
  smart sanctions on, 186–190
  United Nations Security
    Council, 189

domestic policies
  instrumentality and, 282–285
DRC
  governance indicators for, 202
  political terror score of, 240
drug mules, 117
drugs
  crime and, 93–97

Egypt
  governance indicators for, 246
embargoes
  United Nations Security Council and, 50
End Child Prostitution in Asian Tourism
  (ECPAT), 158–159
England
  homicide rate in, 153
environmental uncertainty, 85–89,
  204–206, 249–252
  conceptualization and, 85–86
  operationalization and, 86–89
  Vienna Convention and, 114–117
Estonia
  potential stockpiles in, 238
EU Joint Action and the ECOWAS
  Memorandum, 232
European Central Bank, 48
European Community Directive for the
  Prevention of the Use of the
  Financial System, 143–144

Financial Action Task Force (FATF)
  anti-money laundering efforts of, 10
  establishment of, 139
  Forty Recommendations of, 145–148
fire alarms, 52–53
Forest Stewardship Council Certification
  Scheme (FSC), 204–205
Forty Recommendations
  versus Vienna Convention, 174
France
  governance indicators for, 246
  transfers of arms to, 235
Fuerzas Armadas Revolucionarias de
  Colombia (FARC), 94–95
functionalist theories, 67–69

Germany
  drug-related deaths in, 109
  governance indicators for, 246

homicide rate in, 153
transfers of arms to, 235
Global Survival Network (GSN),
  158–159
Global Witness, 189–190
globalization
  illicit products and services and, 7
  organized crime and, 7
  regulatory challenges and, 20–21
  transnationalization of illicit products
    and services, 7
go-it-alone power, 70
governance incapacity, 157–158
  behavioral uncertainty and, 111–114,
    244–248
governmental monitoring
  reliance on, 158–159
Greenpeace, 51

Hague Convention of 1912,
  The, 98
hard law
  types of rigidity and, 27
  Vienna Convention on the Law of
    Treaties and, 134–138
hard law *versus* soft law, 26
  boundaries of, 29
  complementary roles of, 28–29
heroin, 107
homicide rates, 153
Hoyos, Carlos Mauro, 94
Human Rights Watch, 247–248
Hungary
  governance indicators for, 246

independence
  as first aspect of delegation, 49–51
  delegation and, 216–217,
    260–262
India
  governance indicators for,
    202, 246
  political terror score of, 240
industry opacity
  behavioral uncertainty and, 114
"institution" *versus* "regime," 11
institutional design
  competing theories of, 60–61
  domestic policy-based theories of,
    63–65

institutional design (cont.)
  explained, 9–15
  functionalist theories of, 65–67
  implications for, 117–119, 165, 180,
    252–255, 263–266
  implications for model validity
    and, 220
  power-based theories of, 61–63
instrumentality, 278–285
Inter-American Drug Abuse Control
  Commission of the Organization of
  American States, 52
Interlaken Declaration, 208
International Action Network on Small
  Arms (IANSA), 158–159, 247–248
International Alert, 247–248
International Campaign to Ban
  Landmines, 247–248
International Convention for the
  Supression of the Financing of
  Terrorism, 173–174
International Court of Justice, 129
international initiative, 226–230
international institutions
  design of, 13–15
  Koremenos, Lipson, and Snidal's
    definition, 9–10
  methodology of design, 15–17
International Narcotics Control Board,
  51, 132–133
interstitial law, 10–11
Iran
  selected governance indicators for, 112
Iraq
  political terror score of, 240
isomorphism, 274–278
Israel
  governance indicators for, 202, 246
Italy
  drug-related deaths in, 109
  governance indicators for, 246
  heroin in, 107
  transfers of arms to, 235

Kaldor–Hicks, 70
Kerry, John (quoted), 5
Kimberly Process. *See* Kimberly Process
  Certification Scheme (KPCS)
Kimberly Process Certification Scheme
  (KPCS), 11, 12

Korea
  governance indicators for, 246
  political terror score of, 240
  potential stockpiles in, 238

Lake, David, 68
Laos
  selected governance indicators for, 112
Latin America
  drug-related deaths in, 106–109
legal bindingness, 54
  defined, 31–41
  obligation and, 209
legalization
  concept of, 20–21
  degree of, 119–125, 165, 208, 255,
    268–269
  delegation and, 46
  levels of, 29
  lobbying efforts for, 63–65
  term defined, 14, 20
  three dimensions of, 29–30
Liberia
  political terror score of, 240
Lipson, Charles, 66, 68
Luxembourg
  heroin in, 107
  homicide rate in, 153

Medellín and Cali cartels, 94–95,
    106–109
Middle East
  asset specificity, 148–157
Model Regulation for the Control of the
  International Movement of
  Firearms, 52
money laundering
  as international policy problem,
    140–142
  defined, 139–140
Money Laundering Prosecution
  Improvement Act, 142
Morocco
  homicide rate in, 153
Morrow, James, 66, 69
multi-purpose instrumentality
  bounded rationality and, 285–286
Myanmar
  political terror score of, 240
  selected governance indicators for, 112

Nine Special Recommendations
  on Terrorist Financing of
  2001, 173
1925 Geneva Convention, 98
1936 Convention for the Suppression
  of Illicit Traffic in Dangerous
  Drugs, 98
North Korea
  governance indicators for, 246
  political terror score of, 240
  potential stockpiles in, 238
Norwegian Initiative on Small Arms
  (NISAT), 247–248

obligation, 54, 166–171, 208–213,
  255–257
  compliance mechanisms and,
    208–213
  defined, 30–31
  delegation and, 56–57
  legal bindingness and, 209
  precision and, 56
Office of the United Nations High
  Commissioner for Refugees
  (UNHCR), 50
operationalization
  asset specificity and, 75–80
  behavioral uncertainty and, 82–84
  environmental uncertainty, 86–89
opium
  leading producers, 105
organized crime
  globalization and, 7
Oxfam, 247–248

Pakistan
  governance indicators for, 246
Panama
  US invasion of, 6
parchment institutions, 12
Partnership Africa Canada (PAC),
  189–190
Peru
  drug mules and, 117
  selected governance indicators
    for, 112
Poland
  governance indicators for, 246
policy issue
  novelty of, 160–161

precision, 55, 125–128, 171–174,
  213–214, 257–259
  coherence and, 259
  coherency and, 213–214
  delegation and, 57–58
  determinacy and, 213–214, 257–259
  obligation and, 56
Presidential Decision Directive 42
Principles of International Law, The
  (Lawrence), 26
problem constellations, 148, 191–192,
  233, 269–270
  interaction between variables, 89–91
  overview of dimensions, 87–88
  three dimensions of, 72–89

Qatar
  homicide rate in, 153

rationality, 271
regime
  term defined, 11
  versus "institution," 11
Resolution 1373 of the United Nations
  Security Council (UNSC), 174
Romania
  governance indicators for, 246
Russia
  governance indicators for, 202, 246
  homicide rate in, 153
  transfers of arms to, 235
Rwanda
  genocide in, 4
  political terror score of, 240

Saferworld, 247–248
Sierra Leone
  political terror score of, 240
Singapore
  governance indicators for, 246
  homicide rate in, 153
Single Convention on Narcotic Drugs, 99
small weapons
  as international policy problem,
    221–222
smurfing
  defined, 161–162
soft law *versus* hard law, 26
Somalia
  political terror score of, 240

South Africa
governance indicators for, 202, 246
homicide rate in, 153
South African Institute for Security
Studies (ISS), 247–248
South Korea
governance indicators for, 246
political terror score of, 240
potential stockpiles in, 238
Spain
governance indicators for, 246
Sri Lanka
political terror score of, 240
state
criminalization of, 6
Statute of the International Court of
Justice of 1945, 30
Sudan
political terror score of, 240
Suriname
homicide rate in, 153
Switzerland
drug-related deaths in, 109
governance indicators for, 246
homicide rate in, 153

Taiwan
governance indicators for, 246
potential stockpiles in, 238
Taylor, Charles, 187
terror
war on and narcotics, 92–93
Thailand
governance indicators for, 202
Turkey
governance indicators for, 246
political terror score of, 240

United Arab Emirates
governance indicators for, 202
United Kingdom
drug-related deaths in, 109
governance indicators for, 202, 246
heroin in, 107
transfers of arms to, 235
United Nations Commission on
Narcotic Drugs, 130–132
United Nations Convention against the
Illicit Traffic in Narcotic Drugs and
Psychotropic Substances, 13

United Nations Department for
Economic and Social Affairs, 52
United Nations Model Regulations
on the Transport of Dangerous
Goods, 52
United Nations Narcotics Laboratory,
129–130
United Nations Office on Drugs
and Crime (UNODC), 52,
129–130
United Nations Security Council
diamonds and, 189
embargoes and, 50
United States
drug-related deaths in, 109
Foreign Assistance Act of 1961, 134
governance indicators for, 246
homicide rate in, 153
Money Laundering Control
Act, 142
potential stockpiles in, 238
transfers of arms to, 235
United States American Center for
Defense Information (CDI),
247–248
United States National Air Interdiction
Strategy, 116–117

vague rules
consequences of, 41–43
Vienna Convention on the Law of
Treaties, 30, 51, 100–101,
106–109
as example of hard law, 134–138
environmental uncertainty and,
114–117
Forty Recommendations of FATF,
145–148
level of legalization, 135–137
versus Forty Recommendations, 174

Wales
homicide rate in, 153
war
small arms and, 222–226
war *versus* crime, 3
weapons
as international policy problem,
221–222
crime and war and, 222–226

defined, 223
potential stockpiles of, 238
trafficking summary assessment, 254, 267
unexplained loss of, 224–225
Wolfsberg Group, 213
Woolsey, James (quoted), 5
World Bank, 48

World Trade Organization, 63
Dispute Settlement Body of, 53
World Wildlife Fund (WWF), 51

Yarbrough, Beth, 68
Yarbrough, Robert, 68
Yugoslavia
political terror score of, 240